WORKING WITH VOICES AND DISSOCIATIVE PARTS

A Trauma-Informed Practical Approach

SECOND EDITION

Dolores Mosquera

Institute for the Treatment of Trauma and Personality Disorders (INTRA-TP)

Cover design: Luis Baldomir
Editor: Miriam Ramos Morrison
Copyright © 2019: Dolores Mosquera
Web: www.intra-tp.com
E-mail: info@intra-tp.com

ISBN-13 9788409082162

TABLE OF CONTENTS

PREFACE

Whenever we try to find a satisfying definition to describe what is a voice, we need to accept that there is an intrinsically relational quality to it. The other option is to stick to the concrete, and ultimately weird, approach found in dictionaries (e.g., a voice is the sound made in the larynx through the vibration of the vocal cords) that obviously does not fit with any psychological work or sensitivity.

If I hear a voice, I will immediately assign it to an owner. The connection between the owner of the voice and me is the basis of the relational quality of this sensation. Moreover, since a voice is much more than a simple noise, what I am hearing is meaningful, because it carries a message from that person; message which is up to me to accept or not.

Sometimes, through his or her voice, I can recognize the owner clearly, and this adds more depth and substance to this sensation. The voice reminds me of that specific person, and nobody else, and the message gets enriched because it becomes "the message of *that* person, who I know personally."

These general observations about voices as signs of a meaningful relatedness are valid even when the experience of hearing one or more voices is considered hallucinatory. Historically, the whole "psy" field (psychology, psychiatry, and psychotherapy) has made two serious mistakes regarding the so-called auditory hallucinations (AHs, auditory perceptions without an auditory stimulus). The first error has been considering all AHs automatically pathological. Many surveys in the general population have proven this idea wrong. In fact, quite a number of people, ranging approximately between 5% and 15%, report to have this kind of experience on a regular basis, without necessarily fulfilling any psychiatric diagnosis. The second error, which can be seen as a continuation of the first one, has been creating an automatic link between hearing voices and suffering from schizophrenia. Auditory hallucinations are often a symptom in this disorder, but not always. Looking back on the work of Emil Kraepelin and Eugen Bleuler, the two historical founders of the studies on psychotic disorders and schizophrenia, we can easily see that *neither one of them* considered *any kind* of hallucinations as a fundamental or necessary symptom for diagnosing this severe condition. It was Kurt Schneider's work in the '50s that created the basis for this partly wrong connection. Among a group of symptoms that he defined as "first-rank symptoms" (FRS), he proposed some types of AHs as particularly important to distinguish schizophrenia from other psychiatric syndromes.

Since the '90s, there has been a consistent and unequivocal result from clinical research: Schneider's FRS are present in many different psychiatric conditions and are *not reliable* for the diagnosis of schizophrenia. In fact, they are more prevalent (present) in dissociative disorders and, more in general, in people with higher scores on the Dissociative Experience Scale (DES) who have experienced physical and/or sexual abuse in childhood. This comes as no surprise since these last three aspects are linked together.

Taking a closer look to FRS, we find some interesting dissociative features, especially when we consider single voices that comment on the client's ideas or behaviors or multiple voices discussing or arguing with each other, excluding the client, as if the voices were independent "individuals," acting in spite of the subject who experiences them. The same can be said for other typical FRS, called "made symptoms" (made feelings, made actions, made thoughts) characterized by the fact that the person feels like his or her actions, thoughts and feeling are not his/her, but instead are "somebody else's" (loss of ownership) and are imposed upon him/her (loss of agency).

From many trauma studies and scholars, and especially from Pierre Janet and the authors of the theory of the structural dissociation of the personality (Van der Hart, Nijenhuis, & Steele), we know that traumatizing events produce their dis-integrating (e.g., dissociative) effects proportionally to their intensity, age at onset, duration, and repetition. One fundamental, dis-integrating effect of traumatization is on the cohesiveness of the personality, that is broken in two or more parts, formerly integrated and now dissociated. Following this approach, it is understandable that the earlier, more pervasive, repeated and horrible the abuses, the more complex, fragmented, conflictual and entrenched will be the dissociative inner world of the client and his/her symptomatology. For this reason, the presence of relatively independent and articulated dissociative parts is the sign of a very probable, early, and severe traumatization. One of the main ways these parts will manifest themselves will be through "their" voices.

In this brilliant and groundbreaking book, Dolores shows us how to maximize the presence of voices as the way to reach important clinical goals. Instead of being afraid of the voices, or seeing them as a sign of schizophrenia, or something to get rid of, she explains to us, step by step and in the clearest way, how to work with these voices with our clients. Throughout the book, she teaches us to encourage our clients to start exploring and listening to the voices instead of avoiding them; to lower the dissociative phobias towards the voices and understand and validate their functions; to identify alternative ways of responding, and to address the "voices' needs" and missing pieces. By doing so, the system reaches agreements, cooperation and, ultimately, starts working as a true team.

This general structure of the clinical work is interwoven with an explanation of the structure of the single clinical session. The reader will be able to identify each one of the aspects by following the many transcripts based on real therapy sessions. The richness of clinical material is incomparable, augmented by the precise comments of the author, always present throughout the text.

The wise, constant, and expert use of a trauma-informed approach creates an effective framework so both therapist and client can understand the importance, the reasons, and the protective goals of the different part of the Self. This helps to keep the right pace, without hurrying any trauma-processing work, and avoids the reprise of phobic blockages or triggered re-experiencing. It is instead possible to create a relational container that offers safety while "moving forward."

The reader will also find explanations of the application of specific procedures and techniques that come directly from the author's experience as a trauma therapist, such as the Meeting Place, the Tip of the Finger, or the Freckle Technique.

Five long and detailed clinical cases follow the first, more theoretical part. I consider them a must-read, and "a book within a book" thanks to their richness and clarity, and Dolores' capacity to be always present with the client and with what happens moment-by-moment. I am sure that, in the end, every reader will feel that this book is a wonderful gift for psychotherapists, and anyone interested in the healing of people with complex trauma and dissociative disorders.

Giovanni Tagliavini
Psychiatrist/Psychotherapist Milano, Italy
President, AISTED (Associazione Italiana per lo Studio del Trauma e della Dissociazione)

ACKNOWLEDGMENTS

To my clients, for being my teachers and my source of inspiration in this journey. A special thanks to the clients whose experiences have served as the foundation of the case examples included in this book. You are very generous, and I am very proud of every one of you. Thank you for your trust.

To Natalia, for encouraging me to write up the work I do with this population. For being a true friend and always being there for me.

To Paula, for encouraging me in every project I begin and for always finding time to review my work. Thank you for giving me genuine, constructive feedback, suggestions and for your unconditional support.

To Miriam, for editing this text from the very beginning and giving me spot-on suggestions, helping me improve the contents of the book during the entire writing process. Thank you so much for "making me think;" it was fun and extremely useful. I really appreciate all the work you have done, the time and energy you have invested in this project, and the advice you have given me.

To Giovanni, for reviewing the book in such a professional way and writing the preface. Also, for giving me honest feedback and encouraging me to share my work and ideas. Thank you for helping me realize some of the things I do.

To Ainhoa, for reviewing this book, for helping me organize and clarify some of the information and for giving me fantastic suggestions to improve different chapters and sections of the book. Thank you for helping me think and for suggesting the inclusion of a specific conceptualization and treatment planning chapter in the clinical part.

To Andrew Moskowitz, for the feedback about my work and for encouraging me to write up my ideas.

To Onno van der Hart, for helping me value my ideas and for everything you have taught me throughout the years.

To Kathy Steele and Suzette Boon, thank you for your willingness to give me feedback on my work and for the good times we have spent together traveling around the world conducting joint trainings. You are excellent teammates.

INTRODUCTION

This book is meant to be a practical guide for working with clients who hear voices or have dissociative parts. The idea of writing about this topic has been in the back of my mind for quite some time, sparked by comments from colleagues who encouraged me to write something practical describing the interventions that are necessary to understand and work with this population.

When breaking down the steps I follow in therapy, I realized that many of the interventions are interwoven throughout the session, and their application depends on the clinical situation. The idea of writing a practical book that could serve as a guideline for this work started to make sense; a book that would include transcripts of case examples to illustrate the different clinical situations and common complications we often encounter when working with dissociative parts and, specifically, with dissociative voices.

The book is divided into five sections. The first section aims at laying the foundation for the work with dissociative voices and parts. It includes a brief explanation of important key concepts; introduces some of the models that have influenced the framework used in the book; and outlines some of the procedures and techniques that will be illustrated in the case examples.

The second section focuses on three basic interventions: helping the client develop their inner Adult Self, exploring the inner system, and understanding the internal conflict. We will see how conflicts among parts are the fundamental issue in the maintenance of symptoms. The key elements that will allow us to address these basic interventions and reach goals that make sense for the system in different moments of therapy are described in detail and pointed out throughout the clinical cases. This section also includes some general guidelines that will help us to organize the clinical sessions and the treatment in general.

Section Three is focused on the work with challenging parts and voices. It is divided according to the types of voices and parts that we often encounter in the inner world of these clients. They have been classified in hostile and aggressive voices, suicidal parts, critical voices, perpetrator-imitating parts, and fearful parts. The reason for breaking down the different voices and parts is that there are many similarities when it comes to applying the work with the various types of parts, although there are also important differences.

Section Four focuses on three fundamental issues: differentiation, co-consciousness, and integration. Lack of differentiation is one of the main problems encountered by clinicians when working with this population, since the internal and external realities of these clients differ greatly. A common issue that sometimes goes unnoticed is how parts remain stuck in their past traumatic experiences, unaware that the past is over and that they are safe in the present. This blurs the line between being focused in the present moment and reliving what happened as if it were still happening. And last but not least, clients tend to confuse some of their most aggressive parts and voices with those of their real perpetrators and have a hard time understanding that these parts are actually parts of themselves.

As the internal conflict diminishes, we can start working towards developing co-consciousness and integrating these parts and voices. At times, co-consciousness develops naturally and gradually, without specific interventions. As is pointed out in the final section, integration takes place from the first session. The way we conduct our interview, checking-in with the parts, and keeping in mind the system as a whole are already integrative interventions. However, some parts need more help with integration, or the client needs more help integrating some of the parts they fear most. Co-consciousness, time orientation, and working with differentiation facilitate this process.

In most chapters, a short transcript of a case example is included so that the theory included in each specific chapter can be integrated into the reader's clinical practice and used as reference material when faced with these difficult situations. In addition, the fifth and final section includes longer transcripts so the reader can follow a series of clinical cases that adapt and combine the different interventions described in this book. The various steps and procedures explained throughout the chapters will be highlighted in the case transcripts. Needless to say, all personal information from the clinical case examples has been thoroughly modified to maintain client confidentiality.

SECTION ONE:

LAYING THE FOUNDATION

CHAPTER 1

KEY CONCEPTS, THEORETICAL MODELS, AND CLINICAL PROCEDURES

The foundation of the practical tools explained throughout this book lays on various theoretical and psychotherapeutic approaches that work with key concepts related to dissociative parts and lack of integration, both in dissociative disorders and in personality disorders, especially borderline personality disorder. Additionally, this work is also based on other approaches that deal directly with traumatic experiences, such as Eye Movement Desensitization and Reprocessing (EMDR) Therapy (Shapiro, 2001, 2018).

The scope of this chapter is not to describe in detail each of these concepts and models. There is an ample body of literature on these different approaches available for the interested reader. However, briefly introducing some of these key concepts and psychotherapeutic theories and models can help us understand the work that will be discussed in this book.

In addition to introducing some concepts that may be relevant for the reader, some of the therapeutic procedures that apply to specific issues in the treatment of clients with dissociative parts or voices will also be described in this chapter and later illustrated in the different case examples throughout the book.

KEY CONCEPTS IN THE WORK WITH DISSOCIATIVE PARTS AND VOICES

There are a few relevant concepts with which we must familiarize ourselves, since they are an important part of the foundation upon which lays the rest of the information that will be presented throughout the book. For practical reasons, they are presented in alphabetical order.

Adult Self

The Adult Self represents an emergent set of self-capacities that are usually not yet developed in any part of the personality. The concept of the Adult Self used throughout this book is based both on the Future Self developed by Korn and Leeds (2002) and the Healthy Adult from Schema Therapy (Young, Klosko, & Weishaar, 2003). The self-capacities of the Adult Self will include empathy, nurturing, validation, and caring towards the different parts of the personality. These capacities will be developed through the modeling of the therapist. The development of the Adult Self through the therapeutic work will be explained in depth in Chapter 3.

Bilateral Stimulation

Bilateral stimulation (BLS) is the use of visual, auditory, or tactile external stimuli occurring in a rhythmic side-to-side pattern (Shapiro & Solomon, 2010). BLS is one of the key components of EMDR therapy (Shapiro, 2001, 2018), a common treatment for Post-Traumatic Stress Disorder (PTSD). In the most common form of treatment, the client focuses on a traumatic memory and the negative thoughts or feelings associated with that memory. The client then follows with his or her eyes while the therapist moves a finger or some other object in front of them from left to right. Alternatively, the therapist may choose to use other types of bilateral stimuli such as tapping or sounds. The treatment originally used only left-to-right eye movements as the bilateral stimulus, but other forms of stimuli, such as bilateral alternating tones, are now commonly being used as alternatives.

The hypothesis is that this stimulation allows the client to access and reprocess negative memories, eventually leading to decreased psychological arousal associated with the memory. In this book, the use of BLS will be illustrated in the case examples in Section 5, with adapted procedures for clients with complex traumatization (Gonzalez & Mosquera, 2012; Mosquera, 2014; Knipe [2015]).

Any procedures that include BLS are meant solely to be applied by trained EMDR clinicians. Those without specific training on this approach should NOT attempt to use these specific procedures with their clients.

Co-Consciousness

The term co-consciousness is used to describe the sharing of experiences among ego states and/or dissociative parts. Co-consciousness is one of the key aspects of the integrative process. From the Ego State Theory perspective, Phillips and Frederick (1995) propose different stages in this pathway toward integration: recognition, development of communication, development of empathy, cooperative ventures, sharing of inner experiences, co-consciousness, and continued co-consciousness. This is related to the process of overcoming the phobia of dissociative parts of the personality and the internal conflict. Co-consciousness will be explained in detail in Chapter 11.

Differentiation

Differentiation has been understood in many different ways by a variety of authors. In this book, however, differentiation is understood not only in relation to self and others, but mainly as the client's capacity to differentiate between inner and outer realities, what happens inside of the person and what happens outside. This affects many different aspects of the daily life of people who live with complex trauma and dissociation. Differentiation between present and past is crucial, since when there are parts that do not know the danger is over and continue to live in trauma-time, it is easy to become confused regarding time orientation. When there are parts that mimic the perpetrators or voices that tend to repeat what they said, it is also easy to get lost in the inner chaos and confuse these parts with the real perpetrator. Chapter 11 is devoted to the various issues dealing with differentiation.

Dissociative Parts and Voices

This term is commonly used to refer to the internal structure in dissociative disorders. Dissociative parts are each one of the distinct identity or personality states. They are not "things," "people", or "personalities;" they are relatively enduring patterns of thoughts, feelings, perceptions, predictions, intuitions, and behaviors organized into multiple, and at times contradictory, self-states (Steele, Boon, & Mosquera, 2019). A first-person perspective is, then, an intrinsic quality of a dissociative part (Van der Hart, Nijenhuis, & Steele, 2006). When these parts are able to take executive control in daily life, their first-person perspective is highly developed. Simply stated, they experience themselves as separate from the other parts and the client as a whole. However, this perspective can also be very rudimentary, as in parts that hold, for instance, just a fragment of a sensorimotor experience of an accident. Richard Kluft (1988) indicates that dissociative parts, as opposed to ego states, have their own sense of identity and self-representation, as well as autobiographical memory and personal experiences they consider their own.

The reader will see the terms voices and parts when going over the different clinical sections. Some clients will mainly speak about voices and refer to their parts as *a voice* or *voices*; other clients may have a combination of both and talk about *a voice/voices* and *a part/parts*. Note that all voices are parts, but not all parts are voices, and, in many cases, we will need to work with both. The type of intervention used is very similar in either case. The main difference is that working with voices focuses on the type of dialogue that is taking place between the client and the different voices, and the work with parts is mostly based on the kind of interaction (e.g., behavior, symptom) that is taking place.

Dissociative Phobias

This term originates from the Theory of Structural Dissociation of the Personality (Van der Hart, Nijenhuis, & Steele, 2006). The authors describe a model in which structural dissociation is generated by trauma and maintained both by a series of phobias that characterize trauma survivors and by relational factors (Nijenhuis et al., 2002; Steele et al., 2001, 2005). The term "phobia" is understood as a dynamic that often takes place in traumatized individuals, which contributes to the internal conflict and prevents the resolution and re-integration of the personality. Though the authors describe a variety of dissociative phobias, the following chapters will focus mainly on the dissociative phobia between voices and parts of the personality, the phobia of traumatic memories (i.e., trying not to think about the traumatic experiences), and the phobia of mental actions (i.e., trying not to think or feel at all).

Ego States

The concept of ego states, as defined by John and Helen Watkins (1997), refers not only to dissociative parts of posttraumatic pathology, but also to those comprising the healthy self of each individual. These are the parts of the personality that make up the entire self. Ego states offer the ability to adapt, think, act, and respond differently in different situations. From the Ego-State theory perspective, Phillips and Frederick (1995) indicate that in the ego-state continuum, ego states are normally separated from one another by something that can be thought of like a semipermeable membrane.

An important distinction to keep in mind is that all dissociative parts are ego states, but not all ego states are dissociative parts (Steele, Boon & Van der Hart, 2017). Ego states do not have a first-person perspective, since they are aware of being a part of the person and are experienced by clients as "me," unlike some of the more developed dissociative parts.

Integration

The simplest definition would be to think of integration as an act or instance of combining into an integral whole. But integration is neither a single event nor the end of a journey. It is a dynamic state of being that is in constant flux, yet stably constant (Steele, 2017). According to the ISSTD guidelines (2011), *Integration* is a broad, longitudinal process referring to all work on dissociated mental processes throughout treatment. Other related concepts, such as fusion, that sometimes get confused with the term integration, will be explained in in Chapter 12, specifically dedicated to this subject.

Internal Conflict

This term describes the existing conflict between all aspects or parts of the internal system, which will be especially intense in an individual who hears voices or experiences parts as "not me." Both experiences are extremely challenging for clients whose tendency is to try to ignore or get rid of these different parts. And as we will see throughout the different sections, the more clients try to ignore or get rid of the voices or parts, the more intense the conflict. For this reason, the main goal in working with voices is to reduce the intensity of the existing conflict and improve cooperation. We will be speaking at length about this concept in Chapter 4.

Internal System

This term refers to the mental representation of the various aspects or parts of his or her own mind made by the patient whose mental structure is fragmented. The internal system includes dissociative parts, memories, feelings, and any other dissociated aspects of an individual. Understanding the parts as a system rather than as separate personality states provides an important frame of reference for treatment. Chapter 4 explains in depth how to explore the internal system.

Internalization of Messages

Internalization is directly associated with learning and recalling what has been learned. In psychology, internalization involves the integration of the attitudes, values, standards, and opinions of others into one's own identity or sense of self. Through the case examples in the book, we will illustrate how clients and their voices learn and internalize the messages and attitudes of others that they will tend to repeat toward themselves later in life.

Metacognition & Higher-Order Thinking Skills

John H. Flavell (1979) used this term to describe a higher level of cognition, which literally means cognition about cognition, or more informally "thinking about thinking." There are two components of metacognition: knowledge about cognition (i.e., becoming aware of one's awareness) and regulation or control of cognition, related to higher-order thinking skills.

Some types of learning require more cognitive processing than others, but also have more generalized benefits. Higher-order thinking involves the learning of complex judgmental skills such as critical thinking and problem-solving. Higher-order thinking is more difficult to learn or teach but also more valuable, because such skills are more likely to be usable in novel situations (i.e., situations other than those in which the skill was learned).

Modes

This is a concept from Schema Therapy. Modes are states, or facets of the self, involving specific schemas or schema operations (Young, Klosko & Weishaar, 2003) –adaptive or maladaptive– that are currently active for an individual. They identify four main types: child modes (the vulnerable child, the angry child, the impulsive/undisciplined child, and the happy child), dysfunctional coping modes, dysfunctional parent modes, and the healthy adult mode. The latter mode is virtually absent in many borderline clients; therefore, it would be something to achieve in the course of therapy. The main mode we will focus on developing in the course of therapy is the healthy adult mode (see Chapter 3).

Switching

A term used mostly to describe the changes between dissociative parts of the personality in Dissociative Identity Disorder (DID). Some switches are very subtle and hardly noticeable for the observer, others are very obvious and might include tone of voice, posture, or behavior. Some people with DID have very little communication or awareness among the different parts of their identity and hardly notice these switches, which usually means that amnesia is present due to highly phobic conflict among different parts. Others, instead, experience a great deal of cooperation among alternate identities and may be fully aware of the switching or able to control it.

All of these terms will be crucial in describing and understanding the different internal processes occurring for the clients and their voices, as well as the procedures that will be applied throughout the different stages of therapy.

PSYCHOTHERAPEUTIC THEORIES AND MODELS BASED ON THE EXISTENCE OF PARTS AND VOICES

Ego State Therapy

A psychodynamic approach oriented to the treatment of different pathologies, in which, among other tools, we use a variety of interventions based on hypnosis. The development of this therapy has been attributed to John Watkins (1997). This model uses techniques from group and family therapies and applies them at an individual level to the internal system of the client. For the author, ego states are present in each person and represent the different aspects of the personality. In dissociative cases, separation and differentiation between these states are higher, which is even more extreme in the case of dissociative identity disorder.

The working method of this model is based on identifying the different features and functions of each differentiated ego state and applying a variety of interventions to achieve a good relationship between all states.

Internal Family Systems

This integrative approach developed by Richard Schwartz (1995) proposes a model in which the mind is composed by relatively discrete parts or subpersonalities, each one of them with their perspective, memories, interests, and characteristics. In working with this model, the organization of the subpersonalities is explored, as well as the possible conflicts among them. Schwartz describes three categories of parts: managers, firefighters, and exiles. The first two make up a broader type of protector parts. Exile parts, instead, contains the painful and traumatic emotions that the system was unable to bear.

A central idea of this approach is that all parts have positive intentions, even if their actions or their effects are self-defeating or disturbing. The goal of therapy is to achieve inner harmony and connection, without eliminating any of the parts.

Theory of the Structural Dissociation of the Personality

In 2006, Van der Hart, Nijenhuis, and Steele published *The Haunted Self*, developing an approach in which knowledge of psychotraumatology and neurobiology links to classical theories on dissociation. This theory is not about dissociation understood as a symptom or disorder, but as a strategy that would be at the basis of all post-traumatic disorders. This theory provides a compelling theoretical framework for understanding the lack of integration and the conflict observed in clients who have dissociative parts and hear voices.

The theory of structural dissociation of the personality postulates that in trauma (including both traumatizing events and early attachment disruptions) the personality is divided into two or more subsystems or dissociative parts. Each one of these parts is mediated by different action systems: apparently normal parts of the personality or ANP mainly by those related to daily life, and emotional parts of the personality or EP mainly by those related to defense during traumatic experiences.

The client as EP continues to relive the trauma, continues to be in the "there and then." Since the threat is still active for this part, the defensive response also continues, and, in this state, individuals will not be able to continue functioning or interacting. To do so, they disconnect from the emotional part and start to function from the ANP. As ANP, survivors experience the EP and at least some of the actions and contents of the EP as ego-dystonic, as something that "happens" to them but does not feel entirely as their own. This ANP is fixed in the avoidance of traumatic memories and internal experience in general and tries to appear normal. However, mental functioning is altered, and the normality of the ANP is only apparent, presenting negative symptoms of distancing, numbness, and partial or complete amnesia for the traumatic experience.

Schema Therapy

This therapy was developed by Jeffrey Young for personality disorders (Young, 1990) and integrates elements of Cognitive-Behavioral Therapy, Object Relations Theory, and Gestalt Therapy. It focuses directly on the broader aspects of emotion, personality, and schemas from which the individual functions. It describes several fundamental ways in which people with personality disorders categorize, perceive, and react to the world. Childhood traumatic experiences generate schemas and modes, which link to the client's reactions in the present.

This approach is useful for offering psychoeducation, so clients can quickly establish bridges between past and present that help them understand the relationship between what they learned in the past and how they presently relate, interact, and respond to others.

Transference-Focused Psychotherapy

Transference-focused psychotherapy has a psychoanalytical orientation. It was developed in the '60s by Otto Kernberg (1967) and has been refined over the years. It is a developmental theory of the organization of the borderline personality, conceptualized in terms of affects and representations of the self and the other, which have some similarities with the dissociative parts described above. The partial representations of self and others are associated in pairs and linked by affect in mental units called relational object dyads. According to Kernberg, the therapist's task is to "identify the actors" in the inner world of the borderline client, using countertransference as a guide for understanding the client's experience. Representative pairs of actors that are included in the client's inner life are the "destructive, bad boy" and the "punitive, sadistic parental figure;" the "unwanted child" and the "neglected, self-centered parental figure;" the "defective, useless child" and the "dismissive parental figure;" the "abused victim" and the "sadistic perpetrator;" and the "sexually attacked prey" and the "rapist."

The dynamic of change in clients treated with transference focused psychotherapy is the integration of these polarized affective states and representations of self and others into a more coherent whole. Integration is a goal shared with the therapeutic approach for dissociative disorders.

Mentalization-Based Therapy

Anthony Bateman and Peter Fonagy (2004) focus on attachment distortion due to problems in parent-child relationships in childhood, hypothesizing that failures in the maternal task of mirroring the emotional states of the baby lead to mentalizing deficits. Mentalization is defined as the ability to intuitively understand the thoughts, intentions, and motivations of other people and the connections between their thoughts, feelings, and actions. Thus, treatment focuses on the development of this mentalization capacity.

When these attunement and regulation failures are chronic and severe, they profoundly affect the development of the child's self. Children are forced to internalize the distorted mental states as if they were a part of themselves. These internalizations and the internal construction of mental representations derived from early attachment problems run parallel to the ideas of dissociative parts and dissociative phobias against certain parts of the personality defined by the Theory of Structural Dissociation of the Personality. One element provided by psychoanalytic theories, which integrates with these concepts, is that of projective identification: some internalized parts that the individual cannot assume as his/her own, are projected onto and into the other.

EMDR Therapy

Given the high prevalence of traumatizing events in clients who hear voices, therapies oriented explicitly toward trauma offer exciting possibilities for these clinical situations. Eye Movement Desensitization and Reprocessing (EMDR) Therapy is a promising approach with extensive empirical support in the treatment of trauma (Shapiro, 2001, 2018). The Adaptive Information Processing model on which EMDR therapy is based proposes that traumatic memories, including not only situations of abuse or maltreatment, but also daily experiences related to insecure attachment or adverse events of various kinds, are the foundation of pathology. According to this model, these disturbing experiences remain dysfunctionally stored in the nervous system, blocking the innate system with which our brain processes experience.

EMDR facilitates the processing and integration of dysfunctionally stored information. To achieve this, perceptive, cognitive, emotional, and somatic elements of memory are collected, which correspond to different levels of information processing (Shapiro, 2001, 2018). Once this memory and all its components are activated, eye movements are used to unblock this information, which is considered to set in motion the innate information processing system of our brain. The therapist follows the process, helping the client to make eye movement sets, until all the emotional and somatic disturbance associated with that memory disappears, and a new adaptive belief about the self is associated with it. In addition to eye movements, the use of alternating tactile or auditory stimulation has been proposed. All of these modalities are referred to as bilateral stimulation.

EMDR consists of eight phases, including a previous stage of history taking and stabilization, in order to later access and process the disturbing memories. Specific adaptations have been developed for the application of EMDR Therapy to dissociative disorders and personality disorders; for example, some authors have combined EMDR with Ego State Therapy (Forgash & Copeley, 2007; Paulsen, 2009) and others have combined it with the Theory of Structural Dissociation (Gonzalez & Mosquera, 2012; Mosquera & Gonzalez, 2014). In this book, we will describe some of the procedures used in Phase 2 of EMDR Therapy, some of them based on the Progressive Approach (Gonzalez & Mosquera, 2012).

CLINICAL PROCEDURES AND TECHNIQUES

When clients are ready and able to confront and work with their trauma history, processing traumatic memories can be the most powerful stabilization maneuver. However, most clients who hear voices or have complex internal systems are not ready to do this work at the beginning of therapy and need proper preparation. In order to know whether it is safe for clients to process trauma with standard procedures, at the very least, the following conditions should be present:

- Sufficient knowledge about the system of parts.
- Adaptive information: without adaptive information, the client is not ready to integrate any trauma work.
- Some capacity to self-regulate or the capacity to be regulated with the therapist (co-regulation).
- Capable of maintaining dual attention, even if it is only possible with the help of the therapist.
- Capacity to notice the body and tolerate physical sensations.
- Co-consciousness among dissociative parts or having reached agreements within the system.
- Some containment outside of therapy. Social support is ideal; if not, at least having the capacity to ask for help.

However, the goal of this book is not to get into the details of trauma processing. Instead, it focuses on those cases that need other techniques before they can move forward in their work in a safe and titrated way. When it is not possible to use standard procedures, we can still use some of the following techniques and process either particular types of memories (e.g., intrusive memories, memories related to dangerous situations for self and others, nightmares) or certain elements related to the trauma. Some of these elements can be fragments of memories; intrusive elements of the memory such as images, sounds, smells, sensations, etc.; peripheral elements of the trauma; or trauma-related phobias.

The procedures detailed in this section can be used throughout the therapeutic process to achieve different goals and each one will be illustrated in some of the numerous clinical case transcripts in Section 5. Several of these procedures are directly related to trauma processing, but others are designed for exploring the system of parts and stabilizing the client. The procedures used for processing and micro-processing (Mosquera, 2016) are derived from EMDR Therapy.

Grounding techniques

Grounding techniques can be very useful when clients feel really distressed, particularly when the distress makes them feel unreal or detached. They can be very helpful to deal with dissociation and flashbacks and help regain a sense of safety and control in life. Through these techniques, clients can learn to anchor themselves in the here and now and avoid getting lost in their past or reliving an experience as if it was happening again. Some examples:

- **Visual:** Have the client look around the room and notice certain objects, shapes, colors. Ask the client to describe them.
- **Auditory:** Help the client notice the sounds around (e.g., the traffic outside the office, the ticking of a clock).
- **Physical:** Have the client notice his/her body, how the clothes feel on the skin, feeling how the chair or floor is supporting them, how that feels in their feet, legs, and body. Practice breathing exercises. Mindful breathing. Noticing the belly.
- **Movement:** Have the client walk around, move legs, arms or do any other movement that can help them be more grounded.
- **Combined:** Any exercise that combines two or more of the previously described categories. Have the client stand up and put their feet firmly on the ground (physical and movement). Toss a paper ball or a pillow back and forth (movement and visual).

The Journalist Technique

When using the journalist technique, the patient is instructed to act as a journalist who is gathering information without making judgments or filtering information. This technique is created after realizing that many patients get confused when instructed to pay attention to the voices and think that they have to do what the voices tell them to do.

<u>Description of the procedure:</u>

1. Ask the patient to take note of their experience without judging it.

    - *I'll propose an observation exercise for this week. It involves trying to show curiosity about what is happening to the different parts and voices without doing anything about it. In other words, just because you listen or pay attention to a part doesn't mean you have to do what it says or react to what you observe. The idea is to be able to take notes as a journalist would and then bring those notes into the session so that you and I can try to understand what is happening.*

2. Prepare the patient for possible difficulties.

    - *I know that this exercise can be difficult to do. When voices are scary, we tend to try not to listen to them or do our best to keep them quiet. The idea of this exercise is for me to be able to gain access to information about what is going on with the different parts and voices so that I can help you understand what is going on.*

3. Make sure the patient has understood the exercise, with questions like:

   - *Why do you think I'm asking you to do this exercise? What do you think the point is?*
   - *Have you understood that you don't have to do what the voices say? Have you understood that the goal is to gather that information so that you can try to understand what they are trying to communicate through those messages that scare you?*

The main goal of this technique is to help patients to distance themselves enough to be able to show curiosity about what is going on with the different parts and voices, without having to do what they say, and thus encouraging exploration of the internal system.

Meeting Place Procedure

The Meeting Place Procedure (Gonzalez, Mosquera, & Solomon, 2012) evolved from earlier procedures to explore the system: Internal Group Therapy (Caul, 1984), the Dissociative Table Technique (Fraser, 1991, 1993), and the Conference Room (Paulsen, 1995, 2009.) In these procedures, the client is usually placed inside the meeting as another part, and any part can play a mediator role. In the Meeting Place Procedure, the Adult Self is placed outside and all the interventions are done through the Adult Self. All of these procedures are based on creating a comfortable place for the different parts to meet, so their needs, their functions, and the relationships between them can be explored.

Description of the procedure:

1. Ask the client to describe the meeting space: They can imagine a place with a table and chairs, like in the Dissociative Table Technique or they can think of a space that feels comfortable and safe enough to be able to have an imaginary meeting with all the parts and voices of the Self.

2. Set up the meeting through guided imagery exercise.

   - *You can keep your eyes open or closed, whatever is more comfortable for you. Now let's invite all the voices, parts, anything in you, to be in this place. Remember this is a place for dialogue, it is meant for understanding; it is not a place for arguing or fighting. All parts are welcome, but nobody is forced to be here or to participate. Parts can be there observing too; they don't have to say or do anything.*

3. After making sure the client understands the exercise, we help exploration by introducing questions like:

   - *What is this place like? What do you see around you?*
   - *How many chairs/spaces do you see?*
   - *Which parts/aspects are represented in those seats/places?*

13

4. Once we have an idea of the parts/voices that are represented in the meeting, we explore different aspects such as feelings, thoughts, needs, function, and how they can help:

    -   *How does this part feel? And this one? How about the other one? And the one hiding in the corner?*
    -   *What does this part need?* (If the part does not answer, engage the Adult Self by asking, *what do you think it might need?*)
    -   *Let's go over the parts and see how each one is trying to help* (exploring the function).
    -   *Do all parts know that the danger is over and that it is safe now?* (This question can be very useful when there are parts that are still stuck in trauma-time.)

The main goal of this type of intervention is to help the client and the whole system, including the Adult Self and other parts, to understand better, to change the defensive attitude for curiosity and observation, and to develop reflexive thinking. This helps improve communication, empathy, collaboration, and cooperation, which are keys aspects in reducing the conflict. The procedure will be illustrated in several examples in Section 5.

Processing Phobias Procedure

The procedure for processing phobias (Gonzalez & Mosquera, 2012) was developed for EMDR Therapy to facilitate the work when therapists encounter trauma-related phobias, especially phobias between parts, within the inner system. This procedure was originally published as bringing together two elements (dysfunctional emotion and physical sensation) but in many cases, bringing the two together proves to be excessive. In cases of patients with a high phobia of internal experience, it is recommended to omit the somatic part.

It can be used with any part that is experiencing a dissociative phobia and is willing to work with it. We usually begin with the Adult Self, since it models the work for the other parts. By the time we suggest other parts to work with this procedure, they are already familiar with it.

Description of the procedure:

1. Focus on the emotion that a dissociative part is experiencing towards another part (or a voice towards another voice, or the Adult Self toward a voice or voices), as well as on the accompanying somatic sensation. It can be presented as follows:

    -   *Can you focus on the fear/rejection/disgust you are feeling towards this part?*
    -   *Can you ask this part to focus on the fear/rejection it is noticing now towards the other part (or the Adult self)?*

2. Apply this procedure for one or two sets of very brief BLS, 4 to 6 movements, not longer.

The primary goal of this procedure is to slightly reduce the conflict between parts. It is meant to be used in combination with other procedures, such as exploring the system and working with the system of parts, not as the main intervention. The procedure will be illustrated with the case example in Chapters 10 and 11, and in some of the cases in Section 5.

Tip of the Finger Strategy (TFS)

The term "Tip of the Finger Strategy" (Gonzalez & Mosquera, 2012; Gonzalez, Mosquera & Fisher, 2012) comes from the hand metaphor used in EMDR Therapy to explain the processing of a traumatic memory. Phase 3 of the EMDR standard protocol starts with the memory itself (the palm of the hand) and follows the different associative chains (the fingers) throughout phase 4, returning periodically to the original memory. The Tip of the Finger Strategy intentionally targets information related to the traumatic content; the target is not the traumatic memory in itself, but a small part of a disturbing sensation or emotion that is a **peripheral consequence** of the memory.

Trauma often generates a series of consequences, such as symptoms or other secondary problems that, over the years, can end up being stored in a dysfunctional and isolated way in the neural networks, with little connection to the traumatic memory from which they originated. This information may be so far removed from the rest of the memory networks of the original trauma that it may not activate the intolerable traumatic memories with which it is associated. In these cases, an effective way of facilitating the desensitization of the current symptom or problem and, at the same time, preparing the patient to progressively approach the more delicate material would be to work with this "outside in" perspective, starting with the peripheral and gradually approaching the central aspects. Metaphorically, in this case, it would be like peeling the layers of the onion, one by one.

When working with the Tip of the Finger Strategy, we do not select the traumatic incident or any element too close to the intolerable memory as a target. What we use as a target is one of those peripheral consequences, by choosing a single element (emotion, thought, feeling or impulse) and using a couple of very short rounds of BLS (4 to 6 movements per round, at most, or until we notice that the activation is sufficiently diminished), because we want to avoid the connection with the traumatic material. The more elements we introduce or the longer the sets, the more possibilities there are that the isolated material will connect unexpectedly with the initial memories.

<u>Description of the procedure:</u>

1. Propose the procedure: Once we identify information that can be conceptualized as a peripheral element/consequence of the traumatic memory, we propose the procedure. An example could be a patient who feels disproportionate anger towards men when confronting a current situation connected to a traumatic experience that she either remembers but cannot confront, or she knows that something happened but cannot remember. Another example would be a fear of knifes in neutral situations, such as cutting up vegetables, that both therapist and patient know is related to past traumatic experiences that the system cannot deal with at this point.

- *Is it okay if we try to work with* (whatever we have identified as a good example with which to apply the intervention: anger towards men in general, the impulse to grab the knife or the idea of using it against others, etc.)*?*

2. Explain the benefits:

   - *You explained how you would like to be able to cook and use knives naturally. The goal of this work is for you to be able to cook normally, without being triggered by knives. We are not going to work with the past; we agreed not to go there yet. However, we can work with this problem that we know is related to your experience.*

3. Engage the Adult Self in target selection: The idea is to explore options with the client and the system of parts and start with limiting elements that can improve the functioning of the system

   - *From what we just discussed, what do you think is more limiting for you in the present moment?*

4. Ask for permission to make sure all parts agree.

   - *Check if there is something in you that is not okay with doing this.*
   - If there is a part that does not agree, we can say, *Let's just do a test, what does this part need to be able to allow us to try this out? And if it doesn't feel right, we'll stop.*

5. Once we get permission, we give specific introductions:

   - If working with the Adult Self: *You are going to focus on that...* (identified peripheral element). *Just on that, we are not going to work with any memories, nothing from the past, just on what we agreed to work on.* (Example: You are going to focus on the fear you notice when you see your sister cut up vegetables, just that, nothing from the past.)
   - If working with another part or voice: *You are going to ask this part/voice to focus on that...* (identified peripheral element) *Just on that, we are not going to work with any memories, nothing from the past, just on what we agreed to work on.*

The goal is to progress towards processing the traumatic experience. However, when this experience is extremely overwhelming, those memories should be approached in small steps, starting with the most tolerable interventions and processing small quantities. This is a good procedure to use when we can plan this type of work with clients. When we cannot plan this type of work, we can use other procedures such as CIPOS (Knipe, 2001) and the Freckle technique and even combine them.

Constant Installation of Present Orientation and Safety (CIPOS)

The CIPOS procedure (Forgash & Knipe, 2001; Knipe, 2002, 2007, 2010) is a way of facilitating clients in learning the important skill of coming out of the trauma and back into the present. Through practice, this becomes easier over time. This skill is crucial in cases with strong phobia of traumatic material. Through alternating back and forth between safety and carefully titrated exposure to trauma, the client can learn, often very quickly, the valuable skill of emerging from a traumatized part back into a safe orientation to the present. It works on the principle that, by expanding and developing an individual's ability to remain oriented to the safety of the present situation, that person, then, is much more able to safely access and resolve highly disturbing memory material.

Bilateral stimulation (BLS) is used to constantly strengthen or install in the client's awareness a clear subjective sense of being present in the immediate real-life situation (i.e. the therapy office). By strengthening the person's present orientation through BLS, and carefully controlling the amount of exposure to the trauma memory, the individual is more easily able to maintain dual attention. Through the use of the CIPOS procedure, processing of the memory can proceed more safely, that is, with much less danger of unproductive, dissociated reliving of the traumatic event.

Description of the procedure:

1. Explain the procedure. The client needs to understand why and how the CIPOS procedure might be useful. Sometimes it is enough to offer the client just a couple of examples of his or her phobic avoidance and/or tendency to relive trauma and lose dual attention. Once the client understands this, we go through the steps, explaining what can happen and what is expected throughout the procedures.

2. Ask for permission. Obtain full permission from the client to work on the highly disturbing memory in a gradual and safe way, with ample time in the therapy session to complete the work regardless of whatever unexpected traumatic material may emerge during processing.

3. Assess level of perceived safety. As with any therapeutic intervention, it is important that the client be aware of the objective safety of the therapist's office. If the client seems unsure of the physical or interpersonal safety of the present situation, this issue should be addressed directly.

4. Strengthen present orientation. To assess and further strengthen the person's sense of present orientation, the therapist may ask a series of simple questions relating to the client's present reality in your office. Sample questions are the following:

   - *Where are you right now, in actual fact?... Think of that* (then do a short set of BLS).
   - *Can you hear the cars driving by? ... Think of that* (then do a short set of BLS).
   - *How many tissue boxes do I have in this room? Think of that* (then do a short set of BLS).

5. Use the Back of the Head Scale (BHS). The CIPOS procedure is intrinsically linked to the use of the BHS, which is a simple subjective scale developed by Knipe (2015) to assess how oriented the client is to the safety of the present situation and how present they feel in the work

we are doing. It is also a way to assess the effectiveness of the CIPOS intervention moment to moment throughout the session. In this way, we can ensure that the client is remaining sufficiently grounded in emotional safety, so that reprocessing of the trauma can occur. The BHS is a way of making sure the client remains safely in the zone of dual attention: continuing to connect with present safety while accessing traumatic memory information. The script for the BHS goes like this:

- *Think of a line that goes all the way from here* (therapist holds up two index fingers about 14 inches—about 35 cm—in front of the person's face), *running right from my fingers to the back of your head. Let this point on the line* (therapist moves fingers) *mean that you are completely aware of being present here with me in this room, that you can easily listen to what I am saying and that you are not at all distracted by any other thoughts. Let the other place on the line, at the back of your head, mean that, even though your eyes are open, in your mind you are completely in a memory from the past.* (Since even mentioning the trauma memory may create, for some clients, some additional loss of present orientation, I usually repeat the description of the scale, using a tone of voice that is calm and matter of fact.) *The place out here* (wiggles fingers) *means you are completely present; the other place at the back of your head means you are in the memory. Point with your finger where you are on this line right at this moment.* (Knipe, 2018, p. 199)

6. Begin trauma work slowly. When present orientation is established, the client can be invited to bring a memory image to mind for a very brief period of time –as little as 2 or 3 seconds at times– while the therapist keeps track of time.

The goal of this procedure is to enhance the capacity of the client to stay present and tolerate entering safely and gradually into the traumatic memories.

The Freckle Technique

The Freckle Technique (Mosquera, 2014) is another example of fractionated and gradual processing. Unlike the Tip of the Finger technique, instead of focusing on a consequence of the trauma, isolated in a separate neural network and with little chance of activating the traumatic memory itself, it focuses on a **fragment of the nuclear trauma**. The starting point is a frame or a specific element that has acted as a trigger for a traumatic experience (e.g., a picture, a word, an odor, etc.) that the patient or some part of the system do not feel ready to deal with in its entirety.

The application of this technique requires that we are familiar with the internal system of parts and that we have done enough work to increase empathy and cooperation between the different parts. The patient must be able to maintain dual attention (or to recover it with the help of the therapist) and have, at least, the ability to connect with emotions, to feel them without becoming overwhelmed or disconnected, and to regulate himself on an emotional level. The patient and the different parties must also have learned to say "no" or "stop," which will allow them to refuse the procedure if any part is not prepared to do so, since asking permission is crucial.

This technique is not used in a premeditated way, but only in response to a need that arises suddenly during the session. As a general rule, this work does not arise when there are parts of the body that are trapped in trauma-time that contain painful memories and other parts of daily life without neither access to these memories nor the ability to contain them. In these cases, we work with the system of parts following the guidelines that will be described in the following chapters. Even so, there will be times when the patient connects with the trauma by some external or internal trigger and this cannot be contained. Only in these cases will we use this procedure with this type of patient.

Description of the procedure:

1. Propose the procedure:

    -   *Is it okay if we focus on that...* (emotion, image, smell, sensation)?

2. Check with the system and ask for permission:
    -   *Check if there is something in you that is not okay with doing this.*
    -   *Would this this part/voice/ "this something in you" be okay if we do a test? If it doesn't like it, we'll stop.*

3. Once we get permission, we give specific Instructions:
    -   If working with the Adult Self: *You are going to focus on that...* (pain, sensation, image, etc.) *Just on that, we are not going to work with any memories, nothing from the past, just on what they are noticing/feeling.*
    -   If working with another part or voice: *You are going to ask this part/voice to focus on that...* (pain, sensation, image, etc.) *just on that, nothing else. Nothing from the past, just on what it's feeling/noticing right now.*

The goal of this intervention is to reduce the emotional activation caused by the sudden appearance in session of traumatic material, in those cases in which this material is either intrusive and poses a risk to the patient or others, or the patient is not yet prepared to work with the processing of the trauma using the EMDR therapy standard protocol.

CHAPTER 2

SETTING UP THE THERAPEUTIC WORK AND STRUCTURING CLINICAL SESSIONS

Clients usually need varying degrees of help in learning to understand and relate differently to their voices and parts. It is known that clients who develop a meaningful understanding of their voices usually do better than those who avoid, criticize or reject their voices (Romme et al., 2009). But this is no easy task. Clients are often frightened of their voices and parts, or fear the possible response from others if they talk about their existence (e.g., hospitalization, medication increase)

As we will see in the following chapters, the initial steps in this work should be aimed at establishing a trusting environment, where clients feel they can openly talk about what happens inside of them, and where their voices or parts feel safe enough to allow this. After this essential achievement, the work should focus on improving the relationship with the voices and parts.

GENERAL STRUCTURE OF THE THERAPEUTIC WORK

The following section outlines the essential steps to keep in mind throughout the overall therapeutic work. This general structure –based on Mosquera (2014), Mosquera & Ross (2016) & Moskowitz, Mosquera, and Longden (2017)— is meant to be a brief introduction that will be expanded in Chapter 6, when describing the work with the more complicated parts. These steps are not meant to be rigidly followed; instead, they are meant to be a flexible guide to the work. At times, depending on the clinical case, we may skip steps, ask some questions and not others, or introduce variations based on our clinical judgment.

Step 1. Exploring the voices and parts

The first step is aimed at getting an idea of the internal representation of the voices and parts and how clients make sense of what happens inside. If clients indicate hearing voices, it will be necessary to explore the tone, content, and messages that the voices or parts are trying to express. It can either be a repetitive message that apparently does not make sense, or a clear message geared to achieving a certain goal. This goal will become clearer as we explore the function of the voice (step 6). When exploring voices and parts we can also ask how old the voice seems to be and any other details that might help us get an idea of this internal representation. We may also explore the moment of onset and when voices appear in the present moment (related to exploring triggers, step 3).

Step 2. Encouraging clients to listen to the voices and pay more attention to the parts

The second step is closely related to Step 1. To gather the previous information, we also need to help clients become more curious and interested in their inner world. This may be a relatively easy task with certain types of voices. However, it becomes more complicated –and for that same reason, much more crucial– with challenging parts. Helping clients understand that the voices and parts are actually trying to help will be one of the main ingredients needed in developing curiosity.

Step 3. Exploring triggers

The third step must include exploring when voices or parts show up. As we will see in different sections of the book, this is related to the triggers and therefore, the function. The main goal of this step is to explore what was happening when the voices or parts showed up. Eventually, we will link this information to exploring the function and identifying the needs (steps 6 and 7).

Most of the time voices get triggered when the client feels bad, frightened, or concerned. Also, when something happens that reminds them of the past, especially those voices still stuck in trauma-time. There are some exceptions; for example, when clients have been punished for feeling good, voices will also get triggered when in pleasant or enjoyable situations.

Step 4. Exploring and processing dissociative phobias

Phobias among parts are one of the main obstacles that prevent the natural flow of treatment. We should always check how the different parts and the Adult Self feel towards each other. We identify dissociative phobias between parts when the feelings towards other parts are dysfunctional, such as when one part is scared of another part or feels disgust, shame or rejection. Once the phobia has been identified, the work can be better organized and it can be decided, based on the information obtained, whether it needs to be processed before proceeding to the next step. In turn, such processing favors exploration, since it is a tool developed to diminish fear, and any other emotion that is interfering with the process.

Step 5. Assessing the degree of differentiation and time orientation in client and parts

Distinguishing between internal and external elements is not easy for clients with complex traumatization. Sometimes problems with differentiation are related to boundaries, not knowing what they are supposed to tolerate from others and how far they can go with others.

They may also include having difficulties separating what others think or feel from how clients think and feel, or distinguishing the messages they have internalized from what is real.

A crucial issue with differentiation is related to the ability to separate what is happening now from what was happening then. Parts and voices might be stuck in trauma-time, frequently not knowing that the danger is over and continuously responding as if the danger were still happening. Assessing time orientation in different moments of the work will be necessary as well as helping clients be oriented to the safety of the present moment when they lose dual attention. This is especially important when there are parts that never experienced dual attention and still need to learn that they are safe now –or at least start to consider the possibility that this may be the case.

Step 6. Exploring and validating the function of the voices

Voices are there for a reason and finding out what they are really trying to do is a core aspect of treatment. Each part has its reasons for doing what it is doing, and we must always validate these reasons, whether or not they are adaptive in the present. Remember that they were initially created to perform a certain role and functioned to help the person survive what they had to go through in their earlier years.

However, what was adaptive in a given situation in the past does not necessarily continue to be adaptive in the present. In fact, much of the time it evens becomes dysfunctional and makes the person as a whole feel even worse. For this reason, clients may initially have a hard time believing that parts are trying to help, since some of them –particularly the hostile parts– make them feel really bad. This is such an oxymoron that it may make no sense to them in the beginning.

By respectfully asking questions about the parts, we are modeling healthy curiosity towards them, which the client will integrate as therapy progresses. This will help him or her understand how the function of each part was adaptive in the past, as they tried to help the client survive in one way or another.

Validating the responses from the parts of voices is also important. Clients tend to get upset about the voices or the actions, without really being able to appreciate how important this was for survival.

Step 7. Identifying and validating resources, feelings, and needs

Clients with different parts and voices, often have mixed and even opposite feelings. The same goes for their needs; one part may have needs that could be in direct conflict with the needs of another part. This is why identifying and validating feelings and needs is a crucial part of the work; it can help all of the different voices and parts to feel heard and understood, which tends to be a missing experience for these clients. The key in this type of validation is to make sure we accept all the different emotions and needs and help both clients and the system of parts to understand them as well as accept them. To internalize a new way of responding to their feelings and needs, parts need to experience a completely new attitude, which is done through modeling, so it can end up sinking in.

Exploring the needs of the different parts of the system can help us identify some of the resources that need to be developed, as well as those that already exist, even though they may not be seen as such by the client. When clients are able to understand the adaptive function of the voice or part, we can begin to see its capacity to help and identify existing resources within the system that are shared by the different parts and the client. This process can be quite straightforward with those parts that are more simple and easy going. For a conflicted system, however, things can be more complicated. Sometimes, clients spend so much energy dealing with the system that they miss relevant resources owned by some voices and parts. Once we are able to engage the client's curiosity, we can explore the resources of each part and explain how these can be useful for the rest of the system. For example, one voice might have the capacity to help defend the system, another to identify possible danger, and a third to enjoy life. Exploring these resources will reinforce curiosity and pave the way for coop-eration and teamwork. This will lead to a more integrated Self, where each voice represents something useful for better overall functioning.

If the therapist is trained in EMDR Therapy, resources can also be installed when needed, as a way to reinforce any relevant insight that the client and the system of parts achieve as a result of the work. The clinician will generally use short sets (between 8 and 12 movements) of bilateral stimulation for this purpose.

Step 8. Exploring, modeling, and practicing alternative ways of responding

Whenever any of the current strategies used by any of the parts or voices is not working to help the client feel better, we should help the system to think of alternative responses and suggest more useful or adaptive ways in which the voice can truly help the person. This is a good time to continue helping clients to realize they now have options and can make deci-sions based on their needs and wishes.

Most of the time, voices or parts are not aware of the effect their comments have on the rest of the system and of the fact that their behavior is not currently adaptive. Given that their main goal is protective, they are usually not trying to harm, but quite to the contrary, and they will be willing to try new suggestions. Encouraging clients to communicate with them about comments or behaviors that are frightening or bothersome is a key aspect in the prog-ress towards better functioning. Sometimes the simple fact of checking in with the voice will have a positive effect because they are not used to having anyone check in with them. When clients can communicate what works and what does not work for them, voices and parts can modify their way of responding.

Initially, this has to be done with the therapist's help, using questions aimed at helping them realize this:

- *Does this voice know how much this upsets you?*
- *Is this voice aware of how frightened you become when he says those things?*

Most of the time clients will say something like, *Of course it knows, it just doesn't care,* but this is just an automatic reply reflecting the way the system is used to functioning. In these cases, it is important to say something such as,

- *I understand you see it this way, but could you please check if this voice knows how upsetting this is?*

Psychoeducation can be useful but will not be enough with some of the parts; the best way for the new attitude to sink into the system of parts will take place through modeling. Many clients have not had healthy models to learn from, so many of the basic elements we all learn as we grow up still need to be developed. A frequent situation that we encounter in the work with this population is that some parts have a very small repertoire. As the therapist models a new way of responding, the Adult Self and other parts that are listening in, can observe how a new interaction would look and sound. This is something that cannot be learned from reading or explanations or internalized without practice and observation.

With some voices, it is an easy step because they only needed to know that their behavior or comments are not helping in the present. With other voices, however, this will take time, especially with the hostile and critical ones, as we will see in chapters 7 and 9, respectively.

Step 9. Identifying and exploring missing pieces

Another aspect that can be relevant is to explore the missing pieces. For instance, clients who never get angry or sad would be informing of this difficulty or communicating a need in a very indirect way.

Sometimes it is obvious that there are missing pieces; other times, we find out later on in therapy, as we get to know the client and the system of parts. When something does not fit it is important to point it out and check if there are any other parts or voices. This can be done in a general way ("Is there any other part or aspect that is difficult for you to talk about?") or while using some of the exploration tools such as the meeting place, ("Do you think we should leave any empty chairs for other parts that might me more difficult for you to look at?"). Clients might also tell us about missing pieces when they draw their inner system; foggy areas or shades that do not allow to see what is underneath would be some of the frequent examples. Some clients might say things like, "A lot of people are shouting underneath the fog" or "There is something dark that I can't even look at, all the parts are hiding from it too".

In addition, clients do not speak about some parts or voices due to fear, or because they are so used to censoring those aspects that it's unthinkable even to bring them up.

Step 10. Reaching agreements, developing cooperation and teamwork

As a last step, the system must reach agreements or compromises that all voices can accept, for the benefit of the entire system/person. This step is one of the final steps, but we can begin introducing this idea with the previous aspects. This is why it is so important to model new ways for the system of parts in general, so they can eventually learn to cooperate together towards achieving these goals.

All of the previous steps are geared towards promoting understanding and empathy between client and voices. Increased understanding leads to greater compassion and empathy, which in turn allow for cooperation. We will have a chance to see examples of each of these steps throughout the clinical cases in the following chapters of the book.

GENERAL STRUCTURE OF A CLINICAL SESSION

Within this general outline of the therapeutic process, and once we start working with voices and parts, it is important to keep in mind some guidelines that could be applied in each clinical session. This will help keep our work organized and structured, as well as offer us a clear understanding of the effects our interventions are having in the internal system of the client.

The general structure of a clinical session can be divided into three sections, each of which should include various aspects to explore, depending on what comes up during the session. All of these can be applied when working both with voices and with quiet parts.

1. **Explore the effects of the work done in the previous session**

   1.1. Explore how the client and the parts/voices left the previous session (e.g., better, worse, confused, motivated). This will provide some feedback as to what may have worked or not.

      - *How did you feel after you left the previous session?*

   1.2. Check how the week has been for the entire system, not just the Adult Self or any of the parts. It is important to check both with the voices or parts that we were working with in the last session, as well as with the rest of the system. This intervention shows respect towards each and every part of the system and models a cooperative way of functioning.

      - *How did* (voice/s or part/s) *feel with the work we did?*

   1.3. Explore whether during the week the client as a whole has followed the suggestions or indications offered in the previous session and how they felt about them. If any homework was given, it is important to follow up. The system needs to know that we are serious about their treatment, so we keep our word, and we remember to check or ask about pending issues. This will help clients and their different parts to see they are important, that their opinion matters and to develop trust in the therapeutic relationship.

- *How did the system feel about the indications/suggestions given?*
- *Did you find the suggestions useful* (easy, hard, did they make sense, etc.)?

2. Work on issues that came up during the week or come up during the session

2.1. Explore whether the voices and parts were active or not during the week. Check how the parts are doing. The more we consistently inquire about the parts, the more we help clients develop healthy curiosity toward them.

- *Did you hear any voices this week? /Were any parts active this week?*
- *Were they voices/parts you already know or were there any new voices/parts?*

2.2. If the voices appeared during the week or during the session, we must explore what triggered them:

- *When did the voices appear? How did they appear?*
- *What was happening when they showed up?*
- *What did the voices say or what did the parts do and why?*
- *What was the goal or what were they trying to achieve?*

2.3. Explore the reaction of the system towards the voices (e.g., tried to listen, got upset, told them to shut up). By being curious about the other parts, we are modeling a new way of relating to the rest of the system. And only by exploring can we get a clear idea of which part/s of the system are responding in adaptive ways and which ones still need help.

- *What does the client think about what happened with the voices/parts? What do other parts or voices think about it?*
- *Whatever the voices said or whatever the parts did, was it helpful?*
- *What was the result for the voice, part, and system as a whole?*
- *What was the reaction from the rest of the system? How did they manage or respond?*
- *What do other voices or parts think about this reaction?*

2.4. Address any issues or difficulties as they appear. When we identify any important issues or problems, we can either explore them or, at least, suggest working on them.

- *Please, can you ask this part whether it would be okay to work on this* (e.g., anger, frustration, guilt, rejection, etc.) *that just came up?*
- *Check if there any parts that are uncomfortable now or need to express anything.*

2.5. After any intervention, check how the rest of the parts feel about what just happened.

- *After talking about all of that* (in the previous section), *what do you notice now?*
- *What do you think about this? Does it make sense?*
- *What do you notice when I suggest/say this? How about other parts or voices? What happens with them when I suggest/say this?*
- *Is there anything inside that does not like what we are doing now?*
- *Is there anything inside that does not agree with doing this* (whatever we are suggesting or exploring)?

2.6. Check whether currently non-adaptive learned messages or behaviors continue to take place after the voice or part has started practicing new adaptive behaviors. If so, we remind clients that this voice or part is still learning new ways.

- *I understand this is difficult for you or this part, but remember this voice/part is still learning to communicate differently.*

3. Closure for the session

The closure of a session has the potential of being one of the most relevant moments of the work. It is important not to finish abruptly, without taking the time to explore how the client and the system are doing. Many clients seem to be doing fine, but remember this is a learned strategy. More often than not, we will find out that they are not completely present, or another part is not doing well with the work. Most of the time, what is required is nothing more than offering some attention, clarification or help with whatever is happening. Sometimes clients need time to take in the work or a little help understanding the key points of the session.

3.1. Reinforce the work done throughout the session, and validate the efforts made by each part of the system that was active/participated during the work.

- *You have done a great job today! Despite all the fear you noticed, you were able to try being curious about other parts/voices.*
- *I would like to/Let's thank this voice or part for allowing us to explore these issues. This is very helpful.*

3.2. Check on the usefulness of the interventions applied during the session. This can help us review the work we do, repeating what is working and changing whatever is not working.

- *What was useful so we can consider repeating it? What was not useful and would be interesting to avoid repeating?*
- *What needs to improve?*

3.3. Check whether the client is stable and grounded, oriented in time.

- *How are you doing right now?*
- *How is everything inside? Do you notice any agitation inside?*
- If the client says anything that implies not being oriented: *Where are you now? Do you know you are with me in my office?*

3.4. Summarize what has been learned in order to help clients organize the work done during the session and to set goals for future sessions. Highlighting any agreements and realizations helps to organize the information for the client and promote realization, an important aspect of integration. However, we need to remember that most of these clients spend large amounts of energy in their internal struggle, so organizing and remembering can be very complicated in the early stages of therapy. In some sessions, we can naturally set up the work that seems to make sense for the following session. For some clients, this feels like a way to have continuity and to know that we will follow up on what came up during the session.

- *Notice how important it is for you to realize that all the little girl needed was to be seen. Let's make sure we continue to help the little girl feel that she is being seen in our next session.*

3.5. Anticipate potential obstacles and problems. It is important to prepare clients for future difficulties with parts of themselves, since the process may not always go as smoothly as they would wish. This intervention will support them in being more open and understanding to challenges from parts of their system (e.g., hearing critical comments or commands to self-harm, or voices that wish to avoid therapy) (Mosquera & Steele, 2017). Anticipation normalizes therapeutic challenges, helps the client hold the dialectical tension between acceptance of where parts are and the need for change, and attempts to avoid going back to conflictual responses between parts. However, if we detect there may be potential problems during the session, we should not wait until the very end of the session to bring it up. Note that similar questions are also included in point 2.6.

- *If you hear the voice saying negative comments again, remember it is still learning the new ways.*

- *Remember this is very new for all of you. We are asking these voices to do something that they still need to learn and practice. One of the key aspects is how you respond to the comments too.*

Once again, these steps are not meant to be followed in a rigid way. They are meant as a guideline to keep in mind aspects that are relevant to explore. This does not mean we will explore all of these issues in one session, only when needed and when it makes sense. As the work evolves, the client will need less help from the therapist and will realize some of these issues automatically.

GENERAL STRUCTURE OF THE THERAPEUTIC WORK (TW)

1. Exploring the voices (content, tone, message, age, moment of onset, etc.) and parts
2. Encouraging clients to listen to the voices and pay more attention to the parts
3. Exploring the triggers (what was happening when the part showed up or when the voice spoke)
4. Exploring and processing dissociative phobias
5. Assessing the degree of differentiation and time orientation in client and parts
6. Exploring and validating the function of the voice
7. Identifying and validating resources, feelings and needs
8. Exploring, modeling, and practicing alternative ways of responding. Offering suggestions when needed
9. Identifying and exploring missing pieces
10. Reaching agreements, developing cooperation and team work

GENERAL STRUCTURE OF A CLINICAL SESSION (CS)

1. **Explore the effects of the work done in the previous session**
   CS #1.1. Explore how the client and the parts/voices left the previous session
   CS #1.2. Check how the week has been for the entire system
   CS #1.3. Explore whether during the week the client has followed the indications offered in the previous session

2. **Work on issues that came up during the week or come up during session**
   CS #2.1. Explore whether the voices and parts were active or not during the week. Check how the parts are doing.
   CS #2.2. If the voices appeared during the week or during the session, we must explore what triggered them
   CS #2.3. Explore the reaction of the system towards the voices or parts
   CS #2.4. Address any issues or difficulties as they appear
   CS #2.5. After any intervention, check how the rest of the parts feel about what just happened
   CS #2.6. Check whether learned messages or behaviors continue to take place after the voice or part has started practicing new adaptive behaviors.

3. **Closure for the session**
   CS #3.1. Reinforce the work done throughout the session and validate the efforts made by each part of the system that was active/participated during the work
   CS #3.2. Check on the usefulness of the interventions applied during the session
   CS #3.3. Check that the client is stable and grounded, oriented in time
   CS #3.4. Summarize what has been learned in order to help clients organize the work done during the session and to set goals for future sessions. Enhance realization
   CS #3.4. Anticipate potential obstacles and problems to prepare clients for future difficulties

Table 1. Quick reference table of the different steps to be followed in the treatment work and clinical sessions, which will be found throughout the clinical examples in the book. NOTE: Throughout the transcripts of the clinical case examples, both types of steps will be highlighted so that the reader can see more clearly how they are applied in clinical practice. The steps of the general structure of the therapeutic work will be noted as the initials of Therapeutic Work, followed by the number of the specific step, in parenthesis (e.g., TW #1, TW #2, etc.). Those belonging to the structure of the clinical session will appear with the initials of Clinical Session, followed by the corresponding number (e.g., CS #1.2, CS #2.1, etc.).

SECTION TWO:

THE BUILDING BLOCKS

CHAPTER 3

DEVELOPMENT OF THE ADULT SELF

The Progressive Approach model (Gonzalez & Mosquera, 2012) suggests working with dissociative clients through the Adult Self. As mentioned in Chapter 2, the concept of the Adult Self used throughout this book is based both on the Future Self developed by Korn and Leeds (2002) and the Healthy Adult from Schema Therapy (Young, Klosko & Weishaar, 2003). The Adult Self represents an emergent set of self-capacities not yet developed in any part of the personality. The self-capacities of the Healthy Adult include nurturing, validating, and affirming the vulnerable child mode; setting limits for the angry and impulsive child modes; and promoting and supporting the healthy child mode. The Healthy Adult also neutralizes or moderates the maladaptive parent modes and replaces maladaptive coping modes. In addition, this mode is in charge of performing appropriate adult functions such as working, parenting, taking responsibility, and committing, as well as pursuing leisure adult activities such as intellectual and cultural interests, health maintenance, and athletic activities.

Initially, the therapist serves as the Healthy Adult whenever the client is incapable of doing so (Young, Klosko, & Weishaar, 2003). During the course of treatment, clients internalize the behavior of the therapist as part of their own Healthy Adult mode. Most adult clients have some version of the Healthy Adult mode, but there are tremendous variations among individuals in regard to its effectiveness. Logically, higher functioning clients have healthier adult modes than lower functioning individuals, but the underlying idea is that, to some extent, all clients have this capacity.

Based on these ideas, we proceed from the implicit understanding that the seeds of the healthy, well-functioning, and integrated Adult Self are already present. In working through the Adult Self, one of our main goals is to show the client how to talk and communicate with all the different voices and parts. Instead of talking directly to them, the therapist models a new way of relating to them. However, some direct interaction with parts may be necessary at times or may occur due to spontaneous switching, especially in clients with amnesia and little or no co-consciousness.

On the contrary, if the Adult Self is not present and has no awareness of what happens in therapy, and if the therapist also works directly with the parts, younger parts who feel at ease with the therapist and need attention, will tend to show up more often, not necessarily in a controlled adaptive way. Other types of parts, instead, will only tend to show up in session if they consider that it is necessary to offer some protection. When there is not an Adult Self, integration will likely take much longer. Keeping these adult self-capacities in mind and modeling them throughout the treatment will facilitate the gradual development of an Adult Self in the client, who will be the one through which the work will be done during the sessions.

KEY ASPECTS IN THE DEVELOPMENT OF THE ADULT SELF

The work with parts and voices requires clinicians to be aware of some key aspects that are implicit as the session unfolds. These will aid in the development of the Adult Self, since we will be modeling new ways of relating to the parts and voices. In addition, they will facilitate the exploration of the internal system and the inner conflict. By developing awareness of these implicit aspects, we can then make them explicit during the therapeutic work. Let us take a closer look.

Keep the whole system in mind

When we explore the internal system of parts, we must think of the whole picture and try to include all parts and voices. It is important to always help clients understand that the different parts represent the various aspects of a person, but are not different people. This may be difficult to understand for some clients since voices at times model after people that they knew from childhood. It is common for some parts to take after their abusers, imitating their behavior, tone of voice, and expressions, which may make clients believe that these parts may truly be the abusers.

We should keep in mind that there will be parts that are not easily identified. Some parts, such as the hostile ones, may be ignored by the client because they can be terrifying, but we should make a point of not ignoring them ourselves. In Chapter 6, we will focus specifically on the work with hostile parts. After doing some work, we should be able to recognize whether any pieces may be missing in the system. These pieces are usually related to missing needs and are partially related to hidden parts or parts that can sometimes be more complicated for clients to disclose. In Step 9 of the general structure of the work, we suggest exploring these missing pieces.

Always be respectful

Respect is of utmost importance in helping us explore the internal system of parts. We must show profound respect both for our clients and for every one of their parts. This will serve as an example after which clients can start to model their own behaviors and attitudes toward themselves and their parts.

In order to convey respect, our attitudes and behaviors must be guided by the following principles:

- We must accept how the client experiences what happens, even if we may not necessarily agree with it. For example, *I understand why you would see it that way, it has to be very difficult to listen to a voice that keeps saying things that are frightening* or *I see why you feel that way.*

- Respect the feelings and thoughts of every part and do not take sides since this would only increase the conflict. Each part has reasons for doing what it is doing, and it is important to help clients see the whole picture and understand each and every one of them.

- Use the language preferred by the client to talk about their inner world. Some clients do not feel comfortable using the terms "voices" or "parts," and may instead choose to speak of "aspects" or "things in me." In any case, we must adapt our language to match the client's choice of words.

- Avoid name-calling and dismissive comments by helping the client rename the parts that he or she considers to be "negative." Clients will frequently use negative names or comments when referring to some of their voices or parts. Though this has been their choice of language, in this case, we do not follow their lead. Instead, we must help them understand that continuing with the name-calling will only maintain the inner conflict. It is not likely that a voice that is referred to as "bastard," "asshole," "devil," or "bad" will be at all interested in cooperating. We help the client to rename them and eliminate any negative, disrespectful, or threatening adjectives.

- Respect the timing of the different parts. We also need to model respect in regard to timing, so clients can understand that each part has its own pace. Sometimes clients are so eager to get better that they try to force working with trauma or they get upset because other parts that keep secrets do not share the information. This is one of the key aspects to keep in mind during the whole process because it is related to some of the most complicated phases of therapy.

- Encourage clients to make decisions. Many clients have not had any choices when growing up, and they tend to do what others expect or ask others before deciding. A way to model respect is to help clients value their capacity to think, reflect, and decide what might be best for them. Also, learning that they have choices can be a powerful tool that helps them differentiate past from present.

- Avoid interpreting as much as possible. One of the most frequent ways of being inadvertently disrespectful is when therapists interpret what the client, voice or part is doing, instead of simply exploring to achieve understanding. The main idea of exploring the system is helping clients understand what is taking place inside, without introducing anything that can condition the response.

Develop healthy curiosity through modeling

Respect and curiosity feed off each other. By expressing curiosity about why the parts behave the way they do, we model a new and more respectful way of looking at them, which will in turn increase curiosity in the client and in the parts. Once the client can listen to the voice and start to understand the needs or motives of the different parts, they become more attuned, and the attitude towards the parts may start to change. They can begin developing healthy curiosity about what the voices and parts have to say, what they might need, and at what pace they are able to work. This will help in understanding that the work is not about "getting all the information out quickly" so they can feel better soon. They become able to see that the process will unfold as the system of parts becomes ready to share and work with the more delicate aspects.

Questions such as the following can be helpful:

- *What is the voice trying to achieve with certain comments or behaviors?*
- *What is the voice concerned about?*
- *Is the voice trying to help in some way?*
- *What does the voice think would happen if you did _____?*
- *How would the voice feel after that?*

Validate! Validate! Validate!

Validation is perhaps one of the most important tools to be used throughout the therapeutic process. We should always validate any effort the client makes to understand the system of parts, and any effort parts make to be understood. A person with a conflicted system is not used receiving validation, noticing positive attitudes or cooperation, or having anyone model a respectful way of interacting. It is very important to always validate the entire system, the protective intentions of the different parts (whether the actual attempt is functional or not in the present), the aspects that are working, and any resources that the parts may bring to the system. Validating is also something we must always do before any intervention. This is a crucial aspect that helps the therapist model a new way of looking at parts and voices, from which the different parts can observe and learn. This new way of relating can only be internalized through practice and new experience.

Be compassionate

Once clients are able to start being curious and respectful toward the different parts of the system, they can begin to understand why the system became organized in such a way. Understanding gives way to compassion and empathy, which is a necessary step to create an inner environment where communication and cooperation can take place. For some clients, this can be a real challenge. Most people can easily feel compassionate toward the suffering of a child. However, if they think of themselves as children, they become unable to feel compassion and instead may blame themselves. Clients may say thing such as, "I can do that with other people but not me," "if I think of any little girl, I can understand what you mean, but if I think of the girl in me, I can't."

Promote dialogue, communication, and understanding of the intention to help

One of the main difficulties in the work with parts and voices is related to the lack of dialogue and effective communication. As commented before, many clients have very little mental efficiency due to their internal conflict. It is common for voices to keep stating repetitive messages that are frightening or threatening, or just difficult to understand. We cannot say that there is no communication, but we can definitely say that there is no effective communication. It will be necessary to help clients realize the amount of mental energy that is spent trying to avoid parts or voices. A good way to begin is by exploring what is happening when the voices show up. This usually happens when the client is overwhelmed or cannot deal with a situation. But clients rarely make that connection and are genuinely surprised with the logic of this simple aspect: if voices or parts were simply trying to hurt them, they would not only show up when they are feeling bad; instead, they would mostly show up when they are feeling happy and calm. A second question can be aimed at exploring how the client or other parts respond to the voice. The most common responses are some form of "I make it shut up" or "I try to ignore it." Using these two basic questions, we can begin to introduce the idea that this dynamic has been learned in the past and is not working very well for the system in the present.

It's all about teamwork!

Introducing the idea of teamwork from the beginning is crucial for the development of a more integrated self. When clients are able to understand how parts have been trying to help and can feel compassion for them, it becomes easier to see that they were initially designed to work as a survival team. Therefore, the team can return to cooperating as a true team.

Through modeling a communication style based on respect and healthy curiosity, we are helping the Adult Self to start understanding what parts need, how they are feeling, and why they say or do what they say or do. Eventually, the Adult Self becomes the observer and reflective self, learning to relate with compassion and acceptance and changing how clients relate to themselves as a whole, which will lead to our ultimate goal: the client, from the Adult Self, will learn to meet their needs.

BENEFITS OF WORKING THROUGH THE ADULT SELF

By understanding both the needs of all the voices and dissociative parts and how to get these needs met, clients develop capacities for self-care and self-soothing and will feel more confident using these skills outside of consultation. This leads to gradually developing co-consciousness and higher levels of integration.

In summary, working through the Adult Self provides the following benefits:

- Enhances metacognitive processes because the client has to think about his or her thoughts and also notice what the voices and parts are thinking.
- Clients learn new ways of communicating with all the voices and parts, and this serves as modeling for all of them.
- Increases the client's capacity for self-reflection.
- Improves integrative capacities in the client and the system as a whole.
- Clients become able to identify the needs of the different voices and parts and learn to meet these needs.
- Fosters the development of healthy self-care patterns.
- Promotes autonomy in the client, which generates empowerment and security.
- Parts are less likely to switch during sessions.

NOTE: Throughout the following case example, we will be highlighting in bold both the key aspects for the development of the Adult Self and the benefits of working through the Adult Self. This will offer the reader a visual cue which will help us in seeing how crucial these aspects are in the clinical treatment of these clients.

CLINICAL CASE EXAMPLE

Valerie: Doesn't Everyone Hear Voices?

Valerie is a 28-year-old client who was referred to our center due to impulsive behaviors, self-regulation problems, and occasional angry outbursts during which she became aggressive. She was diagnosed with Borderline Personality Disorder (BPD) and Conduct Disorder. After the initial intake, it became clear that Valerie fit criteria for BPD and the main problems were related to her trauma history. After working with significant improvement for about two months on specific traumatic events that were triggering many of the symptoms and behaviors, she finally decided to open up and talk about her voice. She had not spoken about the voice before because she thought everyone heard voices.

In this transcript, the therapist is attempting to help the client develop the Adult Self while exploring the internal system. Asking the client how her week went after the last visit is always a good way to start a clinical session in order to obtain some feedback on the effects of the different interventions that were applied.

> *T: How was your week?*
> *C: I'm fine... I was thinking about the last session.*
> *T: What were you thinking?*
> *C: I thought that I should take better care of myself.*
> *T: That's interesting. How did you realize this?*
> *C: Well because of the work we did, I think something in me liked what we did. But my head is a mess.*

By having asked the client to think about her thoughts, we are helping to **promote self-reflection and integrative capacities**, as well as to **enhance metacognition**. Notice that the client says, "something in me," so we **respectfully use her own language** to explore.

> *T: Something in you liked what we did?*
> *C: Yes, when we worked with the little girl.*
> *T: Great, but you say your head is a mess. What is happening in your head?*
> *C: Well, there is something there that doesn't allow me... (Client is immersed in her thoughts.)*
> *T: Maybe that something (referring to the part) is concerned about some issue.*
> *C: It's not letting me...*
> *T: Why do you think it's not letting you?*
> *C: Because, on the one hand, it thinks I don't need this therapy anymore.*
> *T: Aha, and on the other hand?*
> *C: On the other hand, she does need it.*

Notice the client says, "On the other hand *she does* need it." This seems like a good time to explore this "something," which apparently represents a part of her that is in conflict about therapy. We want to see if she is able to realize that this "something" is as part of her while at the same time helping her develop **healthy curiosity** toward this part. This is meant, once again, to **increase self-reflection and integrative capacities**.

> T: *Can you tell me about that "something?"*
> C: *It's a voice in me.*
> T: *Okay, and what does the voice say?*
> C: *I don't know. She doesn't allow me to think, she doesn't allow me to get sad or anything. (Client starts crying.)*
> T: *Can we ask this voice what can help her right now?*
> C: *She doesn't know.*

Since the voice does not know, we begin to develop the Adult Self and the client's capacity to **identify and take care of her own needs and those of the voice**. This intervention encourages the Adult Self to **pay attention to the needs of the parts** (TW #7), which, in turn, helps **develop autonomy** and **increase self-empowerment**.

> T: *What do you think could help this voice?*
> C: *Getting rid of her body.*
> T: *Why does she think this would help her?*
> C: *Because then all the bad things would go away.*
> T: *Do you realize that the body of this voice and your body are the same one? We can't separate them.*
> C: *I know. (Client starts crying.)*
> T: *So, as the adult you are now, what do you think this voice might need?*
> C: *I don't know.*
> T: *Okay, let's try to find out together. What do you notice about that voice now?*
> C: *It sounds bossy.*
> T: *Is she concerned about something?*
> C: *She is on alert.*
> T: *Tell her that it's okay to be on alert. (Client nods.) Can we ask her why is she on alert?*
> C: *She doesn't want to cross the barrier.*

As we try to help the client to listen to the voice (TW #2) and explore its possible function (TW #6) and needs (TW #7), we encounter a phobia of traumatic memories (TW #4). This is a great opportunity to keep practicing **self-reflection**, as well as to **model communication and respect** towards the pace and the needs of the voice.

> T: *So, she is afraid of crossing this barrier.*
> C: *Yes.*
> T: *And I understand that there is a lot of pain behind this barrier.*
> C: *Yes.*
> T: *I understand that it's not a good time to go there.*

C: I don't know.

T: Ask this voice that doesn't want us to cross this barrier.

C: It doesn't matter.

T: Is this what the voice says or is this what you think?

C: It's what I think.

T: It does matter. She's an important part of you, and she's warning us about something, so it's important to listen to her. Does she think that working on this issue today may not be a good idea?

C: I don't know.

T: Check with the voice.

C: Yes, she doesn't want us to go there.

T: So, there is a voice there who is helping us to stop when it's too much. This is great! And you know what? We don't have to go there until everything in you thinks it's a good idea.

C: Okay (calmer).

After encouraging the client to listen to the voice (TW #2), we have started to explore its function in the system (TW #6) and **validated** its efforts to help the client. This simple intervention helped the client become much calmer, so we can then explore more details about the voice (TW #1).

T: Do you hear this voice often?

C: Of course.

T: Why didn't you talk about this voice before?

C: Because she is always there.

T: How long has she been there?

C: Forever.

T: Since your early childhood?

C: Yes.

T: Is it always the same voice or is there more than one?

C: It's always the same voice, there's just one.

T: And is her tone usually bossy?

C: Yes. It's not really bossy, it's more like alert. She is there...

T: ... protecting.

We acknowledge the protective function of the voice (TW #6) and model an attitude towards the part that is new for the client. By **showing respect** and **validation**, we are encouraging a **new and more efficient communication style**.

T: We are going to thank her and tell her that she is doing a great job. She is very important. It's essential that she can talk to us and that we can get to know her. Notice how much time she has been there, protecting you.

C: I guess so (smiles.)

Exploring the phobia of dissociative parts (TW #4) is another good way to **increase self-reflection**. It also helps us to know how to proceed from this point forward.

T: How do you feel about this voice?

C: Well, I would like her to disappear. I don't have anything against her, but...

This last comment helps us see that the Adult Self is phobic of the voice. Even though the dissociative phobia is not a very strong –her inner system is quite simple and has no elaborate parts–, she will need help in becoming aware of this conflict, so she can continue **developing her integrative capacities**.

T: Do you realize how contradictory this is?

C: Yes.

T: How do you think this voice feels knowing that you want her to disappear?

C: I don't care, I just want her to leave me alone. I just don't pay attention to her, but she keeps coming back.

Modeling an attitude of **curiosity** and **respect** allows a shift from avoidance and inner conflict to **collaboration**. This is an important step towards **empowerment of the self,** as a whole and a good way to facilitate further exploration (TW #1, TW #3).

T: Well, it's important not to ignore her. She probably has important things to share, and that's why she keeps coming back. What happens with the voice when I say that?

C: She likes it. She says, "See? She gets it."

T: Great. It would be interesting for you to understand what she has to say and how she is trying to help. Would you be willing to explore this?

C: Yes, I guess.

T: Does the voice always talk during the sessions?

C: Of course, she is always talking. Now she is quiet; she is listening to what we're saying.

T: And what does she think about what we are doing?

C: She agrees, but at some point, she doesn't allow me... she doesn't want anything to happen. Sometimes it feels that she can take over.

T: What is she afraid might happen?

C: She doesn't want anything to happen because... you know... it's like when people say: "I don't want to talk about this anymore." I don't want to talk or do anymore about this, because it can't be solved. It's better to keep things in the filing cabinet and although some people can file issues, I can't.

This offers an excellent opportunity to use the metaphor from the client to introduce psychoeducation and build on the metaphor towards **respecting** the pace of the system.

T: Who is doing the filing?

C: The voice.

T: The filing cabinet is one way to deal with issues and when people file things it's because it made sense at the time. The idea is to be able to work with the content of that filing cabinet without you being overwhelmed. You know what a filing cabinet looks like, right?

C: Yes.

T: *It has many file folders. We can open one file folder at a time, so the voice doesn't become overwhelmed. How does this sound?*

C: *It makes sense, but sometimes she frightens me, and I don't like that.*

Once again, we **validate** the intention of the voice (TW #6), **model communication**, and foster the attitude of trying to develop a **healthier way of taking care of the self and the needs** of the system.

T: *This voice has been with you for a long time, and she has learned to protect you in a certain way. For now, she doesn't know how to communicate differently, but she can learn with our help.*

C: *You think so?*

T: *Yes, I do. Notice how important it is that you can say what you don't like. What does she think about that?*

C: *(Checking with the voice.) She says she doesn't want to scare me. She's upset.*

T: *It's good to know that, isn't it? Let's thank her for letting us know. (Client nods.)*

T: *Could you ask this voice what she needs to feel a little calmer?*

C: *She needs someone to take care of her.*

T: *And what does she need so she can feel that she is being taken care of?*

C: *To be pampered.*

T: *How old does this voice feel?*

C: *Young.*

T: *How young?*

C: *It's like a little girl.*

T: *Imagine this voice as a little girl. What would you say to her?*

C: *I would tell her to calm down.*

T: *Imagine what you would do with a little girl who is anxious, feeling bad, and thinking negatively.*

C: *I would kiss her and hold her.*

As we can see, this client has a positive attitude towards the voice, with a little help she is able to be **compassionate** and engage in a **new way of responding**. But the fact that she can identify the need and have a suggestion to meet this need does not mean that the system is ready. So, before we decide to follow up on the suggestion from the client, we need to explore if the part thinks this is a good idea.

T: *Can you ask her if she would like that? (Client starts crying like a little child.) What just happened?*

C: *She wanted that, and I imagined it.*

T: *And what happens when you imagine that?*

C: *That everything falls apart.*

T: *What falls apart?*

C: *Everything. If the only thing that the voice needed was loving care...*

This is an important realization and an opportunity to keep working with the notion of modeling new ways of responding (TW #8) and developing **cooperation** and **teamwork** (TW #10).

T: She needs loving care, so it's important to give it to her. What do you think? (Client nods.)

T: Where do you notice this voice in your body?

C: In my chest.

T: Let's do something. Place your hands there, close your eyes, and imagine she is a little girl that only needs you to be there. (Client places her hands over her chest, very engaged in the exercise.) Have her notice that you will be there for her. (She seems much calmer, still with her eyes closed, very much connected to the part.) Stay that way for as long as you need. Tell her that she's very important, that we'll keep her in mind, that it's okay to let us know that she needs more attention, and that we are very sorry we didn't realize this before. Stay like this for a while. (Client seems increasingly calmer and, after a few minutes, we check the result.)

T: How was that?

C: Good (smiling).

With this intervention, both the Adult Self and the voice calm down. The client is very surprised by this realization. Although "everything falls apart," her Adult Self had enough integrative capacities to do this work. Of course, this is a simple internal system with a younger part that just needed to be heard and seen. This led to an important change in the system; the client felt empowered and more capable of understanding and meeting the needs of her young self, represented by this voice. Other cases have more parts that might get in the way, as we will see in the next section of the book.

As we have seen through the case example, keeping in mind and modeling the key aspects for the development of the Adult Self generates numerous benefits, which will help foster a new attitude in the client. This new attitude becomes the foundation for our work and the best way to teach our clients new ways of relating to themselves and their parts and voices.

CHAPTER 4

EXPLORING THE SYSTEM AND UNDERSTANDING INTERNAL CONFLICT

When working with clients who hear voices, both therapist and client will need to understand the representation of the internal system, its structure, and the most significant dynamics requiring interventions. In addition to taking a thorough clinical history of the main symptoms and presenting problems, it is important to explore their inner dynamics. Learning to listen to these voices or parts of the self and understanding the function and meaning behind their disruptive behaviors becomes a crucial aspect of treatment. This process is facilitated when clients are already familiar with working through the Adult Self. The combination of all these factors creates an excellent foundation on which to start building an actual alliance with the whole system.

INTERNAL CONFLICT WITHIN THE SYSTEM

Many of our clients live in a constant battle with themselves, and their inner experience is not easily understood without specific training on the topic. When clients experience intolerable thoughts, feelings, memories, and impulses, their inner system tends to organize itself into dissociated parts. Some of these dissociated aspects tend to be angry and may be experienced as hostile and critical inner voices conversing with each other and with the part of self in executive control. These interactions usually generate such intense internal conflict that the person may even have difficulties carrying on ordinary conversations.

Research on the phenomenon of hearing voices has found that traumatic experiences –including sexual and physical abuse, extreme belittling over extended periods of time, persistent neglect, aggression, and inability to accept one's sexual identity (Romme & Escher, 2006)– could be the leading cause of symptom maintenance. Another reason for symptom maintenance could be the resulting unresolved internal conflicts. The system of parts will naturally reflect the type of conflicts that have been experienced by the client as he or she was growing up.

One of the main problems that voice hearers encounter is that some professionals tend to focus on the symptom without understanding the underlying issues or causes. Conventional approaches in psychiatry to the question of voice hearing have been to avoid the issues or emotions the voices are expressing and to ignore the meaning of the experience for the voice hearer, thus concentrating on removing the symptoms (auditory hallucinations) by the use of medication (Romme & Escher, 1989.)

When clients tend to ignore the voices, these will, in turn, tend to scream louder or escalate their actions in a desperate attempt to be heard. This dynamic creates a vicious circle that only increases internal conflict. The more intense the internal conflict, the stronger the dissociative barriers need to be, and the fewer integrative capacities the clients will develop.

USEFUL QUESTIONS TO EXPLORE THE SYSTEM

The following are some examples of questions we may ask the client about the different aspects related to the voices when exploring the internal system through the Adult Self.

- Moment of onset

    - *When did the voice appear for the first time?*
    - *How long has the voice been there?*
    - *When did you become aware of this part?*

- Information about the characteristics of the voice

    - *Is there more than one voice?* If so:
        - *How do you know they are different voices?*
        - *How do you distinguish them?*
        - *How is this voice different from the others?*
    - *What is the tone of the voice?*
    - *Is this a male, female, or child voice?*
    - *How old does this voice sound?*
    - *Does it sound familiar? Does it remind you of anyone?*

- Identifying the message from the voice

    - *Does the voice say things?* If so: *What type of things?*
    - *What is the voice saying now?*
    - *Why does the voice think that?*
        - *And what do you think about that?*
        - *Did the voice know this? Was the voice aware that this was so scary for you?*

- Exploring communication/interaction style with and among the voices

    - *Do the voices mostly give commands, or do they try to reason?*
        - If they try to reason: *What kind of arguments do the voices give?* Ask for examples.
    - *Do you have internal or external communication with the voices?* Ask for examples.
        - *What do you think about this?*

- *Do you hear voices conversing between themselves?*
  - *How is this interaction?* Ask for examples.
  - *What is the tone of the conversations?* (friendly, threatening, arguing, whispering, etc.)
  - *When does this normally happen? How long can this take?* Ask for examples.
  - *What do you think of this? Why do you think this happens?*
  - If other voices are having a conversation: *Do they know you can hear them?*
  - *Do you ever try to participate in the conversations? If you do, what happens? How do they respond?*
- *When the voice talks to you, do you answer back?*
  - If so, *what do you answer?* Get examples.
  - *How does the voice respond to your answers?* We want to get an idea of the dynamics.

- Identifying where the messages were learned

  - *Does the message sound familiar?*
  - *Where could this voice have learned to communicate in such a way?*
  - *Is it possible that the voice learned to repeat these messages?*
  - *How did others respond when you got angry/sad/frightened/happy?*

- Exploring the function of the voice

  - *Have you noticed when the voice tends to show up?*
    - *Does it show up when you are feeling upset?*
    - *Does it show up when you are feeling good?*
  - *What do you notice about how the voice may be feeling?*
    - *Is the voice feeling angry, upset, afraid, sad, etc.?*
  - *Can you ask the voice how it is feeling?*
    - If no answer from the voice: *How do you think this voice may be feeling?*
  - *What is the function of the voice?*
    - If the client answers "None": *If it were trying to help, with what would it be helping?*
  - *What is the voice trying to achieve by doing...?*

- Exploring needs in the different parts and in the Adult Self

  - *What do you think the voice needs?*
    - If the client has an answer: *Why do you think that?*
    - If the client does not know: *Can you ask the voice?*
  - *What would you need from this voice?*
    - *How would that help you?*

- Exploring alternatives

  - *I know this voice can learn to communicate in a way that is more helpful, but it might need our help*
  - *Can we think of a different and more functional way to communicate?*
  - *What type of messages are more difficult for you?*

- *What type of messages would help you?*
- *How can we help this voice to communicate this type of messages?*

- Exploring the logic of the changes in the voices

  - *Are there moments when the voice does not show up?*
    - *When does this happen?*
    - *Why do you think this happens?*
  - *Do you know what was happening when the voice went away?*
  - *Do you know what was happening when the voice got more aggressive?*

- Building resources and reminding the client that this is a learning process

  - *If the voice repeats some of the scary messages, remember it is still learning.*
  - *I know you would like the voice to respond differently, but at the moment we need to focus on what you can do and how you can respond.*
  - *If we focus on what depends on you, you will be modeling new adaptive ways for the voice.*
  - *The fact that we are trying to listen to the voice does not mean you have to act on what it says, especially while we are still trying to understand what is underneath those messages* (need, function, etc.).
  - *When you feel confused about what the voice says, try not to interpret the message or what it's trying to do. Use the Journalist Technique. Remember that this technique consists of paying attention to what the voice says in order to discuss it with me, but that you don't have to do what the voice says. Write down what it says or what you find confusing and we will try to understand it together.*

Other questions:

- *Do the voices know each other?*
- *Do these parts have anything in common?* This question aims to help identify possible shared resources, function, qualities, needs or goals.

These questions are not meant to be used as a one-size-fits-all questionnaire. Instead, we should adapt them to each situation while trying to understand what is happening in the inner system. A key aspect of this type of exploration is to be curious and try to understand without interpreting. If we add our impressions or interpretations, it is more likely we will condition the response or get in the way.

EXPLORATION METHODS

One of the more straightforward ways to explore the internal system of parts is asking questions through the Adult Self. In different parts of this book, curiosity is mentioned as one of the main ingredients of this work.

Exploring whatever comes up for the client, regardless of how they refer to their parts or voices, is a good way to begin. For instance, a client says, "*I can't stand myself! I am crazy! I don't understand why*

I do the things I do! No wonder I drive everyone away, I think of doing one thing and end up responding in a completely different way."

The therapist responds, *"Okay, let's try to understand what happens inside of you when you respond differently than expected."*

From here on, we can go in different directions.

1. Guiding the client through specific questions, such as:

    - *How do you know that you responded in a completely different way from what you expected?*
    - *What was happening inside of you? What were you feeling or noticing?*
    - *Was there anything in you feeling differently?*

2. Listening to what seems to point to internal conflict

    - *You say you function in a way that is confusing for you, and there seems to be a lot of conflict inside. Can you try to describe this conflict so I can try to understand it better?*

3. Asking clients to draw this conflict in a piece of paper

    - *Try to draw what happens inside when you notice this conflict. Just draw whatever comes up for you.*

4. Using small toys or action figures (e.g., Playmobil, Disney, Lego) and asking the client to select those figures that represent the different aspects, voices, or parts of the Self, either in a general way or using a specific situation to explore:

    - *Do you see these figures? I would like you to select those that represent the voices in you.*
    - *I am going to place these figures here and you can select the ones that represent what happens inside of you when you notice _____.*

All of these tools help externalize the conflict and create some distance, which is helpful when dissociative phobias are very strong. In addition, we can use the Meeting Place procedure described in Chapter 1.

CLINICAL CASE EXAMPLE

Sharon: Feeling good is not allowed

Sharon was referred to our unit due to frustration from the previous therapist because the client had a difficult time engaging in therapy, barely talked, and avoided any type of eye contact with the therapist. She would often become dysregulated and hurt herself after the sessions. In the previous session, the client had become completely blocked when selecting action-figures to represent her inner system. She had connected one of the action-figures representing a child with her own history. She now says that things are very confusing, and that remorse and guilt are very present. At times, she hears voices and becomes very distressed. We begin with exploring the internal system to understand what happened.

In this example, we are exploring the system through drawings and Playmobil action-figures, always showing healthy curiosity toward the part and its functioning. We begin with exploring the voices (TW #1) and encouraging the client to be more curious (TW #2).

> T: *Should we explore this voice?*
> C: *Okay.*
> T: *How does the voice sound?*
> C: *Well, I don't know.*
> T: *Is it a male voice? Is it a female voice?*
> C: *Male.*
> T: *Male.*
> C: *I don't know if it may be... Well, I don't know, but it's like the same voice as when he (referring to the perpetrator) was with me. Yes, it's the same tone of voice.*

When the client says this type of things, we could proceed with exploring the degree of differentiation (TW #5). In this case, she is still too phobic and agitated, so we postpone this piece of the exploration for later. One way of helping when the phobia is intense is to externalize the conflict, so we ask the client to make a drawing of her inner world. This is one of the options that can help us start exploring the inner system.

> C: *I don't know how to explain it very well; some things are repetitive.*
> T: *What type of things?*
> C: *Bad thoughts and feelings.*
> T: *Can you give me an example?*
> C: *The voice says that everything is my fault and that's when the other part shows up.*
> T: *Which part shows up when the voice says that?*
> C: *I think it's a little one.*
> T: *How old is that part, more or less?*
> C: *She's old; I don't know how old.*

This is a very common response from clients when asked about the age of the part. Quite often, the longer the part has been around, the younger it is, even though clients may initially perceive them as older because they have been around for so long. We continue exploring the voices (TW #1), modeling healthy curiosity, in order to understand the system as best as possible. This helps the client to enhance metacognitive processes and increase self-reflection.

> T: *Has it been there for years?*
> C: *Yes.*

T: *But what age sounds right? Is it a part of you that looks older? Is it a part that seems like more of a child or a teenager?*

C: *I think I didn't have those these feelings back then, or I didn't understand them like this. I don't know... Perhaps it was after I got out of there.*

T: *Are there two different parts or is it the same one?*

C: *One is the consequence of the other, I don't know...*

T: *Very good. What else are you drawing?*

C: *The fears that paralyze me and go against me. I am trying to give you an example, such as what I said before, that I would never be happy,*

Exploring when the voice shows up is necessary in every case since it gives us crucial information about the possible function and goal. We need to know what is triggering this voice (TW #3) because it will help us to determine its function (TW #4).

T: *And is that when the voice shows up?*

C: *Yes.*

T: *Okay.*

C: *And then there's another sensation... Something that often makes me act according to what is around me in different contexts and that causes me... well, let's say, the pain.*

T: *These are things you have trouble managing, and when you have trouble managing them, you separate from yourself and adapt to what the situation requires. And what about that last one? What does it say there?*

C: *Well, it's more or less the same, a sense of disconnection when I feel very burdened. But I don't know how to explain it.*

T: *When you feel very overwhelmed you disconnect from yourself.*

C: *Yes.*

T: *And is that when it feels like you stop being you?*

C: *I think so, yes.*

T: *Do you have the feeling that certain behavior is controlled by another part of you?*

C: *Yes, I think so.*

T: *What part would that be?*

C: *Well, I guess the emotional one.*

T: *If this is your inside (therapist draws a circle around the words the client wrote down before) where would you place it? How much of this circle is taken up by the guilt?*

C: *I can't separate it; it's as if it were all mixed up.*

T: *The feeling you have is that everything is mixed up. Do you have the feeling that things become activated in different ways? (Client remains silent.) For example, you sometimes see yourself acting from here (pointing at the figure). And when you see yourself acting from here, from "I will never be happy," is this (pointing at the figure that represents another part) active?*

C: *Well, that's what it feels like, this is what leads to me being stuck with those two things.*

While keeping in mind the entire system, we have been inquiring about the relationships between the different parts in order to have a sense of what is triggering each one of them (TW #3) and how they relate to one another (TW #1). This could help us determine the dissociative phobias among parts, if there were to be any (TW #4). At the same time, it helps the client understand the function of the voice (TW #6), which is a crucial part of exploring the system and one of the strategies that will help the client look at their own system from a completely different perspective. Although we must remember that, initially, it may be hard for clients to see that the part has any positive function whatsoever, so we need to be very patient and consistently model a new way of responding (TW #8).

> T: *Okay, this* (pointing at the figure that represents the part) *sometimes makes you react in that way, even if you have to disconnect.* (Client nods.) *What do you think is the function of the part that holds the guilt?* (Client remains silent.) *Try to think that these are ways to try to help you, okay? Try to see the positive. What function could it have?*
>
> C: *I don't know, I don't see it.*
>
> T: *And what about any other part? Do you see it? For example, the function that the disconnection may have.*
>
> C: *I just don't know where each thing takes me.*
>
> T: *You don't know where it takes you. But would you like to find out?*
>
> C: *Yes.*
>
> T: *Would it be interesting for you to delve deeper and really understand the structure so that you can have a higher sense of control?* (Client nods.) *The feeling that you have right now is that all of this is somehow separated, and, at the same time, it's all mixed up. As if it were a knot or something like that?*
>
> C: *Yes.*
>
> T: *Then it would be interesting to undo that knot, right? To really understand both what is there and the function of each of these aspects.* (Client nods.) *Because it is important to keep this in mind when working. Do you have the feeling that there are different Sharon in you or not?*
>
> C: *Yes.*
>
> T: *That's what we want to understand. We want to see the different Sharons to see how you function differently or from a different perspective than the one you have... From one state, you can see and experience things in one way, and from another state, you cannot. For example, from one part you can have the feeling that you deserve to enjoy something and that it's okay to do so, right?*
>
> C: *No, I don't have any part like that.*
>
> T: *You don't have a part like that, I see, but imagine it was there. I think that part is somewhere in you. Maybe that part is very repressed in there. Maybe it's very hidden. Maybe it's a very small part of you, who thought you deserved it when you were younger. We all have a moment when we can feel that, you know?* (Client nods.) *Then maybe that's a smaller part of you, and there would be another part telling you that you don't deserve it or that you will never be happy. Could you try to think about that?*

By doing this, we are keeping in mind the entire system and starting to help the client consider the possibility that there may be other parts with which she is not so familiar (TW #9).

> C: *Yes.*
>
> T: *Do you find it difficult?*
>
> C: *I don't know. It's not so clear now... No...*
>
> T: *Do you think it's been clear for you at some point?*

C: *It's as if I had had some loose pieces that were clear.*

T: *Could you try to rescue those loose pieces, just so you can describe them?*

C: *Yes, but it's not easy for me.*

Using the metaphor of the puzzle is helpful because it is easy to visualize and helps to understand the chaos as we validate the entire system and introduce the idea that each part of the system is important (TW #6).

T: *Well, if this were very clear for you, we wouldn't have to do it anymore. I wouldn't have to ask you these things. There may be things that are clearer for you and others that are more confusing. The idea is to start understanding, you know? It's about putting the pieces of the puzzle together. Just imagine that your whole personality is like pieces of a puzzle. Sometimes these pieces are all disorganized, especially when a person goes through everything that you have gone through, and what we want to do is to start reorganizing them and understanding them; how one is connected to another, how one can be separated from another. Does it make sense?*

C: *Yes*

T: *Do you think that may be useful or not?*

C: *I think so, because one thing I would need is for everything to be in place. I don't know.*

T: *Perfect. And above all, what is crucial about this is that each piece is important. Sometimes, when you work on this, there may be a part that feels uncomfortable, but it has an important function and that's what we want to understand. All pieces of the puzzle are important, we don't want to eliminate or remove any one of them, you know? What we want to understand is why, at a certain point, you have to act in certain ways. Is that okay with you?*

C: *Yes.*

In this example, we have seen the use of drawings and action-figures, which has helped both therapist and client explore and increase understanding of the system. The interventions have been geared mostly toward exploring what has been triggering the voice (TW #3), understanding the protective function of the voice (TW #6), and realizing that inner phobias and not listening to the voices result in more discomfort for the client and the system of parts.

Throughout the chapters of this book and, specifically, in Section 5, you will find a variety of clinical case session transcripts. Most of them include one or more of these different ways to explore the inner system.

SECTION THREE:

CHALLENGING PARTS AND VOICES

CHAPTER 5

SPECIAL ISSUES IN THE WORK WITH CHALLENGING PARTS

Most of the work shown in the previous two chapters of this book was aimed at both developing an Adult Self and understanding the internal conflict among voices or parts. In order to do this, we must keep in mind a few basic ideas, such as regarding the system as a whole, being respectful of each part and its timing, developing healthy curiosity, exploring the adaptive functions and the system's resources, and fostering empathy, cooperation, and negotiation.

These elements have become the building blocks that will help us reach our ultimate goal when doing this work: to *reduce the internal conflict* among parts and voices. This process may be relatively straightforward with simple systems or compliant parts. However, we must place special attention on learning to understand and work with those voices that are distrustful, hostile, aggressive, suicidal, or suspicious, since they are much more complicated and challenging.

WHAT MAKES SOME VOICES OR PARTS MORE CHALLENGING THAN OTHERS?

Many of the challenging voices seem to repeat —over and over again, like a broken record— the messages they learned in the past. And in all truth, playing a new song will not be easy for them. These voices need to understand and internalize two important facts. On the one hand, they need to see for themselves that the danger is over, the past is gone, and the present circumstances are very different. On the other hand, they need to learn that there are other ways of protecting the system. New protection strategies are usually well received by all parts, including the most hostile and suspicious ones. But these new ways need to be realistic. We cannot expect a voice that has exclusively learned to repeat insults to suddenly develop great communication skills. We cannot expect a voice that was born to be suspicious to start trusting from one day to the next. This will take time.

It is usually easier to work with the rest of the voices and parts, since they are less difficult to engage and tend to cooperate sooner. However, starting with the more compliant parts is not usually the best option. Yes, it is one option and it will help. But my recommendation is that, if possible, we should try to show interest in the most reluctant parts. Sometimes they will not be willing to engage and will refuse to collaborate, but as long as we try to communicate with them, we are introducing a crucial message, *"I am interested in you, and I understand that you are an important part of the system."* This will allow for better development of the work with the other voices or parts.

We should also keep in mind that starting by working with the most fragile or needy parts, such as child parts, may be tempting for therapists, but it can lead to complications. First, because these parts are often protected by some of the more challenging parts in the system and, second, because trying to work with the core parts of the system might be too invasive for some clients. Showing interest in these fragile parts may be experienced as a threat by other protector parts. We need to have achieved both a good enough therapeutic alliance and some degree of cooperation from protector parts for us to be able to dive into working with these essential parts.

Achieving cooperation from these parts will greatly depend on the healthy communication skills that therapists can model for clients so that they, in turn, can model these skills from the Adult Self to other parts of the system. It is necessary to achieve positive changes in the dynamics of the internal system. If the Adult Self learns to communicate differently, even the most challenging parts can incorporate the information and learn from this experience.

Let us see some specific aspects to keep in mind with challenging parts and voices:

- They were born from the most painful experiences, allowing the person to dissociate the most traumatic aspects and continue dealing with daily life.
- They often have little or no time orientation. They live in trauma time, unaware that time has gone by and the present is currently safe. When parts are not time oriented, they are unaware that danger is over and remain stuck in defense. They may either be suspicious of others or be focused on repeating damaging behaviors to avoid pain or punishment from others (thinking that by inflicting pain themselves, they have more control over what is still perceived as an out-of-control situation.)
- They often do not have much of a repertoire; they repeat what they have learned to do. When exploring the type of messages, we will frequently run into repetitive sentences or a variation of the same message. In some cases, this might seem like a psychotic or Obsessive-Compulsive Disorder (OCD) presentation, but it is just a lack of resources and adaptive information.
- They are usually ignored and rejected either by the client, other parts, or both. If clients have received any previous treatment, they often have been actively ignored by clinicians too, who may say things such as, *"Do not listen to them, try listening to music instead,"* *"Just try to ignore them,"* or *"Remember they are not real, they are a product of your imagination."*

HOW DO WE BEGIN OUR WORK WITH THESE PARTS?

In working with this particular type of parts, we will follow the same steps of the general structure of the therapeutic work outlined in Chapter 2 and they will be expanded based on how they apply to challenging parts. We will also see how the essential aspects from Chapter 3 fit in quite nicely and become even more relevant, given how much we will need to insist on them.

Step 1. Exploring voices and parts

Getting clients to talk about complicated voices and parts is often a challenge, and it is not rare for clients to even deny their existence. Gathering details about these voices might be even more complicated than with other voices or parts because they often remind clients of people that were abusive and frightening. Acknowledging how difficult this can be is a must, as well as using a language that clients can accept.

Step 2. Encouraging clients to listen to the voices and pay more attention to the parts

When working with clients who have complicated parts and voices, it is necessary to recognize the fact that listening to the voices can be very such an unpleasant experience for clients that they prefer to ignore them or wish that they would disappear. In many cases, these voices give suggestions or commands that may be frightening for the client, and we should remind them that listening to these parts does not mean having to necessarily comply with their orders, which may be related to harming themselves or other people, or also to keeping silent and not speaking. The fear of the Adult Self is usually the biggest obstacle to being able to listen to these parts and be curious about them. Keeping the system in mind, respect, and healthy curiosity become even more important when working with these challenging parts, and we must show consistency and persistence.

The main idea –which is crucial in the case of hostile voices– is for the Adult Self to understand that ignoring these voices will not help. The less we listen and the more we ignore them, the more they will tend to get louder or escalate their behaviors in a desperate attempt to be acknowledged.

The same thing happens in regular human interactions. When the person with whom we are desperately trying to communicate listens consistently to us in a respectful, considerate way and shows healthy curiosity for what we have to say, we will be willing to communicate more amicably. Thus, being as respectful and curious as possible with the entire system becomes even more crucial in the work with challenging parts and will eventually lead to understanding what is happening with these parts and how to help them and the rest of the system.

Step 3. Exploring triggers

As clients understand that parts or voices become active when they are triggered, they can begin to grasp the idea of how these voices are trying to help out. By exploring when voices speak up, get louder or send messages that seem threatening or frightening for clients, the system can begin to understand that these apparently dysfunctional ways are a genuine attempt of helping out which also allows clients to identify the function of these hostile voices better.

Hostile voices often get triggered when the client must address or deal with something in particular. Their reaction can either be in response to a perceived threat or to noticing that other parts are not up for the job or cannot handle what needs to be done. Remember, parts and voices that are still stuck in trauma-time will respond as if the threat or the danger is still happening. In addition, the voice can also be protecting the system from overwhelming memories, by diverting attention from trauma contents or cues. Generally, the Adult Self and other parts cannot understand these attempts to help and tend to perceive them as attacks or abuse.

As pointed out in the general steps in Chapter 2, most of the time voices will show up when the client is feeling under stress, pressured, and unwell. However, some exceptions are worth mentioning, such as when clients have been punished for feeling good and have developed parts to protect them from these feelings, as a way to avoid further punishment. Some of the hostile voices and parts have the function of keeping "forbidden feelings or situations" under control, such as joy or pleasure. This is especially true in cases of sadistic abuse, for instance, where clients were sexually aroused and then blamed and punished for being "filthy pigs."

Step 4. Exploring and processing dissociative phobias

Phobias among parts are frequently one of the main obstacles that prevent the natural flow of treatment, but in complicated parts or voices, this becomes more relevant. Phobia towards hostile and critical parts will be very intense, and even when it is undeniable, it should be explored to help clients realize how the phobia is getting in the way of understanding and cooperation. We should always check how the different parts and the Adult Self feel towards the parts that are more threatening for the system and help clients to begin to develop curiosity towards the motive behind the scary or threatening behaviors or messages. Another critical aspect of this work is helping the most challenging parts and voices to understand that the way they are communicating or trying to help is causing more problems within the system and, thus, increasing the dissociative phobias. Processing the phobia between parts is particularly helpful when dealing with parts that generate intense fear, rejection, shame or despise.

Step 5. Assessing the degree of differentiation and time orientation in client and parts

The ability to differentiate between internal and external elements is not an easy task in complex traumatization. In cases with challenging voices, making a proper assessment of the client's degree of differentiation becomes crucial, since it may affect a variety of parts at different levels. Complicated parts and voices seem to be stuck in trauma-time to a higher degree than other, more simple voices. Since they are born from the most painful experiences, they have to work harder at their job to keep the client "safe." They usually do not know the danger is over, so distinguishing the past from the present is even more difficult for them. There are also some parts that may take on the role of the perpetrator, and the client may have a very hard time differentiating between the real perpetrator from the past and the internalized perpetrator.

Step 6. Exploring and validating the function of the voice

As with all parts or voices, we must help clients explore the role played by the challenging part and learn to recognize the adaptive function of the voice and its capacity to help. Remember to keep in mind the basic questions from Chapter 3 and explore with the client what the voice is trying to achieve with these comments or behaviors, and if the voice is concerned about something or it is simply repeating what it has learned in the past. Of course, figuring out these questions will be much more challenging than with other voices, since their response tends to be very negative and frightening for the client or the other parts.

Parts and voices have mostly protective functions, though this may be harder to see when the voice is aggressive and frightening. Most of the time, clients will say things like "I don't think it is trying to help, it's just ruining my life!" or "What do you mean help? It makes me feel miserable!" In addition, we will often encounter problems related to distrust. For example, clients do not like it when one or more parts do not seem to trust therapy, the therapist or other relevant people. And this is a great protection in those who were hurt by people who they were supposed to trust. Validating distrust is the best way for these parts to give us the benefit of the doubt.

It is important to keep in mind that questioning the protective function of the voice is a natural response for the client, either because the voice is experienced as frightening and dangerous or because fearful parts are blocking the client and making him or her feel powerless. Thus, we must insist on this point, and a good way to do so is to help them explore what is triggering the voice. By analyzing the triggers, the client will eventually see that voices tend to appear when things become complicated and the client or other parts of the system are feeling distressed or unable to manage difficult situations. We can say, "I know it doesn't feel like this part is trying to help because it is very frightening, but remember that it usually appears when things are difficult for you." We must always validate the protective function of the voice, even if it is currently ineffective, helping them see how it could have been useful in the past.

Once we start moving forward in therapy and understanding better, voices usually become quieter; this is a sign that things are calmer. When the conflict is reduced, voices might show up to help in a more positive way, helping clients to be careful when faced with situations that might be perceived as threatening by the system. Or they might show up when there is a phobia of change and normal life.

As we try to identify and acknowledge the function of the different parts, clients might even think we are taking sides and feel misunderstood. All of this is expected, and clinicians should be able to identify such issues as typical responses due to internal conflict. When clients feel misunderstood, we should not become discouraged nor give up quickly. We can actually use this information to clarify our message and say, "My intention is not to take sides. Remember, this is about helping all of you as a whole. I am just trying to help both you and the voice understand how you can function better as a team."

Step 7. Identifying and validating resources, feelings, and needs

After communication has been improved, if the voice decides to cooperate or give us relevant information such as "I am not trying to hurt her," "I don't want him to talk or think about the past," or "We have to be perfect or bad things will happen," we should thank the part and validate its willingness to help. This will increase understanding of how the voice has been a resource in the past, and resources can be derived from their function.

Validation is a very powerful tool for parts that have been functioning through power struggles and fights, so validating the feelings and needs of these parts becomes especially important. We will often need to help the client and the system understand that it was, and nowadays also is, valid to be angry or defensive, that it made sense back then and has helped them survive. The client and other parts might be frightened or ashamed of some of the intense feelings, but once they understand –mostly through modeling and working with the phobias– that fear can be reduced, this can open up space for acceptance and even gratitude. Identifying and validating needs might be somewhat more difficult since these parts often hide and are ashamed of even having needs. For instance, parts or voices that are fixated on being strong and tough may have a hard time realizing that they need acceptance and support.

Anything that we pick up that is meant as an attempt to understand or to help should be pointed out since it is not easy for clients, parts or voices to identify positive aspects in the behavior or comments of other parts. However, given the complicated nature of these voices and the fact that they have usually been very disturbing for the client for long periods of time, the Adult Self or other parts might get confused with this type of intervention. We should always check with the system after each intervention, asking questions that help us clarify what the client or the other parts think about what the voice is saying and making sure that everyone understands how the function can actually be considered a resource.

Step 8. Exploring, modeling and practicing alternative ways of responding

Once we have an idea of why voices are saying what they are saying, and how their comments concern, frighten or block the client or other parts, we can start introducing more adaptive ways to communicate. To reduce dissociative phobias of the Adult Self toward the parts and between the different parts, we either suggest or encourage the client to think about more useful or adaptive ways in which the voices can get their message across to better help the whole.

Since these complicated voices have been playing their protective role in one very specific way for a long time, we should assume that it will take them some time to learn the new ways and consistently use the new suggestions. For this reason, we must prepare the client for future messages from the voice that are similar to the old messages, helping them to develop appropriate response strategies to deal with these old learned messages.

Step 9. Identifying and exploring missing pieces

Being attentive to holes within the system is a good way of identifying the missing pieces. This can be particularly important in hostile voices since they are often related to aspects that are not accepted by clients such as experiencing rage, anger or shame. For instance, the desire to hurt others can be hidden by clients due to the fear of acting on those thoughts, as well as to feeling shame about their thoughts and urges and fearing the possibility of others seeing them as monsters or bad people if they share these thoughts. Unless we explore this openly, it might take some time for clients to bring it up. These parts are usually related to a huge conflict within the system that takes up a lot of the available energy to keep it contained.

Step 10. Reaching agreements, developing cooperation and teamwork

As a final step, we must try to reach agreements or compromises that all voices can accept, for the benefit of the entire system/person. Remember that it will be much simpler to reach agreements with parts that can cooperate than with parts that are still learning that cooperating is a possibility.

We should encourage clients to explore whether other parts can help them achieve their weekly goals, noticing if any parts feel these agreements or compromises are not a good idea. We must remind them that this is about teamwork, and we are interested in goals that feel right for every part or voice. If there is something that seems difficult during the week, we ask the client and any part to be curious about the difficulty, so we can analyze how to deal with it in the next session.

These steps are general guidelines for working with complicated parts or voices. However, each different part may have its own peculiarities. In the following chapters, we will delve into the specific work with the different types of complicated voices.

COMMON ISSUES IN COMPLICATED PARTS AND VOICES

Several issues are common in complicated parts and voices. To organize our work in a way that can be perceived as non-judgmental, we explore different interventions for each one of them:

Issue #1: Repetition. Parts protect the individual in the same way they learned to protect themselves. They have never been taught a different way of functioning. Endless repetition is then used as a defense to manage affects and emotion. This issue takes place in many types of voices, but it is especially disturbing when the voices are hostile, suicidal, critical or imitate the perpetrator in some way.

> ➤ Intervention: Acknowledge the protective function of the parts, while at the same time validating the experience of rejection or worry from the rest of the system. We must convey that we believe they can acquire new ways of managing their emotions, which will make them even more useful and powerful.

Issue #2: Anger. Parts are afraid of disappearing and tend to think that therapists want to destroy them or get rid of them since this is usually what the client wants initially. Showing anger is a great way to compensate for fear of disappearing. Hostile and aggressive parts, critical parts, and perpetrator-imitating parts tend to show anger more often.

> ➤ Intervention: One of the key messages that will need to be repeated many times is that voices are important parts of the Self and we do not want to get rid of them. On the contrary, we want them to guide us in the work because we know they are protector parts that can be very useful. Anger is important, but they should know that it can be expressed adaptively.

Issue #3: Distrust. Parts believe that therapists will never want to work with them; nobody, including the rest of the parts, ever showed any interest in them. Distrust helps them deal with the fear of rejection. Distrustful parts have a hard time trusting, but so do the rest of the different parts.

> ➤ Intervention: Another relevant message is that we are interested in their needs and what they have to say; this implies that they can complain, show distrust, disagree, and ask for help. We want to listen to them.

Issue #4: Control. Underneath the defenses lies a great deal of pain. Appearing to be in control is the perfect facade to hide extreme vulnerability. This issue is common to many different parts. However, in hostile parts, especially those that imitate perpetrators, it is more challenging because control is done in extreme or rigid ways that are limiting and very frightening or remind clients of their trauma history.

> ➤ Intervention: Keeping the pain in mind helps us understand why they need to resort to such complicated defenses. We must find a way to let parts know that they can have real control by not having to control everything and be even stronger. They need to know that they can keep control and will not become weaker or lose strength if they cooperate.

Issue #5: Power vs. submission. This is another side of keeping control. Usually, hostile voices and parts tend to insult, threaten, or harm the client or other parts, appearing powerful to keep them in line. Often, both the client and some of the voices or parts (e.g., fearful parts) go into submission to avoid conflict or retaliation.

> ➤ Intervention: Working with the system of parts and voices as a whole, explaining that all parts aim for the same goal. Explaining the importance of being assertive since the danger is over and there is currently no need for neither exerting power through scaring others nor submitting. Engaging the voices and parts so they can understand that there is no need to repeat this type of behavior and helping them understand that they will be more powerful as a whole.

Issue #6: Power struggles. In response to the insults and threats from the voices, the client or some parts may fight back, instead of going into submission. They end up feeding and maintaining the power struggle –and thus the internal conflict– by being as aggressive toward the voices as the voices are towards them.

➤ Intervention: Whenever clients talk about the voices in a derogatory way, we ask them to be respectful; and if they have given some of the parts or voices nasty names, we will ask them to rename them and refer to them respectfully. It is important to set the basis for the beginning of respect and cooperation.

Throughout the different cases presented in the book, especially in Section 5, we will find examples of working with all kinds of challenging voices. We will also be pointing out the different issues as they come up. And, as we have already done in the previous case examples, we will also be paying attention to the general steps of the treatment structure and the key elements for the development of the Adult Self.

CLINICAL CASE EXAMPLE

Susan: My Different Selves

Susan is a 30-year-old woman who has been diagnosed as BPD. In the moment of this intervention, she describes several parts of herself that are in conflict. In the beginning of therapy, there were many complicated symptoms, and the conflict between parts was high; she did not perceive all of them as parts of herself. After a period of working with her therapist, she becomes more aware of her internal system, which begins to function with more acceptance and collaboration between parts and patient. Although some of the more problematic symptoms improve, the outbursts of anger remain, which are a concern for both the patient and her therapist. For this reason, the professional requests clinical supervision of the case, resulting in this session between therapist, supervisor and patient. The client has already previously explored her system through the use of drawings, which is one of the exploration methods described in Chapter 4.

T: *I am aware that throughout this time you have done different drawings of how your inner world is doing.*

C: *Yes.*

T: *Would you be able to tell me how you are doing inside now?*

C: *(Sighs.) In general, it's Me, Myself, and She. Me is the part, let's say the rational part of myself, who the world sees, right? Me is the one that cooks, cleans, shops, and smiles at people. Myself is a teenager who is about 18 years old and is in charge of the attic.*

T: *The attic?*

C: *Yes, Myself has everything in boxes, and everything is organized, my memories, my history. It's all behind closed doors. Myself is in charge of everything being locked up and put away.*

T: *And what do you think about that?*

C: *Let's just say that Myself is who deals with my emotions.*

T: *And she deals with emotions by putting things away in boxes?*

C: *Yes. But I think that Myself is not doing well, because everything is all over the place and disorganized. The entire attic is a mess.*

T: *And the attic is something that you see in your head? Something that you visualize?*

C: *Yes, it's my interpretation of Myself.*

T: *It's how you perceive it. You perceive that Myself is in charge of protecting you from emotions by keeping them put away.*

> C: *Yes. Myself has been with me for a long time. She's always been a teenager. And the attic, well, she always said, "When I can't deal with something, it goes into the attic."*
> T: *And what do you think about the job that Myself is doing putting everything into boxes?*
> C: *It's hard work; it's difficult.*
> T: *And do you think it helps you?*
> C: *Well, yes. If it weren't for Myself, I wouldn't be able to manage. I would get too overwhelmed by all of it.*

The client already understands the function of this part, so further exploration can occur. If she had no concept of how this part functions for her, the work would focus initially on exploring the function, so understanding and cooperation can be encouraged. However, she does not understand what generated the changes, so further exploration might improve reflective abilities.

> T: *Why do you think everything is so disorganized now?*
> C: *She has been present a couple of times. She is like a three-year-old girl with a temper tantrum, and she just wants to let anger out. When she speaks, what she says is, "Why? Why do I have to be rational? Why can't I throw a rock at that man if he's bothering me? And why do I have to be quiet if I want to scream? And why, why?"*
> T: *How do you respond?*
> C: *Well... huh... I... I tell her that... that she just can't do that. I answer "Of course it would be satisfying to throw a rock at that man if he's bothering you."*
> T: *So, do you think it would be satisfying for you?*
> C: *Yes, of course. I could release the anger.*

Notice how we respectfully confront this information. Instead of telling the client that this is not adequate behavior, we help her reflect by asking her how she would feel. The client describes several situations where she had the impulse to hurt others. She also describes several episodes since childhood when she lost control and hurt others. She has good reflective abilities and can distinguish between a wish or impulse, and an action.

> T: *So, there's a lot of uncontrolled anger, and She has a hard time thinking logically and managing her anger. It's normal for all of us to have those types of thoughts because of unexpressed anger inside, but this does not mean you will actually do it.*
> C: *Yeah, yeah... I know.*
> T: *It's great that you can talk about it, so we can understand what is happening and why. Do you remember how you felt after those situations where you lost control?*
> C: *Yes, how couldn't I? I felt horrible.*
> T: *I wonder, do you think that anger is connected to She or to some other parts of you?*

We are attempting to make connections in understanding and working with anger (Issue #2). Further questioning reveals that even though there is a temporary loss of reflection and thinking capacity, there is no amnesia. It becomes noticeable that she has a very negative mental representation of herself.

> C: *Let's see. She did not exist until very recently, or I had no insight about her, so, it didn't seem connected to anything. It's as though I had a mental short-circuit and everything disappeared in those moments of rage.*

T: So, at that moment it's like you don't care, but do you remember what happened?

C: Yes, Yes.

T: What was next?

C: The monster showed up.

T: The monster?

C: Yes, the monster is what Myself was keeping away. She had it hidden in the attic behind a door. I think that monster is now She. I have the impression that Myself couldn't deal with the monster any longer; it got to be too much, too big. And then I think the monster turned into She.

Already the client demonstrates some integration, moving from a primitive image of her anger as a monster, to the anger of a little girl that represents the client as a child. By having been able to do so, she was able to partially resolve the power struggles among parts on her own (Issue #6). We continue exploring how the client perceives the different parts.

T: When you talk to me about Me, Myself, and She —who used to be the monster—, do you see them as aspects of yourself?

C: They are me, yes, but they're not me at the same time. Let's see, they're not like how I would be, but they are part of me, I guess, parts I don't like very much. I don't want to be that person.

T: Okay, so then you know that they are you, but it isn't how you want to be, so they feel different from you.

C: Exactly, they are part of me, but they are not exactly me. The me that I recognize as me is Me, let's say the part who is the most rational one of all.

T: So, on the one hand, She shows up now because Myself couldn't deal with it anymore.

C: Yes.

Once there is a better understanding of the internal system, we can use this information to help the client understand why She became triggered (TW #3) and appeared in the present context, which, in turn, will clarify the function of the voice (TW #6).

T: Does it seem like She is trying to help?

C: I think that She just wants to let the anger out.

T: Yes, getting out the anger can feel very urgent, and also if She gets out, she has the opportunity to be seen and understood by us. That is also so important. I wonder if perhaps another possibility is that She shows up because Myself is overwhelmed, and she's trying to help.

C: Uh-huh, yes, I understand.

After introducing the possibility that the part is trying to help (TW #6), the Adult Self can feel more empathy and compassion towards She. It then becomes easier for the client to acknowledge the needs of the parts (TW #7). From there on, we can work on cooperation, encouraging teamwork (TW #10) so the client can try to reach agreements between the parts regarding how to meet these needs and other possible common goals.

T: If this is it, what is She trying to do?

C: Lighten the burden.

T: She understands that in order to lighten Myself's burden, she has to do things, such as throw things at others, hurt others, etc.

C: Yes.

T: And what does Myself think about this?

Exploring what the parts and voices think and feel about other parts and voices (TW #4) is a great strategy to determine the existence of dissociative phobias between the parts. As we see, the way in which She is functioning may be, in fact, increasing the dissociative phobia. It is important that both the client and the part can see this clearly, so new alternative ways of functioning can be explored (TW #8).

C: If She came out like she wants to come out, I think that Myself would not feel good.

T: So, this is very important for She to know. Do you realize this? If She is trying to help Myself be less burdened, but acts out her anger in order to make that happen, you are actually going to have a much heavier burden and will need to put even more feelings in the attic.

C: Yes, I can see that.

T: So actually, she would not be helping with the burden. But it would be interesting to see how she could help in a way that can help lighten this burden.

C: Well, the only way that She can be helpful without Myself feeling bad, is if She was able to come out little by little, in an organized and buffered way, in a way that is not hurtful.

T: Yes, that makes sense. You know, I think it's a hefty load. It sounds extremely tough for a three-year-old girl to have to alleviate the burden of both a teenager part and an adult. What do you think about this?

C: Yes. (Client has a sad look on her face.)

Determining the needs of the different voices and parts (TW #7) is crucial. This cannot be achieved if the client has not previously started to develop some compassion for the part through her Adult Self.

T: What does She need? What could this three-year-old part of you need?

C: Love, I guess, lots of love.

T: And when you realize this, what happens?

C: Sadness.

T: Sadness, yes. It's sad, isn't it, to realize how much she–you—lack love. It's so good that you understand what she needs. What else is going on in your head?

C: I realize I know why she needs love. She needs love because Me and Myself are very harsh.

T: Oh, I see. What is it like to realize this? Do you think it can be useful to realize this?

C: Well, it's hard to realize this, but it's useful.

We are continuing to promote empathy towards the part by thoroughly describing her function in the system (TW #6). This helps the client to fully realize that there may be alternatives that need to be explored within the system (TW #8), that things can function differently, in a way that better helps to meet the needs of the parts and the client herself.

T: Okay, so you can see that She needs that love now. And you understand that also Me and Myself are being too harsh on the little girl. Yes?

C: Yes, with the girl, with Myself, and with Me.

T: Okay, so what does that help you understand about what needs to be changed?

C: That we need to change the judge that lives in this house.

T: What does the judge need?

C: To stop judging once and for all and start loving a little bit more.

T: Okay, what is that like for you? Would that possibility be interesting for you?

C: It's what I should do. I just don't know how to do it.

Here is an integrative lag between what is known and what can be accomplished with actions. The therapist understands that more work should be done to support this integrative step. It may be interesting to check if there are any dissociative phobias present that may be getting in the way (TW #4). The fear of losing control is a common one in these types of voices (Issue #4) and it is necessary to help them see that by getting her needs met (TW #7) and increasing cooperation in the system (TW #10), the client and the part are, in fact, less likely to lose control.

T: From the perspective of Me, what do you feel towards the girl?

C: Fear and sadness. I am afraid of losing control.

T: Yes, that's a pretty big fear. And you said the girl needs love, so if she receives a little bit of love, I wonder, is it possible that she will not need to lose control?

C: Yes, because more than likely, since the girl needs love, the intensity of the anger will decrease through love.

Continuously promoting an adult perspective by modeling new ways of responding (TW #8) with acceptance and compassion, is a must throughout the sessions. Clients may become easily frustrated when parts are distrustful (Issue #3) and do not believe their efforts to change the relational dynamics within the system, and it is important to normalize these responses.

T: Could you try thinking about what you would say to a three-year-old girl? What would you say to her?

C: I would tell her that she deserved to be loved.

T: And when you tell her that, what happens to her?

C: The problem is that she doesn't believe it. T: Well, that's fine, she probably has good reasons not to believe that. Can Me understand it?

C: Yes.

T: From the adult that you are nowadays, do you understand that it's hard for your three-year-old self to believe that?

C: Yes. T: What do you imagine she needs from you in order to believe it?

C: First I have to believe it from Me and Myself, or else She will never believe it.

T: Yes, somehow all of you need to believe it. And what do Me and Myself need in order to start believing that a little more?

C: I have no idea. Well, first I have to stop being so mean to myself.

> *T: Well, that would be quite an interesting step. I already see that you have compassion for that little girl and thus for yourself today. That's a wonderful start, don't you think so? Do you think you could try taking care of yourself a little bit more these days and not be so harsh on yourself? And see how your inner world responds to that?*
>
> *C: I can do some "thought stopping."*
>
> *T: Do you imagine that will help?*
>
> *C: It helped me once when I was depressed.*
>
> *T: Perfect, so then it would be good that you use whatever helps you not to be so harsh. And if you are harsh, just notice the circumstances that activated that inner judge. Maybe you could remind the judge that you are safe and okay now? Something like that?*

Before closing up the session, we prepare the client for possible negative reactions and help her connect with her own resources (TW #7), so she can learn to respond more adaptively to herself and her inner system (TW #8).

> *T: You're an adult now, and you have a son.*
>
> *C: Yes. T: When your son is restless, how do you usually respond to calm him down?*
>
> *C: Hugging him and kissing him.*
>
> *T: Does it work?*
>
> *C: Yes, most of the time.*
>
> *T: Okay, so then from your adult, when She is restless, what could you do?*
>
> *C: Calm her down, tell her loving things.*
>
> *T: How great that you know just what to do! So, it would be very important that if She responds by not believing she is loved, that you respond by compassionately understanding why she doesn't believe it, from your adult self. To say something like, "I understand that you don't believe it, but I'm trying to understand and help you feel accepted." (Client nods.) In order for She to truly believe that she deserves to be loved, you have to show her these kinds of things little by little.*
>
> *C: Right. So, let's see if the thought stopping works.*
>
> *T: Great. Try it out, because you know it has worked before. And if it doesn't work, no problem! We'll explore other ways and find the ways that are right for you. The important thing is to simply practice and notice what happens. You have many options, something the adult part of you can remember. What is important is to understand that when there is a part of you that loses control, it's usually because you don't yet know that there are other options. Now that you understand why She loses control; you can help her see other options. Above all try not to get frustrated with the messages, just try to understand, "I understand that she's feeling sad or angry, that she doesn't feel love." And from there, you can start to understand and learn how to manage better.*

This case example of a client with a high integrative capacity illustrates how to move from the symptoms to the origin of the problem. We see how exploring the system can help both client and therapist understand that the client's angry impulses are related to a part. This angry young part is trying to help the system in the only way it knows how. The client can achieve more clarity about the impulses, about the related part and its function within the system, and also about the dynamics between this and other parts. She is also able to understand that the older parts have been too harsh on the little one and how the little one is actually trying to do something too big for such a young age. The work that was done resulted in the decrease of internal conflict, an increase of empathy, and the beginning of a search for common goals within the system

SUMMARY

Working with complicated parts and voices requires the therapist to insist even more on working through the Adult Self in order to increase understanding of what is happening in the system. Dissociative phobias will be stronger, and it will be more difficult to see how the part or voice has a positive protective function. Issues such as anger, control, distrust, or power struggles, among others, makes working with these parts much more challenging.

Most, if not all, of the examples in the following chapters of this book deal with one or another type of challenging voices and parts.

CHAPTER 6

WORKING WITH HOSTILE AND AGGRESSIVE PARTS AND VOICES

Working with all parts of the system is important, but the specific work with hostile and aggressive voices and parts is a crucial aspect of the therapeutic process because they generate much discomfort, confusion, and fear in our clients. Therefore, helping the client to listen to these voices can be especially challenging since they may have invested much time and energy doing exactly the opposite: trying as hard as they could to ignore them.

As a first step, then, we must acknowledge how frightening and confusing it must be for them to deal with these parts. As stated in the previous chapter, in the case of voices that frighten the client by giving aggressive and harmful orders (e.g., hurting themselves or others), clients may think that listening to the voices means having to comply with what they are saying. Explaining that listening to these parts does not mean having to act necessarily on any of their suggestions or commands may be surprising for the client and may help put them at ease.

THE ORIGIN OF HOSTILE AND AGGRESSIVE PARTS

Many hostile or aggressive parts came to be in traumatic and abusive environments and originated through a learning process. As we will see through the different case examples in the book, they are often just repeating the behaviors they learned from their childhood perpetrators. If we think about it, the only way in which the client can feel that they have some strength or control is developing a part (or parts) that seems as strong as the people who hurt them. This is why they might mimic the same comments, type of thinking, belief system, tone of voice, and attitudes. The sad truth is that they do not have healthy models to teach them other options. A person who grows up surrounded by verbal, physical, or sexual aggression, negligence, threats, etc., cannot internalize positive behaviors and attitudes towards the self or think of other possibilities since no one is there to model them. This is why it is crucial to help clients understand the rationale behind these voices; to let them know that anger and threats are often how they learned to feel some control over their environment; and to teach them new ways of looking at the voices and themselves. And, as we know now, new ways *can* be learned.

THE FUNCTION OF HOSTILE AND AGGRESSIVE PARTS

For the client to understand how these parts are trying to help, it becomes necessary to explore the function that the part is serving in the system. As commented before, one of the most common responses from clients when exploring the possible function is that there is no function at all, that the part or voice is something that is ruining their life. In other cases, clients might be able to see that this is a protector part, but the phobia will still be there. In these cases, clients will say things such as, "She was always there when I could not handle the situation anymore." To help clients understand how these parts are trying to help when exploring the system, we should always ask about the triggers, "When does this part show up?" knowing that the answer will most likely be that the part shows up when the person feels bad or is going through a difficult time.

These parts may be serving other purposes as well. On the one hand, they may be holding anger and traumatic memories that the client or the Adult Self cannot assimilate. On the other, they may be trying to generate suspicion in the Adult Self, since this keeps the client vigilant for potential perpetrators in the present. Also, these parts may be only trying to adopt the perpetrator position to avoid the victim position (Blizard, 1997; Ross, 1997; Ross & Halpern, 2009.)

SPECIFIC INTERVENTIONS

As clinicians, we need to remember and remind clients that these uncomfortable parts are usually trying to protect and help. So regardless of their presentation, we always need to keep this in mind and remember that, initially, this statement is often met with disbelief by clients, especially when it comes to voices that tell them to hurt themselves or hurt others. It is hard to fathom how something that is hurting or scaring them daily could be at the same time trying to protect them. This seems inherently contradictory. However, as stated before, as we help them understand the dynamics –and once the client realizes that the part shows up when they are feeling bad– it starts to make more sense that the part would be trying to somehow make them feel better. Realizing that if it were simply trying to make them feel bad, it would more than likely show up randomly, especially when the client is feeling well, is often experienced as a relief, despite the phobia still being present.

Since most of these parts and voices remain stuck in traumatic memories, they often do not know they are safe in the here and now. It will be crucial for them to develop time orientation, so they can begin to realize that the present is safe and there is no reason to protect themselves now. Time orientation is not easy for parts that have been stuck in trauma-time for years and who are still afraid of the possible consequences from their perpetrators.

Initially, the work with these voices will take place as they come up in therapy or outside of therapy sessions. Often, exploring the symptom becomes one of the ways to encourage clients to start speaking about these voices, allowing us to introduce this work.

CLINICAL CASE EXAMPLE

Hope: No way out

Hope is a 32-year-old woman who was referred to our center from the emergency room (ER) due to many complicated symptoms like impulsivity, aggression towards other people and things, and dangerous and convoluted self-harming behaviors. She feels like a lost cause and does not expect to live better in the present and, much less, in the future. During the first intake, she describes a life filled with trauma. In this fragment, she explores an episode when she had to go to the emergency room.

> C: *Do you know what happened? I had an argument with my best friend because I was drinking. I was raising my voice more than usual, and he wanted me to lower my voice, but I couldn't, so then he slapped me. I said, "It's OK, it's normal." I didn't want it to be a big deal, but it seems that my subconscious did, and I had a panic attack. It was one of the convulsive seizures, suffering for hours and days, and going to the emergency room. There was no way to calm down, even with strong medication. I don't know if there are other drugs that can work, I think I've been given everything.*

This is a typical example where the client will give us a lot of information, and we can be confused about what to focus on. But if we are clear about one of our main goals, understanding the conflict and triggers, we will be able to filter the information better.

> T: *What do you mean with subconscious?*
> C: *Well, apparently, it did not affect me. But it really did, because otherwise, I wouldn't have ended up like that.*
> T: *It did affect some part in you.*
> C: *It sure seems like it.*
> T: *With your previous therapist, you had been exploring inside, and you had identified different parts of yourself. Has that changed? Can you tell me how it is now?*
> C: *I still see myself more or less the same, but more aware of things and calmer, because I also hang out with people who are much calmer.*
> T: *That's good.*

We ask her to draw a picture of her inner world –one of the ways to explore the internal system of parts– even though the client has a hard time drawing because of a critical inner part.

> T: *I know you have a hard time drawing, but could you draw your inner world? Just so I can get an idea of how you're doing inside now.*
> C: *Like drawing a circle and the parts you mean?*
> T: *Perhaps. However it comes up for you.*

She describes each part as she draws. Mainly there seem to be three identified parts: Hulk, Doll, and Child.

C: *The most impulsive, violent, and irritable part now takes less space than before. Even the Doll part is also smaller than it was, which is the part that is responsible for being absolutely perfect at all times with people I don't know, or at work; responsible for doing everything right. I'm not paying so much attention to that anymore, so this part could be even smaller. And then the Child part, this is the person who is hiding there and who has a hard time coming out. She is very vulnerable but is starting to become stronger, not much, but it seems like she has grown up a little. (Looks at the drawing and makes a change.) Maybe the Doll part is bigger, yes. Let's see, these two are armors that protect this one, but they're not so big now. Child used to be a tiny thing you couldn't even see. She's me when I was little, that lost little girl, sweet and funny.*

T: *Which part do you identify with now?*

C: *Right now, I'm a bit Hulk. I'm quite upset. I am so upset right now that I'm considering not going to work today because I don't want to end up breaking anything.*

T: *Well, you don't have to end up breaking anything. Let's try to understand what's happening so that you can be calmer.*

When there are aggressive parts, exploring the possible dissociative phobias towards and among the different parts, becomes even more important (TW #4). Inquiring about dissociative phobias can be done by simply checking how the client feels about each of the parts.

T: *What do you feel towards each of these parts of you right now? How do you feel about Hulk?*

C: *What do I feel towards those parts right now? Do you mean whether I consider them good or bad? T: Yes, if you see them as good or bad.*

C: *I think they are bad.*

T: *You do know that they all have their function, right?*

Exploration of the function of the parts (TW #6) is also very important, especially given that it becomes very hard for clients with aggressive and hostile parts to understand that there can be anything positive about the behavior displayed by the part.

C: *Well, I really don't see Hulk's function. I can see something in Doll, but Hulk's function seems pretty ridiculous. Yes, it is protective, but it is a very impulsive and violent protection, both verbally and physically, because I can break anything.*

T: *She tries to protect you when you cannot deal with things.*

C: *Yes, but it doesn't make sense, because she explodes in an uncontrolled way, like what happened the other day when the ambulance came to my house. It's ridiculous.*

T: *Was that Hulk?*

C: *Yes, that was totally Hulk, whether it's self-harm or damaging objects.*

T: *So, it would be ideal if Hulk could help you in a way that didn't scare you.*

C: *I used to make some sense out of her before, but she doesn't make any sense now, I believe it's an armor that should disappear.*

Although there is partial realization about the possible intent of help, the phobia towards the most impulsive part is maintaining the conflict. In fact, the issue of anger (Issue #2) can often become a vicious circle associated with the desire that either the client or other parts have for a certain part to disappear from the system. The therapist is trying to help the client and the part understand that Hulk can help in a more adaptive way (TW #6). This sets the stage to start exploring alternatives to other and more functional ways of helping the system (TW #8).

> T: *More than disappearing, it's about her being able to help you more adaptively.*
> C: *But that's what Doll is for, I believe. Because Doll is also responsible for being perfect all day long, but she also knows how to be calm and relaxed, to have a good conversation, to do things well. I know it's not about being perfect, because perfection doesn't exist. Doll at first started out with perfection, doing everything perfectly and looking perfect at all times, everywhere. It's an armor and, at the same time, it's a way to protect the self, not letting other people get to know you. And she also stabilizes, I think that she works well.*
> T: *But everything has a function. So, Hulk needs to learn to regulate herself differently too.*
> C: *Yes. She comes out less and less.*

At this point, the therapist continues trying to understand Hulk's function (TW #6), exploring the triggers that determine when she shows up (TW #3). Keep in mind the importance of helping the client see that parts do not usually show up when she is calm and the fact that this means they are trying to help. Clients are usually surprised by this realization.

> T: *When does Hulk show up?*
> C: *She shows up in chaotic moments, like the other day.*
> T: *So, she doesn't come out when you're calm, right?*
> C: *No.*
> T: *She comes out when you're not doing well.*
> C: *Of course, she comes out when I'm completely hysterical.*
> T: *That means that she's trying to help you; otherwise she wouldn't just come out when you're not doing well.*
> C: (Seems surprised.) *Oh, really?*
> T: *Of course.*

Once the client starts showing some curiosity about this protective function, even if there may still be some disbelief, we can continue introducing the idea that there may be alternative ways to protect the system that are more adaptive and effective in the present (TW #8). Functions that were protective in the past may be very dysfunctional in a present where there is no real danger.

> C: *And what do you consider good about what happened? I ended up breaking things, I ruined the garden, and then I started to wrap myself around an electrical cord that could have electrocuted me.*
> T: *It's not about seeing this action as a good thing. It's about trying to understand how Hulk is trying to help you, so she can do so more effectively. It is obvious that she has a lot of strength, but it is such an out-of-control force that, in the end, it hurts you. It's likely that she may not even realize that doing this ends up hurting you. I think this part can help you by channeling that strength, without having to blow up or walk around breaking things.*
> C: *And how is it channeled?*
> T: *This is something that can be learned here.*

Since the client is paying attention, it is a good time to continue developing healthy curiosity toward this part that is so challenging. As we can see clearly, anger is a central aspect of this part (Issue #2).

T: Do these parts ever talk to you?

C: Hulk is always talking.

T: Does Hulk have a voice?

C: Yes, I think it's my voice. But it's also the hate. Hulk is all of that.

T: There is a lot of accumulated anger.

C: Yes, it's all anger.

T: It's the fight, the defense, and she has so much anger that sometimes she cannot even see clearly.

C: Doll is constantly saying, "control yourself, control, perfection, control..."

This last comment points to a possible conflict between these two different parts of the internal system, so we must explore it (TW #1).

T: Do they know each other?

C: I don't think so.

T: You don't think so. But you do know the three of them.

C: Yes, I do, but I think those two don't know each other, or if they do, they don't care. They might know each other because, now that I think about it, they do speak to one another. The problem is that sometimes Hulk is stronger. I really believe that Hulk is the strongest one of all.

T: Hulk has a lot of strength.

C: Sometimes Doll can control Hulk, but this is more the exception.

This comment from the client clearly points at the conflict between the parts. There are a few issues that perhaps could be taking place and are worth exploring or pointing out: the issue of control (Issue #4) and whether there are any power struggles among these two parts (Issue #6). This would be a good time to offer suggestions (TW #8) and introduce the idea of teamwork since collaboration among parts is paramount for the good functioning of the system (TW #10).

T: More than controlling, it's about working as a team. When you say they speak to one another, what kind of things do they say?

C: Trying to soothe her, saying "it's OK, calm down, breathe..."

T: Who says this to whom?

C: I think it's Doll, the one who speaks about control. (Changes the drawing a bit). Maybe we could do another Hulk-Doll-Child. Child is me, let's leave it that way, but I think we could also draw another part. I had never thought about this, but now I am thinking that it's a sense of constant uselessness. Doll has worked a lot on this in a positive way, and so has Hulk, but in a negative way.

T: So, what positive things does she say? About the feeling of uselessness?

C: Well, she says positive things.

T: Like what?

C: I don't know, for example, "No, you are not useless; we all need time; patience, patience, patience; you have to work, and work, and work..."

T: So, she gives you some positive messages.

C: *Yes, the problem is that I don't know if the messages are sent by Doll or Child, I'm not sure.*

T: *Try to think about that.*

C: *Because Doll is now looking at it as if it were a good thing ... to make sure that it's control and perfection. And perfection is not good. It also includes control because perfection reaches a control point; that is, to be controlling at all times in order to be perfect and to do everything well. But the most normal control, let's say more rational, I think maybe it comes from Child, because Child is rational.*

T: *Child is rational.*

C: *I think so.*

T: *Could you specify a bit?*

C: *Let's see, at first, she started out as a little girl, who came out from time to time. She was a nice and sweet, but very vulnerable, little thing. Now she can reason, she can have some control, but in a healthy way.* T: *What age would she be?*

C: *What age?*

T: *Yes. When you think of Child, how old does she sound?*

C: *Maybe we should change Child's name. She's still vulnerable, yes, but Child does not mean really "child," it means "the inner self."*

T: *The inner self.*

C: *The real me.*

T: *Your authentic self.*

C: *My authentic self, yes. My authentic and very vulnerable self, but over time maybe it may be evolving a little and offering some positive messages. Hulk has strength, lots of strength. But of course, I'm not all Hulk, because if I were only Hulk, I would be completely out of control, I would be in jail.*

Even though our way of interacting with clients should always be geared towards developing an Adult Self within the client, since it is the beginning of a more integrated way of functioning, at this point the therapist chooses to introduce this idea directly, both as psychoeducation and as a goal for therapy.

T: *In a way, you would be interested in developing a healthy adult. The healthy adult is the one who can take care of everything, the one who can protect the vulnerability of Child, the one that can tell Hulk when she is going overboard, when she is getting way too triggered. And she's the one that can tell Doll that not everything has to be perfect, that it's great to want to improve and bring out the good in you, but when there are so many demands, in the end, it's not helpful.*

C: *It just blocks me.*

T: *Being able to have the adult present —considering everything that is inside of you— is what can help you make it all work in a more integrated way. Does this make sense to you?* C: *Yes, totally.*

Helping the client understand the function of the parts is an ongoing task that should be kept in mind in every session (TW #6). One of the issues that is very much related to the angry parts is the fear that both the client and the therapist want them to disappear (Issue #2). The therapist returns to what the patient had said before about wanting the part to go away.

T: *What worries me a little is that you want Hulk to disappear.*

C: *Well, I used to see her usefulness, but not anymore. She is useful if someone wants to rape you or hit you, right? Anger is really the one that saves you from that.*

T: It's a protection, yes.

C: It's the defense that saves you there, so you don't get stuck in "duh" mode.

T: You cannot defend yourself if you freeze.

C: Yes, and it happened to me once when a guy tried to rape me. I was completely blocked, and I already had my pants down. And then I would try to hit him, I mean, I wanted to ask for help. So I did, but there was so much noise that no one could hear me. I tried to get out of there by knocking on the door, punching the door. At that point, I thought, "Stop, stay still for a moment and think," and then I said, "Well, think, what can you do to get out of here? Because you have to do something, otherwise it's going to happen." So, I don't know, but I got some strength out of somewhere and "boom," I pushed him against the door, and then I ran away.

T: Sure, and that was with Hulk's help.

C: Yes, and reasoning helped a little.

T: But that is your adult self –the adult in you–, the one who has grown up and knows that things can be handled differently.

C: Well, that was an extreme situation.

Whenever possible, it is important to validate what the parts are doing, by pointing out and reinforcing her resources (TW #7) and helping her see how the parts assist her in managing difficult situations. Also, offering suggestions about new ways of dealing with difficult situations (TW #8) helps the client to start considering new ways of coping that are more adaptive in the present and neither maintain nor increase the inner conflict between the parts.

T: You have a lot of resources, especially if your mind is calm, if you are not triggered emotionally by anything. Then, you know what is right, what is not right, what you can tolerate, what you cannot. The problem is when something gets triggered inside.

C: Sure, I think I have to learn to say no and be able to say, "Look, I'm fed up, I cannot deal with this now, just talk to me about something trivial."

T: And Hulk can help you there, but without having to explode. She can give you a warning beforehand...

C: She learned to say, "Enough!"

T: Sure, but that "enough" should not scare you or generate more problems. She can give you a hint kind of like this, "Hey! Not this!"

C: I remember an incident at work when I felt I wanted to rip a co-worker's head off. I think that Hulk must've been the one who told me, "Leave now, there are 20 minutes left. Leave now because you are going to explode." It must've been her, right?

T: Well, if it was her, then she is learning to manage things better.

Although we might think that it was probably not this part, we take the opportunity to validate what would be adaptive, since the part is listening.

C: That's important.

T: Everything is important because everything is a part of you trying to help.

C: In a way that is out of control.

Since the client has trouble understanding her own reactions, it can be very useful to introduce psychoeducation on defense systems. Biology is easy to understand when it is linked to reactions and behaviors that the client does not fully understand or control. In this case, the Hulk part is related to the fight action system, and helping her understand the protective function (TW #6) is crucial for better functioning and to develop empathy and compassion.

T: *We have fight, flight, submission, attachment —which is bonding with others— and then we have freeze.*

C: (Very surprised and engaged.) *That's the blockage.*

T: *So, this is biological. This is what happens in all human beings and animals. An animal uses all these types of biological responses to protect itself.*

C: *Sorry for smiling so much. I'm fascinated by these things.*

T: *We want to understand what happens at a biological level, so that you can also give yourself messages and understand what is happening. If you were able to say, "Wait a moment, think about this," then you definitely have the ability to do it.*

C: *Uh, and I was completely high and drunk.*

T: *We know that this pretty much cancels your ability. Usually, when we are in a dangerous situation, we can activate fight or flight, depending on the situation. If there's a danger, we escape if we can, or we defend ourselves if we are in a position to defend ourselves. When this is not possible, submission or freezing must step in.*

C: *But what is submission useful for?*

T: *Well, so they don't hurt you more.*

C: *When?*

T: *This usually happens when one is younger and has no way out.*

C: *For example, when they hit you and you get blocked, right? But that would not be...* T: *That's a mix.*

C: *I believe this is not submission. Let's see, sexually, it would be submission, but this would be more of a block.*

T: *Freezing.*

C: *Yes. I don't understand submission yet.*

T: *Submission is like pleasing. Usually, as adults, we have more options, and we try to avoid this. Perhaps Hulk and Doll become activated to protect you from that. But when one is growing up in a complicated situation, fight and flight cannot usually be put into practice. They are two impossible responses, given the existing helplessness; the only thing left is to submit, to put up with it because there is no way out, to think that everything is my fault. That is the most intelligent response in a no-win situation: the child assumes that it's all his fault. If the child should realize that there is no way out, he would be terrified. Are you following me?*

C: *Yes, go on.*

T: *So, it's better to think that "I do bad things," "This is my fault," and "If I do everything right one day, this will stop happening." We learn this here. And what happens later when we become adults? This keeps repeating itself. Things are triggered, but they don't make sense now because we are no longer in the same dangerous situation. What your brother explained to you at some point, I can't remember the exact words, something like "the war..."*

C: *The war is over now.*

> *T: Yes. What you said is somewhat related to this. Sometimes, in current situations that remind you of things you've experienced, possibly one of these responses is triggered, and this is where these two parts come in to help you out. The difference is that now you are no longer in a no-win situation. You are an adult; now you can protect yourself, you have resources. This is what your inner system has to be able to understand in order to help you.*
> *C: In other words, I basically have such low self-esteem that I don't believe in myself. Well, sometimes I do a little.*
> *T: You're starting to believe more in yourself.*
> *C: Yes, a little bit more.*
> *T: And in your abilities. But what has long been with you is what you have learned, which is to think that everything is your fault and that you have to put up with it.*
> *C: And that I'm unworthy.*
> *T: And that you're unworthy. Then there is internal conflict, because other parts of you don't want to think you're unworthy, and they don't want to tolerate things that shouldn't be tolerated. Now that you're taking better care of yourself, these parts have to learn to help you in a way that is more adapted to your current reality, because you are not at war with anyone now. If you are at war right now, it's with yourself.*
> *C: Yes.*

Once the client is able to understand what happens with this part, we can begin suggesting a different way of responding to the part (TW #8). On the one hand, we are interested in promoting collaboration between parts (TW #10) as we will see in the following segment of the session. Another key aspect is to help the client understand that listening to this part does not imply doing what it says (TW #2).

> *T: The idea is to see which part of you could give Hulk a warning when she's going overboard.*
> *C: At that point?*
> *T: It has to be before, because...*
> *C: Then I go completely crazy and there's no way...*
> *T: Do you like animals?*
> *C: Oh, yes, I love them.*
> *T: Do you like cats?*
> *C: Yes, I have cats, and dogs too.*
> *T: When a cat is scared* (the therapist makes the gesture of a cat in defense move), *you cannot even get close to pet it.*
> *C: No, because it'll hiss and scratch you.*

We naturally flow into offering alternative ways of behaving in certain situations (TW #8), while helping the client communicate with the voice and help increase realization of a very common topic: lack of differentiation between past and present (TW #5). What was useful in the past, may not be useful in the present. In fact, it may be even harmful.

> *T: It cannot accept it because it's in full defense mode. When Hulk is in full defense mode, she has already gone beyond the limits of realizing, her inner system cannot say, "Hold on, let's see, what can we do*

now?" So, the issue is to give her a warning beforehand, so she can understand that it's great that she can help you, but it is not necessary to go to extremes.

C: *It's just not necessary.*

T: *Sure, but maybe she doesn't know it differently yet. Do you think Hulk knows it's not necessary?*

C: *No way! She's impulsive.*

T: *But she can learn to be reactive while being in control. That would help you with setting boundaries.*

C: *Yes, the basis is setting boundaries, well, almost...*

T: *There is something inside that warns you when something is not right. When you are working, for example, and you are about to blow up and something in you says, "You better get out of here," the important thing is that you don't ignore it. If you pay attention to this warning, you can take a step back before reaching your limit. Maybe you can tell yourself something like, "I'm just going to do it right."*

T: *They cannot say anything if you do a good job. Instead, they will have something to say if you try to do it fast, but in the end, you lose more time fixing your mistakes and then you feel more stress. So, you say that you would like to do what others do (have control) ...*

C: *Yes, I see my colleague at work going, "Oh look, I'm not a professional, I'm going at my own pace." I see he's just chilling and I go, "Fuck! Why can't I do that, man?"*

T: *Well, maybe you can't do that either because it's not in you. If there are things that do not go with you, you won't feel comfortable either; but you can say, "Well, I am learning, I am going to do it well, as I like to do it." Not perfect.*

C: *Well, my last hair dye was done slowly and well.*

It is always a good idea to introduce psychoeducation on mental efficiency, so the client can understand that she has little energy to function in daily life when so much energy is spent on the internal conflict.

T: *But that may have to do with managing mental energy. Do you know what that is?*

C: *I know what energy is.*

T: *Well, think of mental energy. In order to do something well, we need a certain energy concentration.*

C: *Yes, but a lot of it. I can't be doing something and talking at the same time.*

T: *Of course, because right now there is a lot of internal conflict. When there is so much internal conflict, a lot more energy ends up getting spent. If you learn to manage this conflict, you will not spend so much energy, you will be able to be aware of two things at once. But for that, you have to understand everything that has been triggered in you.*

Increasing understanding of the parts and validating what each one is trying to do (TW #6) is a continuous piece of our work. Here, we end the example by starting to suggest alternative ways for the different parts to help the client (TW #8). This is meant to, in due time, increase cooperation between them (TW #10).

C: *So, Hulk is important?*

T: *Yes, Hulk can help you in a non-explosive way.*

C: *And Doll?*

T: *And Doll can help you, too. In fact, both of them are helping you. The problem is that they are doing so in extreme ways and we need to soften what is not useful.*

C: And the feeling of uselessness? Is it there because it's been there forever and the two of them also increase it sometimes, right?

T: Do they increase it?

C: Yes, I think so, because if everything is not perfect...

T: Exactly, if Doll learns to give you positive messages without everything having to be perfect, the feeling of uselessness will really diminish. If she is trying to help you with your sense of uselessness by doing everything perfectly, this in the end does not help you. Instead, it could be more useful if she were to say, "Well, try it later." That could be another way to help.

C: Yes, because it wasn't really that important.

T: In our next sessions, we can keep exploring this. We want to see how they can help in a way that calms you. (The client nods, looking happy and calm.)

As we could see in this example, initially the client did not think the aggressive part could have any function and thought it was best to get rid of it. But by helping her become aware of when the part shows up and how she shows up, she was able to become more curious and begin to understand that it had been trying to help her for a long time. By the end of the session, the client is still afraid of this part, but feels more empathy and curiosity, and we can observe in her willingness to try to understand it. She is even able to ask, "So this part is important then?" and acknowledge how the part has not only tried to help but has actually been protecting her for a long time, including from a rape.

SUMMARY

Aggressive parts are very challenging for clients because they engage in behaviors that could easily be frightening. Anger becomes one of the main issues here because clients and other parts would very much like for these parts to disappear. This, of course, makes the part even angrier. Remember that exploring how aggressive parts are trying to help becomes an even more important task since, initially, it is not easy for clients to believe that these parts are actually helping at all. As usual, exploring what triggers this part will help us determine the function it plays in the system.

CHAPTER 7

WORKING WITH SELF-HARMING AND SUICIDAL PARTS AND VOICES

Self-harming and suicidal voices are a variation of hostile voices and can be extremely frightening for clients. Although they share some similarities, there are some differences between them as well. As we saw in the previous chapter, hostile voices are usually repeating messages they have learned to try to achieve a change in the client or other parts. However, they frequently do not understand that this is making the situation worse. In the case of self-harming and suicidal parts, this becomes particularly dangerous, since they are both fixated on behaviors that can pose significant safety concerns.

Both hostile and suicidal parts can be conceptualized as fight parts. The comments and behaviors of hostile parts are openly aggressive, either towards others or towards the self. Suicidal and self-harming parts, on the other hand, can be aggressive towards the self and, besides, the defensive action system of fight is needed in order have enough energy to take action and complete the potential suicidal or self-harming act.

Nevertheless, and in addition to fight, suicidal parts also involve the action system of flight. They have often given up and do not see any other way out of the current situation. Their main focus is on finding a way out, hoping that they can finally rest and be at peace. Self-harming parts can also be a combination of fight and flight; even though these parts do not necessarily want to die. Instead, they may focus more on getting relief or helping the client divert the attention from more painful feelings or memories.

When dealing with both suicidal and self-harming parts or voices, one of the biggest challenges the therapist will encounter is the issue of countertransference. It is easy to feel frightened by some of the intense situations in which therapists can find themselves with these hopeless parts or voices. Both types of parts have difficulties seeing any other way out of the current situation and can be of great danger for the client. Even self-harming parts –which might not be focused on dying, but fixated on hurting themselves, other parts, or the client– can end up provoking the death of the client.

One of the most important recommendations for this type of situations is for the clinician to stay focused on the reasons why suicidal parts do not see any other way out.

THE ORIGIN OF SELF-HARMING AND SUICIDAL PARTS

There are many pathways to the development of self-harming and suicidal parts. Although they frequently go together, they can involve different aspects. Clients with self-harming parts have often not learned basic healthy habits of self-care. Some were ignored when expressing emotions or needs, and many were even punished for it. Because of this, one or more parts of the client have learned to repeat the same type of treatment they have received. Those clients who have developed suicidal parts may have learned that suicide is a way out of pain. They may have learned this through witnessing important figures in their lives trying to kill themselves –and perhaps succeeding– after leaving a note explaining that they would be in peace from now on.

The idea of self-harm and suicidal ideation can begin to take form in many different ways. Some clients learn these behaviors from peers, artists, actors, the news, etc. Other clients find relief in self-harm simply by mistake, when they realize that an injury is actually making them feel calmer. These will develop parts that can even give positive messages when encouraging self-harm ("Just cut yourself, you will feel better"). Other clients will create parts that encourage self-harm as a way to distract the client from other thoughts that are unthinkable, such as hurting others.

THE FUNCTION OF SELF-HARMING AND SUICIDAL PARTS

The function is quite easy to identify in some cases, and clients can even appreciate the help of these parts when they understand this. Other clients, however, are unable to see any useful function and clinicians may also have difficulties with it, as well. Some of the parts that are focused on self-harm have developed the behavior to avoid contacting painful memories or to bring some relief to the system. Parts can be trying to avoid trauma memories or realization of reality. If we think about it, when somebody self-harms, all the attention goes to that behavior (especially if this is a voice or another part that is in charge of it). So, if trauma memories are getting triggered, bringing self-harm into the picture is a very effective way to divert attention.

Suicidal parts offer a last and definite resource, a way out of pain and hopelessness. These parts get triggered when no other resource is working. In some cases, self-harm parts can precede suicidal parts; if the behavior works, suicidal parts can stay inactive, but if it does not work and things get too overwhelming, this final resource may begin to kick in.

SPECIFIC INTERVENTIONS

Clients often describe the behaviors from both of these parts as being out of control. This is why we must help clients identify and understand the triggers, see what type of resources might be needed to help these desperate parts, and involve other parts of the system that feel differently.

One of the main goals will be around reaching agreements regarding the type of alternatives that are available.

While keeping in mind all of the more general interventions for challenging parts detailed in Chapter 5, it could be necessary to let clients know that the body is shared by all parts and trying to get rid of any one of them will endanger the whole system. As obvious as this might seem, it is often a shocking discovery for these hopeless and suicidal parts that do not see any other way out.

Since these parts or voices are stuck in behaviors that could be lethal for the client, focusing on the possibility that there is a different way out is crucial. They must understand that death is not the only solution. In addition, we must pay special attention to certain points, which are already included in the specific steps for a clinical session.

- Understanding why the voice or part is showing up. Suicidal parts do not show up or become active for no reason. Something is triggering this part, and both therapist and client must be aware of what this is.

- Clients need to understand that the messages or behaviors are taking place have been learned at some point in the past. If we are working with a new client, it is important to introduce the idea that the part is likely trying to help in a way that is very scary and that it is important to understand this. However, if we have already been working with this client, we need to remind them that the part or voice is still learning new ways.

- Checking how other parts of the system were/are feeling regarding the behavior done by the suicidal part. Most of the time, the client is so terrified of suicidal parts that there is little room to reflect on how this can be affecting the whole system. Engaging other parts and getting a sense of how they experience the thoughts and behaviors of the suicidal parts can be a good way to help the client understand they need to take charge of the situation from a different standpoint other than fear and resignation.

Throughout the work with these parts and voices, it will be important to (1) practice the guidelines about communication and empathy, exploring how other parts experience whatever information is coming up or the information the clinician is introducing, and (2) process dissociative phobias (Gonzalez & Mosquera, 2012) when it can help reduce the conflict and there is agreement from the different parts involved once they are identified. Processing phobias aims to reduce the conflict between parts or voices and is to be used when conflict is identified.

Self-harming and suicidal parts have priority regarding the work, even when they are not very evident. Whenever we see a case that presents previous suicide attempts, we should explore these attempts to understand the dynamic involved. It is not the same to get triggered and become suicidal in a specific moment as it is to have a part or parts that are very driven towards to goal of annihilation. There is only one exception: when clients are very unstable and suicidal ideation is shared by the whole system. In these instances, we will proceed with regular interventions for suicidal ideation. Questions should be asked regarding how they are planning on doing it, what methods are they thinking about using, when are they considering doing it, and why would they do it. All these questions are meant to assess the degree of suicidal ideation and risk.

Even though exploration of suicidal ideation should be part of the intervention when suicidal parts are triggered, this is not always simple in cases of complex trauma and dissociation. The person might not remember the details of what happened due to amnesia or some parts might not want to disclose this information for different reasons.

CLINICAL CASE EXAMPLE

Lisa: Pieces of Me

Lisa, a 43-year-old woman diagnosed as Borderline Personality Disorder and Dissociative Disorder, has been in treatment for about a year. The initial work was focused on reducing the intense conflict between different parts; everything seemed to be fine, and there was more understanding about the system of parts. Both therapist and client were confused when the client woke up in the hospital after ingesting what could have been a lethal dose of pills. The client was very angry and stated, *"I did not try to kill myself; this was an attempted murder by one part towards another."* The therapist seeks supervision, and the supervisor meets with the client to try to understand what is happening within the system.

The following is an example of exploring the internal system to understand what the client describes as "an attempted murder." We are inquiring openly about the part that the client tends to avoid because it is so scary for her, trying to be curious about the whole system in a respectful way.

> *C: I got really scared once when I overdosed on pills.*
> *T: You got to the point of realizing that it was sort of attempted murder.*
> *C: Yes, there was one part that wanted to kill another part. That really scared me.*
> *T: And which part was that?*
> *C: I have a very strong part that is pretty quiet lately, but when she takes over... Let's say that more than taking over, she takes control; she becomes extremely strong. She's an exact copy of my mother's voice: the same tone of voice, the same sentences, and the same expressions.*
> *T: She has learned to repeat the same type of messages.*
> *C: Yes. It's exactly the same.*
> *T: Notice how much sense that makes. She scares you very much because when she shows up, she reminds you of your mother. You see that now.*
> *C: Yes.*

Once we understand that the voice has modeled after her mother, we try to find out which situations trigger the voice to appear (TW #3). Helping the client see that voices tend to appear when they think they are needed, that is in stressful moments, helps understand that their true intention is to help (TW #6).

> T: *Have you noticed when the voice tends to show up?*
> C: *At times of a lot of tension and distress. It comes in through the back of my head, places herself in the middle of both ears, and starts talking. She starts quietly but, after a while, she's talking louder than my own voice.*
> T: *Does she shows up at times of great distress and not when you're fine or when you're feeling calm?*
> C: *Yes.*

Once we confirm the hypothesis that the voice is actually showing up in moments of distress (TW #3), we introduce psychoeducation about this possibility. This is a way of validating the voice and its intention of helping as we guide the client in becoming more aware of these aspects. Remember that validation is one of the key aspects of the work with voices and must take every opportunity we encounter to do so. When exploring the function of the voice (TW #6), this key aspect becomes very important.

> T: *When these hostile parts show up, they're usually trying to help. I'm guessing you've seen this already with your regular therapist.* (Client raises an eyebrow in disbelief.) *But her way of helping is scary because she's using the same sentences and tone of voice your mother used when she scared you. So instead of feeling better, you become more blocked.*
> C: *Yes.*
> T: *One of the most interesting goals would be for that powerful part to learn how to give you messages that helped you feel better.*
> C: *That would be great, but I think this part has never helped me.*

This is a very important point on which we may have to insist. Clients will tend to show disbelief because it is an oxymoron that something that is supposed to be helping is actually making her feel worse (TW #6).

> T: *She scares you because of how she learned to respond. Her ways are very scary and unsettling. The stronger parts often copy their ways from the people who were stronger when one was younger, right? They imitate those in control. Years later, when they think you're not doing well, they come out to help, but they become so scary that you are unable to see their true intention. Notice what you said before: she shows up when you're not feeling well, and she shows up quietly. What do you usually try to do when she shows up quietly?*
> C: *I try to make her shut up.*

Once again, the main problem here is how the client's response worsens the part's response, thus increasing the dissociative phobias among parts (TW #4). It is important to help them understand that how they respond to the voices will have an impact on how they respond to them. If we are to follow the rule of respect, listening to the other seems like the natural thing to do.

> T: *That's why I am asking this, you see? She shows up quietly when you're not feeling well. It would be interesting to find out what she wants to tell you. Since you can't listen to her because you're so scared of her —given that her messages and her ways remind you of very difficult things—, you tell her to shut up, so the voice becomes even louder, and ends up yelling louder than you. It would be interesting to*

see how this part of you —who doesn't need to say anything right now because you're calm— could help you during those difficult times, without scaring you and creating even more problems for you. Does that make sense?

Dissociative phobias are one of the main reasons for the maintenance of the inner conflict and are usually expressed through maladaptive emotions towards parts of the system (fear, disgust, rejection, shame, and distrust) (TW #4). This is one of the reasons it is important to always keep the whole system in mind. In the previous interventions, we can see how we are helping the Adult Self pay attention to the voice (TW #2) so we can understand what it is trying to say. In addition, we are helping the client notice the function of the voice (TW #6) and searching for alternative ways of functioning (TW #8) to promote dialogue between them. And at the same time, we are helping the voice realize that this way of responding frightens the rest of the parts.

C: *Yes, but that's very weird for me because I feel very repulsed by this part.*

T: *Of course, and that's part of the conflict that maintains the existing division. You were not so scared of the other parts and you understood them better, so you were able to integrate them. Perhaps, if you try to understand this scary part better, the same thing will happen.*

C: *It just can't be right, not that part! It's not true! I don't believe you!*

T: *The goal is not so much for you to understand everything right now or to believe me. It's just to see if it would make sense to you. If this were the case —even if you don't see it now— would it make sense to try and understand it?*

C: *Yes.*

T: *If there is a part that shows up and takes control, maybe it's because in those moments you become blocked to the point that you're unable to be in control. Perhaps the part that tells you these things is not noticing that her way of showing up is what is blocking you the most. And I think we can work on that, and it would be great to understand it. How are you feeling as we talk about this?*

C: *A bit distressed, because I have many reservations about this part and many conflicts.*

We can now see how to validate the function of the voice (TW #6) and start suggesting alternative ways of responding (TW #8) that do not frighten the client. By doing this, we are also promoting empathy towards the part, helping the client understand that this is how the part learned to behave and the fact that the part is not her mother, which facilitates to start working on differentiation (TW #5). Introducing the idea that the strength of the part could be used as a resource in a positive way (TW #7) is one way to increase curiosity and encourage cooperation and teamwork (TW #10). The effect of the intervention on the system is also explored (CS #2.3).

T: *Based on what you were saying, this part is very strong. If at any point you feel bad and this part can be there to help you, the issue is for her to do so in a way that you can maintain control. If she were to learn to come out more gently, you could feel that "this part of me can help me because she is strong," and you would clearly see that she is not your mother. Right now, she reminds you of everything you've lived through, but it's just because that's how she learned to do it.*

C: *Yes, yes, and how do I teach her?*

T: *Well, that's why we are here. With a positive attitude of curiosity –trying to understand and being open to the possibility that it might be an attempt to help– and our guiding questions, you can reach an understanding, and we can give her cues, so she can take them into consideration whenever you need that help.*

As curiosity continues to increase, she becomes more able to talk about the part she fears the most, and this will increase her willingness to pay attention to the system (TW #2).

C: *Another part, another piece, another who knows what –I mean the one who showed up to get rid of this part that was hurting me– is a very basic and primitive primal instinct.*

The therapist picks up on the language used by the client ("piece") and continues using her preferred terminology to explore the system.

T: *Of course, and especially because at the time that piece –or whatever it is– didn't know this other one was also a part of you. It saw it as something foreign, something terrifying and hurtful.*
C: *Yes, yes, yes.*
T: *So, the attempted murder makes sense if you see it from this perspective. The issue is that, ultimately, you all are one and you are the one putting yourself at risk.*
C: *Yes.*

In this example, we are helping the Adult Self understand the function of the voice (TW #6), how this part came to be, and how it has learned to respond. We are also helping the parts understand that they are ultimately one person; therefore, if any part attacks another part, they are placing the whole system, including themselves, at risk.

SUMMARY

Suicidal and self-harming parts can be particularly challenging for both therapist and client. One of the key aspects to keep in mind regarding the interventions with these parts and voices is how the client is making sense of the behavior. If there is compassion from the Adult Self towards other parts, the work will tend to flow naturally; if there is rejection, fear, anger or disgust, we will need to do more interventions such as working with the system to reduce the conflict and improve cooperation and, more than likely, process the dissociative phobia between parts. One of the most important interventions for this type of parts is making sure they all understand that they all share the same body.

CHAPTER 8

WORKING WITH CRITICAL PARTS AND VOICES

Some voices or parts are very focused on criticism. They are not overtly aggressive; they neither want to die nor want any part of the system to die, and they are clearly trying to help the client or other parts. The main problem with these voices is that they are very stubborn in their messages and have trouble being flexible or using constructive criticism that can help the system. What usually starts as a warning for the client becomes a stuck circular interaction between the critical voice and the client, as well as within the whole system. The different parts will respond to this criticism in different ways; some parts get upset and feel a lack of motivation, others get angry and try to fight the critical voices.

These voices might be less problematic than other voices that are openly aggressive. However, some clients have limited functioning due to these voices, so it is very important to work with them from the early moments of therapy. The relevance of understanding and working with this type of voices will be illustrated by case examples.

THE ORIGIN OF CRITICAL PARTS

How do we learn right from wrong? How do we learn to accept what we do or criticize it instead? Critical parts have learned from critical models. When we explore how these parts come to be, we will always run into a figure who was focused on doing things better, for whom nothing was ever good enough, and for whom comparisons with others were the norm. Overt criticism can be easier to detect than covert critical attitudes, where the caregiver is not directly abusive or critical but is always reinforcing what others do, and never validating anything the client does.

THE FUNCTION OF CRITICAL PARTS

Critical parts help clients to protect themselves from exposure to further criticism or shame. If a part that imitates the critical figure is created, its job will be to anticipate future criticism from others in an attempt to help the child avoid the pain resulting from these interactions; interactions that are often a reminder of unresolved attachment trauma and painful memories.

In addition to avoiding further pain, critical voices are trying to help the person improve and do things better, in the only way they know how: by criticizing. They are desperately trying to help the person become good enough in whatever they do so they can finally be accepted. The problem of constant repetition turns this dynamic into a vicious circle: nothing is ever good enough, and the strategy ceases to be functional.

SPECIFIC INTERVENTIONS

Identifying the job of these parts is always a good way to begin. Because of the strong criticism received, this part was never validated. For this reason, validating the critical part turns into a new experience.

Critical parts observe and analyze the client's behavior to catch anything that can be improved. So, we could easily validate their observation skills and their capacity to analyze what the person is doing. However, their way of criticizing is often linked to a harsh tone of voice, which has been learned directly from the attachment figure that used to be critical with the client. The way of expressing themselves usually frighten clients and other parts of the system. By modeling new ways of getting the message across, so the client can actually benefit from it, damaging criticism can be transformed into constructive criticism, and both the client and the critical part can become best allies. In Section 5, most of Hugo's transcribed sessions are good examples of the work with critical voices.

CLINICAL CASE EXAMPLE

John: I need some quiet time

John is a 35-year-old man who comes to therapy due to a critical voice that is always talking to him and telling him nothing is ever good enough. Although he can understand that the voice is trying to help, he is bothered by it and would like to have some quiet time. We start this part of the interview exploring the physical characteristics of the voice (TW #1) to try to understand its origin and help the client become aware of it.

> T: *So, you were saying that you understand that this voice is trying to help but that it got to a point where you need some quiet time, did I understand correctly?*
> C: *Yes, that's right. I really need some space. I get very tired, my head hurts, and it is very uncomfortable when I am around other people trying to engage in a conversation.*
> T: *Is it always the same voice or is there more than one voice?*
> C: *No, just one voice.*
> T: *Can you describe this voice?*
> C: *It's a male voice, it's very authoritarian.*
> T: *Does it remind you of anyone?*
> C: *Yes, it is very similar to my father's voice. And it uses the same type of insults and expressions.*
> T: *This is interesting. You know, usually, voices learn their ways from important figures in our life.*
> C: *Hmm... It could be.*
> T: *Does it make sense?*

C: *Yes, my mother was very critical too. I know they both tried to make a responsible man out of me, but they were too harsh.*

T: *So, it makes sense that this voice would repeat the same type of messages. Don't you think?* (Client appears thoughtful.) *What happens when we explore this? What do you notice inside?*

The client seems to be doing fine at this point, but we decide to explore the possible dissociative phobia just in case (TW #4). We also check how the voice is responding to the intervention (CS #2.5) since this can help us guide the work. If either the client or the voice is getting upset or frightened, we can resort to using dialogue to promote understanding, modeling new ways or processing the phobia.

C: *I feel sad.*
T: *How about the voice?*
C: *I don't know.*
T: *Do you notice any changes in the voice?*
C: *It is quiet right now.*
T: *Alright, that might mean that what we are saying seems reasonable for the voice.*
C: *Hmm.*

After briefly checking the phobia, we can proceed with exploration (TW #1). The next step is to try to find out when the voice shows up or becomes more complicated (TW #3). This is a first step to exploring the function of the voice within the system (TW #6). Throughout the process, our way of inquiring and relating to the part and the client will help the client to develop healthy curiosity towards the part, which will increase understanding and empathy (TW #8).

T: *Have you ever noticed when the voice tends to show up? Is it when you are doing fine or when something is upsetting you?*
C: *Well, now that you bring this up... Yes, it shows up when I am feeling insecure; it tells me what to say and what to do.*
T: *I see. Does this help?*
C: *It depends, when it's calm and does not shout, it does. But it usually shouts, and then it becomes very difficult to talk with others as if nothing were happening inside.* T: *Does it usually show up shouting?*
C: *Hmm, no. I guess not.*
T: *So, what happens inside? Can you describe it?*
C: *No, not really.*
T: *How do you respond when it shows up?*
C: *I try to make it shut up.*

This is another example of how clients are frequently stuck in permanent conflict, trying to ignore the voices or have them shut up. This attitude only makes things worse inside, increasing dissociative phobias (TW #4). Exploring the dynamics of the interactions between the different parts is a good intervention that helps the Adult Self and other parts become more aware of how their reactions are maintaining the conflict in place. This, added to an increased understanding of the fact that the voice is trying to help (TW #6), allows increased understanding and empathy within the system and is a good way to begin cooperation (TW #10).

> *T: I see... If the part is trying to get a message across that it believes to be important, and you try to make it shut up, maybe this is why it needs to shout. Would that make any sense?*
> *C: It does. I never thought about that.*
> *T: I am wondering if we can find a way for this voice to help you in a way that is not bothersome for you or scary.*
> *C: That would be fantastic, but I don't think it's possible.*

Clients may be used to having the voice speak to them, but sometimes are not fully aware that they can also interact and dialogue with the voice. It is common that dissociative phobias are what keeps these calm interactions from taking place because whenever they do happen is usually in the form of shouting or desperately trying to shut the voice up. (TW #4). This simple question may surprise our clients and model a new way of communicating with the voice (TW #8).

> *T: Can you ask this voice if that is possible?*
> *C: How do I do that?*
> *T: Check inside, ask that voice or what this voice represents if it can help you differently.*
> *C: It doesn't say anything. Now it's quiet; this is very weird.*
> *T: Maybe it does not know what to say or what to answer.* (Client seems thoughtful.) *Just saying...*
> *C: I guess it can be. It is strangely quiet.*
> *T: Well, maybe it needs our help to figure out what you might need.*
> *C: This is really weird.*
> *T: I know, just bear with me for a little bit, okay?*
> *C: Hmm.*
> *T: You say this voice is always speaking, that it is often very difficult for you to hold an ordinary conversation.*
> *C: Yes.*
> *T: And somehow, when I try to point out that maybe it is trying to help it stays quiet. It almost feels like it is listening in.*
> *C: Yes, I agree. It would be really helpful if it gave me some space to think.*

Once the voice and the client seem to be engaged with curiosity about what is happening (TW #2), we may then continue suggesting new alternative ways of communicating or interacting (TW #8). An important aspect of communication is the tone of voice in which messages are conveyed. Since this is a part that reminds the client of his father, helping the part change the tone could be helpful. This is one of the details in which the modeling of a new way of communicating from the therapist may be crucial, given that these parts have taken after caregiving figures that usually have treated the client harshly. As usual, always check in with the part after any intervention (CS #2.5).

> *T: So, I am wondering if you can tell this voice what would help you most. We already know that shouting is not useful, that it blocks you more.*
> *C: Exactly, but I can't think of anything*

T: Perhaps one of the things that would be helpful is if both the part and you could try to change the tone of the voice you use with one another and speak with a softer and more gentle tone. Maybe you can even think of sentences or actions that can help you.

C: That sounds like a good idea. I think I can do that.

T: What does the part think about this? Is it willing to try?

C: It seems to be listening in still, and I would say that it feels some relief... hmmm...

In order to encourage the part to consider exploring alternative ways of functioning (TW #8), it is important to explore and validate the resources (TW #7) that the part brings into the system which will improve cooperation within the system (TW #10).

T: What do you think this voice is good at doing?

C: Well, I'm not sure. It seems to be pretty good at noticing what to point out at me, what needs to improve.

T: Well, the part seems to have great observation skills. It seems to be able to analyze the situation and figure out what needs to improve. These are great skills and valuable assets for you.

C: Yes, I hadn't thought about it in this way,

T: I wonder if by using this part's skills in this new way, unhealthy criticism could be transformed into healthy and constructive criticism.

C: Wow, that would definitely be a great change.

T: So, do you think you could you ask the voice for help if you need it and perhaps it could give you some good advice?

C: Yes, I think I could do that.

T: Can you check what the voice thinks about this?

C: (Laughs) The voice just said, "It's about time!".

T: This is great! So, let's try this out, and in the next session, we will check the results.

By the next session, things had improved dramatically between the client and this critical voice. They had both started treating each other with respect instead of continuing with the old shouting dynamics. For the client, reframing the communication and behaviors of the voice as a way of helping and extracting such positive resources from it was determinant of a new attitude towards the voice. The client came in stating that they had gotten into a routine of "running together" and during the run, amicably discussing, in a realistic way, some of the things that could use some improvement.

SUMMARY

Critical voices are usually very powerful within the system and have the potential of being extremely disruptive for the client. However, due to this great strength, they also have the potential of becoming great allies once the relational dynamics can change within the system and the internal conflict can be reduced. As we have seen, validating both the protective function of the voice and the resources it incorporated into the system, are good ways to open the door to new ways of relating and communicating.

CHAPTER 9

WORKING WITH PERPETRATOR-IMITATING PARTS AND VOICES

Parts that resemble perpetrators are commonly referred to as introjects. In psychoanalysis, introjection refers to the process through which the individual replicates in him or herself behaviors or attitudes of others. The concept of internalization is very useful in understanding this process since it involves the integration of attitudes, values, opinions, and rules of others into one's identity or sense of self. Research suggests a child's moral self starts to develop around age three (Emde, Bringen, Clyman, & Oppenheim, 1991.) According to the authors, the early years of socialization may be the underpinning of moral development in later childhood. This is how children who are victims of early traumatization internalize the attitudes, thoughts, and views of others. Getting clients to understand this process is extremely important.

Working with introjects is a difficult part of the therapeutic process because it implies learning about the parts that were developed to survive and how they are attached to the main perpetrators. Even though clients frequently confuse them with the real perpetrators, they are not, and should not be treated as such.

THE ORIGIN OF PERPETRATOR-IMITATING PARTS

As the name clearly indicates, perpetrator-imitating parts (Van der Hart, Nijenhuis, & Steele, 2006) usually look, speak, and act like the perpetrator/s. They are related to pathological attachment and are born out of the most damaging and frightening relationships human beings can experience, often including horrible, unimaginable abuse. The fact that these parts are so frightening for the client and generate so much rejection is very sad because they are extremely ashamed of the things they had to tolerate or do and are in desperate need of being seen and accepted for who they really are.

According to Nathanson (1994) for many of us, almost any affect feels better than shame. This author describes what he calls the Compass of Shame, with four poles, each one describing one way to deal with feelings of shame: withdrawal, avoidance, "attack self," and "attack other." Those dissociative parts that attack other parts of the self, fit into the "attack other" quadrant of the compass and they are easily confused with the perpetrator.

Let us think for a minute about the logic of these parts. People who develop these types of parts have lived through situations in which those who are supposed to be caregivers or protectors are the same people who are inflicting hurt, abuse, exploitation or torture. Feelings of shame are inherent to these situations. Helplessness and vulnerability are such that the client truly has no control and no possible sense of safety, so the only possible explanation the child can find is that "there must be something inherently wrong with me." Given the intensity of these emotions, dissociation becomes an effective and necessary coping strategy. Specific parts are created with the purpose of becoming allies of the perpetrator, who is the person perceived as strong and in control. This is the only way for the client to generate a certain sense of control and safety and becomes a way to deal with the intense feelings of shame and a constant reminder of how things "have to be done." The sad part is that, at the same time, these parts or voices represent the very thing they fear and despise the most, generating excruciating shame. These perpetrator-imitating parts then become both a source of shame and a way to deal with shame.

THE FUNCTION OF PERPETRATOR-IMITATING PARTS

These parts are created to vigilantly maintain behaviors and attitudes that the perpetrator wants or to avoid behaviors and attitudes that the perpetrator punishes. By having a part that takes care of this, the system is trying to avoid more punishment or further abuse from the perpetrator/s.

According to Suzette Boon (2017), the functions of perpetrator-imitating parts are:

- Protect the client against threats or imagined threats from the perpetrator.
- Protect the client against new imagined attachment trauma ("Don't get attached, because if you do, you will see that you will be left alone/ridiculed or traumatized/abused again.")
- Defend client (but also themselves) against the unbearable realization of being helpless and powerless as a child.
- Defend against shame through attacking the client and avoiding inner shame.
- Hold unbearable traumatic memories/feelings in bodily sensations.
- Provide an outlet for clients' disowned sadistic and punitive tendencies.

In most clients there is an internal hierarchy, perpetrator-imitating parts being considered by other parts (and themselves) as "the boss or inner leader" and most powerful. They often have younger parts (that had the same function at a younger age) in their system who they can order to do certain things (servants, slaves, assistants). Often, they also play a role in ordering self-harm, prostitution, suicidal behavior, and other unsafe behaviors (Boon, 2017).

These parts or voices can end up believing that they are the real perpetrators; they can even have the same name as well as the same voice and behavior as the original perpetrator. But they are also very confused about themselves; they have to defend against terrible shame and rage, and deep inside they hate their own "repetition of perpetration." It is important to remember that these parts or voices often guard the most difficult feelings of shame, rage, guilt, and powerlessness for the person (as a whole) and frequently substituted for victim parts during the worst abuse (but mostly have developed amnesia for their own memories of being abused and feelings of intense powerlessness).

SPECIFIC INTERVENTIONS

One of the first interventions with this type of parts or voices is to offer psychoeducation to help clients understand how these parts come to be. Simply pointing out that they are not the real perpetrators will not be enough.

Two key aspects of the work with these parts are related to differentiation, which we will explain in more detail in Chapter 11. The first one refers to the ability to distinguish between parts of the self and real perpetrators. To do so, we want to help clients understand that their inner experience is affected by their traumatic experiences and what they experience as a real external person or the perpetrator is a part of them that resembles the perpetrator and what they went through.

The second one is to differentiate past from present. It is important to keep in mind that these parts are necessarily stuck in trauma-time or they would not be resorting to comments and behaviors that are not needed anymore.

CLINICAL CASE EXAMPLE

Rose: The wolf that haunts me

Rose is a 45-year-old client who was sent to our unit due to self-harming behavior and lack of selfcare. She had been in a religious organization in which maltreatment and abuse happened regularly. She had been diagnosed with many different disorders and had been in therapy for over 25 years. At the time of this interview, she still has many difficulties functioning in daily life and is frequently triggered by her traumatic memories. She has a hard time understanding and accepting her parts, especially the ones that remind her of the perpetrators. In the week before this session, she had read an article about dissociation after meeting another woman with severe trauma during a hospitalization. She explains how she feels more curiosity, but still cannot accept that those parts can be parts of her: a dark wolf with sharp teeth, a dark figure with a blurred face and angry eyes, and a woman who uses a soft voice in charge of telling the part she fears most to punish her. The part she fears most looks and sounds exactly like one of her main perpetrators.

> T: *You told me that the Black Wolf is something that is constantly lurking and activates other parts of you generating fear, annulment, and a blocking sensation.*
> C: *Yes. And even though you say it's a part of me, I cannot accept that; it really repulses me.*
> T: *You say that you cannot accept that part of you, that you feel repulsed by it.*
> C: *Yes.*
> T: *Do you understand that what you feel towards this part is a big part of the problem?*
> C: *Yes, but I feel that way.*

> *T: If we do not understand why this part came to be or the function that it had and that it has now, and if we do not give it a more adaptive function, it will feel bad and stir up.* (Client nods.) *If you want to get rid of something in you, this something is going to get very restless. And we are interested in understanding it because it was created for a reason.*

Rationally, the client can understand this, but she still has difficulties accepting that these parts can actually be hers. Her response toward this part is perfectly natural, but it is maintaining the current difficulties/internal conflict. As obvious at it may seem, the issue of anger (Issue #2) is a big problem with these particular parts and voices. We must remember that it becomes even more important to help the client understand the reasons behind the behavior of this voice (TW #6), so the inner conflict can be reduced, and the client can see the important role these parts have been playing within the system. The therapist does some psychoeducation about this type of parts.

> *T: Usually the parts that are seen as more negative arise as protective parts. Do you understand that?*
> *C: How can they be protective parts? No, I don't understand that.*
> *T: What do you see in the wolf? In that part that you associate with the wolf. Think about who does that part remind you of in your life.*
> *C: It reminds me of him* (one of the perpetrators).
> *T: This part has copied the characteristics of this man because there was no other way out, and that gave you some control. Now it is not necessary, but when you were in that situation, one way to be in control was for that part to do exactly the same things this man did.* (Client pays attention.) *But that part is not him; it's a part of you that looks like him. Do you understand that?* (Client shakes her head.) *No?* (Client shrugs her shoulders.) *You do know that he is not inside of you.*
> *C: Yes, now I do.*

Differentiation is a big part of the work with clients that have these types of parts in their internal system (TW #5). Helping the client to understand the difference between her inner and outer realities is a crucial step of the process.

> *T: That you do understand, you know he is a person from the outside world.*
> *C: Yes.*
> *T: That you understand, okay. How about the Wolf? Do you think it's yours or not?*
> *C: I see it as a part that is acting against me.*
> *T: You see that he is acting against you. How is that so?*
> *C: He is always there lurking.*
> *T: What is he looking at?*
> *C: I think he looks at the girl.*
> *T: He looks at the little girl, okay. Do you know why?*
> *C: No.*
> *T: Can you ask this part why is it doing that?* (Client shakes her head.) *Okay, it's fine, you don't have to do that now if you can't. I wonder if the part is concerned about something.*
> *C: I don't know, maybe.*

T: What do you think this part might need?

C: I don't know.

With the previous question we were trying to explore and identify the needs of the part (TW#7), but the dissociative phobia in the adult is so intense that it is not possible. Since the client is too phobic to do any exploration, the therapist decides to process the dissociative phobia she is feeling towards the Wolf part (TW #4).

T: Let's do something, if you think about that part that you identify with the wolf, can you focus on your sensation so we can try to process it a bit? (Client nods.) Yes? (Client nods again.) When you think about that part, what do you notice right now? What is the physical sensation?

C: I feel overwhelmed.

T: Where do you notice that in your body?

C: In my breathing.

T: Focus on that a bit and follow my fingers, can you? (Client nods.) Think of that overwhelming feeling, notice it a bit, just that burden, nothing more. (Very short set of BLS.) What do you notice?

C: Nothing.

T: Should we do a bit more? (Client nods.) (Very short set of BLS.) How about now?

C: I don't know.

As always, after any intervention, it is good practice to check how the different parts of the system have reacted (CS #2.5). When clients are not familiar with communicating with the different parts, or when the dissociative phobia is too high, checking the physical sensations can be a good approach.

T: Check your body. Do you still notice the same overwhelming sensation?

C: Inside, I do.

T: Is this yours or does it belong to this part?

C: I don't know how to distinguish that.

T: You don't know for now, that's fine, this is why it is so important to understand little by little. Close your eyes for a moment and check inside to see what part is agitated.

C: Sometimes I see the Wolf part, and it's as if it were like coercing. I don't know how to explain it.

T: You are explaining it well. Do you have the feeling that this part is coercing you or are you doing it yourself?

C: I think it's this part.

T: This part, okay. Then close your eyes and check whether this part can focus on this sensation to relieve it a bit. You let me know if it's possible.

C: No (The client closes her eyes but opens them quickly.)

We respect that the part does not want to do this. We are interested in modeling new attitudes of respect for the system (TW #8) and in addition, validating the client's experience and reminding her of some aspects of psychoeducation that have previously helped both her and the system. As we continue, we may also resort to interventions or resources that are familiar to her and may be helpful. In this case, we suggest introducing a gesture of care with the idea that this may calm the client and, at the same time, the part, based on some previous experience in which both the client and other parts would have calmed down.

> T: *I know that you are quite scared for now and you notice rejection, but that is not the way for you to feel better. Just as you do not like to feel rejected, this part doesn't like it either. Especially if it is a part of you that has a lot of charge. So just try to think about where you notice that part and place your hands there. We will try to show interest and see if it calms down a bit. For now, we do not understand, but we want to understand. We agree on that, right?* (Client nods.) *Think about that.* (Very short set of BLS.) *What do you notice?*
> C: *That... that it is intense.*
> T: *And is it positive or negative?*
> C: *I don't know.*
> T: *When I was doing tapping, what happened with the intensity? Did it go up or down?* C: *It's there, I don't know.*
> T: *Can we try again? Can you notice that a bit more?* (Client nods.) (Very short set of BLS.) *What do you notice?*
> C: *I notice as if it's something external.*
> T: *And this makes you anxious.*
> C: *Yes.*
> T: *Can you notice that?* (Client nods.) (Very short set of BLS.) *What do you notice?* C: *This other part just doesn't leave me alone.*

Notice that every time the client calms down or notices something positive, another part gets triggered. This is an opportunity to explore missing pieces (TW #9).

> T: *Let's try to understand the other things a little more, because sometimes it helps you to go little by little so that you can digest it. There was another email in which you told me that whatever you had experienced as positive in the session, it seemed as if it sometimes activated a part that tried to cancel it. Is this what is happening now?*
> C: *Yes.*
> T: *And which is the part that wants to cancel it?*
> C: *I don't know.*

The dissociative phobia seems to be very intense, which results in the client responding "I don't know" very often. In these cases, there is very likely to be a low level of differentiation (TW #5), so introducing information that increases the client's capacity to differentiate past from present is a very important step toward decreasing the existing phobias.

> T: *Sometimes when there are these sensations, it might be because this part does not know that you have already gotten out of that situation and that you lead a different life now. Especially if you have learned what you have been taught: that experiencing anything positive is not allowed. Think about what you have read of the text: if there is a part of you, whatever it is, that does not know that you are no longer there, that part will be disturbed by anything positive. As we get to understand your inner system, this part will know that both of you are no longer there. But maybe it doesn't know it for now. Does that make sense?*
> C: *Yes.*

T: *And that's why there is this rejection of the positive. But you do know that you are no longer there, right?*

C: *Yes.*

T: *And there are parts of you that also know it.*

C: *I think so.*

T: *Until everything in you understands that there is no danger, that you are no longer in that place, there are parts that are going to be agitated.*

C: *What I also read in the article, and I notice it happens to me, is that I see myself reacting more from the here-and-now.*

T: *Hmmm* (validating).

C: *Instead of reacting from the there-and-then.*

We explore triggers (TW #3) since they are a key element that will give us a lot of information about is the function of the different parts (TW #6). Understanding the function of the voice helps increase compassion and empathy towards what the client had to endure, decrease the dissociative phobia towards the different parts, and improve cooperation (TW #10).

T: *Indeed, it's great that you can understand and identify it. Do you realize what an important step this is? Because that is what happens. Sometimes, when there is this desire to ruin the positive it is due to fear because the positive was punished before. So, if you understand where it comes from when you get triggered, you can feel calmer. I know that sometimes it helps you to have a vision of yourself through me. That is something you can try in those moments. Try to remember that we are in 2016, that you are working with me, that you are no longer in that situation, that there are things within you that we do not understand yet, and that we will eventually understand everything. Do you think this can be useful?*

C: *Yes*

T: *How is the wolf now?*

C: *It's not doing anything now.*

T: *Do you think that might mean it is okay with the work we did?*

C: *I think so, yes*

T: *Great, let's thank all the parts for the work they allowed us to do today.*

This intervention is mainly focused on helping the client and parts differentiate between past and present. The client has trouble in different moments throughout the day because the parts stuck in trauma-time keep getting triggered when faced with apparently neutral stimuli, and she feels she is going crazy. Some of these parts act like the perpetrators, which makes it even more challenging for her.

SUMMARY

When working with perpetrator imitating parts, issues of differentiation will be crucial. In the next chapters, we will discuss this subject specifically. The client will eventually learn to differentiate between the real perpetrator and the internal part who imitates the abuser, understanding the reasons behind it taking on such a despicable appearance. It will also be necessary to differentiate between the dangerous past and the safe present. The degree of these types of dissociative phobias is usually very high, and it is important to remember that the process of working with them takes time.

CHAPTER 10

WORKING WITH DISTRUSTFUL AND FEARFUL PARTS AND VOICES

Human beings need others in order to grow and feel they exist. The development of personality, identity, and relational patterns in human beings begins in the family and later expands to other relationships, shaped by the perspective and style of care that the child receives from his or her attachment figures. According to Erikson (2011), development of basic trust is the first psychosocial developmental state that occurs or fails to occur during the first two years of life. Success results in feelings of security, trust, and optimism, while failure leads to orienting towards insecurity and distrust. The dispositional tendency to trust others can be considered a personality trait and, as such, is one of the stronger predictors of subjective well-being. This can help us understand why people with early traumatizing histories have such difficulty when it comes to trust.

In psychology, trust means believing that the person who is trusted will do what is expected. Trust has three different connotations (McKnight & Chervany, 1996). First, trust implies being vulnerable towards someone even when it is still uncertain whether they are trustworthy; second, trustworthiness is based on the characteristics or behaviors of one person that inspire positive expectations in another person; and third, trust propensity is about being able to rely on people (Mayer, Davis & Schoorman, 1995; Bamberger, 2010). All three are severely damaged in survivors or chronic neglect and abuse. Once trust is lost, by obvious violation of one of these three determinants, it is very hard to regain.

THE ORIGIN OF DISTRUSTFUL AND FEARFUL PARTS

As mentioned at the beginning of the book, when starting to discuss the internal conflict, the system of parts reflects the type of conflict that has been experienced by the client as he or she was growing up. Sadly, most of these voices and parts of the Self have never learned the meaning of the word "trust" and are naturally distrustful and very fearful. If basic trust is never learned, the system needs to adapt to an environment that is not trustworthy and is often dangerous. A client who has never felt safe cannot learn the meaning of safety until it is experienced. And since feeling safe is the exception, fear takes over and becomes an unwelcome companion.

THE FUNCTION OF DISTRUSTFUL AND FEARFUL PARTS

Developing a distrustful part is a perfect way of making sure that the client is not hurt again. Little kids do not lose hope unless the situation is chronically unsafe and it becomes impossible to trust. It then makes sense to create a part that will make sure not to expect anything or have any hope whatsoever.

Another way of developing this type of parts has to do with the effects of feeling invisible. Invisibility –not being seen– prevents the essential development of the person. When children are not seen or are only seen when adults need something from them, they will try their very best to be invisible (Mosquera, 2018).

Becoming invisible in a dangerous environment is a good option for protecting the self. The more the child can become invisible to others, the higher the chances of preventing danger and surviving. One client explained how she used to hide behind the stairs most of the day, inside a very narrow closet that nobody used. This was her way of avoiding verbal and physical abuse from her mother, who would often insult and hit her for no reason.

SPECIFIC INTERVENTIONS

Trust improves the functioning of a conflicted system and has a positive influence on the overall behaviors, perceptions, and functioning of a person. The process of building trust, thus, becomes an essential piece of the work, given that only by being able to trust others, including other parts, can we start approaching the work with these very hurt and damaged parts of the Self. The clinician's response to a lack of trust from any part of the system will model a new way of being in relationship. A general way to begin this process is to meet their distrust with acceptance. As fearful parts become able to develop trust, we will be allowed to reach and work at deeper levels.

Working on differentiation is also a fundamental intervention with these parts. For them to even consider the possibility of trusting, they must learn to differentiate between past and present, so they can realize that the danger is over, that new ways of relating are possible and there are currently options that did not exist before.

CLINICAL CASE EXAMPLE

Rose: Everything is stirred up

This is an example of working with a conflicted system. This session began by working with a child part that the client is now able to look at with more interest and less fear or rejection. However, while exploring this younger part and her possible needs, another part stuck in trauma time gets in the way. We begin the example from the moment when the client realizes that something else is interfering and she cannot notice the little girl anymore. Much of the work is related to time orientation, one of the important differentiation points (see Chapter 11), as a way to help her become more oriented to the present. We try to explore the inner system through drawings.

T: Do you still notice the girl here or not?

C: Not now.

T: And what happened for you not to notice her anymore?

C: I don't know.

T: Try to describe what's inside. What do you see?

C: Well, right now I don't know how to draw it.

T: What do you notice inside? Are there more parts there or is there just this one part?

C: I just don't know if something is getting in the way, I don't know.

T: What is it that you don't know?

C: How to identify what it is.

T: What do you think is getting in the way?

C: I don't know.

T: What do you see there?

C: I don't know, it's like... I don't know. (Slowly gives the paper back to the therapist without saying a word, containing her distress.)

T: Remember, I can't know what's going on inside if you don't tell me. So, why are you giving this back to me?

C: Because I don't know how to draw what I see inside.

T: Why not?

C: Because I see a part of the girl, but... I don't know.

T: You see a part of the girl, you do see that.

C: Yes, I just can't identify why she's gone, I don't know.

Helping the client to be curious about what is going on inside (TW #2) will help decrease her possible anxiety about not being able to identify what is interfering inside. Curiosity, as it has been mentioned multiple times throughout the different chapters of this book, is one of the main aspects that help develop the Adult Self and change inner relationships within the system.

T: Can you close your eyes and check inside? Let's see what happened with the girl. Just look at the girl with curiosity and see what's there.

C: I just don't know if she believes me when I tell her that the man is not there.

T: Well, could it be that she doesn't believe it yet?

C: It seems that she doesn't. She thinks I'm deceiving her.

When parts are stuck in trauma-time, they really have difficulties trusting new information. In this example, we decide to work on time orientation after having assessed differentiation issues (TW #5) and we try to show the girl where she currently is. To do so, we offer an object from the present moment that she can see and perhaps even feel. This will increase mutual awareness between the Adult Self and the little girl. In addition, we offer psychoeducation to increase differentiation between past and present.

T: Check if it would help her to see the things that are in the office, if you can show them to the girl. See if you need to hold something in your hand. Is there anything that calls her or your attention?

C: (The client looks around the office.) *I don't see anything...*

T: *None of these things were there. The fact that she can see anything that is here is positive, because it was not there for sure.*

C: *No, it wasn't.*

T: *This week, you have noticed that the girl has been quieter, except when you started to read yesterday.* (Client nods.) *What helped her feel calmer? Can you ask her?*

C: *What helped her was to know that neither he nor I can hurt her.*

Helping the client differentiate inner reality from outer reality is a must. In the present moment, the reality is that the perpetrator cannot access the little girl or the client; therefore, he cannot hurt either of them anymore. The client can now choose to protect the little girl. Before she could not do this, there was no way out. In the present moment, there is (TW #5).

T: *Well, see, but these are two different things. You don't want to hurt her, but he just cannot hurt her anymore. We're not going to change the story; it's not that he didn't want to hurt her. This person hurt her a lot; this person hurt you a lot in the past. But now he can no longer hurt either one of you. Do you understand?*

C: *No, not really.*

T: *Let's see, given everything that you experienced, we can't ever say that this person didn't want to hurt you or the girl, because that would be lying. That person hurt you and hurt the girl, so the girl was scared in that room. You don't want to hurt the child, and you want to help her know that she is no longer there, that this man can no longer hurt her. Do you understand what I'm saying?* (Client nods.) *So, what happens inside when I tell you this about the girl?* (Client starts pinching herself.) *Try to focus here with me. Don't pinch or scratch yourself, because then you disconnect. If you start doing other things, you cannot be aware of what you and I are doing here. Try to see how the girl is doing now when we talk about this.*

C: *Well, I see chaos in there, I don't know.*

The chaos that clients notice inside is usually related to some dissociative phobia (TW #4). The dissociative phobia is very clear in this case, and it consists of a combination of phobia of inner experience and phobia of parts. The intervention chosen is the processing phobia procedure.

T: *Would it be okay to process the chaos and see if it clears up a bit? What do you think?*

C: *Yes.*

T: *Let's focus on the feeling of chaos. Where do you physically notice the chaos? If you were to notice this chaos somewhere in your body, where would it be?*

C: *In my head.*

T: *I would like to ask you to place your hands on the table and think about the chaos you're noticing, and we're going to try to process it a little bit to see if something clears up. You let me know when you are ready.*

C: *Ready*

We initially try to encourage the client to simply pay attention to what is happening inside (TW#2), listening with curiosity instead of trying to avoid it, which is a very recurrent way of dealing with the discomfort.

T: *Let's listen with curiosity to what it's trying to say. (BLS.) Were you able to listen to it or not? (Client shakes her head.) Should I do a little more bilateral stimulation to see if it gives you more time?*

C: *Yes. It is as if it wanted to say something (BLS.) I just don't understand.*

T: *Can you tell her that you want to understand her and that we are here to listen to her?*

C: *It's just a little strange.*

T: *Try not to judge it.*

C: *It feels as if she thinks that I still blame her because of what happened with that man.*

T: *And what do you think? What would you answer?*

C: *That now I am really sorry.*

T: *Okay, explain that to me. For what are you feeling really sorry now?*

C: *For the fact that she had a very difficult time.*

T: *Ah, okay, perfect. I understand that you don't blame her anymore and that you feel very sorry she had such a hard time. Should we tell her you feel sorry that she had such a hard time and that she's not doing well?*

Several sessions later, Rose is much more aware of what the little girl had to endure. This involves more realization, but with realization, reality sinks in. Rose is upset because she feels she has not done anything to help the little girl since she has been rejecting her and blaming her for years. In general, Rose has developed more curiosity towards her little girl part and is thinking of more active ways of helping her (TW #8). But things get a bit tricky when the little girl does not respond as Rose was expecting.

C: *I feel guilty.*

T: *That is part of the problem. The most important thing is for you to understand where to place the responsibility. It would be important that you, from the adult who is here with me, can see that the little girl is not guilty.*

C: *No, but I feel guilty myself.*

T: *Let's go one step at a time. So, when you think about the little girl in the dark closet, you don't blame her anymore. Did I understand correctly?*

C: *Yes.*

T: *So then, what do you feel guilty about?*

C: *Well, because she has had a very hard time and I haven't done anything for her to be better.*

T: *You didn't? You got out of there. (Client makes a gesture as if saying that it is not enough.) Can you let her know that you don't blame her anymore? (Client nods.)*

C: *(Internal communication.) Well, she doesn't trust me.*

One of the main interventions with distrustful parts is not to try to get them to trust us. Instead, modeling acceptance (TW #8), validating and normalizing the fact that not trusting makes sense at this point, given what the client has been through, is a much more effective intervention. Trust is something that needs to develop over time; it cannot be forced.

T: *She doesn't trust you. Well, it's normal that she doesn't. Where does she notice that she doesn't trust? (Client looks confused.) Remember when you were afraid of the girl too? (Client nods.) We processed it, remember? (Client nods.) Well, now we would try to have the girl process that fear, that feeling of "I cannot trust." Can we ask her to focus on that fear of trusting you? Let's see if we can both help her process this fear. (Client nods and we start* tapping.) *What happens to the fear?*

C: *It's as if she were asking me to help her.*

As expected, when focusing on processing the phobia (TW #4), the little girl part can feel more safety and ask for help. The part asking for protection demonstrates an adaptive shift toward accepting connection, which is the beginning of increased collaboration (TW #10). We explore the voice (TW #1) and continuously encourage the client to pay attention and listen to the part (TW #2).

T: *What is she asking for?*

C: *I don't really know.*

T: *Well, let's listen to her a little bit more. Let her ask you; we're here to listen, and it's okay to ask.*

C: *It's just that it feels heavy.* (Client starts losing the connection and looks down.)

T: *Look at me. What do you mean heavy?*

C: *It's like I didn't do anything to stop it.*

Self-blame is a deeply-rooted defensive strategy that clients have usually used since childhood, so it is not easy to let go of it. In this case, it continues to emerge. We can offer a psychoeducational interweave and proceed to reprocess self-blame in the Adult Self. On a different note, asking clients to look at the therapist, in this case, is a way to activate a relational resource when there is excessive dissociation and it becomes difficult to remain present. However, we must be cautious with this intervention, given that eye contact is particularly difficult for these clients.

T: *Yes, but you did; you left. So now we're going to focus on your sense of burden, okay? (Client nods.) Focus on your sensations, considering you got out of there when you could. (Very short set of BLS) What happens when you focus on that?*

C: *Like the last time, here in therapy. It's been the only time I've seen it as something I could reject.*

T: *Explain that to me. What has been like the last time? What have you seen?*

C: *Well, I could tell her that she wasn't there and that I want her to feel it, so she doesn't feel so bad.*

T: *Can you tell her that? (Client nods and closes her eyes. Internal communication.) That is great, notice that (Short set of BLS.) Okay, and how does it feel to be able to tell her that?*

C: *Well, it makes me feel calmer towards her.*

T: *Can you notice that feeling? (Client nods.) Yes? Very good, very good. (Short set of BLS)*

T: *How is the girl now?*

C: *She's still in the corner of the closet, though she's calmer.*

T: *She's calmer in the corner. Do you think we can try to help her get out of the corner a little bit? Would she be okay with that? I am thinking that maybe she needs our help to get out of there.*

C: *I don't know how.*

Since we have done this type of work with Rose before, we suggest doing visualization techniques to help the little girl feel less frightened and more oriented to the safety of the present moment. This will help the client to consider interacting with the little girl part in new alternative ways (TW #8).

Regardless of the intervention, we always make sure all interactions are carried out respecting the pace of the part.

T: Do you see yourself being able to step into that corner and get her out of there? To reach your hand out to her so she can leave? Can we do that visualization exercise?

C: It's a little scary.

T: Well, but we can stop at any time. Remember we never force anything here. (Client nods.) Then let's imagine it. Close your eyes. (Client closes her eyes.) Do you see the girl? (Client nods.) We're going to reach our hand out to the girl, and we're going to tell her that she can leave if she wants, that she doesn't have to stay there. We just want her to know that we are here for her, that she can get out of there and leave the closet behind now. (Internal communication.) Are you able to reach your hand out to her?

C: Yes, but I am not sure I know how to do this.

T: Just reach you hand out, okay? Imagine you're stretching your hand out to see if she wants to hold on to it. And it's okay if she can't; the hand is going to be there, and we will reach out as many times as we need.

C: She doesn't seem to trust me too much, but she trusts you. (Client looks down.)

T: She doesn't trust you. Do you understand that? Look at me for a second. (Client looks up.) She trusts me, right? Well, I am very happy that she feels she can trust me. Do you understand why she can trust me?

C: Perhaps because you don't hurt her.

T: Maybe, and does she think you do?

C: Yes, she doesn't trust me.

T: And when you notice that she doesn't trust, what do you feel?

C: A little bit of frustration.

Frustration is a very common occurrence when a client expects or tries to take care of her child parts and they do not respond as easily and quickly as the client would like. Since frustration is a disturbing element related to the effects of trauma, we can process it.

T: Frustration. Look at me for a second: that's the problem. The problem is the frustration you notice when she doesn't trust. You see, when she doesn't trust me, I understand. (Client is paying attention.) I understand that she's a girl who's stuck in a difficult situation and has a hard time believing that she is no longer there. She can see that I am not frustrated, you know? (Client nods.) What we can do now is process your frustration. Is that okay with you? If you lower your frustration a little bit, then you can understand that it's normal for her not to trust.

C: What can I do for her to trust me?

T: Well, we can process what you notice when you feel frustration, and maybe you can tell her that it's okay, that she can take all the time she needs to trust you. That you understand that it's hard for her. Let's first process your frustration and see what happens, because sometimes things fall back in place on their own. What do you think? (Client nods in agreement.) Where do you notice the frustration?

C: Well, a little bit all over, but more on my chest.

T: Let's process your frustration, only your frustration, nothing else. (Client nods, so we start tapping.) What do you notice when we focus on that?

113

> *C: I feel a little less frustration, but I still don't know how to help her very much.*

Once the phobia is reduced, we can proceed with the intervention. With less fear getting in the way, the client is more likely to be able to listen to the information and let it in. As always, it is important to validate the client by pointing out, in this case, how she has already been able to improve her relationship with the little girl part (TW #7).

> *T: Well, but do you realize that you can learn? You can learn how to help her, and that's what we're working on. In fact, there's a huge change already, because before you couldn't even look at her, and now you can both look at her and tell her that you don't want her to suffer. Do you realize how important that is?* (Client is paying attention, much calmer than before.) *How is the girl now?*
> *C: She's still hiding.*
> *T: She's still hiding, okay. Should we try offering her some help one more time? See if you can think of a better way to do this, to increase the chances of the girl accepting. Maybe the hand is too much, you know? See if you can show her something you have at home. What do you think can help the girl? C: Well maybe... It's a little silly...*
> *T: I'm sure it's not.*
> *C: Maybe offer her your hand instead of mine.*
> *T: Do you think this might help her?*
> *C: Yes, because then she won't be afraid that I may hurt her.*

This is an interesting idea. The client is suggesting something that she would like to experience, but that she is may not be able to do herself. She seems to believe that the little girl will be able to do what she cannot. It is important to validate this idea, and we can even try it out as a learning opportunity for the client (TW #7 & TW#8). No matter how much we explain certain issues –such as, in this case, why the little girl cannot do this– the idea will not sink in as well if the client herself does not have the direct experience of why this could be difficult.

> *T: Well, this is interesting, we can try it out, but it's important that you also participate in that visualization* (Client nods.) *Could you imagine yourself accepting my hand too? Think about it.* (Client makes a gesture indicating, "No way!") *Well, exactly. Do you realize that even though you trust me, if I were to reach my hand out to you, you wouldn't be able to accept it?* (Client makes a gesture indicating, "No way!") *Well, exactly, Do you realize that even though you trust me, if I were to reach my hand out to you, you wouldn't be able to accept it?*
> *C: Maybe after the last time, I could, but I don't know.*
> *T: But the first thing that comes up is the thought that it would be difficult.* (Client nods.) *Let's try it, anyway, and see what happens.* (Client nods in agreement.) *So, let's think together about the best way to do this exercise. What would be the best way to check if you are able to accept the hand when I reach out to you? Would it be best to do it only in your imagination? Would it be best to try it out for real? How could we best do this?*
> *C: I think that I reject it more in my head.*
> *T: And what does that mean?*
> *C: That maybe I could change the way I think now.*

T: *And what could you change now?*

C: *Being able to see it as something that won't do me any harm.*

T: *Can you imagine how it would it be for you?* (Client nods.) *Should I do some tapping?* (Client nods.) *Great, imagine that.* *(BLS)*

At this point, it becomes obvious that the client cannot do the visualization, and she starts getting very agitated due to the frustration. She is shaking, looking down, and losing contact again. Respecting the pace of the client and parts also helps her to learn to be patient with herself and her inner system (TW #8).

T: *Look at me for a second.* (Client looks up.) *Do you see that I'm not worried about what just happened? I understand that you can't do that yet and it's perfectly fine. Keep in mind that when we're talking about the girl, we're talking about you. The girl will not be able to do something you cannot do, you know?* (Client looks up, calmer.) *Let's try something else instead of the hand, okay?* (Client nods.) *I'm thinking that maybe we can use the rubber foam things from the other day. What do you think?* (Client appears restless.) *Look at me for a second, what's going on inside?*

C: *I feel bad.*

T: *But why do you feel bad? Try to look at me.* (Client tries to look up.) *Why do you feel bad? Because you can't imagine yourself accepting my hand?* (Client nods.) *What does that mean to you? Try to look at me. What does that mean to you?*

C: *Well, I don't know, it's contradictory.*

T: *Explain it to me, so I can understand. How is it contradictory?*

C: *Well, that I know I can trust you, but I couldn't do the exercise* (Client looks down and starts crying.)

T: *It's okay, try to look at me for a second.* (Client looks up.) *This is important, just think that I suggested this, right? For me, it's a matter of how to approach it. I'm trying to see what can help, right?* (Client nods.) *When I asked you to reach out with your hand, the little girl couldn't hold your hand, but you were able to reach out to her, right?* (Client nods.) *You tried to imagine it and the girl couldn't hold it, so you thought of the possibility that I reach out with my hand, yes?* (Client nods, listening attentively.) *But when we imagined that, you couldn't do it either, and this helps us understand the little girl better, you know? So, it's important to choose our options better, so the girl is able to do it, do you realize this?* (Client nods, looking calmer.) *Perhaps, instead of the hand, we can both take one of those rubber foam things we used the other day.*

C: *Okay.*

One of the key points in this example is helping the client understand that she cannot expect her little girl to accept and tolerate something she, as an adult, cannot tolerate. The exercise proposed by the client was way too activating for either one of them to accept. The therapist is now introducing an intermediate way to get close and be in contact, without being excessively close. Here, the therapist models a different way to respond when her little girl cannot react as the client would like (TW #8). In addition, it generates co-consciousness and time orientation by combining them with play. This combination is useful when we are working with young parts and want to activate the exploration system.

T: *We could do something in between, you know? I hold one end and you hold the other. Can you do it?*

C: *Yes.*

T: *You can do it like this, right?* (Therapist is modeling.) *And you can look at me, right? You can look and notice this, and you can notice that you hold it from there and I hold it from here, right?* (Therapist is moving the rubber foam so she can notice the pulling.)

C: *Yes.*

T: *Perfect, and what happens when you notice this?*

C: *That maybe she trusts more, I don't know.*

T: *Great, so let's try it out. Notice how you're on that side, and I'm on this side. And we're both connected. If I pull a little bit, you notice it, right?*

C: *Yes.*

T: *And if you pull, I notice it too* (Client nods.). *So, can we try to do this with the girl?*

C: *Yes.*

T: *I won't let go, so try it out. While you and I do this, try to imagine letting the little girl notice it, and then check if she can notice it. We'll try for as long as you need, okay?* (Client nods.) *You see that if I pull a little bit, you notice it, right?*

C: *Yes.*

T: *Perfect, I'm here, okay?*

C: (Client pulls rubber foam.) *She is trusting more.*

T: *She is trusting more, great, and then what happens?*

C: *Nothing.*

T: *Well, what do you notice when she trusts more?*

C: *Well, I think that... I don't know...*

T: *Is it positive or negative?*

C: *Positive.*

Once the phobia is reduced through this visualization exercise, we can go a step further and try to do the same exercise while both parts are being co-conscious.

T: *Positive, okay. Let's do something. I'll just put it out there, but remember that you're the one who has to tell me whether it fits or not; and if it doesn't fit, no big deal, we'll just find another way.* (Client nods.) *So, while I hold this, you can hold on too and be in contact with me, and you know this is from 2016 and was not there in the past, right?* (Client nods.) *Now we are going to ask the little girl again to notice it, you're going to show it to her. Telling her that this belongs here, not there, okay?* (Client nods.) *And you're going to ask her to take it knowing that she can be here in 2016 with you and me because she's inside of you. And while you reach out to her, I'm going to hold on to it with one hand and tap with the other. What do you think? Is it possible?* (Client nods.) *Then check and see how it's more comfortable for you.*

C: *Like this.* (Client holding one side, therapist holding the other side.)

T: *Like this, perfect, so notice it and keep on observing that if I do this, you notice it. Well, when you're ready, you're going to reach towards the girl with it too, okay? And you let me know when you are ready, and I'll do a little tapping. C: Ready*

T: *Very good.* (BLS)

The therapist is tapping with one hand, and holding the rubber foam with the other hand, while the client is holding on to the rubber foam on the other side, and the girl notices it. The client seems much calmer. After every intervention, we always check in to see how the client and the part have reacted to it (CS #2.5).

> *T: What did the girl think about that?*
> *C: It makes her feel safer.*
> *T: And what do you think about that?*
> *C: Well, maybe I need help, so I can learn to help her.*
> *T: Perfect, well, and do you think this is a good place for us to practice?*
> *C: Uh-huh.*
> *T: Okay.*

Before closing the session, it is interesting to check how things are internally just in case any other parts are not feeling settled or need some attention (CS #3.3). We don't need to go one by one; we can check in a general way. If we were to check on the parts one by one, we might ruin a perfect moment for the client and the little girl. Remember this client is still very phobic of other parts, so if we bring up any other part, her reaction could be negative, even if the part was not active at the moment. This also helps us check the usefulness of the interventions that have been applied during the session (CS #3.2).

> *T: How is everything inside now? How do you feel?*
> *C: Well, a bit shook up.*
> *T: A bit shook up how?*
> *C: It's not bad, it's not against me, I don't know how to explain it.*
> *T: Oh, I see, shaken but in a positive way, right? This is very new. (Client nods.) Being so new, it's also hard to know very well what it is, but now that you can see what happened, you identify it as something positive. Is that right?*
> *C: Yes.*
> *T: And what do you notice about the girl?*
> *C: She's more attentive, she is calm.*
> *T: Perfect.*

We close the session anticipating potential obstacles and preparing for problems that could show up in the near future (CS #3.5). After this type of intervention, clients might think that things are going to stay in this positive state, but this is highly unlikely when parts are still learning to understand each other. The idea is to anticipate future difficulties, so the client feels she has more resources to respond when the girl is triggered.

> *T: We will keep on practicing until the little girl can get out of the dark closet. And remember, if at any point you notice that the girl becomes agitated, just try to observe what is it that you're doing that could be triggering her. It could be something you're reading or the news or a certain comment. If you identify the trigger, you can perhaps start doing something different. Or you can simply tell yourself, "No, look, this is a book from now. This is a character from a book." The fact that you can give yourself these messages also calms you down. Does this make sense?*
> *C: Yes.*

It is important to reinforce the work done throughout the session (CS #3.1) and validate the efforts done by the client and the part that participated in the exercises. In addition, we may briefly summarize what has happened in the session (CS #3.4).

> *T: You can try it out to see how it goes, and we'll continue working until you can do it on your own, because I know it's hard for you to do it outside of our sessions.* (Client nods.) *Well, good job! These are important steps you're taking, right? Look at me for a second, because it's important that you remember this. Can you try not to get frustrated with yourself when things don't flow as fast as you would like?*
> *C: I can try.*
> *T: And remember that it was me who proposed the hand exercise when the other day the girl still couldn't even look. The idea is to try and see if something works or not, and if it doesn't work, we just try something else. So, don't get frustrated, you get easily frustrated with yourself when perhaps my proposal has been too much. The time will come when the girl will be able to accept the hand. If she can't do it now, there are intermediate steps we can take, do you understand?*
> *C: Yes.*

This is a good example of working with distrustful parts and how modeling can make a big difference in the work we do. By helping the client understand her own difficulties in doing this exercise, she could better understand the little girl in her and become less frustrated when things do not move as fast as she would like. The client also became more aware of the relevance of respecting pacing for all the parts of the system, not just the Adult Self. By happing the therapist assume responsibility, the client learned that mistakes can be made and that this is okay, that whenever something does not work, there are always other options.

SUMMARY

Working with distrustful parts can be very frustrating for clients. It is nearly impossible for a part that has learned not to trust others to suddenly with ease start trusting. For this reason, the most effective interventions are aimed both at normalizing this difficulty trusting and accepting that this is where the client and the part are at the moment, while always being respectful of the pace of the different parts.

Another crucial point brought up by this example is that even when we know an intervention can be too much for the client, we can still try it out as a learning experience. In complicated issues like distrust, simply talking about it does not allow integration of the experience. It is much more effective if we can help clients experience how difficult it is for these parts to trust, by using their own experience. Doing so also encourages co-consciousness, which can be a great resource for clients who have parts that are still stuck in trauma-time.

SECTION FOUR:

DIFFERENTIATION, CO-CONSCIOUSNESS, AND INTEGRATION

CHAPTER 11

WORKING WITH DIFFERENTIATION, TIME ORIENTATION, AND CO-CONSCIOUSNESS

Differentiation, time orientation, and co-consciousness are different concepts that clients often get mixed up. The main focus of this chapter is to clarify the relationship between them and emphasize the need to distinguish them during interventions. Clients who have difficulties with differentiation and staying present may get stuck in a variety of ways. When different parts are triggered at the same time and are still experienced as separate parts that are very phobic of each other, clients can become very confused. Introducing differentiation interventions, helping clients to orient in time and adding little experiments where parts can be noticing or engaging in something at the same time is a good way to reduce the chaos.

DIFFERENTIATION

Chapter 1 introduced the idea that differentiation can be a confusing concept which has been understood in many different ways. Differentiation of self has been defined as the ability to distinguish between thoughts and feelings in an emotional relationship system (Bowen, 1974, 2004). Undifferentiated people cannot separate feelings and thoughts; when asked to think, they are flooded with feelings, and have difficulty thinking logically and basing their responses on reason. Furthermore, they have difficulty separating their own feelings from those of other people; they look to family members to define what they think about issues, how they feel about people, and how to interpret their own experiences. According to Bowen, differentiation is the process of freeing oneself from the family's processes to define the self. This means individuals will be able to have opinions and values that may differ from those of their family members, while still being able to stay emotionally connected to them. It means being able to reflect calmly after a conflicted interaction afterward, becoming aware of their role in it, and then choosing a different response for the future. This can also be applied to clients with complex traumatization, whose emotions, thoughts, and behaviors are very much influenced by how they grew up and what they were encouraged to feel and think.

Differentiation has also been defined as the separation of parts from a whole, necessary for conscious access to psychological functions. Without differentiation, direction is impossible, since the direction of a function towards a goal depends on the elimination of anything irrelevant (Jung & Baynes, 1921). So long as a function is still so fused with one or more other functions –thinking with feeling, feeling with sensation, etc.– that it is unable to operate on its own, it is in an archaic state. This means that the function is not differentiated, not separated from the whole as a special part that exists on its own. A person with undifferentiated thinking is incapable of thinking apart from other functions; thoughts are continually mixed up with sensations, feelings, or intuitions; just as undifferentiated feelings are mixed up with sensations and fantasies. An undifferentiated function is characterized by ambivalence (every position entails its own negative), which leads to characteristic inhibitions in its use.

Otto Kernberg's (1984) developmental model –built on the developmental tasks one has to complete to develop healthy relationships– establishes differentiation as related to stage 3, going from 6-8 months to 18-36 months of age. In a normal personality organization, the individual has an integrated model of self and others, allowing for stability and consistency within one's identity and in the perception of others, as well as a capacity for becoming intimate with others while maintaining one's sense of self. Such an individual would be able to tolerate hateful feelings in the context of a loving relationship, without internal conflict or a sense of discontinuity in the perception of the other.

When one fails to accomplish a particular developmental task, there is an increased risk of developing certain psychopathologies. Under high stress conditions, clients with integrative deficits fail to appreciate the "whole" of the situation and *interpret* events through the filter of their traumatic history. Therefore, they might fail to discriminate the intentions and motivations of the other and tend to perceive threat in neutral situations or events. For many traumatized individuals, thoughts and feelings about self and others are often split into dichotomous experiences of good or bad, black or white, all or nothing. This also happens in clients with inner fragmentation, where voices and parts are usually described as *good* or *bad*. The lack of integration in representations of self and other leads to identity diffusion (inconsistent view of self and others), and unstable reality testing (inconsistent differentiation between internal and external experience). This might lead to a very complicated way of functioning.

Some of the aspects with which clients have difficulties in differentiation are quite basic and can go unnoticed if not explored:

- Me and others
- Internal and external elements/My inside world and the outside world
- The trauma and me
- Past, present, and future
- The perpetrator and the part of me that resembles the perpetrator
- What I think about doing vs. what I do

TIME ORIENTATION

As we have seen in previous sections of this book, one of the first important aspects to explore is time orientation, since some of the parts and voices tend to remain stuck in trauma-time even if many years have gone by. The Adaptive Information Processing model (Shapiro, 2001, 2018) postulates that the brain is often unable to adaptively process highly charged traumatic experiences. These experiences, then, remain isolated in neural networks containing the thoughts, emotions, and sensations that were experienced during the traumatic event. Parts and voices related to these experiences will then remain "frozen" in the time of the traumatic event feeling that they are still in danger.

For this reason, helping clients to connect to the present will become a crucial aspect of treatment. We must help clients understand that whatever they experienced, happened *in the past*, but it is not happening *now*. And, as mentioned, one of the main difficulties we will find with complex traumatization is that some parts might not know that the *danger is over.*

The following questions are useful in helping clients to consider this fundamental issue:

- *Where are you right now?*
- *What day/year is it?*
- *How old are you now?/How old do you feel right now?*
- *Does this part of you know that it is the year X and that you are no longer in that place?*

CO-CONSCIOUSNESS

Co-consciousness is the sharing of experiences or tasks among ego states and/or dissociative parts. When our life experience is fragmented, developing co-consciousness becomes a fundamental tool that will help clients and parts of the system in a variety of ways. First, co-consciousness helps them realize they are safe now; the client and some of the parts or voices may know the present is safe, but others may not. Second, it also helps them experience receiving and accepting help, which is something that is usually difficult for these clients. Overall, it helps them to become aware of the difference between functioning from a conflicted system with isolated responses or functioning from a team experience, where they can start to feel the power that comes along with joining resources.

Co-consciousness might happen spontaneously with parts that are not phobic of each other and may also happen when there is less separation between parts. However, the parts toward which the client feels more phobic tend to be more isolated and conflicted and often are not invited to participate in shared experiences. Promoting the capacity to experience neutral stimuli is a good way to begin when clients or parts are still learning to relate in a healthier way.

CLINICAL CASE EXAMPLE

Alex: Don't be so naive

Alex is a 40-year-old man who has worked very hard in therapy for quite some time. He is able to connect more with one of the most wounded child parts that is still partially stuck in trauma time. This intervention takes place while checking the results of the previous session in the inner system after working with the child part and reaching a deeper layer of understanding and compassion.

The session begins with the therapist asking about the effects of the work done in the previous session (CS #1.1).

T: How are you? How did you feel after the work in the last session?

C: Well, the last time I felt very relieved.

T: Yes?

C: The only thing is that, afterward, there was something that ended up interfering, as always.

T: One step at a time. First, let's see what helped you feel relieved. Could you tell me what differences you noticed?

C: Well, I think it was ... I don't know, dealing with the part of the little boy. He seemed more familiar.

T: Very good. And what did you notice differently in your daily life?

C: Well, less tension, although from a certain moment on, it felt as if I couldn't be so present with him and it was as if another part were interfering, telling him he was naive.

T: Another part you say.

C: I think so.

T: But is that part telling you not to be so naive?

C: It's telling the boy.

By exploring when this happened or what was happening at the time, we show interest in the part as we help the client be more curious about the possible intentions (TW #2). It may also help us determine the function that the part plays in the inner system (TW #6).

T: And do you remember when this was? What was happening or what had happened?

C: No. I thought so, but I wasn't able to identify anything in particular.

T: So, you're already trying to notice a little bit.

C: You told me to do so.

T: Very good.

T: And then, at a certain point, it seems as if another part shows up.

C: Yes, something that treated me like garbage.

T: And do you notice that something now?

C: I don't know, I think it's something directed towards the boy.

T: Not towards you. And that something directed towards the boy, what do you think it is?

C: I don't know, it points out that he will never be alone.

T: It points out that he will never be alone.

C: Yes, but ...

Apparently, there is a positive message, but the client becomes agitated. The therapist tries to help the client remain curious and respectful while continuing to pay attention to whatever happens in the system (TW #2).

C: It seems it's against... when it saw that... That I could be calmer without... I don't know how to explain myself.

T: The important thing is that you don't judge it. Say whatever you have to say, it's okay, so we can understand.

C: *There was a bit of relief due to... seeing that he* (Referring to the perpetrator) *can't get to where the little boy is; relieved to see that the perpetrator could not reach the boy, but... As if it had imposed on himself to never leave. I don't know how to explain it better.*

T: *So, what is this imposition to never leave? Is it a phrase, a thought or something else?*

C: *I don't know, because it also tells him that he's naive.*

T: *And being naive is not something that this man would say.*

Although this part may have a protective function (TW #6), it reminds the client of the perpetrator, so we can determine that there is a certain level of phobia that is being generated (TW #4). The therapist continues to help the client keep an open attitude to increase understanding (TW #2). In addition, removing the negative connotation with which the client interprets the message from the part and helping him see it from a different perspective is a way to explore the resources that this part may offer to the system (TW #7). This intervention also helps in reducing the existing power struggle within the system (Issue #6).

T: *When there is something like this, it usually is a part that tries to protect, but it does so in a way that is a bit scary and more critical. The thing about not being so naive seems more like, "Hey, be careful."*

C: *I don't see it that way ...*

T: *How do you see it? Maybe I did not understand it well.*

C: *As opposed to what I saw the last time and the following days, it's as if this part points out to the other one not to be so naive as to think that he can feel better.*

T: *Ok, and do you have access to this part? Do you see it or notice it?*

C: *I notice it when it comes up.*

T: *How is the little boy now? Let's see, let's try to understand.*

C: *I think he's a little scared.*

T: *Do you think or do you know?*

C: *I can see that he is scared.*

T: *What scares him?*

C: *He's scared of things being done without thinking... as if someone were telling him to do so.*

In the previous segment, we are trying to help the client be more curious about what is happening with this part in order to become able to start interacting and communicating with it (TW #2). Notice that by asking the question, "Do you think, or do you know?" we are making sure that the client has actually checked inside and is not simply giving us a quick answer. This will lead to developing cooperation among parts (TW #10). Next, we assess the degree of differentiation (TW #5) by inquiring about time and space orientation and again trying to help the client understand that the part is here and now and no longer there and then.

T: *The other day we saw what you did when facing that man, who is no longer there anymore, so it's impossible. He is not there, and neither is the child. I wonder whether this other part knows that you're not there, or he feels like the little boy.*

C: *I don't know, maybe.*

T: We would be interested in having some access to this part, to see if you notice it, hear it, or see it.
C: No.

This is very common when there is a dissociative phobia. The client usually has a hard time thinking about the part, looking at it, and even being curious about it. This seems like the right time to explore the dissociative phobia (TW #4).

T: No? (Client shakes his head.) *What do you feel towards this part?*
C: It scares me.
T: What is it that scares you about this part?
C: It always shows up when it seems that I'm going to start feeling better.

Asking the client to outline his inner world is another technique that can help us understand better what is happening in the system.

T: Can you tell me what you are noticing inside while you draw a picture of it?
C: Yes. (Client starts drawing.) *Here is the boy, this is me, and then there is this, I don't know how to draw it better.*
T: It's just fine. Here's the boy. And you?
C: There.
T: What does this mean?
C: I notice... as if it were God.
T: As if it were God. You notice this part as if it were God, what makes you think or feel that it's as if it were God?
C: Because it's everywhere.

At this point, it is interesting to help the client be more curious about this part (TW#2). We try to identify the needs of the part (TW #7), but a strong dissociative phobia seems to be getting in the way (TW#4).

T: Let's see what this something needs. Can you ask and see what information comes up for you?
C: No, no.
T: This part is of interest to us, just like any other part that is inside of you. Do you think your fear does not allow you to ask?
C: Maybe, yes.
T: We can try to process that like we've done previously and see if that clarifies a little bit. What do you think? Shall we try?

We propose processing the phobia (TW #4) and, since it is a new part and the phobia is very intense, we remind him of the procedure. When clients are not too phobic, it is usually not necessary to explain the procedure again. But when it is a new part or a part that is not usually involved in therapy, it is important to do so.

T: *We are going to do the usual procedure. You will try to physically locate where you notice the fear towards this part that you believe is everywhere. If your fear is reduced a little, we can see what is left and maybe that allows us to understand better.*

C: *It's just that I don't see that it's helping me. I just notice myself more controlled.*

T: *Exactly. Since you notice that, fear is activated, and it doesn't allow you to look at this part with curiosity. And if you cannot look at this part with curiosity, we cannot know what its worries are, and it cannot learn how to do things differently. That's why I suggest that we work with your fear a bit and see if it helps us clarify, but only if you want, if you think it makes sense.*

C: *Yes.*

T: *Yes? Well, you tell me when you're ready to focus on the fear.*

C: *Okay.* (Short set of BLS)

T: *What did you get or what did you notice?*

C: *Control or something like that.*

T: *You notice control. How do you notice it?*

C: *I don't know, in that I lose control.* (Short set of BLS)

T: *What did you get or what did you notice?*

C: *Well, the only thing I see is that it wants to...*

T: *You can say it.*

C: *To control.*

T: *When you were in that place, there was a lot of control in general, right? Everything was controlled. Is that so?*

C: *Yes.*

T: *What would happen if everything was not under control?*

C: *Well, punishment.*

T: *Punishment, negative consequences. From what I know of your story... Look at me. It makes sense that there would be a part trying to control things due to fear of punishment. This would mean that this part does not know that you are not there either. If this part learns that you are no longer there and that you don't need to control all of that, it may lower its guard and help in a way that scares you less. Do you follow me?* (Client nods.)

After introducing psychoeducation to help the client be less frightened of the part and more understanding, we explore other alternative options (TW #8) for it to continue to use its identified resources (TW #7). By doing this we promote cooperation (TW #10) through trying to develop co-consciousness.

T: *What could this part do to help you? Check what things this part could control, since if it can only exert control, we should give it a function that could be useful for you. Check if there is something in your life that you would like to control more.*

C: *Currently?*

T: *Hmm.*

C: *I don't know, maybe the fear.*

T: *The fear of what? Fear in general or fear of something specific?*

C: *I don't know.*

T: You don't know. How could this part help you control the fear? Can you check in with it?

C: I don't see it.

T: What don't you see?

C: That it can help me like that.

T: But have you asked? (Client nods.) *How do you notice the part now?*

C: It seems that it has surrounded me or something like that.

T: It seems that it has surrounded you. We are going to do tapping again with your fear, but we are going to invite this part to be there noticing the tapping. Is that okay with you? (Client nods.) *Yes? Very good.* (Shor set of BLS) *Could the part notice the tapping?*

C: I think so.

T: Yes? And how is your fear?

C: More or less the same.

T: There was a moment when you signaled me to keep on going a little bit longer, right? What was happening?

C: It was as if the circle had opened.

T: The circle opened a little. Is that good or not?

C: I don't know.

T: So, it seems that the part notices the tapping. And after tapping, the circle opened a little bit. Should we try a little bit more? What do you think? Let the part notice it again. What do you think? (Client nods.) (Short set of BLS) *T: How did it go?*

C: I don't know if it's because of my fears...

T: If it's because of your fears, we will work on it now, but try to tell me what happened.

C: It's as if it closed it up again.

T: What do you mean by closed? Was it you or the part?

C: I think it was me.

T: Can we focus on your fear? We will go back to the part now, but first, we'll go with your fear for a little bit. (Client nods.) *Then we'll try again with the part, we won't forget. Can you tell me what happened just before you closed the circle?*

C: I think the other part was looking at the boy, but I don't know.

T: How interesting! So, your fear was activated. Let's just go with your fear and then we can go back to this part.

C: With the fear that I'm feeling?

T: The fear that you feel when you see this part looking at the boy. Let's work with your fear to see what the part was trying to do. (Client nods.) (Short set of BLS.)

T: What happens with your fear?

C: It's gone.

T: Is the fear gone?

C: No, I was going to say something and it's gone.

T: Don't you remember?

C: That it seems to me that things are coming together.

T: Think for a moment to see if you remember, and, if not, I'll do tapping again on your fear, only on the fear, yes? (Client nods.) (Short set of BLS.)

C: I'm not getting anything...

Although the client does not state getting anything, he seems calmer. We try to help him become more aware of any internal changes and also stay curious towards this part (TW #2). As usual, we check in with the part after each intervention (CS #2.5).

> T: *You're not getting anything, but have you noticed anything? Check your fear, because it seemed that something calmed down in you. Can you tell me how the fear is?*
> C: *Hmm, I notice it less.*
> T: *Less. Let's do something. We again invite this part to open that circle. We are going to be curious about this part too. And you let me know. Ready?* (Client nods.)
> C: *I don't understand how it can help me.*
> T: *It's about checking with the part. What was the part doing to notice the tapping?*
> C: *Again, it seemed that it was surrounding me.*
> T: *And what is it trying to do with that? Just ask. How is the boy doing with all this?*
> C: *Well, I think he's more scared.*
> T: *Can you ask him what he is perceiving?*
> C: *What I said, fear.*

Again, a dissociative phobia comes up, we suggest processing it so we can keep exploring (TW #4). Later on, we are also going to suggest a different way of responding that is not so frightening for the client or other parts (TW #8).

> T: *Shall we process a little bit of the boy's fear? You felt it before, and your fear has lowered a little. Perhaps by processing the existing fears, the rest can become a bit clearer, yes?* (Client nods.) (BLS) *What's happening?*
> C: *He has withdrawn because I can't help him.*
> T: *And why?*
> C: *Because he can see that I am surrounded.*

We are keeping in mind that the system was initially designed to work as a team in order to adapt to a dysfunctional environment. We remind the client to let the parts know that what they are doing is no longer useful and is detrimental instead. Conveying this message is one way to start helping the parties see that, with some changes, they can act as a real team (TW#10).

> T: *Because he sees you are surrounded. Let's ask the other part not to surround you because it's scaring you both. If it's trying to protect the boy, it's just not working. Is that okay?* (Client nods.) *We're going to ask this part not to do that and we can do tapping, in case the part is also worried about something.*
> C: *What part?*
> T: *The part that is surrounding you. Tell the part that this is not helping neither you nor the boy, that this scares you, and that it would be good to work as a team, so you don't get scared.* (Client nods.) (Short set of BLS) *What's happening?*
> C: *I noticed that it also noticed the tapping.*
> T: *Great. Do you notice it's less wrapped around you?*
> C: *Yes, there's more space, and the boy seems relieved.*

T: Let's thank the part for opening up that space and do a bit more tapping. Ask it to keep on noticing that you and the boy need that space. (Client nods.) (Short set of BLS)

Once we confirm that the procedure is helping with the conflict, we check how the part is responding to the intervention (CS #2.5).

T: What happened to this part when I tapped and thanked it for giving you some space?
C: Maybe it's silly, but perhaps the part didn't know that it was scaring me.
T: It's not silly, it's very important. It's great that it can realize that.

We close the session by summarizing what has been done in the session and thinking of goals for future sessions (CS #3.4).

T: Try to assimilate all of this gradually. You don't have to do anything when you are not here other than self-care, which is what we are working on. Little by little, we will be looking at everything that scares you. I will just ask you to remember that you always learn from experience, control is something that is learned. I'm going to make sure that, just as we understood the boy, we will understand what is happening, but you'll do it here, with my help and little by little. Is that okay? (Client nods.)

This case example illustrates the importance of checking on the effects of the interventions from the previous session and how this can guide our next steps. We begin with a part that tells the client he is naive, which generated discomfort and fear. By exploring why the part is saying that and what it is trying to achieve with this type of message, we could begin introducing the idea that this way of communicating is currently not helping. After getting a clear picture of what was happening, we could also continue the work with differentiation and co-consciousness while both part and client are involved.

SUMMARY

Working with differentiation while encouraging co-consciousness is probably one of the most useful interventions for parts that are stuck in trauma-time. Just pointing out that the present is safe will not be enough, especially if parts have been stuck there for years and especially when the Adult Self is not yet strong enough to get this message across. One way to help the system experience the safety of the present moment is to involve the different parts in the work, having them look through the eyes of the client, or notice an object in the office, as we did in the case example from the previous chapter.

CHAPTER 12

REACHING INTEGRATION

DEFINING INTEGRATION

When delving into the definitions of integration, it is easy to get lost. The simplest definition would be to think of integration as the act of combining elements to create a unified whole; which implies, in terms of personality, the coordination of mental processes that give rise to an adequate functional personality. But what does this really mean? Integration is neither a single event nor the end of a journey. It is a dynamic state of being that is in constant flux, yet stably constant (Steele, 2009). Integration consists of an ongoing series of mental and physiological processes such as synthesis, which implies the association of experience and realization, which is the process of developing conscious awareness and extracting meaning from personal experiences. Realization, in addition, implies personification ("That little girl is me!") and presentification ("I am in the present and the past is gone, I am an adult and I can choose now") (Janet, 1928).

The 2011 *Guidelines for Treating Dissociative Identity Disorder in Adults* states:

> There are certain issues that every therapist will run into during the therapeutic work with unintegrated individuals: fusion, merging, blending and unification. A desirable treatment outcome is a workable form of integration or harmony among alternate identities. Terms such as *integration* and *fusion* are sometimes used in a confusing way. *Integration* is a broad, longitudinal process referring to all work on dissociated mental processes throughout treatment. *Fusion* refers to a point in time when two or more alternate identities experience themselves as joining together with a complete loss of subjective separateness. *Final fusion* refers to the point in time when the client's sense of self shifts from that of having multiple identities to that of being a unified self. Some members of the 2011 Guidelines Task Force have advocated for the use of the term *unification* to avoid the confusion of early fusions and final fusion. (p. 195)

THE PROCESS OF INTEGRATION

Integration is often seen as a goal. And although it is a goal, it is also a process that takes place from the early stages of therapy. But, how do we know whether we are on the right path towards integration? Generally, we will know when curiosity is increasing, empathy among parts is developing, and phobic avoidance is decreasing. This generates a greater sense of calm, resilience, and internal peace. Another relevant moment is when there is conscious awareness both of what happened (trauma) and of what other parts had to do in order to survive. A third milestone is when clients can really get a felt sense that the past is over.

The following paragraphs from the *ISSTD Guidelines* (2011) describe some aspects of the process well:

> Many tasks of late-phase treatment of DID are similar to those in the treatment of non-traumatized patients who function well but experience emotional, social, or vocational problems. In addition, the more unified DID patient may need specific coaching about dealing with everyday life problems in a non-dissociative manner. Similarly, the patient may need help with tolerating everyday stresses, petty emotions, and disappointments as a routine part of human existence. Eventually, many patients experience this treatment phase as one in which they become increasingly able to realize their full potential in terms of personal and interpersonal functioning. Patients may acquire a more coherent sense of their past history and deal more effectively with current problems. The patient may begin to focus less on the past traumas, directing energy to living better in the present and to developing a new future perspective. (p. 201)

During the latter part of therapy, we will observe how clients are more capable of engaging in adaptive behaviors, establishing healthy and safe attachments, and using adaptive defensive responses. Little by little this leads to a more integrated person who is able to feel all the emotions that were dissociated, for example. Mental efficiency becomes higher since the energy is no longer spent on the conflict.

THE RESULT OF INTEGRATION

Our self or personality is not the active agent of integration, but rather is the result of integration (Loevinger, 1976; Metzinger, 2003; Van der Hart, Nijenhuis & Steele, 2006). As clients overcome their phobias, there is less need to invest in separateness and fusion among parts can happen spontaneously or with our help.

> The most stable treatment outcome is final fusion—complete integration, merger, and loss of separateness—of all identity states. However, even after undergoing considerable treatment, a considerable number of DID patients will not be able to achieve final fusion and/or will not see fusion as desirable. Many factors can contribute to patients being unable to achieve final fusion: chronic and serious situational stress; avoidance of unresolved, extremely painful life issues, including traumatic memories; lack of financial resources for treatment; comorbid medical disorders; advanced age; significant unremitting *DSM* Axis I and/or Axis II comorbidities; and/or significant narcissistic investment in the alternate identities and/or DID

itself, among others. Accordingly, a more realistic long-term outcome for some patients may be a cooperative arrangement—that is, sufficiently integrated and coordinated functioning among alternate identities to promote optimal functioning. However, patients who achieve a cooperative arrangement rather than final fusion seem to be more vulnerable to later decompensation (into florid DID and/or PTSD) when sufficiently stressed. (p. 195)

Even after final fusion, additional work to integrate the patient's residual dissociated ways of thinking and experiencing may continue. For instance, the therapist and patient might need to work on fully integrating an ability that was previously held by one alternate identity, or the patient may need to learn what his or her new pain threshold is, or how to integrate all of the dissociated ages into one chronological age, or how to regauge appropriate and healthy exercise or exertion levels for his or her age. Traumatic and stressful material also may need to be reworked from this new unified perspective (p. 195).

This chapter, mostly based on the guidelines of the ISSTD, points out the different moments of the therapeutic process. In the next pages, we can see how a client describes her journey towards integration.

EVE'S JOURNEY TO INTEGRATION

Beginning of therapy

I have a twin that takes over when I am blocked.
A dangerous and terrible twin, who destroys everything around when I let my guard down.
No one is safe if I let her out, and she sometimes hurts me.
She scares me so much that I avoid looking in the mirror, just in case I see a bit of her in me.
I see her unfolding in my shadow,
transforming herself,
transforming me from the inside out,
shredding my skin,
reaching out with her claws
and vomiting her rage over all of us.
I fear her even more than accepting the reality of what they are doing to me,
but deep inside I know that thanks to her I am never alone,
even though she hates me so much,
she hates them so much that she would kill us all.

During therapy

My biggest fear? It still is my other half.
It is not the same fear anymore. My life is different now.
No one destroys me, but she still exists, and I fear she will attack the people around me,
because she cannot control herself.
I am terrified that she may hurt the person I love, the person who loves me.
Sometimes I have terrible dreams, and she wakes up before I do.
She does not realize we are not there anymore. And I am scared.
She does not hurt me anymore, though sometimes I am scared of not being able to control her desire to do so.
I want her to leave me alone.
I want her to leave me.
I do not want her to remind me of the past anymore.
Sometimes, I am scared of running into her in the middle of the hallway.
Sometimes, I look at my hands and fearfully ask myself if they are really mine.
If I muster up some courage, I look straight in the mirror for a few seconds,
and I make sure my reflection follows my movements and my smile smiles only if I do.

Later in therapy

The owner of this body is not here,
I have stayed in this world as part of a life that does not belong to me,
in hopes that she will come back to occupy her place.
I do not feel anything for what surrounds me.

I do not understand how no one notices this and how no one realizes
that I am only occupying an empty skin.
If I did not do so, neither one of us would survive what has just happened.
Sometimes I see her, like a ghost
wandering through the house with her nightgown half unbuttoned and dry bloodstains.
I see her, but she does not see me.
I ask her to go back to her body, but she does not hear me or does not want to hear me.
I cannot be here living her life.
I try to smile when in their eyes I see that it is necessary.
I try to take care of her body without changing it too much,
though I feel locked up in it and I do not feel comfortable with the image it is projecting.
This is not my life. I hope she comes back.

Towards the end of therapy

I am alone.
For the first time in my life, I am alone.
She died to save my life. She is not here anymore.
I am here thanks to her.
Because of her, I had enough strength to give birth,
and fill up the life we created with all the good things I never had.
She is not here anymore. Before she left, she said, "You will never be alone again."
It hurts, it hurts... my heart aches like it never did before.
I do not want to live without her, I do not want for her not to be here, I miss her.
I want her back, I want her back... I feel lonely.
I isolate myself, I close my eyes and call her throughout my inner being... throughout my guts...
and I only hear my voice.
It is terrible that just when I learned to listen to her, to love her, to understand her... she went away.

I feel alone, empty, hollow...
I feel as if I had lost the most valuable part of me, the one that most deserved to stay.
Thank you, thank you, thank you... no one ever took care of me more than she did,
no one ever loved me more than she did ...
I do not feel her reflection, I do not feel her pulse ... I do not feel her ...
I woke up one day, exactly the day when the night before I fell asleep hoping to feel,
feeling bad for not having the guts to do so, for not wanting to do so.
I woke up feeling everything again... everything except her.

At the end of therapy

I do not know who I am, which one of them I am.
I am big, strong, a full moon.
I know so many things... I have lived through so many experiences...

I have the best treasures in the world at arm's reach, sleeping next to me every night. Love.
Few people know its true meaning. Few can look it in the eye.
Few can understand everything this word hides.
Most settle for much less.

I can love, I can hate, I can burn others or myself.
They could not defeat me and they never will,
because those who could are the ones who would never want to do it...
and the rest... they are nothing... only shreds of dry skin.

I am thankful for my other half, whoever was the one that split,
for the one who had to grow up amidst atrocity after atrocity,
and for the one who stayed taking care of who I should have been.
I am thankful for the little flames lighting my steps,
with the unshakable silence of the truth in a nonsensical world,
for those that are gone, and for those that still guide me... the many times I lose my path...

I am complete and complex.
I am sweet, and I am a warrior.

I am the storm and the calm, light and shadow.
I am full of scars, from wars, from volcanoes and deserts, from sand and ice.
I get lost in myself, and I find myself, and I get lost again.
I can walk between times searching for hidden pieces of life,
and to look at them until I am bigger than they are.
I am and I feel more than many,
I have lived a thousand lives and fought a thousand battles, and I am only here thanks to me.
No one other than myself has always been with me, no one other than myself has accompanied me in this journey.
My life is mine.
I know I am not like most people, I am proud of this, I have gotten this far,
I am very strong.

EVE

SECTION FIVE:

CLINICAL CASE EXAMPLES

CHAPTER 13

CASE CONCEPTUALIZATION AND TREATMENT PLAN

The work described in the different chapters of the book is based on clinical experience and case conceptualization, a key element in trauma-informed therapies such as EMDR (Shapiro, 2001, 2018). In this section, a way of thinking about the cases and organizing the work depending on the information of each particular client will be explained at the beginning of each of the case example chapters.

CASE CONCEPTUALIZATION

For practical purposes, case conceptualization is organized into five main sections. The first two sections include the basic information that we will gather to understand and organize each case. The last three sections are aimed at gathering information about dissociative disorders.

- History of symptoms and presenting problems
- Resources, capacities, and support network
- Structural elements of the internal system
- Relational aspects of the internal system
- Trauma related phobias and other potential blocks

History of symptoms and presenting problems

1. General presenting problems and/or symptoms
2. Previous diagnosis
3. Attachment patterns
4. Relational problems
    a. Family members
    b. Friends and peers
    c. Intimate relationships
    d. Work and/or school

5. Daily life functioning
   a. Self-care habits
   b. Financial stability
   c. Social, occupational or school functioning
   d. Overall level of functioning
6. Initial onset of problems/symptoms
   a. What was happening then?
   b. What got triggered?
7. When did symptoms worsen?
   a. What was happening then?
   b. What got triggered?
8. When do symptoms increase or worsen now?
   a. Current triggers
   b. Degree of awareness of triggers

Resources

1. Sources of adaptive information
   a. Good enough attachment figures in childhood and/or adult life
   b. Moments of feeling safe and being protected
   c. Moments of feeling cared for
   d. Other relevant positive figures/models (caregivers, siblings, nanny, teachers, coaches, family friends, etc.)
2. Emotional regulation capacity
   a. Self-regulation capacity
   b. Co-regulation capacity
   c. Tolerance for negative and positive emotions
3. Social support
   a. Family members
   b. Intimate partners
   c. Friends
   d. Work colleagues and peers
   e. Other professionals (therapists, support groups, teachers, etc.)
   f. Religious/spiritual resources
4. Other resources
   a. Mentalization capacity
   b. Degree of realization
   c. Degree of integrative capacity
5. Timeline of best memories (realistic, not idealized; include age, places and people)

Structural elements of the internal system

1. Client's degree of awareness of parts
2. Internal structure
   a. Approximate number of parts
   b. Client's description/representation of the internal system of parts
   c. Organization and distribution of those parts that the client can discuss
   d. Any missing pieces in the description
3. Degree of differentiation about the self and others
   a. Can the client distinguish her/his own thoughts, emotions and needs from what has been imposed by others?
   b. Is the client confusing any parts or voices with the real perpetrators?
4. Time orientation and current perception of safety
   a. Is the client confusing what happened in the past with what is happening in the present?
   b. Does the client know that the danger is over?
   c. Which parts are still stuck in trauma time?
5. Mentalizing capacities
   a. Can all parts mentalize?
   b. Which parts have higher mentalizing abilities?
   c. Which parts need help with mentalizing?
6. Adaptive information
   a. Which parts have adaptive information?
   b. Which parts need help with adaptive information?

Relational aspects of the internal system

1. Acceptance of parts
   a. Despite the fear/conflict, does the client describe some parts with compassion, acceptance or appreciation?
2. Relationships among parts
   a. What feelings do the parts have towards each other?
   b. Which are adaptive for the system in the present moment?
   c. Which need to improve?
3. Degree of cooperation between parts of the system
   a. Is the client aware of any parts attempting to help the system?
   b. Can the client accept that there might be an attempt of help even though it may not be clear yet?
4. Parts that may have difficulties with therapy
   a. Is there ambivalence or rejection towards therapy?
   b. What are their concerns regarding therapy?

5. Co-consciousness between parts
    a. If it exists, which parts are co-conscious?
    b. When does co-consciousness occur? Does it vary?
    c. How do other parts respond to this?

Trauma related phobias and other potential blocks

1. Phobia of inner experience
    a. Can the client check inside?
    b. Can the client notice and tolerate sensations?
    c. Is the client afraid of his or her feelings, thoughts or sensations?
    d. Is the client ashamed of his or her feelings, thoughts or sensations?
2. Phobia of parts
    a. Does the client show ambivalence about the parts or does he/she avoid talking about them?
    b. Despite the fear, can the client try to explore parts and be curious?
    c. Do any of the parts feel shame or is the patient ashamed of any of them?
3. Phobia of attachment and attachment loss
    a. Is there ambivalence around trust in the therapeutic relationship?
    b. Do the client or any of the parts have difficulties trusting others, ambivalence between wanting to attach and pushing others away?
4. Phobia of traumatic memories
    a. Does the client insist on avoiding any exploration about childhood?
    b. Does the client show ambivalence about trauma work or even talking about traumatic experiences?
5. Phobia of change and adaptive risk-taking
    a. Is the client afraid of change?
    b. Does the client present difficulties trying suggestions that would improve his or her quality of life?
6. Defenses (minimization, rationalization, avoidance, etc.)
7. Any other identified potential blocks

TREATMENT PLAN

A frequent question among trauma therapist is how to organize a good treatment plan when clients present with so many different complications. A sound treatment plan will need to rest on the foundation of a comprehensive conceptualization of the clinical case. For this reason, one of the goals of the conceptualization described in this chapter is to introduce a way of looking at cases that can help us with decision-making. Once we gather all the information in the previous section, we will have a better idea of where to begin. However, we can list a few possible ways to begin the work as a guide to keep in mind.

The basics

1. **Pacing the clinical history intake**. This is essential in cases with amnesia or limited affect tolerance capacities. It is important to be aware of the difficulties that many trauma survivors have when faced with an exploration that can be experienced as intrusive and/or overwhelming.

2. **Establishing a good enough alliance with all the system of parts**. One of the usual goals in therapy is to establish a good therapeutic alliance with the client. In cases with dissociative parts, we cannot expect a good alliance anytime soon in therapy, but we can develop a good enough, safe relationship based on an agreement to help all the parts in the best possible way as a whole.

3. **Setting therapeutic goals.** It is recommended to avoid just following what the client brings to the session. Clients with such a chaotic and conflicted system need at least some structure. This serves to guide both client and therapist in assessing the outcome. We can establish short, medium and long-term goals and collect all of them. We can even organize them in different areas, such as personal, family, work or academic.

4. **Reaching agreements.** It is important to agree on what needs to be worked on and how it will be addressed. Some parts might understand that it is important to work with their trauma history while also knowing that it might not be the right time. Therefore, reaching agreements according to what is needed *and can be done* can be particularly useful. It is a way of letting all the parts of the system know that we will not lose perspective of what needs to be done, and that we will not avoid it either. We will eventually get there when the moment is right for all the parts.

High-risk behaviors or symptoms affecting self and others

High-risk situations, such as a client being in imminent danger due to suicidal ideation, aggression, self-harm or any other high-risk behaviors, should be addressed first. Other behaviors such as addictions or dangerous sex-related behavior should also be explored. Clients who continue to live in abusive environments need help with addressing the necessary issues that they may need to confront so they can feel safe.

1. **Suicidal ideation.** Clinicians should assess suicidal ideation and intervene whenever necessary. Basic questions to explore are how, when, where, and why. The answer to these questions will help us assess the reason, any triggers, whether there is a specific plan –which always involves a higher risk– and what needs to be addressed. If suicidal ideation is no longer active after the intervention, we continue the work revising therapeutic goals just in case they need to be adapted. If suicidal ideation is still present, we need to take measures to keep the client safe, such as resorting to family members or even hospitalization, at least until the intensity decreases and we are able to continue with the therapeutic work.

2. **Aggression.** Some parts might be fixated on the defense of fight, in charge of protection from any potential threats. These parts need to know that the present is safe and they are no longer in danger. Perpetrator-imitating parts may perceive themselves and be perceived by other parts as the real perpetrators. These parts are frequently stuck in trauma-time, engaging in the same behaviors that kept them safe back then. Sometimes they even hurt other parts or the client, creating more fear and complications. The lack of realization about the difference between parts and perpetrators is one of the reasons why working with differentiation is so important. For the same reason, working with safety and boundaries are the first interventions to be done.

   Anger and aggression can also help clients to avoid contacting more difficult emotions such as shame and fear. In these cases, it will be necessary to understand them as defenses while helping clients to increase their capacity to tolerate other emotions. Occasionally, some parts may get triggered and have the urge to hurt others. Though the system usually finds a way to deal with this impulse, when it is present, we must address it with clients and either work with boundaries or work with the memories that are getting triggered, in addition to introducing time orientation.

3. **Self-harm or any other high-risk behaviors.** Self-harm may serve many purposes. Most of the time it is a regulatory strategy. Other times self-harm can be a type of punishment that is actually a reenactment. Some perpetrator-imitating parts may believe they have to hurt the client or a specific part to avoid something else from happening. Again, parts stuck in trauma-time need to understand that this is not needed anymore.

4. **Any other behavior that can interfere in therapy.** In addition to the above, any other behavior that may interfere with therapy should also be addressed. For example, missing appointments or attending only when one is feeling well or ill can be interferences that need to be addressed.

Working with the system of parts and reducing the conflict

1. Once we have addressed the previous issues, we focus on the work described in this book, with the goal of reducing conflict and improving cooperation, collaboration and teamwork.

2. If there are dissociative phobias, we need to begin with the phobia of inner experience and the phobia of dissociative parts. These are the priority when dealing with dissociative clients with dissociative parts.

3. The phobia of traumatic memories is related to many of the conflicts between parts and to the presence of other phobias. Making sure the pace is adapted to the whole system is the best way to proceed. Other phobias can be addressed as they emerge too.

Resources and emotional regulation strategies

1. Developing capacities for emotional regulation, social skills, and problem-solving. This might seem very basic but is often overlooked due to the many presenting symptoms. To help clients achieve a better functioning in daily life should be a priority.

2. Developing capacities for affect tolerance when this is one of the identified problems

Trauma work. Micro-processing, processing, and reprocessing procedures.

When the client and the system of parts are ready, doing trauma work will be the best stabilization technique we can use. If the client is not ready to reprocess it, we can resort to the different procedures described in this book.

TARGET SELECTION

There are many ways of organizing target selection in EMDR. Special populations might need adaptations depending on the difficulties or limitations presented by each individual. Whenever the client can tolerate speaking about early memories, even those with intense emotions, we will begin working on an early memory that both client and therapist understand is connected with high-risk behaviors or debilitating problems. When clients demonstrate they cannot yet tolerate focusing on the most disturbing targets from the past, we will focus on reprocessing current triggers, alternating this with brief spontaneous or guided contact with targets from the past until the client can tolerate more extensive contact with the past (Mosquera, Leeds & Gonzalez, 2012). In general, it will be crucial to keep in mind the specific characteristics of the client to guide target sequencing and to organize a treatment plan. Here are some examples of the decision-making process and possibilities:

1. **Targets related to high-risk behaviors or symptoms.** To support the client in achieving stability, it would make sense to begin with targets in the present or the past that are clearly associated with the client's most debilitating symptom(s). We would then continue to work with the targets associated with those specific symptoms until the client shows stable gains with a reduction or elimination of the associated symptoms. Any risk behaviors that lead to the client decompensating should be a priority, since they are usually directly linked to unresolved issues that require immediate attention.

2. **Intrusive memories, thoughts or beliefs.** When there are intrusive and recurring memories, it is recommended to address them first, since the client may strongly benefit from reprocessing them. Often, such intrusive memories are so activating that an attempt to reprocess any other material would be ineffective. Persistent negative thoughts or limiting self-referential beliefs can be productive initial targets, followed by searching for specific memories using the procedures previously described. We can resort to contained processing to avoid opening up too much material or used micro-processing techniques described in Chapter 2.

3. **Any other targets that can help with better functioning.** Once we have addressed targets related to high-risk behaviors and any intrusive memories, thoughts, or beliefs, we can identify potential areas of conflict that need to be addressed. This can be related to the system of parts or to information that we think can help the client feel better or function better.

Keep in mind that smaller amounts of work are preferable, while remaining within the window of tolerance, aware of the amount of mental energy available to the client. In cases of complex trauma with early histories of learned helplessness, it is essential and highly therapeutic to give clients an active role in decision making, never forcing and checking regularly to make sure he or she has not become overwhelmed or depleted (Mosquera, Leeds & Gonzalez, 2014).

INFORMATION ABOUT THE CASES

The case examples in this section will be introduced with a brief conceptualization using the model presented in the beginning of this chapter. Then, in each case example, the steps and procedures detailed in previous chapters will be highlighted, so the reader can see their application in clinical practice. In the case conceptualization, we will introduce the information that was available at the beginning of the therapy, whatever was available to organize the work, and in some cases, additional information in brackets and italics will be introduced when we think it can help the reader to better understand the case. As we have indicated, much of the information presented in each of the cases has been modified to preserve patient confidentiality.

CHAPTER 14

ETHAN: THE MAN WHO SPOKE WITH BOATS

Ethan, a 38-year-old male who has received numerous diagnoses, is sent to our service due to severe self-harming behaviors. At the initial intake, he presented with flat affect, second person auditory hallucinations and thought disorder. He was taking a variety of prescribed medication that were not having an effect on the remission of his symptomatology nor on his behavioral control.

Ethan hears different voices, but he mostly worries about the one he calls "Little Motherfucker," who is constantly asking him to hurt himself. The main areas of concern are related to the internal conflict between the voices and his fear of them. With the goal of improving, the patient does great efforts to ignore the voices or quiet them. As we will see throughout the examples, most of the initial work was focused on helping Ethan to understand the voices and what they were trying to achieve with their comments.

Ethan does not have many childhood memories. However, despite not remembering what happened or how it happened, he knew he had been sexually assaulted by a group of men when he was 15.

BRIEF CASE CONCEPTUALIZATION

History of symptoms and presenting problems

1. **General presenting problems and/or symptoms.** In the initial intake, Ethan reports many difficulties with self-regulation, especially around one of the voices he hears, which he calls "Little Motherfucker." This voice leads to self-harming and other dangerous behaviors, to the point of needing to be admitted several times in the ICU, twice in a comma. He is also concerned with the urge to hurt others and verbalizes being afraid of himself and losing control. In addition, he states having occasional sleep problems, also related to the voices. He reports frequent episodes of passive influence, in which "a force" pushes him to do things in which he does not recognize himself.

2. **Previous diagnosis.** Borderline Personality Disorder, Schizophrenia, and Psychosis.

3. **Attachment patterns**. Ethan had an ambivalent attachment with his mother and an avoidant attachment with his father who spent periods of time out of the house for work reasons.

4. **Relational problems**
    a. Family members. The client describes a distant relationship with a few family members; they seem to think he is a "weirdo" and they never understood why he developed so many problems. They believe he is this way because he wants more because "he's full of shit." He has a distant relationship with a brother and a sister, and also an older brother with whom he does not speak, who thinks Ethan just wants attention.
    b. Friends and peers. No relevant issues.
    c. Intimate relationships. Not when he starts attending therapy. [Avoids romantic relationships due to his trauma history.]
    d. Work and/or school. The client is neither working nor in school when he starts therapy.

5. **Daily life functioning**
    a. Self-care habits. The client tries to maintain an organized and simple life. He cooks and tries to keep his house clean and neat. However, he has difficulties from time to time due to the voices.
    b. Financial stability. He is not working at the moment. His boss encouraged him to apply for disability, so now he has enough money to live and does not need others for financial stability.
    c. Social, occupational and school functioning. He goes for a walk on a daily basis and occasionally meets with his friends. At the beginning of therapy, he is not doing any activities.
    d. Overall level of functioning. Low.

6. **Initial onset of problems/symptoms**
    a. What was happening then? The voices started when he was 15, right after he was sexually assaulted by a group of men. The client describes how he went from being a regular teenager to becoming an isolated person that kept to himself and began doing weird things. He never spoke about what happened or told anyone and those around him thought he had gone crazy.
    b. What got triggered? The assault seems to be the breaking point for a person who had already been through many adverse experiences and somehow managed to keep it together. Due to past and recent amnesia, it is not clear whether other previous experiences got triggered.

7. **When did symptoms worsen?**
    a. What was happening then? Symptoms worsened after an important family member died.
    b. What got triggered? In the initial sessions, this remains unclear, mostly due to presenting amnesia.

8. **When do symptoms increase or worsen now?**
    a. Current triggers. He cannot identify triggers. He associates the symptoms to the voices but is does not know what activates the voices when symptoms become intensified.

b. Degree of awareness of triggers. The client is acutely aware of the voices and how they limit his capacity to function, but he is not aware of what is triggering them. Symptoms related to self-harm and sleep deprivation seem to worsen when he hears voices.

Resources

1. **Sources of adaptive information**
    a. Good enough attachment figures in childhood and/or adult life. In childhood, mother and grandmother. In adulthood, father.
    b. Moments of feeling safe and being protected. The client can give many examples of moments of feeling safe and protected with his mother and grandmother.
    c. Moments of feeling cared for. He can also give many examples of feeling cared for.
    d. Other relevant positive figures/models. A teacher in school.

2. **Emotional regulation capacity**
    a. Self-regulation capacity. The client is able to self-regulate, but only when not triggered by the voices.
    b. Co-regulation capacity. He has some capacity to co-regulate, even when exploring and hearing voices.
    c. Tolerance for negative and positive emotions. At the initial intake, he is very disconnected. *[As we progress in therapy, he becomes increasingly able to connect and remain present with his emotions. No issues around positive affect; when he feels good, he does fine; this is not a trigger.]*

3. **Social support**
    a. Family members. No family support at the time of initial intake.
    b. Intimate partners. No.
    c. Friends. Good support with a group of childhood friends who are willing to help and offer him good advice.
    d. Work colleagues and peers. Relevant support by his ex-boss and his wife; they have become friends.
    e. Other professionals. A psychiatrist and his general practitioner who have known him for many years.
    f. Religious/spiritual resources. Not relevant for him.

4. **Other resources**
    a. Mentalization capacity. The client has good mentalizing capacity.
    b. Degree of realization. Limited. He knows his trauma has affected him, but he can barely think of the event. Avoids thinking about it and tries to forget.
    c. Degree of integrative capacity. Initially, it appears to be low. (*High integrative capacity*)

5. **Timeline of best memories.** To avoid disclosing too much personal information we will omit this part. The client is able to do a realistic timeline including positive memories that are not idealized, which in terms of EMDR implies having adaptive information.

Structural elements of the internal system

1. **Client's degree of awareness of parts.** The client is relatively aware of having parts and he can partially understand that they are parts of himself. However, he speaks about them in a third person perspective, as if they were individual people.

2. **Internal structure**
   a. Approximate number of parts. In the initial intake, the client seemed to have mainly two dissociative parts, manifested by two voices: Noise and Little Motherfucker. *[Later in therapy we discovered that he had a few more parts: Noise, Little Motherfucker, Rage, Child, Fog, Conscious Part, Original Voice, and Dude. At some point in therapy, a balloon also came up, but it went away or integrated within a few sessions. A monster also shows up, representing the phobia towards one of the parts. He calls it a monster when he is upset and feels rejection. We will see more about the description, organization, and distribution of the parts in the case transcripts].*
   b. Client's description/representation of the internal system of parts. In the beginning of therapy, the client describes Little Motherfucker as a voice that is always insulting him, asking him to self-harm, and wanting his destruction. He says this is a high-pitched voice that sounds like a cartoon character. The client also describes a noise that he hears most of the time. He explains that he manages this noise by going into noisy places, where the external noise is louder than the internal noise.
   c. Organization and distribution of parts that the client can discuss. The organization and distribution of parts are not clear until several sessions into the work.
   d. Any missing pieces in the description. There seem to be many pieces missing in the beginning. The client does not seem to get angry or sad, for instance, and it appears that other parts take care of that. *[The missing pieces are related to anger. By exploring anger later on, we could reach Rage, a very important part.]*

3. **Degree of differentiation about the self and others**
   a. Can the client distinguish his own thoughts, emotions, and needs from what has been imposed by others? Yes.
   b. Is the client confusing any parts or voices with the real perpetrators? No, but he has difficulties understanding the messages he receives from the voices, often aggressive and hostile.

4. **Time orientation and current perception of safety**
   a. Is the client confusing what happened in the past and what is happening in the present? Not usually.
   b. Does the client know the danger is over? Rationally, he understands he is safe, but when he becomes emotionally triggered, the line between what happened in the past and what is happening in the present becomes blurrier.
   c. Which parts are still stuck in trauma-time? In the beginning of treatment, all parts are stick in trauma-time, except the one he describes as the Conscious Part.

5. **Mentalizing capacities**
   a. Can all parts mentalize? No, only some of them. The parts stuck in trauma time have no mentalizing capacity.
   b. Which parts have higher mentalizing abilities? The Adult Self and the Conscious Part.
   c. Which parts need help with mentalizing? The parts that need more help with mentalizing capacities are the hostile parts: Rage, Little Motherfucker, Dude, and Original Voice.

6. **Adaptive information**
   a. Which parts have adaptive information? The Adult Self has adaptive information. *[The conscious part also has adaptive information. The child part has adaptive information regarding self-care and feeling accepted and seen. This part knows what it is to be loved, taken care of, and have needs met by a good enough parent.]*
   b. Which parts need help with adaptive information? Little Motherfucker seems to need help to access adaptive information. *[The hostile parts need adaptive information both regarding the assault and how to help in a more adequate, healthy way.]*

Relational aspects of the internal system

1. **Acceptance of parts.**
   a. Despite the fear/conflict, does the client describe some parts with compassion, acceptance or appreciation? Initially, there is no acceptance of the parts that he is able to describe. He can only tolerate Noise, because he is not too bothered by it, compared to how much the other voices bother him. *[Later in therapy he is able to feel more compassion, acceptance, and appreciation for other parts. He accepts and feels compassion for his child part.]*

2. **Relationships among parts.**
   a. What feelings do the parts have towards each other? The parts that the client describes at the beginning are in conflict and seem to despise him. *[The client rejects most of the parts he describes, except the child part and the Conscious Part.]*
   b. Which are adaptive for the system in the present moment? The Adult Self has adaptive responses. *[All the other parts were trying to help, but none of them seemed adaptive at the moment of the initial intake. We had to explore to understand them.]*
   c. Which need to improve? All parts needed to improve, as well as the client.

3. **Degree of cooperation between parts of the system**
   a. Is the client aware of any parts attempting to help the system? No.
   b. Can the client accept that there might be an attempt to help even though it may not be clear yet? He can reluctantly accept that there might be an attempt to help.

4. **Parts that may have difficulties with therapy.** Initially, it is unclear. The only accessible voice insults the client or asks him to hurt himself. *[He occasionally has the impulse of hurting others which seems to be related with another part that is later identified.]*

a. Is there ambivalence or rejection of therapy? Initially, it is unclear. The client shows interest from the Adult Self but indicates that they insult him throughout the session. *[There was ambivalence about the trauma, the parts did not want to talk or work on what happened. Little Motherfucker thought coming to therapy was being weak, but we learn this later in therapy.]*

b. What are the concerns regarding therapy? He does not refer any relevant worries in regard to therapy.

5. Co-consciousness between parts
    a. If it exists, which parts are co-conscious? Usually there is no co-consciousness between parts
    b. When does co-consciousness occur? Does it vary? At times, Little Motherfucker is present while the client is describing what happened, but it's not true co- consciousness
    c. How do other parts respond to this? *[Other parts did not seem uncomfortable when we started doing co-consciousness work later on.]*

Trauma related phobias and other potential blocks

1. **Phobia of inner experience.** High.
    a. Can the client check inside? Yes, the client can check inside. He becomes angry and confused by the answers from the hostile parts, but he is able to do it.
    b. Can the client notice and tolerate sensations? Not in the beginning. *[The client was very disconnected initially, but later on, he could notice sensations and tolerate them better.]*
    c. Is the client afraid of his feelings, thoughts or sensations? He was afraid of his thoughts, especially the ones coming from the aggressive voices. *[The client was open to understanding the parts but was very upset and concerned with the aggressive messages.]*
    d. Is the client ashamed of his feelings, thoughts or sensations? *[The client felt blamed by aggressive parts and was ashamed by his reaction to the assault.]*

2. **Phobia of parts.** Very high.
    a. Does the client have ambivalence about parts or avoid talking about them? The client is ambivalent about parts, especially the more aggressive ones.
    b. Despite the fear, can the client try to explore parts and be curious? Yes.
    c. Do any of the parts feel shame in or towards any parts? Initially unknown. *[The teenage par feels shame.]*

3. **Phobia of attachment and attachment loss.** Low.
    a. Is there ambivalence around trust in the therapeutic relationship? The client is able to trust the relationship. *[The hostile parts are hesitant.]*
    b. Do the client or any of the parts have difficulties trusting others, ambivalence between wanting to attach and pushing others away? No big issues around trusting others. *[Does not have problems with relationships already established but avoids new intimate or romantic relationships to avoid being triggered.]*

4. **Phobia of traumatic memories.** Very high.
   a. Does the client insist on avoiding any exploration about childhood? When the client tries to talk about what happened he becomes overwhelmed. *[The aggressive part insists on avoiding any exploration about childhood.]*
   b. Does the client show ambivalence about trauma work or even talking about traumatic experiences? Yes, the client and all the aggressive parts.

5. **Phobia of change and adaptive risk-taking.** Initially did not seem high.
   a. Is the client afraid of change? *[The client wants to change, but some parts are afraid of it. This also makes him afraid of it.]*
   b. Do the client present difficulties trying suggestions that would improve his quality of life? *[No. Quite the contrary, the client is open to this and does his best to put all suggestions in practice.]*

6. **Defenses.** Avoidance, rationalization, and minimization.

7. **Any other identified potential blocks.** He has lost big blocks of time due to amnesia. There is missing information about his trauma history.

EXAMPLE 1. INITIAL INTAKE: WORKING WITH THE SYSTEM FROM THE BEGINNING OF THERAPY

In the first few minutes of the interview, Ethan talks about the voices he hears and how this is a daily problem for him. This is a good point of entry to explore the system (TW #1).

C: *I hear voices in my head and things talk to me.*
T: *So, you have the feeling that things talk to you. What type of things?*
C: *Computers, boats... anything.*
T: *How often does this happen to you?*
C: *I don't know.*
T: *Once a day? Once a week? Once a month?*
C: *It happens a lot. Whenever I go to the harbor, if there's a boat, I'll have a conversation with it.*

We want to start by finding out everything we can about the voices, exploring the system by asking questions, and validating every resource we can find. We ask about things such as how many voices they hear, if they are female or male voices, the content of the conversations, and how they usually take place (TW #1). This will help us understand the logic of the voices, their possible function, and how they are trying to help (TW #6).

T: *What kind of things do boats say to you?*
C: *Just a normal conversation. They ask questions such as what my name is, how am I feeling, etc.*
T: *Is this an internal conversation or do you usually speak out loud?*
C: *I speak out loud, too.*

T: Do you speak out loud on a regular basis even if there are people present?

C: Well, the boats are usually located in isolated areas. Sometimes I just remain silent, but when I get distracted, I find myself speaking out loud. Other times I don't even know how to react. Boats are just a lifeless bunch of wood and metal, and there I am talking to them about my life.

T: Do you think that people around you can hear what the boats say?

C: No, I don't think so.

T: How about the voices, do you ever have internal conversations with the voices you hear, without actually speaking out loud?

C: Not really, I basically try to shut them up.

T: Could you tell me a little more about the voices?

C: I have 2 voices. One is constantly present.

T: Do you hear it now?

C: Yes, it's like noise in a bar, constant and hard to deal with. It's like a crowd of people, and I'm able catch a word here and there.

T: Sometimes you're able to catch words. What type of words?

C: I wouldn't know what to tell you.

T: Do those words convey any messages?

C: Not a clear one, just some words.

T: Does this voice bother you?

C: When it bothers me, I go into a bar to soothe the noise. It has to be a loud bar, so the external noise is louder than the internal noise.

T: Okay, that's a very smart choice. How about the other voice?

C: The other one is "Little Motherfucker." This is a very loud self-destructive external voice, always looking for trouble. He's always saying things like, "Jump out of the window, jump in front of a train, jump in front of a car." Or "take some pills and kill yourself." He wants me to kill myself or hurt myself.

T: Is it the voice of a man or a woman?

C: It's like the voice of a cartoon character. I can't tell if it's male or female. It has a strident and unpleasant tone.

T: What do you mean by strident? Is it loud?

C: Not exactly loud. Let me see... Have you seen Roger Rabbit?

T: Yes.

C: He has that high-pitched voice. It's something like that.

Once we have some insight into the voices (TW #1), we can explore how the person feels toward them (TW #4). Exploring the dissociative phobia towards the voices (TW #4) helps us understand which ones should be worked on first. Non-frightening voices are usually easier to work with because clients can feel compassion and understand them better. On the contrary, frightening voices are hard to listen to and difficult to like. These strong emotions towards the voices become a crucial part of the conflict.

T: How do you feel towards this voice?

C: It terrifies me. I listened to that voice several times and it led to several suicide attempts. I even ended up in the ICU. And what really bothers me is that I hear it from behind, so I turn around, but then I hear it in front of me. It's like now you are talking to me and I hear you in front of me, but if I turned around, I would hear you from behind.

In order to have a clear understanding of how the client has been dealing with the voices in daily life, we need to explore his responses and possible resources (TW #7). This is important because it will let us know the dysfunctional strategies used by the client as a means for self-regulation, the resources the client may or may not have, what has worked for him, and what has not.

> *T: How do you manage this voice?*
>
> *C: It's difficult to handle. If I ignore it, it becomes louder and it brutally wants to cause more damage.*
>
> *T: Well, this is interesting. Normally what happens when we try to ignore voices is that they become louder to be heard.*
>
> *C: Yes, very loud.*
>
> *T: So, we would need to find out other ways of responding.* (Client nods). *What helps?*
>
> *C: Usually hurting myself helps.*
>
> *T: Hurting yourself helps. Does anything else help?*
>
> *C: It depends on how the voice shows up. If it starts slowly and low, I take my medication, so it doesn't get too loud. But if it shows up abruptly, it's like a punch, and that's when I always end up hurting myself, even though I try as hard as I can not to do it.*
>
> *T: Have you tried other options instead of hurting yourself?*
>
> *C: I've tried almost everything.*
>
> *T: Could you give me some examples?*
>
> *C: Taking a cold shower, getting out of the house, and saying, "fuck it."*
>
> *T: Does that help?*
>
> *C: No.*
>
> *T: Does medication help with this voice?*
>
> *C: No.*

We also want to find out when the voices appeared for the first time (TW #3). This information is relevant because clients need to learn to identify the situations in which the voice gets triggered in order to understand it better. Our questions will help us identify the traumatic aspects that need to be dealt with. In the following segment, we explore when the voice appears and why, trying to understand its possible function (TW #6).

> *T: When does the voice show up?*
>
> *C: Nowadays, I hear it a lot, but I don't understand why. Lately things are going well, so it shouldn't appear so much.*
>
> *T: Do you associate this voice with uncomfortable or tense moments?*
>
> *C: Yes, I would say so. It usually shows up when I make mistakes, but now it also appears whenever it wants, and it crushes me.*
>
> *T: Do you remember when this voice appeared for the first time?*
>
> *C: I cannot give you many details since I don't remember many things. I've erased many things from my head.*
>
> *T: You've erased things from your head. It seems you've blocked some memories to protect yourself.*
>
> *C: Yes, those memories are kept in a trunk, but sometimes they get out.*

When clients spontaneously bring up having trunks, closets, cabinets, etc. inside, these are usually ways found by the system to protect the client from painful memories. It is important to validate this resource (TW #7) and introduce the idea that we do not want to open trunks, closets, or whatever metaphor they choose. We also want to use this opportunity to explore whether they try to lock the voices away, which usually does not help and increases the conflict. If this is the case, we introduce the idea that, as a first step, it is best to start to listen to these voices (TW #2) to understand them better.

> T: *Inside of a trunk. So, you have found a way to protect yourself a bit.*
> C: *Yes.*
> T: *Have you ever done that with the voices?*
> C: *I tried many times, but it doesn't work.*
> T: *That's why I was asking; it usually doesn't work. The idea is to try to listen to what the voices say and understand what they are trying to say or why they say what they say.*

We now transcribe the closure of the session, pointing out some crucial aspects that we want the client to remember, such as the fact that the voice is a part of the person and not a separate person and how it is trying to help, and setting therapeutic goals (CS #3.4).

> T: *If you feel comfortable coming here and working with this, one of our goals could be to try to understand what triggers this voice. By doing so, you shall be able to deal with it better, and it will likely not show up in such a harmful way.* (Client nods.) *Do these goals make sense to the voice?*
> C: *Its goal is to destroy me.*
> T: *I can see why you would think this. It must be terrifying to have this voice saying all these things about hurting yourself. But I wonder whether there is another reason. Why would this voice want you to hurt yourself?*
> C: *Well, because of the guilt.*

As we can see in the previous section, we validate the client's experience even though we may not agree with what he is saying. This is a good example of how not to take sides and adopt a respectful attitude towards both parts in conflict.

> T: *Have you thought that this might be a part of you? Perhaps a part of your mind?*
> C: *It has to be, there's nobody there and suddenly I hear it. So, although it might sound like I'm crazy, I'm not as crazy as it seems. I know it's just a voice. I know that nobody else is there.*
> T: *So, it could be a part of you that feels bad, that you associate with your feelings of guilt.*
> C: *Yes.*
> T: *We can find a way to work on this.*
> C: *Okay.*

Although we could explore the guilt, we decided to simply point out the relationship between the information shared by the client and what actually happened, without going any further. Since it is one of the initial sessions, exploring deeper might not be a good idea, especially when we know that he does not remember many moments from childhood. It is better to explore cautiously in the first sessions.

EXAMPLE 2. INITIATING COMMUNICATION WITH A CHALLENGING PART

In the session prior to the one we are transcribing, we did a simple intervention with Ethan, which was asking him not to refer to his voice as a "Little Motherfucker." We asked him if he could just call him something that did not have a negative connotation. Ethan initially responded, *"Well that's what he is! A motherfucker!"* The therapist explained how name-calling is not usually helpful, since voices do not like it when they are insulted (Issue #6). Just as he does not like it when the voices call him names and tell him that he is useless. The client agreed to refer to the voice differently and said, *"I'll try. How about simply Little Guy?"* So "Little Motherfucker" became "Little Guy." This simple intervention led to a very interesting change. For the first time, "Little Guy" stopped name-calling during the session and was able to respond, expressing what he thought instead of just laughing or insulting. In this session, we explore why "Little Guy" keeps telling him to jump out of the window and hurt himself.

Following the general steps from Chapter 2, we begin the session exploring when the voice showed up and why (CS #2.2), which will give us information about the triggers (TW #3) and the possible function of the voice (TW #6).

> C: *The other day he showed up during the night.*
> T: *When did that happen?*
> C: *During the weekend. He came at night.*
> T: *While you were sleeping?*
> C: *Yes, I was sleeping, and he woke me up. He started saying over and over, "Jump out the window! Jump out the window! Jump out the window!" And I said back: "I won't jump! I won't jump! I won't jump!" This went on for hours until he left. It's the first time in my life that I could make him go away, without him getting what he wanted.*

We cannot know for sure, but it is very likely that the voice could be helping him divert attention from a more complicated issue. If the client was sleeping, would it really make sense for the voice to wake him up out of the blue just to tell him to jump out of a window? No, it would not. But if the client were having a nightmare about the sexual assault, which he does not even remember, it would make sense for a protective part to try to divert his attention elsewhere. It is way too soon to point this out, and it is best to avoid interpretations, but we can start to establish for ourselves different hypothesis regarding the functioning of the system of parts. While keeping track of our observations, it is always recommended to be on the look-out for possible resources for the client and validate their positive qualities so they can start to recognize them in themselves (TW#7).

> T: *Uh-huh. So, how did you accomplish this?*
> C: *Being more stubborn than him. He would say "Jump!" and I would say "No." I held on to the pillow, saying, "No, no, no." "Hurt yourself." "No, I don't want to hurt myself." I was sweating blood.*
> T: *But you did it.*
> C: *Yes, it's the first time ever.*
> T: *Are you happy about it?*

C: Yes, but I'm scared because he said he would be back. He said, "Get ready. I'll be back the day you feel bad." So, I'm terrified, because today I don't feel too good, and Little Guy just keeps bothering me. He's not telling me to jump out the window that much, but he does tell me to hurt myself. He calls me names and puts me down. He's driving me mad; I can't stand it. If I could slam him against the wall, I swear I would.

This part has given the client a very important clue when saying, *"I'll be back the day you feel bad."* And although this was interpreted by the client as a threat, the reality is that it is often just pointing out the function of the voice or part, which is usually related to protection. This is why it is important to understand the function of the part and what it is trying to achieve with the behavior (TW #6). Contrasting this information with the reality of the situation is crucial to increase realization. Both client and parts need to see what the behavior is actually achieving and if this is useful in the present circumstances. Most of the time, what was useful in the past has ceased to be so in the present, since the circumstances that created this behavior have now changed, and nowadays the previously adaptive behavior mostly generates discomfort.

T: And what would you accomplish with this?
C: If I hurt myself, he goes away.
T: Uh-huh.
C: I know I can't do that. I'm trying to make sense of everything and understand that it's just me, that they're my voices. I try to tell myself that even though I hear the voices externally, it's my head playing tricks on me. I don't know how to explain this.

As we can see, as we explore what happens inside, the Adult Self becomes more curious and also tries to understand. By encouraging him to pay more attention to the voice and promoting curiosity (TW #2), he is much more capable of doing this type of work. We validate this effort and begin exploring resources (TW #7) so we can start offering suggestions (TW #8.)

T: You are doing great.
C: It's a struggle. Little Guy is against me, and he's hitting me hard, very hard.
T: It does sound like a struggle, and this is precisely what I am trying to help you understand: this is not about fighting against each other, it's about fighting together. If I understood correctly, you want to be okay, but you are afraid of this part and concerned that you won't be able to deal with it. And you feel that instead of helping you right now, it makes you worse.
C: Yes. I don't want to go back to the doctor and tell him, "Look, I made myself another hole." (Client shows his scars)
T: And how do you think you could begin to try to manage those moments?
C: If I'm to be honest, I'm terrified! I don't think I can stand it. He's been at it for too many hours. Sometimes I have to leave the house to calm down and not hurt myself. If I stay in, Little Guy shows up.
T: Well, whenever you find yourself in those situations and feel that leaving the house will help, you should do it. It's positive to avoid destructive behaviors.

When trying to communicate with Little Guy, first the client has to be able to listen to the voice (TW #2). With complicated parts, we should offer lots of encouragement, since listening is usually a hard thing to do and clients are more used to avoiding the voice and trying not to listen to it. Again, in the following segments of the transcript, we are repeating the basic steps: exploring the voices (TW #1), encouraging the client to pay more attention to the part (TW #2); exploring the function of the voice (TW #6); exploring and validating resources, feelings, and needs (TW #7); and offering suggestions, so the client can expand his repertoire and respond differently (TW #8).

> *T: Is Little Guy here with you?*
> *C: Yes, he is busting my balls...*
> *T: What is he saying?*
> *C: He is saying, "You're a loser."*
> *T: Why does he say that?*
> *C: That's what I would like to know.*
> *T: Well, ask him why he says that. Let's listen.*
> *C: He just keeps saying, "Loser, loser, loser."*
> *T: Can you ask him why he is saying that?*
> *C: No answer, just repeats "Loser, loser, loser."*

Since there is no change or cooperation from this voice, we move along trying to understand Little Guy. The client tends to deal with the phobia by fighting against it (TW #4). We need to help him understand that this will likely just increase the conflict and not resolve it.

> *T: Okay, so what is going on with Little Guy? What would help him calm down?*
> *C: I have to keep on fighting him.*
> *T: Could you try to avoid fighting him?*
> *C: Yes, I can avoid it by taking a pill.*

Notice how both part and client have a reduced repertoire at the moment. The therapist tries to remind them that this is not about fighting between them but, instead, starting to function as a true team (TW #10).

> *T: Try not to look at it as a fight against Little Guy, because you're wasting too much energy. It's not a fight against him; it's a fight for your wellbeing.*
> *C: (Client seems thoughtful) Okay, so I have to look at it differently.*
> *T: Yes, I don't know if it's possible, but it would be very interesting to look at it as a fight for your wellbeing, not against Little Guy.*
> *C: Well, like you said the first day, he's not going to go away, so I fight.*
> *T: Little Guy is a part of you; we don't want him to go away; we want to understand how he is trying to help.*
> *C: I fight for me, to feel better.*
> *T: Correct, and we are interested in having Little Guy as an ally, not an enemy.*
> *C: Yes, but right now he's not an ally.*
> *T: Okay, so for now he's not an ally, he still has to learn new ways of functioning; until then, let's try not to be enemies.*

As soon as the client starts showing some curiosity about how to do things differently, we can guide him toward practicing a new style of communication through the Adult Self, offering specific practical tools that are easily applicable through modeling (TW #8). The clearer the client and other parts can see that his old dynamic of fighting just makes things worse, the more willing the entire system will be to change its ways.

> *C: Okay, so how do I do that?*
> *T: Well, we can start with how you respond to his comments or insults. For instance, if he calls you a loser, just tell him, "I'm doing the best I can to feel better." Can you try to say this to him?*
> *C: I try to tell him that I'm doing things to improve, but "loser" has been one of his favorite words ever since I've started to feel bad. Whenever I try to destroy or ignore him, he gets worse.*
> *T: And the more you see him as an enemy or try to destroy him, the more problems he will bring you.*
> *C: Yes, but the problem is I'm not trying to destroy him. I just want him to shut up.*

This is a typical example of the responses we get when clients are not aware of the different ways in which they try to ignore or eliminate parts; wanting him to shut up is another variant that does not invite communication or curiosity.

> *T: So, what is happening with Little Guy now?*
> *C: He wants me to hurt myself.*
> *T: That's the message you get, but what emotions are there? How does Little Guy feel now?*
> *C: He's making fun of me, calling me a loser, "You can't do anything on your own" and such.*
> *T: What is "such?"*
> *C: A list of all my failures, in all areas.*

As we can see, this part is stuck in circular messages. Not only does he not have much of a repertoire, but he is also not opening up to any collaboration at this point. The best way to proceed in these situations is not to insist. Instead search for alternatives and model new ways along with the Adult Self (TW #8).

> *T: Let's go step by step and focus on your response now.*
> *C: Okay.*
> *T: When he calls you a loser, what do you say to him?*
> *C: I tell him that I'm not a loser.*
> *T: And do you really believe this?*
> *C: Well, kind of.*
> *T: How much do you believe it?*
> *C: When he calls me a loser, I answer right back, "You're wrong."*

The idea of the next section is to try to get the client to understand that the comments of the part are actually similar to his feelings about himself. After all, he is one person. And also, to help him respond differently to Little Guy by encouraging him to reflect on why he is not a loser (TW #7 and TW #8). If the Adult Self can understand this, he will have more resources to respond. As we do this type of exploration, we are also modeling new ways of responding (TW #8).

> *T: So, let me see if I understood correctly. When you say "kind of," does that mean that in a way you feel like a loser?*

C: Yes, in a way I do.

T: Why do you think you're a loser?

C: Mainly because I can't do any activities or have a normal life without voices, without medication.

T: But you're trying.

C: Of course. Otherwise, I wouldn't be here.

T: Yes, I know. Let's see what you can say to him when he calls you a loser.

C: That he's wrong.

This type of reasoning generally does not work too well because it does not involve information that can help Little Guy understand why he could be wrong. We want the Adult Self to have arguments about why he is wrong, as a way to stimulate metacognitive capacities.

T: Why is he wrong?

C: Because, even though I go to doctors, therapy, and take medication, I'm still fighting to pull through. Then, it's not a loss, it's a win.

T: Exactly. This is a very positive message and it makes sense: you are fighting to pull through. And this is a success for you, isn't it? (Therapist writes down his exact words).

C: Clearly.

T: Does he think you are weak because you ask for help and go to therapy?

C: Yes, and he tells me, "You don't belong in this world, just find yourself a balcony and jump off."

T: "You don't belong in this world." What do you have to say about that?

C: I am strong, and I'll keep on fighting as long as I have some strength left in me.

T: Do you want to be in this world?

C: Yes, I want to be in this world. The problem is when he shows up in a foul mood.

Again, the client tries to focus on what the part is doing wrong, which is part of the conflict.

T: Let's focus on you. On one hand, there is what he says, and on the other hand, what you think and say. He says things to be heard. We are interested in knowing what he has to say and what you answer.

C: I think I have a future ahead of me to do things that I never dared to do until now, because I feared what people would say. (Therapist writes down his exact words).

The intervention seemed to calm down the system, so after checking in to see how the client is doing (CS #2.5), we repeat this message with the part.

T: How do you feel now? I get the impression that you are a little bit calmer.

C: Yes, it seems like Little Guy is not moving much

T: Okay, it seems like he is also listening to your reasons for being in this world. Try to find a way to communicate with Little Guy and tell him the following (taking the piece of paper and reading out loud the client's sentence): *"I'm fighting to pull through. This is a great success for me and a big effort, but I want to be in this world, I have a future ahead." Just think about communicating this to Little Guy.*

C: The problem is that I don't know how to communicate with him.

This is a very common statement that clients with phobia toward their complicated parts usually express. Helping them to feel comfortable listening to the voice is an important step of our work (TW #2). After making sure that both parts are calmer, the therapist decides to install this new message (adaptive information) with bilateral stimulation (BLS).

> T: *Just think about it. He is a part of you and has a lot of information, so this means that he receives the information somehow. Focus on this: You are fighting, making a big effort, and doing the best you can. (BLS)*
> T: *What do you notice?*
> C: *I think he is listening because he is not saying anything or moving much.*
> T: *Well, neither of you are used to communicating like this. The fact that he is calmer might be telling us that this is a good way to begin.*
> C: *It seems so.*

Finally, the session is closed with an important reminder (CS #3.4).

> T: *Remember you are fighting to get better, not against him.*
> C: *Okay.*

EXAMPLE 3. DISTRUST IN THE ADULT SELF

In the next session, Ethan is surprised because Little Guy has not been showing up. His first interpretation is that the part is planning something to try and trick him. We begin the session by exploring the effects of the work done in the previous session (CS #1.1), and how the system has been (CS #1.2).

> T: *How are you doing?*
> C: *I guess I am doing fine, but everything seems strange.*
> T: *Okay, we will explore how the week went in a little bit. Could you tell me how you left the previous session?*
> C: *Good, things were calm. Little Guy wasn't moving much when I left, and everything stayed like that for a few days.*
> T: *So Little Guy seemed calm after the session.*
> C: *Yes.*
> T: *Did you try to remember that this was a fight for your wellbeing?*
> C: *I understood that, as long as he leaves me alone, I am fine.*
> T: *Well, it is interesting to remember that if you change your ways, he can also change his ways.*

After checking the results of the work done in the previous session (CS #1.2), we proceed to explore what has happened during the week, for example, if the voices showed up (CS #1.2) and how the client responded (CS #1.3).

> T: *Did you hear the voices this week?*
> C: *Yes, but only once and it was different.*

T: It was different?

C: It was softer than other times, not as loud.

T: When was that? Do you remember what was happening?

C: No.

T: It is important to try to pay attention to what is happening when you hear or notice any of the voices. (Client nods.) Do you remember how you reacted when you noticed Little Guy?

C: Now I use headphones to cope with this.

T: Is that what you did when you heard him?

C: Yes.

T: Does that help?

C: It does.

T: How does it help? Did you stop hearing the voices when you put your headphones on?

C: They are less intense.

T: How does Little Guy respond when you put your headphones on?

C: He doesn't mind. I think he likes the music I play.

T: Well, that's interesting. So, this could be a good resource for both of you.

We have tried to explore both what triggered the voice (TW #3 and CS #2.2) and the reaction from the system (CS #2.3), in this case, how the Adult Self responded when he heard Little Guy and how Little Guy reacted to the response of the Adult Self. Once we understand that the reaction (headphones, music) could be a resource (TW #7), we make sure to point it out as an option to use at other times (TW #8).

T: So, does it seem like Little Guy was less intrusive this week?

C: He only showed up once; it's as if he was busy or something.

Changing the name of the part from "Little Motherfucker" to "Little Guy" seems to be working because the part only appeared once during the week. Notice that the client is not aware that this change might be related to a different attitude towards the part or the previous work done in therapy, so we help him realize this.

T: Okay, great, so maybe he understood what we were talking about.

C: Maybe he did, I don't know.

T: You said he showed up differently and only once.

C: True, he was much more aggressive before, and he showed up often.

T: Yes, and that's when you called him "Little Motherfucker" and you responded differently.

C: Yes.

T: So not calling him "Little Motherfucker" and trying to respond in a different way seem to be working better.

C: Yes, it seems like he reacts in a different way.

T: Maybe he doesn't feel attacked.

C: Maybe.

After validating this new attitude from both of them, the Adult Self seems even more confident about his capacity to learn to deal with the conflict differently. We start closing the session reinforcing the work done today (CS #3.1) and checking its results (CS #3.2).

> *T: I must say you seem more focused and motivated. I really appreciate the effort you and Little Guy are doing.* (Client smiles.) *How do you feel about the work we just did?*
> *C: Great! Now I'm all in! We are going forward no matter what happens. I want to improve.*
> *T: Do you notice the changes you are achieving in regard to the teamwork?*
> *C: Yes, I do. I know I still have a long way to go.*
> *T: Yes, but it is important to appreciate the effort you are doing. I am listening to you and there is a big difference between now and the first time we met. It's great to see the progress. Congratulations!*
> *C: I'm really trying.*
> *T: Yes, I see, and I really appreciate it.*

This could be a good way to close the session, but it is always interesting to check if the client and the system are grounded (CS #3.3), to summarize what we covered during the session (CS #3.4) and to anticipate potential future obstacles (CS #3.5).

> *T: How are you feeling now?*
> *C: Calm and motivated.*
> *T: And how is Little Guy doing?*
> *C: He is not saying anything, so I guess he is calm too.*
> *T: Do you notice anything else inside that we need to check with?*
> *C: No.*
> *T: Okay, great. So, remember, I will keep checking in with all of the voices and aspects in you. Try to keep this new attitude up.*
> *C: Yes.*
> *T: And remember to take notes of anything you notice during the week.* (Client nods.) *And if Little Guy shows up saying some of the old things he used to say, remember he is still learning the new ways. You take notes and we can try to understand here.*
> *C: Okay. And if he becomes aggressive, can I call you?*
> *T: Of course, you can.*

EXAMPLE 4. FROM CONFLICT TO UNDERSTANDING

This is an example of dealing with a complex situation that took place two sessions prior to this one. The client was very upset when he went to the bank and realized that his account had been emptied. Little Guy shows up again with very negative messages. As always, we did the CS #1 steps, and he stated that he was fine when he left the previous session. He also reported no difficulties or fights right after the session.

> *C: The first thing I wanted to do was to calm down about that issue. The Little Motherfucker is going crazy. He's calling me all sorts of names; he's been at it for two hours, since I went to the ATM to get*

the money to pay. I took the receipt and saw that they had taken all my money out of the account, all at once.

T: *Remember what we said about calling him names.*

C: *Sorry, yes. I am very nervous.*

T: *So, let's go over what happened. You went to the bank and realized that your account was empty.* (Client nods.) *And when you see that, what do you feel?*

C: *At that moment, I felt helpless. Because, what am I going to live off this month?*

T: *And what else did you feel?*

C: *Powerlessness, anger.*

T: *How about Little Guy?*

C: *He is angry.*

T: *How do you know that?*

C. *Well, he's laughing at me. What I hear is laughter, "useless, loser, son of a bitch..." Mainly those three things. So, he's driving me to the edge.*

T: *How do you think Little Guy has felt about what happened?*

C: *Happy. Because until now, since I was doing things right, I was doing everything with an order, making sense of things. I was trying to avoid the internal struggle, with certain carelessness towards him, I was trying as much as possible not to care too much about it.*

We have to keep in mind to always model curiosity (TW #2) and help the client understand what is happening because it is very easy for the system to fall back into conflict. Due to this, it will be very important to help them anticipate future problems (CS #3.5) that might arise while all parts are adapting and learning new ways (TW #7).

T: *Well, my idea was mutual respect, rather than carelessness.*

C: *Yes, but oh well.*

T: *What do you mean "oh well"?*

C: *He's not respectful.*

T: *He's not respectful, uh-huh. And how about you?*

C: *I try for him to be respectful. I try to be respectful, but I end up calling him all sorts of names, I don't know if that's my big mistake.*

T: *You end up calling him all sorts of names?*

C: *Yes, I end up insulting him, because he doesn't let me be calm.*

T: *Well, yes, I think it's a mistake.*

C: *He doesn't let me, he totally blocks me.*

T: *I understand it has to be difficult. Remember he's still learning new ways.* (Client seems exasperated.) *Do you realize that you're fighting with him again?*

C: *Of course. I just start fighting with him without even realizing it.*

T: *But you have identified it. That's very good.*

C: *Yes, but when I fight with him, he always wins.*

T: *That is why I think we need to improve the way you relate to each other. This is about both of you winning.*

C: *Let's see, I don't understand that part. The only thing that he wants is to hurt me and to kill me. This is his ultimate goal.*

This is a good opportunity to explore what might be underneath those problematic behaviors, and to try to understand how the part is trying to help (TW #6).

> *T: And what do you think is behind that goal?*
> *C: Mostly, destruction.*
> *T: I think there is another goal. What else could there be? Try not to think like an enemy. What else could there be behind what he's telling you?*
> *C: Unless he's trying to tell me something and I'm not understanding it... I mean, because if he would at least say something coherent, then I could understand him. I don't know, just something coherent.*
> *T: But maybe he doesn't know how to communicate something coherent for now, and he has to learn. And you could set a good example.*

Once again, we remind the client that the part is simply repeating what he has learned to do, and the learning process takes some time. We also begin to introduce the idea that the Adult Self can set a good example by responding differently (TW #8). In the next section, we can see how the client will have difficulties accepting the information we just introduced because he is still used to responding in a defensive way. But at least, he can begin to be curious about how to do it differently.

> *C: I just don't know. Primarily, his goal is to crush me. I mean, if you told me how to do it.*
> *T: Think about this: Little Guy shows up when something negative happens to you. So, maybe he only knows how to react in this way.*
> *C: Yes.*
> *T: He doesn't know any other way for now.*
> *C: Then, we would have to look for another way, because it destroys me.*

Once we get enough curiosity in the Adult Self, we can explore the motivation and the function of this voice/part a bit more (TW #1).

> *T: Let's try to understand Little Guy.* (Client nods). *How old does Little Guy feel like?*
> *C: How old?*
> *T: Yes, does he seem older, mature, more childish, younger?*
> *C: He is not mature, because if he were, he would not ask me to do those things.*
> *T: Maybe he would have more alternatives.*
> *C: That's right. I see him as the typical spoiled child who says, "I want this, so either you do it or I'll screw you."*
> *T: Okay. And how old does that sound? More or less.*
> *C: Five years old or something like that. He is very little.*
> *T: So, he'd still have a lot to learn yet, right?*
> *C: Of course.*
> *T: If his sensations are like those of a five-year-old, he has a lot to learn from you.*
> *C: Yes, but I don't know how to teach him.*
> *T: That's why you and I are working together.*

C: Oh, okay.

T: Notice that just with our conversations, he's understanding some things. And that's one way to do it.

C: Of course, but he scares me to death, he makes me panic. I'm not a person who gets scared easily, but this scares me because I don't understand it.

T: I know. What is not understood generates...

C: Fear.

T: Fear, that's right.

By validating how the client feels (TW #7), normalizing his fear and explaining that it is important to understand what happens with other parts despite the fear, the client feels understood and is more able to remain curious (TW #2).

C: Do you understand it?

T: I'm trying, and I need your help to understand what he needs or what he is trying to achieve.

C: If I knew what he wanted from me, I would give it to him. But the only thing that he seeks is destruction.

T: Maybe he has not learned that there are other alternatives for you or other ways of helping you. But I think he can learn with our help. (Client nods.)

Now that the conflict is reduced, we once again check how he left the session (CS #1.1), to make sure that the work we are doing is not triggering these reactions.

T: And how did Little Guy feel after the last session?

C: He felt happy. The last time I felt him was last Tuesday when I was with you.

T: You noticed he was happy. (Client nods). *Did you notice anything else inside that was not happy? C: No, I was calm, no voices, no problems. He showed up again during the ATM incident when I checked my balance, and I saw a big fat zero and the charges.*

T: And that's when he showed up.

C: Yes, that's when he started saying all those things.

In the previous section, we explored the voices (TW #1), encouraged the client to pay more attention to the part (TW #2), and explored triggers (TW #3). We also explored the effects of the work done in the previous session (CS #1.1) and how the week was for the entire system (CS #1.2). In the next section, we will try to help the client understand that the part is actually trying to be helpful (TW #6), explore alternatives (TW #8) and try to develop cooperation (TW #10).

T: Well, it seems that he becomes triggered when things hurt you.

C: Yes, he does.

T: So, maybe his intention is not so negative. Like I said before, maybe he doesn't know there are other alternatives for you. And you and I are going to tell him that there are, okay? (Client nods). *What would help you?*

C: For example, if Little Guy came out when I did something right and said something like, "Good job!" Even if I still heard the external voice and all, but if he could just cheer me up, that would be nice.

T: Sure, but maybe he doesn't know how to do that yet.

C: He doesn't know how to do it, for sure.

T: Well, if he could do something like that, it would be great. But if you think that he is only five years old, he might be too young to understand that. So, for now, I'm just going to ask you to try to remember that he is still learning and to understand this for now and keep it in mind. And if you could try not to see him as the enemy, that would be great, because this a problem for both of you.

C: Okay.

T: For now, keep in mind the following: for some reason, he usually appears when something bad happens to you. So maybe his intention is not negative; maybe there is also some concern. And he doesn't know that there are other possibilities.

C: When I come to therapy, I need to be clear-headed, and if this guy is screaming, it drives me nuts.

T: Can you let him know that his screaming makes you nervous and does not help right now?

C: Yes, he needs to understand that it drives me nuts, because it's as if half of my brain were attending to a bunch of insults, a huge mess, and the other part of the brain were saying, "Focus, I have to do this."

T: It's what he knows how to do.

C: Yes, because one thing I didn't tell you is that the other day, before disappearing, he said "I'll be back on a bad day."

T: Yes, that's what you told me the other day.

C: Did I mention it to you?

T: You told me that he had said that before.

C: And today is a bad day. So, I don't know.

T: How is Little Guy now?

C: He seems a bit nervous. Maybe he doesn't like what I just said.

After checking how the part responds to the intervention (CS #2.5), we can identify the phobia. Since we have been working with the client towards a better understanding of the system of parts and he is becoming more curious, we can begin introducing some of the clinical procedures described in Chapter 1, such as the processing phobias procedure, to address the phobia between parts (TW #4).

T: Let's try something, okay? (Client nods). *Remember what I told you about this therapy called EMDR?*

C: Yes.

T: And how we could use it for different issues? (Client nods.) *Well, we can try to work with the fear a bit. How does that sound?*

C: Okay. What do I have to do?

T: Check if Little Guy is okay with trying out something new.

C: He doesn't answer, but there are no insults either.

T: And what do you think? Does that mean that he is willing to try?

C: I think so.

T: Okay. If you could tell me what Little Guy is feeling, what emotions would those be?

C: What emotions would those be?

T: Little Guy's emotions, yes. He was also surprised by the ATM issue, wasn't he?

C: No, he was not surprised. He said, "Fuck you." And excuse my language.

T: Is there anger?

C: Right now, he's totally angry and laughing at me.

T: Angry.

C: Angry, for sure.

T: And do you think he would like to feel a bit calmer, a bit less angry?

C: I don't know.

T: I think it could help you both.

C: It would help me, personally. I don't know if it would help him.

T: What are you feeling towards him right now?

C: Fear and hatred. Hatred because he will not let me live in peace, and fear because he is asking me to do something stupid.

T: I'm going to ask you to close your eyes, and we'll try something to see if you feel a bit calmer. Okay? (Client nods). (BLS)

T: What do you notice?

C: That he's making fun of me.

T: That he's making fun of you. What do you notice? How does one notice that? Just so I can understand it.

C: I hear him laughing.

T: He was laughing before too. Is there anything different?

C: Let's see, he's telling me that regardless of what I do, he's going to win.

T: And how would you explain that on an emotional level? What is he feeling?

C: Fear.

T: He is afraid too. (Client nods). Let's do one thing. Just keep in mind that he's there. And he can be there because he's not our enemy. Just focus on the fear that you are noticing now. (BLS) What do you notice?

C: On one hand, a little bit of calmness. But on another hand, great torment.

T: Notice those two things at once. And be aware that you're holding those two contradictory sensations at once, just notice that. (BLS) What do you notice?

C: I suffer less, but he's saying something, he's changing his discourse. He's not insulting me; he's changed. It seems as if he feels better. (Client seems surprised).

T: Notice that. (BLS) What do you notice now?

C: Let's see. I feel calmer, but he is still there.

T: Of course, he is, he is a part of you. Do you think we can try to work on his fear a little bit too? Is he willing to try? (Client nods). Ask him to focus on his fear, nothing else. (BLS) What do you notice?

C: The anger has dropped.

T: Notice that. (BLS) What do you notice?

C: He's still angry, but it seems that he's not harassing me like he was until now.

T: Notice that. (BLS) What do you notice now?

C: I notice that I'm calm.

T: Notice the calmness, nothing else. (BLS) What do you notice now?

C: A little calmer. I notice him in there moving around.

T: It's okay. What's important is to go little by little. Do you feel a bit calmer?

C: Yes. I feel calmer, but he is still annoying. He's there as if he were stuck.

After processing the dissociative phobia, both client and part feel calmer. In the previous section, we have been checking how the system responds to the intervention after each set of BLS (CS #2.5), encouraging the client to continue working and helping him stay focused on what we are doing rather than on the internal conflict. In the next section of the interview, we can see how the client misunderstands the information we give him and how we keep modeling different ways of responding until he can think of adaptive alternatives (TW #8).

> T: *What I want is for you to be sure that we will try to do everything we can to understand this part, these voices, these aspects of yourself. And I think that, eventually, we'll get there, so he won't need to communicate aggressively. Because, I insist, maybe he has not learned to do it in any other way. And you can set a good example if you don't respond in the same way.*
>
> C: *Okay, I will try to ignore him.*
>
> T: *We want to take him into account more than ignore him.*
>
> C: *So, if I go for a walk, or listen to music, or talk to someone and he shows up, what do I do?*
>
> T: *We'll try to teach him different things through you. Because you're going to be the best example. Especially if it's a very small part who doesn't know how to do things differently.*
>
> C: *I don't know if I'll be able to teach him.*
>
> T: *This is not something you have to do alone. This is something we are going to do together. I'm going to help you understand and respond better.*
>
> C: *Of course. There's a lot in there.*
>
> T: *And we'll get there when the time is right. First, the most important thing is for you to stay focused on this new attitude and continue taking care of yourself, so we can start working on difficult memories.*
>
> C: *Okay.*
>
> T: *How are you doing now?*
>
> C: *I'm good.*
>
> T: *How about Little Guy?*
>
> C: *He is good too. I don't know why, but he is calm.*
>
> T: *Well, you both did great work today. And, if he shows up again, remember that he is still learning new ways of functioning.*

The processing phobias procedure can be used in this type of situations. Alternating exploration, psychoeducation and this type of work can be very useful, as we could see in this example. Notice we close the session reinforcing the work that was done (CS # 3.1) and anticipating potential obstacles (CS #3.5).

EXAMPLE 5. DISTRUST AS PART OF THE THERAPEUTIC PROCESS

Things are evolving well for the client; he has not self-harmed in several weeks now and is not tormented by the different voices on a daily basis. Although he still feels the desire to hurt himself, he is managing not to do it. This example illustrates the difficulties in adapting to improved functioning and how to continue the work. We begin the session exploring how the client left the session (CS #1.1), how the week was for him and the system of parts (CS #1.2), and if any issues came up during the week (CS #2.4), just as we have seen in previous examples.

> T: *How was your week?*
>
> C: *I am surprised because although I had many difficult situations, Little Guy did not appear. So, I don't know if he's preparing a stronger come-back.*

T: Let's be positive and not lose confidence in him.

C: Okay.

T: So, it's hard for you to adapt to the new ways of Little Guy.

C: It seems so.

T: How did you leave our last session?

C: Good, calm.

T: How about Little Guy?

C: No movement, he is much calmer.

T: Do you still hear him or notice him?

C: Sometimes he says things, but not like before.

T: What type of things?

C: Not insults, now he asks for candy and things like that.

T: That's interesting, and what do you think of that?

C: I think it's weird, but I just buy the candy and give it to him. Is that okay?

T: Of course, it is. And how did you manage to achieve this change?

C: I use some phrases that you told me: "There is still hope, I'm starting a new life...," and I repeat them to myself.

T: Okay. Good.

Notice the usefulness of the adaptive information we installed in sample session #3. He says "some phrases that you told me," when the reality is that the therapist helped him think of alternative ways of responding (TW #8), wrote down the client's sentences when he was able to come up with adaptive answers, repeated them, and installed them. This process is much more powerful than trying to install something that does not come from the client. In the next section, we help him understand the phobia of change.

T: You are not used to Little Guy not being there in this way.

C: That's right.

T: But that's okay; this means that he is calmer.

C: Yes.

T: So that's positive.

C: Yes, it is, but I feel strange and I panic because there were certain periods when he went away, and when he came back things got worse.

T: Okay, but now we are listening to him, so the situation is different.

C: I'm scared that he might appear again in an aggressive way. I could deal with the insults: asshole, dickhead, son of a bitch...and all that. But if he shows up as he did on other occasions, asking for self-harm, it would be difficult.

T: I understand, but let's try to focus on the present moment, one step at a time.

Once we identify the phobia towards the part, we can ask the client to focus on the fear and process it just like we did before, when the phobia in the part became obvious (TW #4).

T: Can you close your eyes and focus on the fear that you are noticing? (Client nods. BLS.) What do you notice?

C: My head saying, "He won't come back... He's not going to come, not going to come, not going to come."

T: Okay, go with that. (BLS) What do you notice?

C: (Client jumps back, looking surprised). I get that he's not going to come because I'm getting better.

T: Okay, notice that. (BLS) What do you get now?

C: The same, he's not going to come because I'm making progress.

T: Okay, notice that. (BLS)

We only do four sets on the phobia. Remember the goal is to desensitize and reduce it a bit, not to do a whole session focused on the phobia, the fear, the rejection, or any other identified emotion that is not adaptive for the better functioning of the system. It is a procedure meant to be used in very specific cases, only when we identify phobias, as we have described in Chapters 1 and 2.

T: How are you now?

C: Good.

T: Okay.

After checking how the system responds to the intervention (CS #2.5), we continue the session trying to prevent problems in the future (CS #3.4) and, given the positive turn after processing the phobia, we decide to install a resource now that the client and the system are working with some degree of cooperation and respect (TW #10).

T: And if he comes back, we will keep on working as we did until now, we will take him into account so you can work as a team. That's the idea and it's working.

C: Okay.

T: Let's begin by trying to strengthen the resources that you already have. I would like for you to think about a situation where you found yourself handling something well. Think about the last time you managed a difficult situation and you felt like you could handle it.

C: It's a little odd. I was with my friend who is a long-distance truck driver, and he let me drive for a while. It was dark out and the road was icy; it was winter. I controlled a situation that could have gotten out of hand.

T: What do you notice when you think about that moment?

C: A sense of satisfaction.

T: Think about that and notice the sense of satisfaction. Are you noticing it? (Client nods.) Ready? (Client nods. BLS.) What do you notice?

C: That I'm useful. (BLS)

T: And now?

C: The same.

T: Notice that. (BLS) What do you notice now?

C: Now I noticed that I can handle situations that are out of my control and regain control.

T: Very well, notice that. (BLS) What do you notice?

C: Insecurity. It's as if Little Guy was saying, "Don't get too confident, these situations can turn against you."

T: That makes sense. Think about how you can handle some situations. Just notice that you have that resource, okay? (BLS) What do you notice?

C: That I can handle tough situations.

T: *Notice that. (BLS) What do you notice?*

C: *That I can handle tough situations, yes.*

T: *Let's stay with that for now. It's good not to be overly confident, but it's also important to know that you can handle tough situations.*

The work transcribed in the previous section illustrates an example of resource installation with a complex case. Although Little Guy and the client have felt nervous after having felt better, this does not mean we cannot continue or that the resource has failed. Actually, it is a good reminder that can help the client not to feel overly confident. By validating the function of Little Guy (TW #6) and the feelings of concern or uneasiness that he was expressing (TW #7), once again we model new ways of responding (TW #8). We close the session reminding the client that we do not want to get rid of Little Guy (CS #3.4), as a way to anticipate potential obstacles in the future (CS #3.5).

T: *I would like you to remember that the goal is not to get rid of Little Guy, this will only make him feel insecure and alert.*

C: *I will try, but, what if he shows up again acting like a bully? What do I do? Do I focus on the message that "I have a new life; I am going to therapy and I still have a lot to learn?" Do I repeat this to myself?*

T: *Yes, you can repeat that, and you can also remember that Little Guy is part of you that is trying to help you by doing the only thing he knows how to do.*

C: *That's harder.*

T: *Yes, it is harder. Remember that this is what he learned to do. The other day you said he was a 5-year-old child.*

C: *Yes, a 5-year-old.*

T: *So, remember that he doesn't know how to express what he feels in a different way. So, one step at a time. If he shows up in a way that is frightening, just try to use what has been working for you; remember the phrases. And also remember that it is information that will help us in therapy and if it does not work, you can call me.*

Although there is still a lot to do with the different parts to reduce the conflict and get them to work and think as a team (TW #10), we are taking small steps in the right direction that will be crucial for our goals. By exploring, understanding, and modeling new ways (TW #8), the client and the other parts can experience little moments of cooperation which can be very motivating for working as a team (TW #10).

EXAMPLE 6. SOMETHING IN ME DOES NOT LIKE PROGRESS

The client comes in saying that things are going well, but there is "something" inside of him that does not like it when he improves. He says it is not Little Guy or any of the known parts. We begin this next section exploring whether the changes are related to any of the other voices that we know; for instance, the buzzing sound described in session one. After the client explains that it has nothing to do with any of the known parts or voices, we proceed by exploring this "something" inside.

T: You were saying that there is something in you that doesn't like positive progress.

C: No, it doesn't. It's like if a part of me still wants to be self-destructive and it's increasingly more sophisticated.

T: But this has nothing to do with Little Guy.

C: No.

T: Do you know what it might be related to?

C: I don't know.

T: Were there any changes this week in the buzzing sound?

C: No, it's still there.

T: So, no changes?

C: No. It's still there. That one is not important because it's under control.

T: Okay. I just wanted to know if there were any changes in the noise.

C: No.

While exploring the issues that are coming up (CS#2.4) the client explains that he is concerned because one day he found himself very confused and disoriented, unable to remember his way home. He also explains that he is afraid that there could be more parts. We begin by normalizing his feelings (TW #7) and his symptoms with psychoeducation about moments of stress and then we proceed with exploration of the system (TW #1).

T: I see. That must've been very scary, but it can be related to many things. There might be other parts besides Little Guy and the ones you already know. Yes, it's a possibility.

C: That's what I am afraid of, that this might be the lid of a pressure-cooker... and if we open it, toads and snakes will come out.

T: I see. Don't worry, we can explore very carefully. Let's try to see what else might be there.

C: I don't know. My head feels like a swarm.

Despite the client's positive attitude towards exploration, it seems that he needs help to identify other parts towards which he feels phobic. This next section is an example of exploring "missing pieces" (TW #9). From the beginning, it was obvious that the client had issues with anger, so we start from there.

T: Do you usually get angry?

C: No, when I get angry I'm dangerous.

T: Dangerous how?

C: I let my fist shine very quickly; I stop being myself.

T: Can you explain this a bit more?

C: I do things I wouldn't normally do, and then I don't remember what I did.

T: Do you think this is another part of you?

C: It's like... how can I put this? It's like the devil.

T: That is how you perceive it.

C: Yes.

T: Can you give me an example?

C: *For example, one day I was waiting for the bus to go to the health center and in front of me were some workers repairing the sidewalk. One of them had a hammer in his hand. I went haywire. I couldn't stop obsessing about breaking his head with the hammer.*

T: *Breaking one of the workers head?*

C: *Yes, you know, a man that was just doing his job, he wasn't bothering me at all. That urge just appears. And I managed to stop myself, but I was going straight for him. This urge comes from inside of me. I know I am about to say something weird, but it's like in the movie The Exorcist, as if I were possessed.*

Once we have identified another possible part, we can explore more details about the inner system (TW #1) and encourage the client to be more curious about this part (TW #2).

T: *How old is this part? Do you have an idea?*

C: *It's intrinsic in me.*

T: *Intrinsic?*

C: *It's always been there. I have been a beast since kindergarten. I had scars on my face, and they were very big, nobody wanted to play with me, they called me "the monster." The other kids threw stones at me, they isolated me. And I turned into the school bully...*

T: *How old were you?*

C: *About 7.*

T: *It doesn't seem that this part had it very easy.*

C: *No. Well, let's be clear about this: my childhood was really fucked up.*

T: *I know. So, let's try to understand a bit more. When does this part usually show up?*

C: *I don't know. I try not to think about this part.*

This is a good opportunity to introduce some of the exploration tools from Chapter 4. The client is asked to draw his internal system, including Little Guy, Noise, and Rage. He takes a few minutes to do the drawing.

T: *Can you explain your drawing to me?*

C: *Yes, this is my head.*

T: *Your head. You mean the inside of your head?*

C: *Yes, inside of me. Here, on one side we have Little Guy that takes up a lot of space. Then the rage that's like the Devil. This part also takes up a lot of space.*

T: *Yes.*

C: *Then we have the conscious part; this one is smaller. There's also another much smaller part, the child part, and then there is a huge part that resembles fog. I know there is something wrong in my head. It feels like I can't use 100% of my brain. And here we have the union-division point. This is where everything gets all mixed up. Then they start to move: if I go in this direction, this line comes down, Little Guy increases and the rage decreases.*

T: *So, when Little Guy grows, the rage decreases.*

C: *Yes, it turns into self-hatred.*

T: *Okay. So, in a way, Little Guy tries to prevent you from hurting others.*

C: Yes, but the cost is that I hurt myself.

T: That's why we are doing this work, so you can function as a team.

C: Yes.

T: So, this part has a very important function.

C: Yes.

This session was a breakthrough in therapy. Regardless of how much we had explored the self-harming behaviors, we could not understand the logic of them. They seemed to come out of the blue, with no connection to specific triggers. But now we were able to understand that they are related to his urge to hurt others, represented by the rage-devil part. This urge seemed to be handled by the system through diverting the attention towards self-harm. By remaining focused on the negative messages from Little Guy, the client avoided becoming aggressive towards other people.

EXAMPLE 7. A PART BURNED MY ARM

Between sessions, the client burned his arm with boiling water, inflicting himself fourth-degree burns. He comes in with the report from the hospital and with his arm wrapped in a large bandage. In this example, we explore what triggered this behavior (TW #3), the parts that were active during the week (CS #2.1) and we try to understand what happened internally (CS #2.2).

T: Do you remember doing that?

C: I remember waking up. My arm was in really bad shape.

T: Biting your watch?

C: Yes, the watch band.

T: Do you remember what happened before that?

C: The last thing I remember is that I had an internal dispute in my head and something new showed up. It was not the five-year-old. It was someone as old as I am, an adult with a very bad temper. I don't know where he came from.

Once we understand that there was a dispute inside his head before the behavior, we explore which parts could be involved and explore the system (CS #2.1) to clarify the actual trigger.

T: Is this related to the rage part we explored last time?

C: I don't think so.

T: So, you say that you see this something as an adult? A man?

C: Yes, I identify him as myself.

T: Yourself at what age?

C: Considering how he was reasoning, I would say he is as old I am now, 38.

T: How he was reasoning?

C: Yes, he had my style of reasoning.

T: I see.

C: Let's see. How can I explain it? It's as if I were arguing with a mirror and the mirror answered back.

T: In your head?

C: Yes, in my head.

T: What was the argument about?

C: I was listening to the radio, I don't know what happened, but it was something I heard on the radio. I was fighting against the monster and he was telling me to hurt myself.

T: Who is the monster?

C: The monster is the adult. Little Guy didn't show up.

The client is referring to a part using a pejorative name. We do not overlook it and make sure to point it out. Since he already knows the benefits of avoiding negative names and insults from the work done with Little Guy, the client can easily understand why we make this suggestion. On the other hand, we use this opportunity to explore the origin of this voice or part.

T: Ok. I'm not sure that the world "monster" is very nice.

C: That's how I refer to him. The kids at school used to call me "monster".

T: The kids at school used to call you "monster". When was this?

C: Always.

T: How old were you?

C: Always, I was the weirdo in class, so I was the "monster".

T: Where would this be in your drawing?

C: This is a combination of Rage and Fog. It was not the child part, because his reasoning was too good.

We have the sense that there may be missing pieces (TW #9), so we suggest using a visualization exercise. In this case, we use the meeting room procedure described in Chapter 1.

T: Let's do an observation exercise.

C: Okay.

T: I'm going to ask you to close your eyes and try to imagine a meeting place where you can invite all the different aspects of yourself to join you. (Client nods.) No one is obliged to be there.

C: Okay.

T: Imagine a place that is comfortable for you. It can have sofas, chairs, it can even have different spaces. Everyone has their own space and there doesn't have to be any contact for now. Invite over all of the voices and parts, they're all welcome. You're just going to observe. Take your time and when you can, let me know what you see.

C: I see my child part playing with a puppet. I see my conscious part fighting to pull through. And I also see the Rage, but he's on one side, isolated from the rest.

As we do the exercise, the client makes a critical comment, judging the behavior of the parts he dislikes the most. We remind him that this is a space for communication and understanding, where all parts can express their opinions and points of view, but it must be done respectfully.

T: The purpose of this exercise is just to observe, you don't have to read into it, just observe what you see. The idea is to try to understand.

C: Okay.

> *T: There are basic rules: parts can't attack each other or fight. All parts are welcome, and all parts will be treated with respect.*
> *C: Okay.*
> *T: So, invite everything inside to come to this place in again and let me know what you see.*

After reminding the client of the rules, we can continue with the exercise and gather more information about the different parts involved in the conflict (TW #1). We do not transcribe this section of the interview because the goal of this example is to illustrate how we can go from one exploration method to another. As a result of this exercise, the client was able to understand the rage part better and how it was trying to help by keeping away painful memories.

EXAMPLE 8. PANDORA'S BOX

A few sessions later, the voices are agitated. In one of the previous sessions, the client suggested he could begin trauma work, but the rest of the parts were not ready, and the system became uneasy. We had reached an agreement that we would not do any trauma work until all the different parts agreed. Instead of trying to understand the voices, the client usually tells them to shut up. We begin this section of the session reminding him about the importance of teamwork (TW #10) and trying to understand what the voices are concerned about (TW #3).

> *T: Remember, it's not about making them shut up; the idea is for them to understand that we don't have to work on it until the moment is right.*
> *C: Yes, but they are obsessed.*
> *T: Ask them what are they worried about.*
> *C: The reality.*
> *T: The reality? (Client remains silent.) The reality.*
> *C: Yes, I don't understand.*
> *T: You seem confused.*
> *C: Because I can't understand it.*
> *T: They might be referring to things that have happened and you don't remember. (Client nods.) That's why I insist on not making them shut up, but instead remind them that we are not going to force anything.*
> *C: Yes, but I don't know what they are talking about, I don't get it. There either is a lot underneath or this (pointing at his head) is not working right.*

The last part of the session has been focused on reminding the client of the relevance of respecting the pace of all parts involved in regard to trauma work. In the next section, we focus on helping the client understand the function of the voice (TW #6) as well as checking the needs of the part (TW #7).

> *T: I think this part has an important role; it's trying to protect you from the painful memories. You are partially aware of these events, but there are many things you still don't know.*
> *C: Yes.*

T: *So, this part did a good job protecting you from those memories. And what you perceive as destructive behaviors now, is probably an attempt to protect these memories.*

C: *So, I might be hurting myself just so I don't think about all of that?*

T: *It's possible. That's why I am interested in having all of you know that there are other ways of working with what happened without having to suffer so much.*

C: *Okay. So how can I get this part to calm down? I can't stand it.*

T: *I want all of you to know that we are going to work with this very carefully, we won't work with those memories until the time is right. Do you agree? (Client nods.) And for that parts that feel uneasy to know that it's not necessary to hurt yourself to avoid going there.*

C: *So, I do all these things to protect myself from everything that's inside my head?*

T: *Maybe, I don't know. Does that make sense to you?*

C: *Yes, it does.*

T: *Okay. Can you ask this part what it needs to calm down?*

C: *How can I put this? It's hard to put this into words.*

T: *Put what into words?*

C: *What the voice wants to tell me.*

T: *What is the voice saying?*

C: *He says that everything has to stay as it is. We have to close Pandora's Box. I opened it, but I have to close it, If I don't close it, the voice will be there telling me to hurt myself.*

T: *Okay, it makes sense. This is similar to what we were just talking about now.*

C: *Yes.*

T: *I think that this voice doesn't know there are other options, and it doesn't know how to handle it differently for now.*

C: *Like Little Guy at the beginning?*

T: *Exactly.*

This session started with a dilemma: the client was wondering what the part was trying to say when he mentioned "the reality." This is one of those situations in therapy where we must be very cautious about using triggering language, such as the words "rape" or "abuse." Finding other words that could help "translate" the message was a key piece of this work. By the end of the session, the client finally begins to understand that this part is communicating in the only way he knows, "just like Little Guy in the beginning." This small realization illustrates how it is easier to proceed with the work after laying the foundation with one of the most complicated parts, understanding it, and helping the client understand its needs and function.

EXAMPLE 9. PHOBIA OF TRAUMATIC MEMORIES

The client arrives feeling very agitated. This section of the interview focuses on reminding him that he will not be forced to do, talk about, or work with anything that he or any of the parts are not ready to face.

C: *After what happened last time, I'm scared that other bad memories might come up.*

T: *We talked about this the other day. Do you remember?*

C: *Yes.*

T: What did we talk about?

C: We said we were going to go slowly, but the fear is still there. So, I started to get nervous on the way here, and I was so distracted that I almost got hit by a car. I didn't even see that the traffic light was red.

Once we introduce the message about pacing the work, we proceed to explore the voices (TW #1). The client has difficulties understanding and managing the 38-year-old voice and needs help understanding.

C: It's as if I am in front of a mirror, and I argue with the mirror. I try to do what you told me to do, to step aside and be like a reporter, but this voice follows me. He is not like Little Guy. The last time I heard Little Guy, he wanted me to sleep with a stuffed animal and, when I did it, he calmed down. But this was different, I was having a cup of coffee, and I felt something like a breeze. I don't know how to explain it.

T: You are explaining it well.

C: A breeze that insulted me. I said to myself," What's going on here?" And I went back to drinking my coffee. Half an hour went by, and the breeze came back again, so I put on some music.

T: You played music. Does that still work?

C: Sometimes. It depends on how much of an asshole the voice can be. First, I turned on the music, looking for something groovy and, with that, it went away. But then it came back. And it was coming back at shorter intervals, so I said to myself, "Use the reporter technique, step aside. Dolores tells you to write down what it says and not to listen to it, so try to ignore it."

T: Well, Dolores doesn't say that.

C: Well, that's how I understood it; maybe that's the problem.

T: What I usually suggest is to pay attention but without taking action or following its commands. Whenever a voice tells you to cut or burn yourself, don't do it. Simply write it down, like a reporter, so that you can tell me, and we can try to understand. But the idea is not to ignore the voice. That's not the point. If you try to ignore it, it will probably become more intense.

C: Yes, exactly.

T: That wasn't what I wanted to suggest. Do you realize that we did not ignore Little Guy? So, we don't want to ignore this voice either.

After reminding the client that the goal never is to ignore voices, but to try to understand, we proceed with the exploration. First, we want to get an idea of what was happening with the voice or part (CS #2.2). We then can explore the reaction of the client to the voice (CS #2.3), to get an idea of what needs to be addressed (CS #2.4).

T: So, what happened after that?

C: He started with his typical, "Dickhead!" Then, he went with, "Son of a bitch," and so on. And when he calls me "son of a bitch," I get all heated up.

T: Yes, it bothers you as much as it can bother him. "Son of a bitch" is an insult that bothers both of you.

C: Yes.

T: So how did you respond? You said you got all heated up. How did you react?

C: I turned up the music and focused on what I was doing.

T: Did you say anything back?

C: I tried not to.

T: Did you answer back? Because sometimes you say negative things about him too.

C: Yes, I know. I took the pills, but he started to win the battle. So, I tried to talk to him, but it was impossible.

T: I think it might be a little too soon to dialogue. What would be great is that you try to show respect and try to understand him.

C: Yes, but I don't know how to tame him.

T: What did we say about taming and things like that?

C: Yes, I know, that I shouldn't do that.

T: Think about it. What worked with Little Guy?

C: We made him an ally.

T: So, how old did you say this voice was?

C: Thirty-eight, like me.

T: And do you really think that trying to tame this voice is going to work?

C: No, because he already won once.

T: This is not about winning or losing.

Once we have an idea of the type of interaction that took place, we can point out the protective function of this voice (TW #6).

T: You said that this voice shows up to protect you from difficult memories by avoiding them.

C: Yes, from what I know. I think he's like the guardian of Pandora's Box.

T: So, he has an important function.

C: Yes, but...

T: And he can help us to find the right moment to work on these traumatic memories.

C: Yes, but that's what I fear the most, that is my biggest fear.

T: Do you think this voice really understands that we are not going to go there until the moment is right?

C: No, I think it's not clear to him or he wouldn't be such an ass.

T: Remember our conversations about name-calling. (Client nods.) Maybe he has to make sure that we are not going to work on this yet.

C: Yes.

T: If he has this guardian function, it's important to respect it.

C: Yes. When I hear the voice, I do get nervous, because the first time I heard it, he made me lose touch with reality.

T: I see.

C: I think that's why, on the way here, I was getting more and more nervous, remembering what happened last week.

T: I see.

C: I thought, "What if another bad memory comes back? What am I going to do?"

T: If you get another memory?

C: Another bad memory, from when I got hurt.

T: If another bad memory comes up, we will deal with it. But we won't try to make this happen. And I think this is what the part is trying to avoid somehow.

C: He wants to protect something, so he says, "Do this to yourself, so you won't have to worry about the memories." He says I won't worry about the content in Pandora's Box if I am focused on the physical pain. After thinking about it a lot, after our last conversation, I reached this conclusion.

T: It makes a lot of sense and remember that we don't have to open Pandora's Box now because it's obviously not the right time. So, there is no need for you to hurt yourself because we are not going to go into the memories.

C: Okay.

T: That's what I want you and this part to understand: it's not necessary to do any of these things because we know for sure it's not the right moment to work with those memories.

C: Okay

Before we continue, it is important to check how the system is responding to the intervention (CS #2.5) and also if this is a good moment to close the session. Following the principle that less is better than too much, we can check and decide what is best. If things are calmer, it is better to close after a small piece of good work rather than push too much and risk the patient becoming overwhelmed again.

T: What do you notice when I say that?

C: I am calmer. He is calmer. Today I feel calm, I'm leaving okay.

T: Ok, so I think this may be a good moment to stop for today. I think it's important to respect our agreement. (Client nods.) So, we will figure out how to work on this at a manageable pace.

C: Okay, yes, but I am very scared of this part.

T: Yes, I know, that is why it's important to keep him in mind and listen to the Guardian.

In this session, we reminded the client how important it is not to ignore the voices, which is what he actually did because he understood that it was what she was supposed to do. By exploring the triggers and the function of the voice, we were also able to help the client understand the function of the part regarding self-harm. We closed the session reframing the function of the part by referring to it as "The Guardian," which gives it a more adaptive and positive meaning than the insults we started with and reminds him of the relevance of respecting the timing of all the parts.

EXAMPLE 10. A CRACK IN PANDORA'S BOX

This session offers an example of the difficulties that clients will probably encounter when they start to be more connected to their feelings. As the therapeutic work progresses, it also leaves both the client and the system of parts in a more fragile situation. The key ingredient is for therapists to remain calm and confident so that clients do not get frightened and can understand that this is part of the natural therapy process and its progress.

C: There is a crack in Pandora's Box and memories about the assault are slipping out. I remember some of the things those guys said, and they keep coming up over and over. (Client is shaking and his voice trembles.)

T: This is overwhelming for you.

C: Fuck! Yes! I can hear them when I'm walking down the street. Now the image of the guys is becoming clearer. Before it was just a bunch of guys attacking me, but now there are bits and pieces coming up, and I can see that the parts are more savage. This is killing me.

T: Can you explain what you mean by more savage?

C: Let's see, Little Guy doesn't just want death; he wants a slow death, he wants me to stop eating. T: Why would Little Guy want that?

C: I don't know.

T: Can you ask him?

C: (Client takes a few minutes to ask the part.) There is nothing here.

T: The parts are still inside of you.

C: Yes, but I don't know how to communicate with them in this situation.

Since we are running into something that neither the therapist nor the client understands at this point, a good strategy would be to do the Meeting Place procedure, as a way to bring some clarity into this new situation.

T: Can you try to imagine the meeting place and invite any parts, voices or aspects that want to be there today?

C: Okay.

T: Check if any parts are coming in. Who is in the meeting place?

C: Terror and me.

T: And terror belongs to ...?

C: Terror is like a partner.

T: Is terror related to Little Guy, to yourself, to Dude, or is it another aspect?

C: I don't know.

T: Take a look at the meeting place, close your eyes and invite all the different parts of yourself. Remember that it's a space where all of them can communicate what they need or express any concerns they might have.

C: Okay.

T: What do you see?

C: Little Guy and Dude are very blurry. I see Terror. It's like a part of me that split off. And nothing else. Actually, there are fragments of memories there. Terror does not trust Dude or Little Guy. They are very blurry and they seem to be drugged on a couch.

T: The one that does not trust them is Terror?

C: Yes.

T: Close your eyes and let this part that does not trust the others know that the meeting place is a place for communication. And that we can add whatever is needed in the meeting place, windows, reinforced doors... anything that can help them to feel safe. And of course, this goes for the other parts too, for Little Guy and Dude. Can you ask Terror why he is so afraid?

C: He does not answer.

This can be a good time to check how the system is reacting to the intervention (CS #2.5.). Since there is a lot of fear, which usually may block the process, we can offer the processing phobia procedure as a way to decrease the fear (TW #4).

T: How do you feel about that?

C: What do I feel now? Fear. I am feeling the terror.

T: Should we process the fear you are noticing?

C: Yes, okay.

T: Focus on the terror that you are noticing now, nothing else. (BLS) What do you get?

C: I get that he wants to get rid of Little Guy and the Dude as soon as possible.

T: Notice that. (BLS)

T: What do you get now?

C: That for him to go back inside of me, those two have to disappear.

T: But that's not our goal.

C: I know, but this is what I'm getting. We need Little Guy and Dude to go back to how they were before. They can be savage, but not so savage. The level of violence needs to go down.

T: That makes sense. Can you ask Little Guy and Dude what they need to be able to decrease the level of violence?

C: To stop the memories.

T: To stop the memories. So, that means they are having a hard time...

C: Hmm, yes. They want to close Pandora's Box.

T: Let them know that we are going to respect the agreement, and we are not going to open the box.

C: They say that it's not closed right, like when a suitcase is too full and you have to sit on it to close it.

T: Let them know that we are not going to work on that until it's the right time for them.

C: Okay.

T: What happens when I say that?

C: They calm down a bit.

Next, we suggest processing the phobia of all parts involved, by asking them to notice the discomfort (TW #4).

T: Can we try something? (Client nods.) I am going to ask the three of you to focus on the feeling of discomfort that you are noticing.

C: Okay.

T: On the suffering, nothing else, and we are going to process it. The three of you together. (Client nods.) Let me know when you are ready. (Client makes a gesture signaling the therapist to go ahead. BLS.)

T: What do you notice?

C: They say that as long as we don't go there (referring to the trauma), it's okay, but if we go there, they will make a mess.

T: Tell them that we are going to respect that. We are not going to go there until the time is right.

C: Okay. (BLS)

T: What do you get?

C: I get "It's okay, guys," just that sentence.

T: Notice that. (BLS) What do you get?

C: Things are calmer, but they want to close Pandora's Box completely. They want to leave that aside and live with the memories that they had from before and after what happened. They want to eliminate all the brutal parts in the middle.

Although the client mentions wanting to forget, it is important to remember that to forget is one of the resources used to cope with traumatic experiences. To close the session we explain that the idea is not so much to forget but to work at a pace that is tolerable for all the parts so we can anticipate future problems (CS #3.5) that might arise when the client insists on working with trauma and the whole system is not yet ready to do so. We also check how the client is doing to make sure he is stable (CS #3.3).

T: *I want you and all the parts to know something. We are going to be very careful, and we will go as slow as necessary so you can all tolerate the work. We are never going to do more than what we can do.*
C: *Okay.*
T: *Do you understand this?*
C: *Yes.*
T: *And what do you think about it?*
C: *I agree. We can set a pace that we can handle so that everything evolves towards a better understanding of this (pointing at his head) and everything that is inside.*
T: *How are you doing now?*
C: *I am calm.*
T: *How is everything inside?*
C: *Also calm.*

EXAMPLE 11. AN AGGRESSIVE VOICE APPEARS: THE ORIGINAL VOICE

This is an example that takes place during a critical time for the client. A lot of work has been done, the voices are cooperating, and the client has not resorted to any aggressive behaviors towards self or others for months. He comes in frightened because he hears a new voice that is very aggressive and "does not reason like the others." What happens in this session illustrates how the system can respond when the client or other parts try to rush trauma work. In the previous session, the client said that, since things were going better, it was a good time to look into the contents of Pandora's Box and work with them. To help the reader understand the following example, this new voice belongs to the part behind the wall, the first voice the client ever heard; the 15-year-old part that has all the memories from the assault. In the beginning of this session, we do not know this, but it can be understood with the guided questions to explore the system and what is happening.

C: *I'm very scared, and the voices have gone wild. Instead of two, I have three now. So, on the one hand, I have the two voices you already know encouraging me to break the barrier; and on the other hand, there is a new one, the "Devil," that wants me to destroy myself. This is killing me!*

The internal conflict becomes obvious by the name chosen by the client to refer to this new part, which reflects one of the common issues with challenging parts already mentioned: an internal power struggle. We make sure to point this out to see how the client responds and to check if there is the need to model new ways of responding (TW #8).

T: *Okay, let's try not to refer to this voice in such a way. What do you think?*
C: *We can call him the Original voice.*

T: That's better.
C: Yes, it is better.

Renaming the voice was quite easy despite the dissociative phobia felt by the client (TW #4). This is a good example of how previous work helps in future similar situations with other parts since the client had already seen the benefits of renaming "Little Motherfucker" and starting to call him "Little Guy." Therefore, we do not need to do more, since the client himself adapts his language.

C: But this voice is really killing me. I can't even smoke in peace, it comes up very easily. If I'm drinking coffee and it's hot, it tells me to pour it on myself. Every time I see anything that I can burn myself with, it tells me to do so. I just can't control it!
T: Let's try to understand this. What happened this week?

By inquiring about what happened during the week (CS #1.2), we are trying to understand why this new part needs to resort to such aggressive and complicated defenses (TW #6), so we can help the client understand as well. Remember that the issue of control in challenging voices is very much intertwined with the pain of those parts holding the most difficult memories.

C: It has to do with the conversation we had last week. First, the two voices from the beginning were saying, "Move on, free yourself, get rid of all that crap." And from the moment they started collaborating more, the third voice appeared. This voice is louder, and it seems much stronger; it's like an explosion. Boom! Boom! Boom! I am very worried because even though the other voices are there, supporting me, this week I was able to put them aside despite everything that was happening, and they responded well. However, this one is different; it's impossible to set aside.
T: The other day you told me you were interested in working with what is so well kept. And I was telling you how we should be careful because this part could feel in danger.
C: Yes.
T: So, what you're telling me is understandable. There's probably a lot of fear there.
C: There is terror. Memories come back and it hurts a lot because... Fuck! Every time I think about that, it... (The client becomes agitated and has difficulty swallowing.)

We point out how the part might be feeling fear, which is both an example of identifying phobias (TW #4), of signaling the function of this voice (TW #6), of helping the client to see that it makes sense that it is showing up after what happened, and at the same time, of validating the feelings (TW #7). Working with trauma generates ambivalent reactions and conflict in the internal system. Just thinking about the trauma makes the client very nervous, but at the same time, he wants to push through. It is important to point out his physical reactions, so he can learn to pay attention to his own body language.

Wanting to get to the trauma too quickly makes the part believe that we want it to disappear, which will increase the angry interactions toward the client, the therapy or other parts. Remember that anger is another of the common issues in challenging parts mentioned in Chapter 5. We must

186

remind him of the importance of respecting the pace of all parts of the system and the agreements that had been reached before (TW #10).

> *T: Do you realize that each time you think about it, you feel overwhelmed?*
>
> *C: Yes, but I must face it!*
>
> *T: Okay, but can you notice that? When you spoke about this incident before, it was blocked. You couldn't connect like this. (Client nods nervously.) I understand that we have to work on these issues, but I also understand that your current feelings of fear and terror can help you understand how this voice could be feeling. And remember that this voice is the one that holds all the memories.*
>
> *C: But we should face this memory, and I want to face it with some calmness. I cannot break down because I have a flashback of a specific moment. This Original Voice bothers me very much; I can't do anything without thinking about throwing myself in front of an oncoming bus or car. The other day I had to take the bus, and as soon as I got to the bus station, it began endlessly repeating, "Throw yourself in front of the bus! Throw yourself in front of the bus!" I used to enjoy traveling by bus, and now I cannot even go to the bus station, because the voice says these things. This is killing me!*

As we commented in the beginning of this example, we continuously model respect for the client's point of view (TW #8), while being respectful to all parts and inquiring with healthy curiosity (TW #2). Our goal is to change judgment for understanding, which is usually achieved by exploring the function of the voice (TW #6) and its needs (TW #7). Exploring the voice further (TW #1) helps us confirm another of the common issues in working with challenging voices: the fact that the voices tend to repeat themselves over and over again, just like a broken record, as the client himself defines it.

> *T: Well, I understand that this voice is very uncomfortable for you because it interferes with you being able to feel calm.*
>
> *C: Yes.*
>
> *T: Could you ask this voice why is it saying this? We would like to understand how it might be trying to help.*
>
> *C: (The client tries to ask the voice but quickly becomes agitated due to the response.) It won't stop insulting me. It's like a broken record plagued with insults, asking me to hurt myself over and over. It won't stop! I can't get in touch with it, it's overwhelming..*
>
> *T: Okay, so ask this part what is bothering him right now.*
>
> *C: Let's see... The pain.*
>
> *T: This part is suffering a lot. (Client nods.) Ask him how he is feeling.*
>
> *C: Angry.*
>
> *T: Okay, angry. And what is he angry about?*
>
> *C: About the past.*
>
> *T: Ask him if he is also angry with you.*
>
> *C: He is insulting me, so I guess he is. I think he continues to blame me.*
>
> *T: Ask this voice if he is angry with me.*
>
> *C: No, he blames me for everything.*
>
> *T: Could you ask this voice how old he feels he is?*

C: Fifteen.

T: And he is suffering a lot. Ask him if he would like to work on decreasing his suffering a bit.

C: Let's see. The other voices are answering; they say they want to be free.

When the client indicates that the response of the part is "15 years old," it is obvious that this is the nuclear part that contains the most painful memories, as we commented in the beginning of the session. We then find ourselves at a choice point: we can either start working with the parts that are responding, or we can remain focused on the one we are working with. Regardless of what we choose to do, it must always be done keeping the whole system in mind and checking how the other parts might be responding (CS #2.5). Validating the protective function of all parts by insisting on the message that they all are important parts of the system is crucial (TW #6).

T: Please, thank them for answering, for being there, and for trying to help. However, we will try to ask this 15-year-old voice what he is feeling and whether he thinks it would be a good idea to work a little bit on his sensation. Tell him that we don't want to work on the memories of what happened, only on the sensation that he is noticing.

C: Everything is getting mixed up.

T: What is getting mixed up?

C: The guilt, the hope of finding some relief, the desire to hurt himself. It's a mix of everything. I feel overwhelmed by this.

T: I know this is not easy for you. But just as you have tried to understand the other parts, the other voices, we also need to understand this voice. This part is also very important, just as the others are. I really appreciate how much the voices are trying to help, but it is essential that all of you try to understand that this other part carries a heavy burden.

C: We all understand it, but he seems stubborn and he appears to be clinging to all of that stuff.

T: Yes, and the more we try to force him to work on it, the more stubborn he will become.

C: So, what can I do?

T: First we will try to communicate with this part to understand him, and then we can try to work with the sensation that he is noticing to see if he can feel some relief. But first, we need his permission.

A more detailed exploration about this voice and what is taking place in the system is allowing us to get relevant information about the voices. This allows us to validate his feelings (TW #7) and help the client, and maybe other parts that might be listening in, to understand that this 15-year-old part has been carrying a very heavy burden. After negotiating with the different parts and getting their permission, we can start working with some of the techniques mentioned in Chapter 1. However, we must pay attention to the signs that may tell us that the clients or some parts are trying to force the work and move ahead too quickly.

T: Ask this part what he is noticing right now. We will try to work with this part, this is important. The others may be there, they are also important, but today we will try to pay attention to this part.

C: Pain.

T: Ask him where he notices this pain right now.

C: There is not a specific place. It's all over my head.

We start trying to apply the Freckle technique, an EMDR procedure described in Chapter 1, using tapping to provide alternate bilateral stimulation.

> T: *Ask him if he allows me, with your help, to work a little bit on this pain. He would be using this device, and he would focus on his pain, not on other issues or memories, just the pain.*
>
> C: *He says yes.*
>
> T: *We will need your help.*
>
> C: *What should I do?*
>
> T: *You can lay your hands flat on the table, palms down, and allow this part to notice it so we can work on his pain.* (Client nods.) *Ask him to focus on that pain, just for a little while. We will do a short test. Is he noticing it?*
>
> C: *I'm the one noticing it.*
>
> T: *Because it's your body as well. Can this part notice it?*
>
> C: *It's generalized, it is as if I was placed in a garbage truck and somebody turned on the grinder. I feel absolutely crushed.*

Working with the sensations of both parts at the same time seems to be excessive at this point. The conflict is not reduced enough due to the phobias (TW #4), and there is no co-consciousness between these two parts. When something does not work, it offers relevant information for us to change or adapt our strategy. We need to know which part is having trouble with the exercise before we proceed. Remember the importance of modeling respect and alternative ways of responding (TW #8) and never forcing any of the voices to work on anything, even if the client is insisting on moving forward. This will help the client increase self-reflection, as well as identify and meet the needs of the different parts. As always, validating feelings, needs and efforts (TW #7) is an important part of the intervention.

> T: *Ask this part if you can do this exercise with him or if he prefers to do it alone.*
>
> C: *He said that step by step, on his own.*
>
> T: *Okay, so ask him to focus on that sensation.* (Client nods. BLS.) *What is he noticing?*
>
> C: *Stop! Stop! It's like going back to the very beginning.* (The client is breathing heavily and his whole body is shaking).

This is another interesting moment, and we need to remain calm and focused. With this reaction, we could easily think that what we did was a very bad idea and could feel tempted to stop the work. But before we do that, we really need to understand what just happened. This is a good example of why it is important not to jump to conclusions and to check with the system of parts to guide our work (CS #2.5).

> T: *It's important to know where this "stop" is coming from. Is it coming from you or from that part?*
>
> C: *It comes from everywhere. The physical sensation from "that stuff" is starting, and those words come up. So, then I don't know if it's me or if it's the other part. I don't know anything.*
>
> T: *Okay, let's ask this part. I understand that this is your sensation, but let's ask this part if he wanted to stop.*

C: *Can you give me some time to calm down?*

T: *Of course, take your time.*

C: *(Client takes a few minutes to breath deep and calm down.) Let's go. He said to go ahead.*

T: *So, this part didn't want to stop. Was it you who wanted to stop then?*

C: *Yes.*

T: *Okay, so how can we do this? Because we cannot force any of the parts.*

C: *I just have to show some balls and go ahead.*

T: *I really appreciate your intention and your interest. There is a big desire to collaborate, but this is not so simple. This is not the way to do it. We will get back to this part and work on his sensation, but first, we are going to focus on your fear for a moment.*

This is a great opportunity to process the phobia of mental actions and dissociative parts in the Adult Self before we go on. If we do not work with these phobias, the fear of the client will likely continue to block the process, even if he is willing to move ahead (TW #4). We use the processing phobias procedure, again using EMDR's bilateral stimulation to process this feeling.

T: *Place your hands on the table, focus on the fear, just a bit. No memories at all, just the fear you are noticing towards what we are doing now.* (Client nods. BLS.)

T: *What do you notice?*

C: *A question is coming to my mind: "Why am I afraid?"*

T: *Should we go with that question?*

C: *Yes.* (BLS)

T: *What do you get now?*

C: *Fear of remembering*

T: *Fear of remembering, it makes a lot of sense. Where are you noticing this fear?*

C: *All over. I notice pressure in my stomach, I feel nausea, I don't know if it's normal. It's as if someone punched me in the stomach. Now I feel bad physically.*

The Freckle Technique is a good approach at this point. Simply focusing on the physical disturbance –which is related to the physical memories of what happened– without gathering any other elements from the traumatic memory may help decrease the sensation, thus reducing the fear as well.

T: *Could we focus on the disturbance that you are noticing to see if it can be relieved a little bit?*

C: *Yes.*

T: *Notice that.* (BLS)

T: *What do you notice? Did the sensation increase or decrease?* (Client remains silent.) *There is not a correct answer, I don't expect anything specific.*

C: *I notice a revolution in my stomach. It's like when somebody punches you. First you feel the pain, then you feel nausea, and after that, you feel sick.*

T: *Okay, but has the sensation increased or decreased?*

C: *It has decreased.*

T: Can you notice it for a little while more, just to see if it keeps on decreasing?

C: Yes. (BLS)

T: What do you notice now?

C: I feel calmer. I notice I am more stable, more present.

T: Notice that. (BLS) *What do you get now?*

C: Pain, desire for vengeance, a weird sensation... I don't know how to define it.

T: Ask this part if we can go on for a bit.

C: Yes.

T: Please, ask the part.

C: Okay. (Checking inside.) *Yes.*

T: Okay, ask him to focus on what he is noticing. (Client nods and then makes a gesture meaning "it's okay, go ahead." BLS.)

T: What does he notice?

C: He is asking why didn't I do anything? Why didn't I press charges? Why did I keep quiet? Why did I keep it to myself? Why did I hide it and build that containment wall?

T: Do you want to answer?

C: I don't have an answer.

T: Try it out. What would you answer?

C: I don't know, what I get is the destruction at the beach.

T: That day, you felt terrible, really bad, right? Under those circumstances, were you able to do anything?

C: No, nothing. Objectively, I did not have the capacity to do anything, because I was blocked.

Introducing past-present differentiation (TW #5) is a crucial aspect of trauma treatment. All parts need to learn that the past is over, even though it may not feel that way, and they are no longer reliving the traumatic past, it is not happening now.

T: Tell him that what can help us the most is to think about what we can do NOW, ask him what you could do now so he can calm down.

C: He says that I could forget.

We often run into this situation in different moments of treatment: the client or a part want to forget. But this is not a real solution. Forgetting is a resource that has been used as a consequence of having lived through an overwhelming trauma that surpasses the person's integrative capacity; a resource that once was adaptive, but no longer is. Once the client is in contact with memories, the system is more integrated and forgetting is not possible anymore. At this point, we help the part to understand the difficulties related to his proposal of forgetting.

T: Ask this part if he can forget.

C: He says he can't forget.

T: So, he is asking you to do something that he cannot do. Ask him if we can at least think of other different options.

C: To relieve the pain.

191

T: *To relieve the pain. In order to do this, we can work with the pain little by little. Try to tell this part that I will be here. I really appreciate how he is trying to help, and I will try to do whatever I can for the pain to go away, at his own pace. Just let him know that and check how he receives this message.*

C: *He's blocked.*

After exploring and identifying the dissociative phobia (TW #4), we suggest processing it. By simply focusing on the pain and processing it with bilateral stimulation, both client and part may start to feel better.

T: *Could you ask him what has blocked him?*

C: *The fear, the fear is coming back.*

T: *So, knowing that we are here, place your hands here and ask him to focus on that fear. (BLS) What do you get?*

C: *Terror.*

T: *How does he feel about us being here, trying to help him? Could you ask this part?*

C: *He says it's something that I should have done before.*

T: *How is he feeling now? Is he still noticing fear?*

C: *Yes. He is afraid.*

T: *Okay, ask him to focus on this a little bit more, just a little more. (BLS)*

C: *He's still as terrified.*

T: *It's normal to be terrified and it's important to let him know that we can work on it. Does he know that?*

C: *Yes, but he can't accept it. Maybe it's because of what happened during the week. He is blocked in that terror, as if he were afraid that it could happen again, and he would have to go through the same thing again. Not that* (referring to the assault), *but it is all related to that fear of the wounds, fear of committing suicide or hurting myself.*

T: *Are you saying this or is it this part saying it?*

C: *The voice says it. He goes back to the insults. He goes back to the blame.*

T: *Insults and blame. Ask him why he is going back to the insults now.*

C: *He left the fear aside and went back to what he knows and has learned to do.*

T: *I am glad you can understand that. I agree. This part is still learning how to respond differently.*

After processing the pain, the part calmed down, but later went back to responding in a defensive way. This is a common occurrence when conflict is still high, and parts are learning new ways. By validating how difficult it can be to do things differently, we are also modeling a new way of communicating and relating between the different parts, one that promotes empathy and mutual respect so we can try to meet the needs of all parts (TW #7) and avoid destructive behavior (TW #8). However, the Adult Self is more capable of understanding that this is learned behavior and is more empathic towards this part and how it responds. This gives us an opportunity to introduce a relevant message that could be very healing: a simple, apology, since usually clients have not received an apology or any other reparation for the pain they have been inflicted.

T: Let's try something, but first you have to let me know if you can, okay? Do you think you could tell him that you are sorry for not being able to respond in a different way and that, at that moment, you did not know how to react, that you were only trying to survive?

C: I can try.

T: Okay, try to let him know this and also that you came here to get help.

C: He says it's too late.

T: Ask him why he thinks it is too late.

C: There is no answer.

T: Okay, so he doesn't know, huh?

C: No.

T: Tell him that I don't believe it's too late.

C: (Internal communication.) He blames me for his suffering.

T: Do you understand why this part does this?

C: Well, no. I don't.

T: I think he is just repeating what he learned. And now it is important to understand and allow this part to express whatever he is feeling. (Client nods and appears calmer.) *I will remember to ask him in each session to give him time and to try to help him feel better. Can you ask him if he can wait to say these things until he is here with me instead of doing it outside? Maybe he can try for a week and then we check on it again.*

C: (Internal communication) No.

T: Can you ask him why not? I would like to know.

C: He blames me again, it's like a circle that I need to break, but I don't know how.

T: Well, this part is very important; he has the key. Ask him how we can break this circle, in a way that is safe for him.

C: He doesn't answer, he goes back to the insults.

Repetition is a common difficulty in working with challenging parts that can be extremely frustrating at times, because clients may lose trust in the possibility that this part will ever change. We should keep in mind this difficulty and not become frustrated ourselves, and of course, remind the client that this is learned behavior, which is mostly automatic and needs a lot of practice to be modified.

T: Maybe he doesn't know how to answer, he only knows how to insult. This is when you need to remember that he doesn't know how to respond in any other way, just as Little Guy at the beginning. And today we gathered a lot of information, he cooperated very much. This is a big step for him. Do you realize this?

C: Well, it was difficult because it's not pleasant to go through this situation, but I have to face it. I can't get stuck in the past because it's destroying me day after day.

T: And it's important that you can think about this differently. Of course, it is not pleasant to be insulted, but for now, he doesn't know how to do it in any other way. And we will keep working on this. It depends on both of you, he is being clear, there are things he is able to do. Today he has allowed us to work a little and afterwards he got nervous, that's fine. He can get nervous and let us know what he needs.

C: Yes, I understand that.

T: How is he doing now?

C: (Internal communication.) *He says the pain is mitigated.*

T: Great. This is very important. We will keep working with this and, in every session, we will talk to this part and to the other parts too. Let's talk to them. How are the other two now?

As usual, after doing an intervention like this, we need to check the effects on the different parts (CS #2.5) which will help you address any other issues that are coming up (CS #2.4), as well as detect whether there are any phobias present (TW #4) that need to be addressed.

C: Frightened. When this Original Voice shows up, the other two went into hiding, as if they didn't want to be with him.

T: Were they present here today? Do they know what happened?

C: Yes.

T: And what do they think about it?

C: They want to go forward, but this other part is much stronger.

In addition to reminding the client that the part is still learning to respond differently, we also anticipate potential problems between sessions (SC #3.5).

T: We are trying to understand this part, and we are not going to ask for radical changes because it's not easy. Let's see how this week goes. I will ask him how it went in the next session, and we will keep on working so he feels better. If you hear insults this week, try to remember that this is what he has learned.

C: Okay.

T: What do you notice now?

C: It feels like the part of me that was being so annoying has gone away. (Client seems relieved.)

T: Notice that. (BLS) *What do you get?*

C: I feel calmer.

T: Do you feel grounded now?

C: Yes.

T: All of you have done a great job today!

C: Thank you.

T: Thank you, and thank all the parts.

We close the session reinforcing the work done by all the parts (CS #3.1) and checking that the client is stable and grounded (CS #3.3) which at this moment of the process can be explored directly without difficulty. He is much more able to identify how he is doing and to express any needs that arise.

EXAMPLE 12. INCREASED COMMUNICATION BETWEEN PARTS OUTSIDE OF THERAPY

After working with the fear of the contents of Pandora's box and helping the parts really understand that the goal at the moment is not to get into trauma work, everything seems smoother. The client has been stable for a few weeks. He comes in saying he needs help to understand and help the 38-year-old part who has been asking for help in different ways.

> C: *As I told you, he showed up at night. He looked like a melting figure.*
> C: *Uh-huh.*
> C: *I didn't see him again, but I did hear him.*
> T: *What did you hear?*
> C: *He asks me for help, but I don't know how to help. He said that, for example, when he told me to burn my arm, he did it so I wouldn't forget about him. He said, "if you don't listen to me, I have to do those things."*
> T: *What do you think about that?*
> C: *I think that he wants to tell me something, but I don't know what it is. And I'm not able to get it out of him. If I knew what he wanted, I would give it to him ...*
> T: *Why do you think there is more communication between the both of you now?*

Remember that one of the special issues in working with challenging parts is fearing that the goal of psychotherapy is to eliminate them, and this can cause strong reactions in these parts, mostly angry reactions. Anger, which could also show up as mistrust, is usually directed both at the therapist and the therapy.

> C: *I think he's asking me not to destroy him.*
> T: *Why does he think that you want to destroy him?*
> C: *I don't know.*
> T: *What was happening when he started to say that?*
> C: *I noticed my scars were healing well.*
> T: *How did you feel when you noticed that?*
> C: *Good, I felt as if I was leaving behind a difficult episode of my life.*
> T: *How did this part feel about that?*
> C: *He doesn't want me to let my guard down.*
> T: *I see, so he is again trying to protect you by using his old ways. Maybe he doesn't know that you don't need to keep your guard up so much now.*
> C: *He doesn't know.*
> T: *So, it's important to let him know. Now you can protect yourself in a different way and there is no need to resort to those behaviors anymore.*

Since the conflict is mostly related to one voice, we just explored th*is* one particular voice (TW #1) and encouraged the client to be more attentive to the inner system (TW #2). In addition, inquiring about what has triggered any specific behavior (TW #3) will always give us clues about the reasons behind it. In the next section, we will work with the phobia (TW #4) of this part and help the client to realize that the part is beginning to cooperate more (TW #10).

C: I know. This has to do with him being in the dark side. How can I explain it? Remember how in the beginning I wanted to destroy both the Dude and Little Guy, but we got Little Guy to change sides quickly?

T: Yes.

C: But this guy is still on the other side, the dark side.

T: Do you realize that there is a change in the way he responds?

C: Yes, he's asking for help and asking me not to forget about him. I get that.

T: And what do you think about that?

C: I will not forget about him. With my arm in this condition (showing the burn), *I don't think I will ever forget him.*

T: Have you tried telling him that you are not going to forget about him because he's a very important part of you?

C: No, I did not try saying that. I told him "I can't get rid of you, you are present."

T: Yes, but notice how different that is from what I propose. It's not that you can't, it's that we don't want to get rid of him. Try telling him that he's a very important part of you and that we are not going to forget about him.

C: I did, I told him that he's very important for us, and I asked him to stay.

T: What happens to him when you say that?

C: He says that he wants to be an important part of me.

T: He is an important part of you.

C: How can I say this? He wants to be present, but he doesn't want to be hurt.

T: Of course, that makes a lot of sense.

C: But he doesn't know what you want to do with him.

T: I consider him a very important part of you. I don't want him to disappear.

C: Okay.

T: He's not going to disappear. What happens when I say that?

C: He listens, but he is still frightened.

After checking the reaction of the part after the intervention (CS #2.5), we can identify the dissociative phobia and suggest working on it (CS #2.2 and TW #4) using the processing phobia procedure.

T: Can you ask him if he would like to work on this fear? (Client nods and takes a few minutes to ask the part.)

C: I talked to him as a friend. I asked him if he wanted to talk about his fear, and it seems he is okay with it.

T: He doesn't even have to talk about the fear. He just needs to focus on the fear.

C: Focus on the fear?

T: Yes, focus on the fear, so we can try to process it. Does he agree?

C: (Client checks inside.) *Yes.*
T: *A ask him to notice the fear, nothing else.* (BLS) *What does he notice?*
C: *He notices fear.*
T: *Ask him to notice that.* (BLS)
T: *What do you get now?*
C: *I get that he wants to live.*

The fact that the voice expresses his wish to live is very new. The therapist reinforces what the part has just expressed to help the client realize that this is important (TW #7).

T: *That's great, isn't it?*
C: *Yes, it's the first time he has ever said anything like this.*
T: *Tell him that he has the right to live and that it is good that he wants to live.* (BLS) *What do you get now?*
C: *I told him that I was part of him, and he was part of me. That if I make it, he makes it too.*
T: *Perfect, both of you notice that.* (BLS) *What do you get?*
C: *I get "We are going to make it; we are going to make it."*
T: *Is this a feeling shared by both of you?*
C: *Yes.*

Installation of a shared positive feeling is a good co-consciousness exercise and a simple way to promote more cooperation and teamwork (TW #10).

T: *Great, notice that.*
C: *Okay.* (BLS)
T: *What do you get?*
C: *We can both make it.*
T: *Is this a shared feeling?*
C: *Yes, he accepts it.*
T: *Ok great, notice it together.* (BLS)
C: *Shit! He got scared.*
T: *Let him know that it is okay to be afraid. We are going to work on whatever needs to be worked on.* (Client nods.) *Ask him if it's a good idea to continue a bit more.* (Client checks in and then nods giving permission. BLS.) *What do you get now?*
C: *I told him to be calm, that we are not going to hurt him, but he is still afraid.*
T: *Ask him to focus on the feeling of fear a little bit more.* (BLS)
C: *I get that he wants to have a life.*
T: *Okay, good. Ask him to think about that, and you can be there with him too.* (BLS) *And now?*
C: *I told him that he already had a life, that he is present, but it's as if he wanted to have his own life. As if he wanted to leave my body and appear next to me as a different person*
T: *Notice that.* (BLS) *What do you get now?*
C: *I asked him not to leave. I told him that he was part of me and that I needed him to survive.*
T: *What does he think about that?*
C: *He says that as long as he is allowed to live, he is okay. But if we try to hurt him, he will hurt me.*

197

T: Well, nobody here wants to hurt him.

C: Of course not.

T: We are going to take care of him and you. If we take care of him, he can also take care of you.

C: Okay.

T: Notice that. (BLS) What do you get?

C: He still doesn't trust us.

T: Okay, I understand. Tell him he can take his time.

We close the session thanking the part for all the work he did (CS #3.1) and exploring ways for him to feel better in therapy (TW #8). Not trying to rush trust is a good way to gain it. Despite closing with distrust, the client is much calmer and did a wonderful piece of work. This is a good example of how modeling sown the seeds for the Adult Self, who eventually will know just what to say or do with the needs of other parts.

EXAMPLE 13. REACHING AN AGREEMENT WITH THE SYSTEM

After a few months of stability and after reaching an agreement to avoid fights and self-harm, one day the client faints on the street and ends up in a coma. This event is very surprising for the client and very concerning as well. It turns out another part had overdosed on medication. Exploring triggers (TW #3) and the inner dynamics that have led to this situation (TW #1) and doing so with interest and curiosity from the client (TW #2) will allow us to understand what happened (CS #1.2).

T: How was your week?

C: Fucking great! Little Guy is laughing and the other one is saying, "You have to hurt yourself, that's what takes the pressure away." And I am trying not to pay any attention to them.

T: What about the agreement we had?

C: Dude broke the agreement.

It is clear that the voice has been active during the week (CS #2.1) and we want to understand the reason (CS #2.2), know how the client reacted (CS #2.3) and address any issues as they appear (CS #2.4).

T: Why?

C: That's what I would like to know.

T: Ask him why he broke the agreement or whether he broke the agreement because maybe it wasn't him.

C: He says that for me to feel good, I have to suffer.

T: Ask him why.

C: Because I stop acting silly, because while I'm suffering, I'm not being ridiculous. He says I acted like an idiot.

T: What does acting like an idiot mean to him?

C: Swallowing about a hundred pills.

T: Dude thinks that if you had hurt yourself, you wouldn't have taken the pills.

C: Yes.

At this point, it is not very clear which part took the pills, so we proceed by directly asking about it.

T: So, which part of you took the pills?
C: That's what I don't know.
T: Ask the Dude to see if he knows.
C: He says that the unconscious part did.
T: The unconscious part.
C: Yes, the unconscious part.
T: So, Dude did not break the agreement.
C: I must've broken it then.
T: I don't know, ask him to see what he thinks.
C: He gives me that crap about suffering, that if I suffer, I don't act like a fool.
T: Which is the unconscious part?
C: That unconscious part is a part that I don't control.
T: Ask that unconscious part why did he take the pills.
C: There's no answer.
T: Do you notice the unconscious part now?
C: Yes, but it's just a vacuum; it's like something white.

Accessing this part seems more complicated. There is no answer and the client is not familiar with it. More than likely, the client is phobic of this unconscious part and will have more difficulties understanding it. We explore whether Little Guy or Dude were present during the suicide attempt to try to get some clarity.

T: Was Little Guy present?
C: No.
T: No? How about Dude?
C: No, just this white part that I'm telling you about. The others were not present.
T: Did they see what happened?
C: No, they didn't see it.
T: Then ask Dude how does he know that this unconscious part took the pills.
C: The answer they give me is that "he's unconscious."
T: But ask him, ask them both why they know he's unconscious.
C: Because he doesn't answer.
T: Ask them how they know there is an unconscious part there.
C: Because they say they don't know what happened.
T: Can you ask them if they want to continue collaborating?
C: You mean to ask them if they want me to move forward?
T: You can ask that too. Ask both of them if they still agree on working as a team.
C: Yes, they want me to lead a quiet, normal life, like anyone else.

We decide to use the meeting place procedure to explore whether other parts might be present. This should help us understand what happened or what needs some attention.

199

T: Should we try to explore this incident through the meeting place?

C: Yes.

T: Remember that it's a space for observation and understanding. (Client nods.) How many chairs would you place there right now for the different aspects of yourself?

C: For the different aspects of myself?

T: Yes.

C: One, myself.

T: Why is that?

C: Because I want to get rid of all the other parts.

T: But then we go back to the conflict. Remember our goal is not to get rid of these parts but to understand them.

C: I know.

The client's tendency is to want to get rid of parts when he is bothered by them. This is a common occurrence and should be addressed by reminding the client that the therapeutic work that needs to be done is more about remaining curious and understanding (TW #2).

T: Let's try to be curious and invite all aspects of yourself, including the unconscious part you mentioned before.

C: Okay.

T: What do you see?

C: Four chairs.

T: How are those chairs distributed?

C: I'm sitting in one, Little Guy in another one, Dude in another one, and the unconscious part in another one.

T: Well, close your eyes. Check and see how these parts are doing. Let me know about anything that stands out for you.

C: Little Guy says that if I behave well, he'll stop bugging me. Dude will not put any more pressure on me if I keep the promise I made to myself, which is not to hurt myself again. And the unconscious part...I don't have a clue.

T: Try to observe and see what you notice, what this part may need, or if it wants to say something.

C: He wants to know.

T: Is this part saying this to you?

C: Yes.

T: What does he want to know?

C: What happened and why. Why we got to this extreme situation.

T: Ask, calmly, what does he mean by "extreme situation?"

C: He would like to know what happened the day I ended up in a coma.

T: Is this the unconscious part?

C: The unconscious part wants to know what happened there, but not from other people. He wants to know it himself.

T: Ask this part who has this information.

C: The subconscious.

T: The subconscious?

C: Yes.

T: Is that another part, different from the unconscious?

C: No, it's as if the brain has a part where it places the bad memories. I don't know if I'm explaining myself well.

T: You are explaining yourself well.

C: Where it places the bad memories and locks them up so they can't get out.

T: Look inside, close your eyes, take your time, try to observe... Who keeps those memories?

C: The brain.

T: The brain?

C: A part of the brain, I would locate it here in the back.

T: You would locate it there in the back.

C: For example, when that happened (the client is talking about the assault he suffered at age 15), *while going from where it happened to the hotel, I started erasing, erasing, and erasing.*

T: And you locate that in the back of your head.

C: I locate it here in the back. It's like a warehouse, it's like a box

T: Okay, but who's in charge of that warehouse?

C: I cannot give you an answer.

T: Ask them, look inside yourself.

C: It looks like a blank space where memories are placed. Then he just locks it up.

T: Who gets them and who locks it up? Ask them.

C: The unconscious, as a protection mechanism to prevent me from criticizing and hurting myself. So, automatically, when something bad happens to me, this part puts it in there and locks it up. As far as I remember, I got home, I took the bag of pills, and began to swallow pills. Just as if I were drinking a glass of water or plugging in my cell phone to charge, in a totally unconscious way.

T: But someone has to be aware of that.

C: Yes, but I can't locate it.

T: Ask the Dude.

C: Dude... Dude is still saying: "If you would've hurt yourself, none of that would've happened."

T: Ask him why is he so sure of that.

C: Because he says that it's my common reaction, that is, hurting myself, for example, like the iron or the burn, paralyzes my so-to-speak murderous instinct.

Although it is not clear which part is related to the suicide attempt, the client and the parts are calmer and willing to keep working together. We close the session by exploring alternatives to which he can resort before the situation gets out of hand (TW #8). Dude even gives a list of alternatives they could use, which is something very new and encouraging for a system that has been in conflict for so many years.

C: Check the pills; if I feel bad, call 911; if I have any problem, call you; if I see the slightest risk in a situation, ask for help.

T: Ask Dude if he could try to remind you of that. It would be great if he could remind you of those alternatives, instead of telling you to hurt yourself.

C: (After checking with the part.) *He says yes.*

T: Perfect, thank him.

T: Can you ask Dude how he feels now?

C: Calm.

T: How about Little Guy?

C: He is calm too.

T: How about you?

C: Well, I'm pretty calm.

T: Do you notice anything inside that is not calm now?

C: No, there is no one else here.

T: All three of you are calm now. Remember that working as a team can help you.

C: Yes, it can help.

T: And we welcome any other part to communicate anything that can help us. We want to understand everything in you. All parts are welcome, even the ones we do not know well.

The result of this session was quite positive, and the agreement was maintained for many months. The client did not go back to the hospital and was able to ask for help before the situation got out of hand. The Dude played an important part in this, reminding the client to reach out when needed, something he did not used to do. This example illustrates how important it is to reach agreements when parts are in conflict, especially when the conflict involves a potential risk for self or others. The only way to begin functioning as a team (TW #10) is to involve all parts of the system to agree on a common goal: improved functioning.

EXAMPLE 14. INCREASED CO-CONSCIOUSNESS

A few weeks after the session previously transcribed, we decide to introduce a co-consciousness exercise since the client and the different parts that are usually active are cooperating more. As commented in Chapter 11, it is a good way to take little steps towards integration and reinforce the power of doing things together. As in other examples, we begin exploring the effects of the work done in the previous session (CS #1), as well as any issues that came up during the week (CS #2). However, in the next section, we will only transcribe the piece of the session related to co-consciousness.

T: So, you said that in the past weeks you have been better, and you noticed that Dude and Little guy were collaborating even more than other times.

C: Yes.

T: How does that feel?

C: It's still weird, but it feels good. It's a very different way of being.

T: I was thinking we could try to do some exercises that can help you collaborate a bit more as a team. What do you think?

C: I think we could try to collaborate so that there is better understanding.

T: Check and see if there is anything that the three of you can feel or notice together.

C: My dog just had a litter. The three of us are looking forward to seeing the puppies. They are at the vet, and we are looking forward to seeing them.

T: And what do you notice when you think about the puppies?

C: *Warmth; I love little puppies.*

T: How about them? What do they notice?

C: *They are happy about that. Dude likes watching them, and Little Guy likes to pet them.*

T: Okay, so now, all three of you try to think about the puppies and notice that sensation together.

C: *Okay.*

T: Close your eyes and let me know when the three of you are noticing it.

C: *Yes, now.*

T: Okay, notice it. (BLS) How was it?

C: *They want to bring the puppies home.*

T: Notice that. (BLS. Client smiles after the set.) How was it to experience something together?

C: *Well, it's strange because there usually was one part that despised another part, or two parts that despised the others, or the three parts that despised me in general. So, the fact that there is something that unites them, gives them strength.*

T: And is that strange in a good way or a bad way?

C: *In a good way, I also notice the strength and union.*

T: Okay, can you notice that union and that strength again? All three of you. (Client nods. BLS.) What do you notice?

C: *I notice the union of the different parts, Little Guy, Dude, and myself feel closer.*

T: Notice that a little bit more. (BLS) What did you notice?

C: *A nice feeling.*

T: Great, now ask each one of them how that felt, what they have noticed doing this.

C: (Client checks inside.) *In general, strength. Union, strength, and the desire to keep moving forward.*

T: Let them know that this is what you can feel in many more aspects and in many more moments if you work as a team. Ask them what they think about this.

C: *Dude and I agree, but Little Guy is afraid, as if he were saying, "You may get rid of me."*

In the last sessions, Little Guy has felt a little excluded; Dude has taken up a lot of space by helping the Adult Self in different ways. Thus, it is important to keep checking in with all the different parts. If we were to notice anything that needed attention, we could explore whether any other parts feel differently. However, there does not seem to be an active part, so we just focused on the main parts that were active in the last week and at the beginning of the session. At this point, we could either explore what is happening with Little Guy or directly use a procedure he is familiar with: the processing phobias procedure.

T: Okay, ask Little Guy if he is willing to focus on his fear a bit.

C: (Client checks in.) *He says yes.*

T: Where does Little Guy notice that feeling?

C: *In general.*

T: Ask him where he is noticing the fear in the body.

C: *In the body, okay.*

T: Ask him.

C: *Here, inside.*

T: Okay, ask him if he wants you and Dude to be there with him or if he wants to do it alone.

C: He wants to do it alone.

T: Okay, ask him to focus on that feeling, only him.

C: Okay. (BLS)

T: What does he notice?

C: He notices terror.

T: Ask him if he wants to work on that terror a little bit more.

C: He is afraid of disappearing.

T: Tell him he's not going to disappear. He is an important part of you, and he's not going to disappear.
(Clients nods and communicates this internally.)

One of the important aspects of the previous section is validating and reassuring the client and the parts (TW #7), especially when any of the parts are highly distrustful and fear disappearing. Even if we have stated that getting rid of the parts is most definitely not the goal, we will need to repeat this at different times during therapy. After introducing the information that he will not disappear, we check how the part responds to the interaction (CS #2.5) to make sure he is understanding or believing us.

T: How did he respond to that?

C: He is listening.

T: Good, ask him if he wants to work a little on that terror to see if he feels better.

C: He says that it's enough for now, that he is afraid.

T: Alright, tell him that it is very good that he can say "no" when he wants to stop and we are going to respect him. He is keeping his word, and we are also going to keep ours.

C: He says it's okay.

T: Perfect.

C: He says that next time he will try to come and cooperate more.

T: Okay, very good, because next time we are going to check and see if it's a good time to do this again. I think you're doing very well in general; you can be proud of the work done.

In this case, the processing phobias procedure led to a completely different attitude in the part. But once the parts that were active calm down, the client talks about a balloon that scares him, so we proceed to explore (TW #1).

C: I am afraid of the balloon. Little Guy is also afraid of the balloon.

T: What balloon?

C: We are seeing a balloon of sorts, but we don't know what it is.

T: Can you describe the balloon?

C: It's round, big, and very inflated, as if it were ready to burst any moment.

T: Can we try to explore the balloon?

C: I'm afraid that instead of deflating, it could burst.

T: Then let's do something: close your eyes and visualize the balloon. Are you seeing it? (Client nods.) What do you see?

C: *I see the balloon with a brown frame surrounding it.*

T: *Can you communicate with the balloon?*

C: (Client checks inside.) *No, it doesn't move or talk or anything. It's just there ready to burst.*

T: *Well now you're going to put a protective layer all around it. How could this protection be?*

C: *It would be like a light layer of cement. The soft kind, so it that can be removed when the time is right, without breaking the content.*

Once again modeling has been useful in helping the client understand the relevance of following the pace of the part or what is represented by the balloon and showing great respect for everything inside. One stabilization technique that can be used when there is a risk of emotional overflow is to build a container with the patient and with the different parts that were active at the time. By doing so, we not only stabilize the situation, but also model for the different parts new ways of responding (TT-8) and use it as an opportunity to work as a team (TT-10). In this example, the client himself is who suggests placing a light layer of cement that can be removed without breaking the content.

T: *Close your eyes and imagine that. Notice how you place this protection around, so if it bursts, every-thing inside can be contained. Visualize how you place the protection and be very careful because you want to protect it, not lock it up. It is a protection that can be removed when the time is right. What do you notice?*

C: *Well, I notice that he does it with his hands. He takes small quantities and spreads them, making the layer. It's moist.*

T: *And who is doing that? Who is placing the protective layer?*

C: *The Dude is.*

T: *The Dude is, okay. So, watch how he does it and let him finish the process. You can use a fan to dry it out.*

C: *He does not need a fan, he prefers to leave it out to dry naturally, he says slow drying is safer than fast drying.*

T: *Perfect.*

C: *He has already enclosed the balloon. Now there is a white sphere where the balloon was before, with a brown edge around it.*

T: *Close your eyes and ask this part if it is possible to add a window, so the balloon can also look outside.*

C: *Okay.*

T: *What does he say?*

C: *If it's small, yes.*

T: *Okay, so let him add a small window.*

C: *Okay.*

This is a piece of work that would have been impossible to do in the beginning of therapy. Co-consciousness exercises can be very useful when parts have learned to cooperate and are willing to try shared tasks together. However, it is important to check the results of the work just in case any parts are feeling upset, uncomfortable, or triggered (CS #2.5). The reason why we suggest a window is because we do not know what the balloon represents, but if it is a new part, the idea is that it can feel protected, not enclosed.

T: How are you doing now? How is the Dude?

C: The Dude is quite calm.

T: He is calmer now.

C: Yes, it is as if he had done his work, his duties, and it seems that he wants to continue working and moving forward.

T: How about Little Guy?

C: The Little Guy is minding his own business. And then there is me. I feel relaxed, I feel good.

T: The Dude has played an important role in this, right?

C: Yes.

T: Let's thank him, okay? You did a good job, too. Now it would be important that Little Guy also collaborates in some way. Close your eyes and ask him, check and see what he can do.

C: He doesn't know.

T: How about you? What do you think he could do?

C: I don't know; it's already done. The balloon is covered and protected.

T: Maybe he can put some color on the cement. What does he think about that?

C: Paint it red!

T: Yes? Great, let him do that. Observe how he does it.

C: It's my favorite color!

This is a good example of working with co-consciousness and developing teamwork and cooperation (TW #10). By having this experience, it is more likely that the different parts can understand how useful it is to do things and experience things together. We close the session reinforcing the work done (CS #3.1) and checking how beneficial this type of work can be (CS #3.2).

T: Very well. Did he do it?

C: Yes.

T: And how is Little Guy now?

C: Calmer. He is still afraid, but his level of tension has decreased because he has seen that he is allowed access to things he could not access before. And now he has done something. He says, "I don't feel so useless or so afraid of the situation anymore."

T: Sure, because you are working as a team and you're all useful. I think it's very interesting. Tell him he did a great job.

C: Okay.

T: What do you think about this type of exercise?

C: I like it.

T: Do you think this is something that can be useful for you and them?

C: Yes, everything is settled inside now.

To close the session, we summarize the primary intervention of the session (CS #3.4) and prepare the client for any future difficulties with this new balloon part that, in many ways, is still a mystery (CS #3.5).

T: The work you all did is important because now, even if the balloon explodes, it is contained. So, whatever might be in there is contained and protected, and we will be able to look into it when the time is right.

C: I agree. (Client smiles.)

This example illustrates some of the situations we can encounter when working with dissociative disorders in different moments of the therapeutic process. Despite having knowledge of the system of parts, something new shows up. Even after exploring this balloon that showed up during the week (CS #2.1, #2.2) and how the client and parts are responding to it (CS #2.3), we do not know if this balloon part is a metaphor of a part of a personality or represents associated mental content: something that the client fears or is unable to observe. However, we proceed to address the issues that came up (CS #2.4) by treating it like a part, just in case it is. After working with the balloon, we check how the rest of the parts are doing after the intervention (CS #2.5) to make sure the client is stable before finishing the session (CS #3.3). We do not check if the client is grounded (CS #3.3) because it is undeniable that he is present and oriented.

EXAMPLE 15. THE CHILD PART

The work done with the balloon proved to be effective as the client had no setbacks and continued improving his daily functioning. The different parts were starting to act as a team and the Adult Self was modeling a completely new way of interacting with them. Self-care routines seemed to be established and the self-harming behaviors were not taking place anymore. In each session after the work done with the container, we checked in with the balloon; there were no changes, it was just there, contained. But after a few sessions, the balloon just disappeared or integrated; the client said the balloon deflated and the only thing left was the brown frame that was protecting it.

Several sessions later the client comes in speaking in a low tone of voice. He is not interacting as much as usual and keeps moving his hands in a repetitive motion, without even being aware of it. We use the movement as a point of entry to explore what might be happening within the system. As in every session, we begin exploring how the client left the previous session and the effects of the work done (following all the steps in CS #1). The transcript will focus on the piece where we work with issues that came up during the week and during the session (following steps in CS #2).

T: I notice that you keep moving your hands. Can we explore that?
C: (Client looks at his hands.) *They tingle today. They are nervous.*
T: How is that tingling?
C: Like fire, hot.
T: When did you start noticing the tingling?
C: Yesterday, when I was going for a walk and saw some workers in the street.
T: Were you aware of the tingling when it happened?
C: More or less. It was one of those moments when I felt the urge to hurt one of the workers.

T: So, something was triggered in you again.
C: Yes. And I managed to stop myself, but the tingling remained.

Once we identify the trigger (TW #3) related to one of the workers, we proceed by exploring the tingling to try to get some insight into what is taking place inside. Notice we do not interpret or explain that this worker is probably triggering traumatic memories. It is too soon for the client to realize that and he would likely get more triggered in the session.

T: How is the tingling?
C: My hands feel weird, as if the tips of my fingers were being squeezed.
T: I see.
C: I know nobody is squeezing them, but I feel the pressure.
T: Check inside and see where the pressure is coming from.
C: I don't know.
T: If your hands could talk, what would they say?
C: (Clients makes a hand gesture.) *They would grab a neck and strangle it.*
T: And how can you translate this into words? What's behind the feeling of grabbing a neck and strangling it?
C: I think it has to do with hurting myself.
T: Just ask inside. We don't want a quick answer. Just listen to your hands. If your hands could speak, what would they say?
C: They would slap me. It's as if they had a life of their own and were saying, "We need to grab something tightly."
T: I see.
C: I don't know whether they need to grab a neck or a cuddly toy instead, just to calm down or something. It feels as if I need to clench my fists.
T: Do you want me to get a cuddly toy and try it out?
C: Okay.
T: Here you go. (Client anxiously takes the cuddly toy from the therapist, holds it tight against his chest, and tenderly rests his head on it)
T: Does it feel right when you hold it? (Client starts sobbing like a little kid.) *It's okay* (Client rubs the cuddly toy against his face and cries even more.) *That's right. Hold on to it.* (Client continues crying while hugging the cuddly toy and caressing it.) *Is that better?*
C: Yes.

We give the client some time to calm down, reassuring him and helping him stay present so he does not lose dual attention. He is obviously in touch with a very young part, we can see it in his body posture, his way if speaking, and his tears. This is a very vulnerable moment, and we are concerned that perhaps some of the protector parts may have gotten upset due to the intervention that brought the child part forward. If we manage to keep the Adult Self present, we can use this opportunity as a self-care exercise where the adult part can regulate the child part while being present and oriented. As we pointed out in Chapter 3, we want to avoid interpreting what is happening, just in case we are wrong. Therefore, before continuing, we need to explore what is happening so we can adapt the work.

> *T: It's okay. What happened? Can you tell me?*
> *C: I don't know. I want out of here* (The client begins to desperately slap his head with one of his hands while he cries and holds the cuddly toy with the other hand.)
> *T:* (In a soft, calm tone.) *It's okay, hold the cuddly toy.* (Client holds the toy with both hands again.) *You know that you are here with me, right?* (Client nods.) *Are you okay here with me?* (Client nods.)

Notice how the client has made a very typical involuntary gesture due to the internal conflict; with one hand he is hitting his head while with the other one is holding the stuffed animal. By helping the client stay in contact using a calm tone, the system is able to calm down enough to continue exploring. We are simply checking that the client is oriented (CS #3.3) and maintaining contact with the client while addressing the issues that are coming up (CS #2.4). In the next section, we will validate the relevance of expressing feelings (TW #7) and explore if the Adult Self or any other parts are concerned about the young part expressing emotions.

> *T: It's okay to express your feelings, it's okay to cry here with me* (Client nods.) *Do you know that?*
> *C: Yes.*
> *T: Are you worried about that?*
> *C: No.*
> *T: Okay, good. Now, hold the cuddly toy and tell me what is happening right now.*
> *C: I don't want to continue living. I'm scared.*
> *T: You are scared.*
> *C: I am really scared. I am very, very scared.*

The client seems terrified, and his tone of voice sounds like a little child. Once again, we can identify conflict: one part of him does not want to continue living, another part is very afraid of this. These are probably two parts, the child part and the Adult Self, who is managing to stay present with the help of the therapist.

> *T: How old do you feel right now?*
> *C: Very young.*
> *T: How old would that be?*
> *C: Very young.*
> *T: More or less?*
> *C: I don't know.*
> *T: How old are you biographically?*
> *C: I don't know.*
> *T: How old are you currently?*
> *C: I am 40 years old.*
> *T: You are 40 years old. You know this, right?*
> *C: Yes, I do know that.*
> *T: And right now, you are feeling like a little child.*
> *C: Yes.* (With a more adult tone of voice.)

Once we are able to help the Adult Self to become more present, we can continue exploring the system (TW #1). We should find out if the child is comfortable, what is happening with him and what he needs (TW #7). When we find out his needs, we can have the Adult meet them if possible.

> T: *Is this child comfortable with me?*
> C: *Yes.*
> T: *Okay, good. What is happening with this child now?*
> C: *He feels lonely.*
> T: *Does he know that he has you?*
> C: *Yes, but I cannot take care of anybody.*
> T: *You are working on it.* (Client nods.) *You are doing your best to learn to take care of yourself* (Client nods, takes out a tissue and wipes his tears. He appears calmer.) *Do you know that?*
> C: *Yes.*
> T: *This part of you that feels so young, has been very brave to show himself.*
> C: *I don't know.*
> T: *What do you think. Is it okay?*
> C: *If he has to show up, then it's okay.*
> T: *And I appreciate it very much.* (Client nods.) *So, you know that this part is very young, but you don't know how young.*
> C: *No.*
> T: *Do you feel that this part can talk or not?*
> C: *Yes.*
> T: *Is he saying something?*
> C: (Nodding.) *He wants his mommy.*

The child part is stuck in trauma-time; he is not aware that Mommy is no longer alive. However, this is not a good moment to bring this information up. In the next section of the interview, we try to focus on the support the client can offer to the younger part through the Adult Self. The memory of his mommy, who was a good enough mother, can be used as a possible resource for the client and the young part (TW #7). If we manage to get this message across, the younger part will be able to feel support from the Adult and calm down; which is a great learning experience for a young part who feels lonely and is still stuck in trauma-time.

> T: *Does this part know that he has you?*
> C: *But I fail. Mommy never did. Mommy was always there, and she supported me, she gave me good advice.*
> T: *Do you remember your mommy?*
> C: *Yes.*
> T: *Do you remember her advice?*
> C: *Yes.*
> T: *Do you know you can learn from that advice?*
> C: *Yes.*
> T: *What advice would your mommy give you now?*

C: To be calm.

T: And if your mommy said that to you, what would you do?

C: I would be reassured.

T: What would happen if your mommy told this to the child to try to calm him down?

C: Yes, he would feel calmer.

T: Can you and I tell the child that he can be calmer? That we are here for him.

C: Yes.

T: May I do tapping on your knees?

C: Yes.

T: Alright, so both of us are going to tell this part of you that we are here for him, okay?

C: Yes. (The client coveys this message to the child part. BLS.)

T: What do you notice?

C: He is much calmer.

T: Ask him to notice that sensation.

C: Okay. (BLS)

T: What does he notice?

C: He is calmer.

T: Let's do a bit more. (Client nods.) Let him know that we are here for him. (BLS) What do you get now?

C: Nothing, he is fine.

T: He is? (Client nods.) How about you?

C: I am fine too. (Client seems much calmer.)

This is a good example of working with a young part through the Adult Self. With the help of the therapist, the Adult Self can learn to calm the younger part. The fact that the client has the opportunity to practice this during the session and achieve such positive results increases the chances of him being able to learn how to regulate himself and other parts outside of therapy.

EXAMPLE 16. TOO SOON TO WORK ON THE TRAUMA

As we approach traumatic contents that were not accessible before, the situation becomes more complicated. Five sessions after the previous example, the client comes in with a dilemma. He blames the part that has the memories, "The Guardian of Pandora's Box," for ruining his life and the part blames the client for not doing anything. This is a situation that we frequently encounter in these cases, after years of struggles and fights. Regarding the structure of the clinical session (CS), as usual, we begin exploring the effects of the work done in the previous session (CS #1) and the issues that came up during the week and the session (CS #2), since the conflict is still active.

Regarding the general structure of the therapeutic work (TW), in this section, we will go over some of the procedures described in Chapter 1. We begin offering some psychoeducation and introducing differentiation (TW #5), pointing out the function of the part (TW #6) anytime we have the chance, as well as exploring and validating needs (TW #7) and modeling alternative ways of responding to deal with the conflict (TW #8). Then we pay attention to helping the client understand how the assault has shaped his way of looking at himself and how the only way to feel some control was to develop a part that blamed him.

> T: *I think this part and you are, in a way, doing the same thing. You blame this part for ruining your*
> *life, and this part blames you for ruining your life. And, in fact, the responsibility is outside, it belongs*
> *to those men that hurt you.*
> C: *Yes, I understand that but...*
> T: *You understand.*
> C: *Yes.*
> T: *How old were you?*
> C: *Fifteen.*
> T: *Ok, and how old were these men?*
> C: *I don't know.*
> T: *Were they kids?*
> C: *No.*
> T: *Were they adults?*
> C: *Yes.*
> T: *What is it that you don't understand about this? Let's try to understand because you see your different*
> *selves as enemies and the enemy is here* (pointing at the drawing the therapist did to introduce
> differentiation.) *The real enemy is on the outside.*
> C: *The first thing I don't understand is the situation, the situation that resulted in... what happened.*
> (Client stutters.)
> T: *I know it's difficult to understand.*
> C: *I had never seen those men before.*

Later in the interview, the client becomes very emotional and begins talking about the fragments of the event that he does remember and starts fitting the pieces of the puzzle with the new scenes that he has been remembering.

> C: (Client very emotional, shaking.) *I don't know what my friends did or didn't do when they went*
> *to the bathroom. What I do know is that when I came out, those men pointed at me and said, "He is*
> *one of them." They took me outside through the backdoor... and...* (Client is visibly moved, crying
> and shaking.)
> T: *Look at me for a second. You don' t have to tell me if you don't want to do so or if you can't.*
> C: *Okay, let's drop it, please.*

We give the client space to calm down and the option of choosing what to disclose. Even though he says, "Let's drop it", it seems like he needs to take it off his chest because he continues describing what happened. After actively listening to the client talk about such a difficult moment, we can try to introduce the idea of this voice having an important function for the system (TW #6) and begin searching for different ways of helping now (TW #8).

C: *I don't know what happened, my friends left me alone, and I couldn't react. I wasn't able to react; it was as if I froze, and then there is the assault. But this in itself is the least painful part. The worst was the mortifying feeling of shame while going back to the hotel. It destroys you and it destroys your whole world, your hope. That's what mortifies me. It's as if my life had broken right there and then, when I was 15. That's when the voices began. That was the beginning of everything and when I started hurting myself.*

T: *Do you understand this voice's function?*

C: *No, I don't. I only know I've been dragging it for a long time.*

T: *I would like you to understand it. Can I try to explain?*

C: *Okay.*

T: *You are explaining a very instinctive reaction in human beings...* (Client starts looking around the room nervously.)

T: *Hold a pillow if you want.*

C: No. (The client gets up as if he was ready to run away from the office.)

T: *Is there something you can do to feel more comfortable?* (Therapist stays calm, with a reassuring and confident tone of voice, which is the best way to calm a flight part.)

C: (After a couple of minutes, the client sits down.) *Yes, erase what's in my head.*

After such an intense moment, and once the level of activation has been reduced, the client is present enough to continue, though he is also very triggered by the body sensations that he is noticing, related to the memories of the assault that are coming up in his mind. We introduce the Freckle technique as a way to help with this activation.

T: *Do you want us to focus on that sensation to try to relieve it?*

C: *Yes.*

T: *Is it okay? Can you do this?* (Client nods.) *Just focus on the sensation you are noticing now, nothing else, nothing from the past, just the sensation.* (BLS) *What do you notice?*

C: *It's as if I suddenly returned to the past, to that beach where... where I destroyed myself... where they destroyed me. I don't know if it was me or them.*

T: *Has the sensation increased or decreased?*

C: *It's less now. What helps me now is that I'm more able to manage my feelings. Even though I slumped and now I'm cold, I don't know why... I'm able to be more logical. So now I can say: "Okay, you were hurt, but there are many things ahead, so you don't have to keep hurting yourself."*

T: *I see.*

C: *I'm afraid because I know that at some point I'll have to remember and bring all this out.*

Remember that the goal of micro-processing procedures is to help just enough for the client to be able to continue moving forward. Once the client has calmed down enough, we check with him to figure out the best way to continue working. We also remind the client that we will do it gradually, in agreement with all the parts (TW #10) and nothing will be forced.

T: *I want to make sure that you understand something: You don't need to confront anything that you don't want to confront, okay?* (Client nods.) *But I have the sensation that all this stuff is already there, isn't it?*

C: *Yes, I don't know if we have cracked open a big bubble that was hiding the origins of all the problems.*

T: *Are you talking about this session or all the previous work?*

C: *All the previous work, gradually. When the moment comes, and this moment is now, the last barrier will have broken.*

T: *I see.*

C: *It was the last protection that I had. I don't know what I will do when I leave your office, because the only image that I have of that situation is just hammering away in my brain.*

This is another choice point. The client is at risk of self-harming or attempting suicide once he leaves the session. We can create a container, or we could process this intrusive piece of the traumatic experience. If the client and the rest of parts agree with doing trauma work, we could take this piece of the memory and process it. But before we do that, we need to check with the whole system and reach an agreement (TW #10). The next section is an example of when clients try to force the work without asking the rest of the parts for their opinion.

T: *Do you think it would be a good idea to work on this image, so it stops hammering you?*

C: *Let's see: we must work on it, we have to, because I should face it, I have to move forward, I can't continue living in an unreal world, hidden, resorting to anything that helps me avoid the final step to confront my past.*

T: *Well, if you can work with this image, then we may be able to do it. But we need to know if you feel safe enough here, with me, to work on it. And we also need to ask the rest of the parts.*

C: *You make me feel very calm, but this is overwhelming.*

Obviously, the therapist's calmness is very relevant, but it may not be enough in highly intense situations such as this one. Introducing more adaptive information through psychoeducation can be useful in this case, even if we have already explained this to the client before. Some parts may have not heard this information before or need to hear it again. Responsibility is adequately placed, and passive reactive defenses such as freezing are explained. After introducing psychoeducation, we explore the system of parts and identify what the client describes as "something inside" that is very agitated. This is another opportunity to use the Freckle technique.

T: *What is this "something inside" of you noticing?*

C: *Pain.*

T: *Does this "something inside" of you agree to focus on his pain, to try to relieve it? Can we try?*

C: *Let's try.*

T: *But does he agree? It's important.*

C: *No, but it's important for me.*

T: *Well, but it's important for me to try to do the best for both of you. Okay? If this part is feeling pain, I think it could be very useful to work on it. But his agreement is essential.*

C: *The question isn't whether he agrees or not, the question is that the work must be done.*

T: Okay, what I would like to know —because this part is there, and I know it can hear me— is whether you notices any resistance inside.

C: *There is resistance.*

T: There is resistance.

C: *Because he doesn't want to confront this.*

T: Can you let this part know that we are only going to do a little bit.

C: *Okay.*

T: That if it doesn't feel right, we'll stop.

C: *Good.*

T: We'll go little by little.

C: *Okay.*

T: It's this part okay with this?

C: (After checking inside.) *Yes.*

T: Ask this part to focus on the pain. (Client starts huffing and puffing.) *And we are just going to try. I'll make sure it's just a little bit. I will keep track of the number of seconds.*

C: *Okay.*

T: How many seconds would this part be willing to try?

The idea of keeping track of time and working for just a few seconds at a time is based on Jim Knipe's work with Constant Installation of Present Orientation and Safety (CIPOS). The difference is that we are not trying to install present orientation and safety; the goal is simply to desensitize one of the elements of the traumatic experience just as we explained in Chapter 1 when describing the Freckle Technique.

C: *Enough to feel a little relief.*

T: Enough to feel relief, okay. So, we have to find a way for this part to let me know when it's enough. I'm going to take my watch and measure the seconds. Let's start with 3 seconds.

C: *Okay, so what should I focus on?*

T: On the pain that this part is feeling.

C: *Okay.*

T: So, should we start with three seconds? (Client nods.) *Notice that.* (BLS) *Okay, 3 seconds...* (Client is breathing heavily.) *That's right, you did it. What does this part notice?*

C: *Fear.*

T: Does this part want to do three more seconds?

C: *Yes, let's go.*

T: Three seconds? How long?

C: *Let's do ten.*

Again, the client is trying to do more than he can possibly take. Not only is he breathing heavily, he is visibly shaking as well, so we try to help him move forward gradually and safely.

T: How about five?

C: Okay, five.

C: Let's go.

T: Okay, notice that. (BLS) *Okay, that's five.* (Client is breathing heavily.) *That's right; take a deep breath.* (Client takes a deep breath.) *Let's make sure you are here.*

C: Yes, I'm here.

T: Okay, it's okay. Now, look at me for a moment. (Client looks at the therapist.) *You are here with me.*

C: Yes.

T: You are in my office. (Client nods.) *And this part was able to focus on the pain, and you both were able to come back to the present. Does this part think it's a good idea to do a bit more?*

C: No, that's the limit.

T: It's great that this part can say "no." (Client seems to be moved.) *Isn't that good? What do you think about the fact that that this part can say "no?"*

C: Well, that there is some control.

The client has done very good work. The part was able to guide us with timing and to say no, which is almost a guarantee of increased control. The fact that a part that tends to resort to destructive behaviors as a way to stop things has started verbalizing "Stop, it is enough!" brings into the system an entirely new way of interacting. This is a new, positive experience, but since the body is shared, it turned out to be quite intense. Since there is still phobia of the part and of the traumatic memories, we have the chance to introduce the processing phobias procedure (TW #4) and continue working with the whole system.

T: Now we are going to work with you. We are going to work with your sensation, but only the sensation, nothing from the past.

C: Okay.

T: For how long?

C: Three seconds, like before.

T: Okay, focus on the sensation. (BLS) *What do you notice?*

C: Try with five seconds.

T: Are you sure?

C: Yes.

T: Okay, five it is. (BLS)

C: Try with ten.

T: Okay but remember you can stop before I stop if you need to. (Client nods. BLS)

C: That's good for today.

T: Alright, good. How are you doing now?

C: Better. (The client shows the therapist his hands because they have stopped shaking).

In the next section, we start to close the session reinforcing the work done in session (CS #3.1.); summarizing the main points on timing, safety, and not going too fast (CS #3.4); emphasizing the protective function of the part (TW #6); and pointing out the cooperation that was achieved in this session (TW #10). We also introduce the idea of eventually doing a full EMDR session when the system is ready. It is important that the client and any other parts that are hoping to work with their traumatic memories understand we are not trying to avoid doing trauma work, but just adapting the pace to the needs of the whole system.

> *T: Great work, all of you (Client smiles.) It's important to go slowly, step by step, unless you and the part think that you can take a full EMDR session. We can do an entire session to work with the trauma when everything inside agrees. Meanwhile, it's better to go step by step.*
> *C: Okay.*
> *T: What is most important now is that you feel safe.*
> *C: Yes, but I'm afraid of what can happen if the barrier breaks completely.*
> *T: The part said "no," the barrier is still there as protection, it's not broken.*
> *C: No, it's not. It's like a dam; it opens a little bit and some water comes out, but it's still there with the doors shut, protecting.*
> *T: That's it.*
> *C: But I'm not really sure who's protecting who.*
> *T: Okay, but there is protection. And do you realize that this part has played an important protective role for a long time?*
> *C: Yes.*
> *T: Do you notice anything different after what we've done today?*
> *C: I see it like something that's protecting something else. It protects my integrity. Like a dam, it prevents everything from being destroyed by a big wave. But sooner or later the dam must be emptied.*
> *T: Ok, so let's allow this part to guide us.*
> *C: Agreed.*

This can be a turning point in the therapeutic process, once the client can actually accept that this part is able to guide the work. Not just in his own benefit, also for the part's benefit since it is an acknowledgment of how important the function of the part is. If the part can cover an important role and is clear about how to function in a more adaptive way so the entire system can, cooperation and collaboration will become easier and more automatic.

> *T: The voice gets more complicated when we don't follow his indications.*
> *C: I know.*
> *T: Do you think that listening to it and stopping when he says so can make him feel safer?*
> *C: Yes.*
> *T: How do you feel now?*
> *C: Off-centered.*

The previous section illustrates the importance of checking how the client is doing before closing the session (CS #3.3). Although he seemed to be doing fine, he is not completely present, and we would not know had we not asked directly. We close the session making sure he is stable and oriented by doing a grounding exercise of ball-tossing.

T: Okay, let's see what we can do to make you a little bit more centered (Client nods.) Where do you feel you are now physically?

C:I am noticing the pain, like a burning feeling inside. I know I'm here in Santiago, far away, from that place, but there is a part of me that's still there.

T: Let's try to bring this part over here, the part that still feels as if he was there. (The therapist crumples a sheet of paper to make a ball.) *This is just a paper ball, I'll toss it to you, and you toss it back to me.* (Client and therapist toss the paper ball back and forth several times.)

T: That's it, good. (More paper ball tossing.) *That's right, very good.* (Tossing the paper ball again.) *T: How do you feel now?*

C: I feel more present, more here.

T: Do you still feel that the part is still there?

C: No.

T: Not at all?

C: No

T: Great.

This session was very important in the therapeutic work. The fact that the part could say no is a good prognostic factor. As mentioned, this means that the part, and hopefully the client, will be able to express his concerns directly, without needing to resort to self-harm, threats, or any of the behaviors that were previously used to express disagreement or concern. From this session on, we kept titrating trauma work and working with the system of parts in a structured, collaborative way.

EXAMPLE 17. AMBIVALENCE ABOUT TRAUMA WORK

We begin this session checking the results of the work done in the previous session (CS #1.1 and CS #1.2), then we explore how the voices did during the week (CS #2.1) to finally insist on respecting the pacing of all the parts.

T: How did you feel after the work we did in the last session?

C: Well, I was not in very good shape when I left, but I was fine.

T: I think you managed very well.

C: Yes, but the problem is not what happened here. The problem came later when I started to remember everything. It feels somewhat overwhelming because I have pushed it aside for too long. Experiencing something like that is much harder than it might seem when you read it in a newspaper or hear it in the news. You can feel sorry for the person and go on with what you were doing. In real life, it's different.

T: That's true, yes.

C: I keep getting fragments here and there. The images are very confusing and unclear. I am very confused.

T: And what do you think about that? Do you think this means we need to work with what is coming up?

C: I personally think that I have to face it. The sooner we deal with the bad stuff, the better.

T: And what do the rest of the parts think about that?

C: The other parts say, "Do not go there."

T: I see.

C: So, I am faced with a dilemma. Do we move forward or not?

This is a completely new way of bringing up the ambivalence about trauma work. We can check with the other parts and get their opinion without any struggles or fights. This is a healthier way of reflecting on the different treatment choices along the way. In the next section, we also check how the system responded after the session (CS #2.1) to explore if anything needs to be addressed now (CS #2.2).

T: How did your inner system respond after the session?

C: Well, like I was saying, confused. I had a thousand images on my head and a thousand possible ways in which I could have reacted and did not.

T: And how have the voices been this week?

C: The voices have been quiet; they didn't bother me much this week.

T: That's a very important indicator.

C: Yes, that is quite noticeable. In the sense that maybe the fact of having learned to handle the voices and to place them in the background, instead of them being the main part of my life, is helping. And above all, except when I left here, was when the "bad" part gave me... Oops, sorry, when the Original Voice was bothering me, telling me to do something bad.

The tendency to insult or refer to the voice in a negative way comes up automatically, but the client corrects himself without the therapist having to intervene.

T: What did he tell you?

C: All the way back home, he kept saying, "Throw yourself under the bus." The opposite of everything you had told me, to distract attention and do alternatives.

T: Well, but you did not. And did the voice calm down?

C: The voice calmed down because it had no choice. I don't know if he just got tired or if he doesn't have as much energy as before when he could be at it for hours and hours.

T: Or maybe, since he sees that you have more control, he calms down.

C: Maybe that's it, I don't know.

Although things are generally better, the client still needs help interpreting the reactions of the voices, which is to be expected after so many years of functioning in constant conflict. In the next section of this interview, we go over the relevance of respecting the pace and maintaining agreements (TW #10). The client is bringing up his desire to move forward –which of course implies working with the unresolved trauma at some point– because he feels better, more stable and in control. But this could be a complicated issue if any part feels that other parts are not respecting internal agreements.

T: But this is a key aspect, to work on things when everything inside is in agreement. We cannot force anything.

C: We must force it, because if it were for them, they would never want to work on it.

T: Sure, that's why I think it's good to wait for this part to feel like it's a good moment to go there.

C: And when will I know?

T: You can ask the voice.

C: I do not want to ask the voice because he's a pain in the ass. He does not provide a clear answer for me to know whether it wants to collaborate or not. He can't make up his mind.

T: Notice that before you know what this voice could say, you don't even want to listen to it. And this is not what we agreed to do.

C: Well, this voice is really difficult to manage.

T: Well, the other day, you did manage it. How did you do it?

C: The other day I managed it. Well, honestly, I don't know how I did it.

T: Try to think about it, because it's important. You handled it. And I think that this part wanted to collaborate because if he had wanted to give you a difficult time, he wouldn't have calmed down.

C: Yes, yes, but from here to my house there is a long way. And he was harassing me. As soon as I saw any little thing that meant a slight risk, he started all over again.

T: That means we need to wait for this part to let us know when it's a good time to work on it.

C: Okay.

T: Because this part has a very clear function. I think that what he did the other day was to try to divert your attention from the pain you were noticing. Once you calmed down, he also calmed down.

C: Yes. But there is also a part of me that wants to get this out and move on.

T: I know, but for us to go there, it is important that there be internal collaboration and a general agreement.

This session illustrates one of the difficulties we will find after working with an aggressive part that is beginning to respond in a more adaptive, collaborative way. Usually, clients feel more stable and in control, which motivates them to think about future options, including doing trauma work. We continue to insist on the need to respect agreements and timing. This is important, but often it is not enough, because other parts might experience this interest as betrayal.

EXAMPLE 18. GROUNDING TO LATER CREATE A STEEL GATE

In this session, the Original Voice, the 15-year-old part, decides to step away for a while and let the rest of the parts do the work. Although this is an improvement for the system, we must be sure to convey to the part that we respect his decision to stay away, but leaving open the possibility that he may change his mind at any time, to prevent him from feeling that we want to get rid of him. We finally reach consensus to move forward and meet the different needs. This session illustrates the relevance of helping the client to be sufficiently grounded and orientated in time. The client is used to certain grounding techniques that usually work, but in this session, for some reason, they are not working. We try different alternatives (TW #8) until we find one that works for the system's need in this particular moment. In this section, we begin when he is speaking about a moment when he got triggered while walking in the streets.

C: I sat down; I was shaking. I felt like I was in a different place. It was as if I was repeating what I did when I got to the hotel; as if I was repeating what happened twenty-three years ago.

T: I see.

C: I don't know. I'm in a period of regression or something like that.

T: What do you notice now? Are you here with me?

C: Yes, I am here, but it feels like I'm not; it feels like I'm there (referring to the place where the trauma occurred). I'm not focused. Instead of being here paying attention to you and the help I can receive, I'm there again, in the past.

T: Okay, let's try to work on you being present here, as much as possible.

C: Okay.

T: Try to describe the office. (The client looks around and describes the office, objects, colors.) See if you feel more present now.

C: No.

T: Do you notice anything different?

C: No, my body is here, and I can describe this place, but my head is going to the past.

T: Let's do something physical, something not compatible with what is happening to you now.

C: Okay.

T: I'm going to toss this paper ball. Just catch it and toss it back. (Client and therapist toss the paper ball back and forth).

T: What do you notice now?

C: I feel like I'm doing something physical, but mentally I'm not here.

T: What is interfering with you being here?

C: The memories of that experience.

T: What are you feeling now?

C: I am frightened. We are frightened. We don't want to remember any of that.

All parts are afraid of the memory (TW #4). We suggest processing the phobia part by part, but the Original Voice does not allow it. We continue exploring what is happening with the part (TW #1), while helping the client to feel more curiosity about what is happening (TW #2) and the possible function of this voice as it is presenting in this moment (TW #6).

C: The Original Voice doesn't allow it. He has taken up almost the entire space, and the other two parts are in a small corner.

T: Okay, we will go back to the other two parts in a little bit. Can you ask the Original Voice what's happening? (Client nods.) Is he answering?

C: Messages of destruction.

T: Ask this part something but ask him and give him time to answer, okay?

C: Okay.

T: Ask him about what we talked about the other day. If he thinks that cooperation is still a good idea? (Client checks inside.) What does he say?

C: I think he can't make up his mind. He says I'm touching something that shouldn't be touched, and he is not going to go away. He is threatening me.

T: Well, we don't want him to go away. We want him to participate, but only if he can and if he wants to. He doesn't have to do it; he can say no like other times.

C: He's not saying anything. He is no longer threatening me, but he doesn't know what to do either. It's as if he doesn't know how to be with us now.

T: Ask him if he wants or needs to be in a safe place.

C: It seems like he wants to put up a barrier and forget about everything.

T: Okay, let's allow him to place the barrier temporarily.

This is a very important message. We are letting him know that we agree *temporarily*, but we will not give up on him and we will not forget about him.

C: Okay.

T: What happens when I suggest that?

C: He seems to calm down a bit. But he still doesn't know what to do. How can I help him? I don't know either.

T: Let's allow him to place the barrier. He can imagine his own safe place. (Client nods.)

T: In your mind, allow him to place the barrier, a protective shield, whatever he needs to feel safe. Let's see what happens.

C: He wants to dominate fear.

T: Dominate fear. Is he feeling fear?

C: Yes.

T: Remind him that he doesn't have to do this. He can do it if he thinks it can help.

C: He wants to do it.

T: Ask him how he wants to place the barrier. Maybe he doesn't want to be totally disconnected. Give him time to think about it and figure out what he wants. (Client takes some time to check inside.) What does he say?

C: He has the idea of building a dam; a very tough and thick wall with a small floodgate, so he can release small amounts.

T: Perfect, that's great. Ask him to visualize that and to let us know when he does so we can reinforce it with tapping.

C: Now.

T: Okay. (BLS)

C: It's a stone wall. It has a steel gate with a knob and a remote-control unit.

T: Is that remote control going to allow us to open the gate when the moment comes?

C: Yes, it's connected to the steel gate.

T: Okay, so both of you notice that, let's visualize that gate. (Client nods and checks inside.) Visualize that gate, its color, its shape, the surroundings. Make sure it's a very safe place. (BLS) What do you notice now?

C: I see it with yellow and black diagonal stripes and it's locked.

T: Okay, visualize that. And notice how all the memories are behind it, ready to be released when the moment is right for all of you. (Client closes his eyes. BLS) What do you notice now?

C: Emptiness.

T: Do you see the gate?

C: Yes.

T: How is the voice now?

C: It's empty.

T: Is it behind the gate?

C: It's closed.

T: Is the voice behind the gate?

C: Yes.

T: So, the voice is there, and in every session, we will ask him if he wants to let out a little bit.

C: Okay.

T: What do you think?

C: Good

This was an important session that allowed the client and the other parts to be calm. No self-harm, no destructive behaviors and no efforts to try to force trauma work. Everything was going well until the client was reading a newspaper and got triggered by a description of a child that was abducted and raped by a group of men. He started getting more fragments of the assault and was very overwhelmed by them.

EXAMPLE 19. FLOODED BY MEMORIES AND WORKING WITH CORE TRAUMA

Three months later, for no apparent reason and coinciding with the anniversary of the assault, the client suddenly accessed everything that was in Pandora's Box. He comes in very nervous and extremely agitated. Given the situation, we should decide between creating a container for these memories or trying to work with them by processing the trauma. We offer different options to the client, so he and the system of parts can decide what is best.

C: It's killing me. (Client is very agitated.)

T: Look at me for a second, can you? Can you look at me?

C: Yes.

T: We have two options, okay? We can create another container for these memories.

C: But I have to deal with them. I can't be like this another 20 years.

T: You are right. The second option, if everything in you agrees, is to work on that.

C: It's a good time.

T: Who says that? You or your inside?

C: Me, everything else is chaos.

T: Okay, check if there is any resistance, please. This is very important. We've agreed to ask, and I have to make sure we comply. Remember our goal is not about forcing things. Take your time, ok? (The client takes a few minutes to check inside.). *What do you notice inside?*

C: I get that any help is welcome.

T: Okay, is everything inside in agreement then?

C: For what I'm able to decipher, yes.

Since there is agreement between the parts, we decide to work with the memory of the assault using Standard EMDR Protocol (Shapiro, 2001, 2018). For the first time in the therapeutic process, we gather all the elements of Phase 3. The worst part of the memory are some words, the softness with which they were saying them, *"Be calm, we won't hurt you, you are going to like it, we love you."* The negative cognition is "I am guilty," and the words he rather think about himself (positive cognition) are

"I'm innocent." The VOC or validity of the positive cognition is a 2, and the disturbance is the highest he can image, a 10 in the zero to ten Subjective Unit s of Disturbance Scale (SUDS). We are not transcribing the processing of this session because we believe the details are not needed. The only variation that we do when working with parts and voices is to check with the system to know if it is a good idea to continue or if someone prefers to stop. Here is an example of this, towards the end of the processing phase:

C: *It's like if it were some kind of protection. I mean, I protected myself by hurting myself, now my body reacted punching my back, but I don't understand it.*

T: *Check if this punch is an expression of something, or if it's a signal that it's best not to continue.* (Client checks inside.) *Let's try to understand. If it's an expression, we'll process it and keep moving along. If it means "I don't want to continue," we will stop.*

C: *It means that I don't want to go on; it's enough for today. The body can't take it anymore.*

T: *Okay. So, we can stop here.*

C: *Good.*

T: *How are you doing now?*

C: *Fine, it was not easy, but I am okay.*

T: *How are the other parts?*

C: *They are better too.* (Client shows his hands, which are not shaking).

T: *Do you need a grounding exercise?*

C: *No, I am here. I am fine.*

We close this session thanking all the parts for the work they did, making sure the client and all the system are grounded in the present moment (CS #3.3) and reminding the client that he can reach out for help and call us if needed. After this session, we continued working with his traumatic memories, occasionally going back to part work when needed. After a few months, the client started going back to school and functioning much better on a daily basis. To close this case, we are going to transcribe a short example of how the client refers to his parts later on, as integration was taking place.

EXAMPLE 20. THEY ARE MY VOICES; THEY ARE ME

Several sessions later, the client comes in looking very good. He is tan, has been enjoying the summer and has been able to do things that were unthinkable in the beginning of therapy. Among them was going to the beach, which used to one of the biggest triggers. The following section illustrates another moment in therapy related to the gradual integration described in Chapter 12.

T: *How are you doing?*

C: *I'm doing good.*

T: *How is everything inside?*

C: *Good. I went to the beach.*

T: *How did it go?*

C: *It was amazing. There was a moment when I got a bit confused, but then I understood what was happening.*

T: *Can you tell me about that?*

C: *I went in the water. It was so incredible; I had not dared to go to the beach for so many years. To feel the water on my skin, to notice the sun... it was great!*

T: *And when did you get confused?*

C: *Well, I went to an isolated part of the beach. It was lunchtime, so it was only me there.*

T: *Uh-huh.*

C: *But then I started hearing somebody laughing. And I thought, "What the heck?" I turned around and nobody was there. And then I heard the laughter again. Until I realized that it was just them, my kids, enjoying the water.*

T: *That's great!*

C: *Yes, that's why I said it was incredible. We were all enjoying the moment together, and it happened spontaneously, I didn't even plan for that to happen. The next day, I was thinking that I don't want them to go away; I would miss them. I know I'm not supposed to be hearing voices, but they are my voices, they are me.*

After this session we kept working towards the goal of integration. A few years later the client was not hearing voices, as they gradually integrated with him. The goal of this book, however, is to address the work with challenging parts, and in that part of therapy, the work with parts was not so challenging. The most difficult moments in therapy were realization about his lost adolescence and grieving when the parts became integrated. But grief is part of the process of integration, as we described in Chapter 12. The only thing left to say about this case is that it has been a great honor to accompany this young man in his healing process.

CHAPTER 15

ADIRA: THE DIFFERENT VOICES IN MY HEAD

Adira, a 25-year-old woman diagnosed with Borderline Personality Disorder, is sent to our clinical services due to severe self-harming behaviors and difficulties in leading a normal life. One of the main problems was the severe self-inflicted cuts, which put her life at risk, having needed surgery for some of them. The client also referred occasional anger outbursts in which she would do things that she later did not remember and felt completely foreign to her, being this one of the motives for remaining isolated for long periods of time. She referred to these episodes as "spells." At the time of the initial intake, the client was in treatment with 3 different mental health professionals and felt very unmotivated.

BRIEF CASE CONCEPTUALIZATION

History of symptoms and presenting problems

1. **General presenting problems and/or symptoms.** Besides the self-harming behaviors, such as cutting, the client suffers from severe social anxiety and phobia. She faints when emotionally triggered and stays home most of the time. She describes second- and third-person auditory hallucinations, which she associates with self-harm.

2. **Previous diagnosis.** PTSD, Adjustment Disorder, Anxiety Disorder, Depression, Social Phobia, and Borderline Personality Disorder.

3. **Attachment patterns.** Avoidant attachment with both parents.

4. **Relational problems**
   a. Family members. Both parents are elderly and need help from the client.
   b. Friends and peers. None who are significant at the beginning of therapy.
   c. Intimate relationships. Does not have a partner.
   d. Work and/or school. Problems when in a large group of people.

5. **Daily life functioning**
   a. Self-care habits. Initially, the client was self-harming daily, and her self-care habits were very deficient.
   b. Financial stability. In the beginning of therapy, dependent on others. Her parents support her financially. *(Later, she starts working.)*
   c. Social, occupational or school functioning. At the time of the initial intake, the client has many limitations in daily functioning. She spends most of her time isolated, can barely leave the house and she had to quit school because she was not able to attend.
   d. Overall level of functioning. At the time of intake, the general level of functioning of the client is very low. She also has many difficulties with basic tasks such as taking a bus or leaving the house.

6. **Initial onset of problems/symptoms.**
   a. What was happening then? The client explains that her childhood was mostly free of problems and that her difficulties began as a teenager when a group of peers started bullying her.
   b. What got triggered? She does not refer prior problems but suffers amnesia and this can interfere with the client being able to identify it.

7. **When did symptoms worsen?**
   a. What was happening then? The voices started when she was an adult, right after she found out that a friend from high school had died in an accident. She had suffered bullying during her teenage years, and this friend was one of the few people who protected her.
   b. What got triggered? She thinks that her friend's death unlocked all the memories from the bullying. After two years of therapy, her symptoms kept escalating. At intake, it is not possible to assess what got triggered.

8. **When do symptoms increase or worsen now?**
   a. Current triggers. She associates the worsening of symptoms to the voices but has no idea what triggers the voices. She says, "they like to hurt me."
   b. Degree of awareness of triggers. She is not aware of what might be triggering her. The client says it depends on the tone and messages of the voices she hears.

Resources

1. **Sources of adaptive information.**
   a. Good enough attachment figures in childhood and/or adult life. Despite the shortcomings, both mother and father have contributed to the client having some adaptive information.
   b. Moments of feeling safe and being protected. The client can give examples of moments of feeling safe and being protected by both parents.

   c. Moments of feeling cared for. She can also give examples of feeling cared for, especially by her mother as a young child.
   d. Other relevant positive figures/models. *[A schoolteacher and a close friend.]*

2. **Emotional regulation capacity.**
   a. Self-regulation capacity. Very limited in the beginning of therapy. She regulates through self-harm, self-destructive behaviors, and avoidance.
   b. Co-regulation capacity. The client is able to co-regulate with the help of the therapist.
   c. Tolerance for negative and positive emotions. No issues around positive affect. She does not get triggered when she feels good.

3. **Social support**
   a. Family members. Both parents and an aunt.
   b. Intimate partners. None.
   c. Friends. Two close friends.
   d. Work colleagues and peers. Not at the time of the initial intake.
   e. Other professionals. A teacher and a psychiatrist.
   f. Religious/spiritual resources. Not relevant for her.

4. **Other resources**
   a. Mentalization capacity. The client can mentalize when she is not emotionally triggered.
   b. Degree of realization. She has partial realization, especially around the effects of her experiences of bullying.
   c. Degree of integrative capacity. The client has good integrative capacity when she is not emotionally triggered.

5. **Timeline of best memories.** To avoid disclosing too much personal information we omit this part. The client is able to do a realistic timeline with positive memories, which in terms of EMDR implies having adaptive information.

Structural elements of the internal system

1. **Client's degree of awareness of parts.** The client is aware of having parts. She can understand that they are parts of her, but she says that the voices do not think they are part of her. She speaks about her voices from a third person perspective and experiences them as "not me" most of the time.

2. **Internal structure**
   a. Approximate number of parts. At the time of the initial intake, the client seemed to have mainly two dissociative parts, which she describes as a bad voice and a demanding, dark voice. But she also describes different voices that were no longer active: a voice of a woman with a German accent, the voices of four young guys, and the voices of an older man and a younger guy that hold conversations about her.

b. Client's description/representation of the internal system of parts. In the beginning, it was not clear. The reader will be able to learn more about the description and representation organization and distribution of the parts in the case transcripts.

c. Organization and distribution of those parts that the client can discuss. Not clear in the beginning either.

d. Any missing pieces in the description. *[The missing pieces are related to anger. She has difficulties with feeling anger and expressing it.]*

3. **Degree of differentiation about the self and others**

a. Can the client distinguish her own thoughts, emotions and needs from what has been imposed by others? Yes. However, she has difficulties accepting all of her emotions.

b. Is the client confusing any parts or voices with the real perpetrators? No, but she has difficulties understanding the hostile voices and what they tell her to do.

4. **Time orientation and current perception of safety**

a. Is the client confusing what happened in the past with what is happening in the present? The client is oriented in the present moment, except when she is in large groups of people. Though she can understand that everything is okay, her fears and insecurities in social situations affect her to the point of fainting.

b. Does the client know that the danger is over? The client knows that she is safe in the present, but states that she sometimes feels very insecure, as if she were in danger or something bad was going to happen. The client can understand the past is over, but the voices seem to be stuck in trauma-time.

c. Which parts are still stuck in trauma-time? All of the parts of the patient seem to be stuck in trauma time.

5. **Mentalizing capacities**

a. Can all parts mentalize? No. The apparently normal part can mentalize when the client is not emotionally triggered, but the emotional parts cannot.

b. Which parts have higher mentalizing abilities? The apparently normal part.

c. Which parts need help with mentalizing? All of them. The parts stuck in trauma-time do not have good mentalizing capacities.

6. **Adaptive information**

a. Which parts have adaptive information? The client has adaptive information, but the voices do not seem to have this type of information.

b. Which parts need help with adaptive information? All of them.

Relational aspects of the internal system

1. **Acceptance of parts.**

a. Despite the fear/conflict, does the client describe some parts with compassion, acceptance or appreciation? There is acceptance of the little girl part. There is no acceptance of the other voices or parts.

2. **Relationships among parts.**
   a. What feelings do the parts have towards each other? All parts are in conflict. Some parts talk between them and seem to agree in the nasty and hostile messages they give to the client. The client is terrified of all the voices, she would like them to go away, shut up, or disappear.
   b. Which are adaptive for the system in the present moment? The client does not think any of the parts are adaptive for the system.
   c. Which need to improve? All parts need help with the conflict.

3. **Degree of cooperation between parts of the system**
   a. Is the client aware of any parts attempting to help the system? There is no awareness and no cooperation with most of the parts. Except for the little girl, who helps her feel good because she feels compassion and acceptance towards this part.
   b. Can the client accept that there might be an attempt to help even though it may not be clear yet? She is able to listen to the therapist's explanations about the attempts to help and tries to accept this possibility, but with much difficulty.

4. **Parts that may have difficulties with therapy.**
   a. Is there ambivalence or rejection towards therapy? Yes, from the initial information, it seems as if the voices did not want her to improve. She does not know whether this is related to fear of change or to an interpretation of the client, who does not understand their function. She states that the voices do not like therapy or therapists.
   b. What are their concerns regarding therapy? The client does not indicate any relevant concerns, but the concerns of the voices cannot be explored initially due to the phobia.

5. **Co-consciousness between parts**
   a. If it exists, which parts are co-conscious? The little girl and the Adult can experience things together, such as enjoying spending time with her best friend.
   b. When does co-consciousness occur? Does it vary? Yes, she is only able in very specific situations in which there is no emotional triggering.
   c. How do other parts respond to this? The parts not show problems with the co-consciousness between adult and child.

Trauma-related phobias and other potential blocks

1. **Phobia of inner experience.** High.
   a. Can the client check inside? The client can check inside with help and support. She is very frightened, but she is able to do it in small pieces, as long as she can have some time to check inside.
   b. Can the client notice and tolerate sensations? The client is able to notice her body and tolerate body sensations unless they remind her of her traumas.
   c. Is the client afraid of her feelings, thoughts or sensations? The client is afraid of her thoughts when they are aggressive.

d. Is the client ashamed of her feelings, thoughts or sensations? The client is very frightened of her thoughts when they are aggressive.

2. **Phobia of parts.** Very high.
   a. Does the client show ambivalence about the parts or does she avoid talking about them? The client can understand the voices are parts of her, but she would like them to go away for good.
   b. Despite the fear, can the client try to explore parts and be curious? Yes, she can despite the fear, rejection, and confusion.
   c. Does any of the parts feel shame or is the patient ashamed of any of them? No information about shame in the beginning of therapy.

3. **Phobia of attachment and attachment loss.** Average.
   a. Is there ambivalence around trust in the therapeutic relationship? The client is able to trust the relationship, but her parts cannot.
   b. Do the client or any of the parts have difficulties trusting others, ambivalence between wanting to attach and pushing others away? Yes.

4. **Phobia of traumatic memories**. Very high.
   a. Does the client insist on avoiding any exploration about childhood? She does not oppose it overtly but avoids the topic any time it comes up.
   b. Does the client show ambivalence about trauma work or even talking about traumatic experiences? Yes. When the client tries to talk about what happened, she becomes overwhelmed. She even becomes overwhelmed when talking about present symptoms related to her history.

5. **Phobia of change and adaptive risk-taking.** Initially, it does not seem high.
   a. Is the client afraid of change? Yes
   b. Does the client present difficulties trying suggestions that would improve her quality of life? She has many difficulties, but they are related to her history of bullying: avoiding big groups of people, public transportation, situations where she can would be exposed, etc.

6. **Defenses.** Minimization, projection, rationalization, pleasing others, and avoidance.

7. **Any other identified potential blocks.** There is amnesia, there is a lot of missing information about her trauma history and minimizes attachment related issues.

EXAMPLE 1. INITIAL INTAKE: EXPLORING SELF-HARM AS AN ENTRY WAY INTO UNDERSTANDING THE SYSTEM

Since Adira is referred due to her self-harming behaviors, we begin exploring the symptom from the very beginning. This is how we find out she hears voices, and she explains that the voices are closely related to self-harm. Once we know that this behavior is related to one or more voices, we explore as much as we can about the voices (TW #1), to start gaining some perspective on the inner system. We want to try to understand what is happening in the system beyond the presenting symptom: the self-harming behaviors. Exploring what happens before the cutting will give us some insight into what may be triggering the client (TW #3).

T: *Would you be able to tell me what happens before the cuts?*
C: *There's a voice inside who is always telling me that everything is going wrong. "Everything is going wrong, you're worthless."*
T: *How long has the voice been there?*
C: *I'd say about two and a half years.*
T: *Was this the first time you heard voices?*
C: *No, I actually had two voices before. Now I have one that's been there longer. This is the voice that has stayed.*
T: *Can you tell me more about the voices?*
C: *I have two voices: a good one and a bad one. Well, I call them good and bad because one is always angry, arguing, and telling me horrible things. The other one seems to want to confront her but can't do it.*

It is important to ask when the voices appear for the first time (TW #1). This can give us relevant information about what was happening in the client's life at the time. Since in this case there is a series of voices showing up, it would be interesting to understand why each one of the changes took place and what was happening at the time. This is relevant information for therapy and for the client since they usually do not think much about these issues due to the phobias. In the event that they were to think about this, their interpretation usually becomes part of the conflict.

T: *Do you remember when the first voice appeared?*
C: *The first one was the voice of a German girl who just ordered me to cut myself. Back then, I knew things about Goethe and other German writers, which I have now forgotten. But my brain seemed to activate additional knowledge of German literature that I didn't even know about. And I thought it was crazy. Where was all this information coming from?*
T: *Is there someone from Germany in your family or social context?*
C: *No. I guess we must have studied German literature in school. I can't figure it out.*

We continue exploring the voice by using specific questions that guide our investigation of the voices (see Chapter 4). Our goal is to gather as much information as possible (TW #1).

T: *So, what did the voice of the German girl tell you?*
C: *She told me to cut myself.*
T: *How was the tone of this voice?*
C: *She had a German accent, and she was really nice and sweet, but she ordered me to cut myself.*
T: *Did you have internal conversations with her?*
C: *Yes, she talked to me.*
T: *How was it for you to have this sweet voice telling you all that stuff that wasn't so sweet?*
C: *It wasn't as horrible as the voice I have now. She didn't scream, she would reason with me.*

T: What kind of arguments did she give you?

C: The same ones she gives me now, but without screaming or anything like that. She would say that things would be better, that I would feel better. She was smarter and knew all about endorphins and how they generate a sense of relief.

When exploring this voice, the client states that she is no longer present, so we ask why the voice disappeared and what was happening in her life when the change occurred (TW #3).

T: So, why did this voice disappear?

C: One day, she just left and did not say goodbye or anything. She left and a four-voice chaos appeared. They were all guys and told me to do horrible things, so I could feel better.

T: What was going on at the time? Do you remember?

C: I think it was exam season, if I remember correctly.

We are also interested in understanding the usefulness, if any, of the message received from the voices and how they might be trying to help. Keep in mind that, initially, the client may not experience it as an attempt to help (TW #6).

T: Did you feel better?

C: No. I felt really bad.

T: Did you also have conversations with these voices?

C: No, they didn't let me participate. They simply told me to do something and I did it, but I felt terrible about myself.

T: How do you know there were four voices?

C: Because they were different, just as my voice and yours are different.

T: Did they all agree on what they were saying or not?

C: Yes.

T: Was it the same message but with different voices?

C: Yes.

It is interesting to explore whether the voices remind her of someone in her life, because this may help us assess issues regarding differentiation (TW #5) and better understand their function (TW #6). Hostile voices often imitate people that had power and control in certain situations and clients often repeat similar behaviors as a way to feel some control. As we identify these issues, we can begin introducing psychoeducation about how the voices learn to protect in ways that may be frightening (TW #6 and #7) but, now that they no longer are in the same situation, they can learn new ways of helping (TW #8). By doing so, we begin to introduce the idea of cooperation and the possibility of working once again as a true team (TW #10). If clients seem too triggered by our questions, we can help them to calm down by explaining that it is important to understand what is happening and proceed with great caution. In this case, the client seemed not to have any trouble talking about the four voices, so we decided to explore further.

T: Did those voices remind you of someone in your life?

C: No.

T: Before you told me that you suffered bullying, did I get that right? Did someone mess with you at school?

C: Yes, a gang of guys.
T: Do these voices have any similarity with the gang of guys?
C: (Thoughtful.) Yes, indeed. I never thought of that.

Although it is important to avoid interpretations, in the previous section, we are helping the client to connect the dots. She is talking about four voices that seem to bully her, which sounds very similar to what she had previously described regarding the guys from school. Once we help the client to understand the connection, we proceed by trying to understand the new voice she described before, the one that "stayed." Trying to understand the logic of the change (TW #3) is a good way to get insight into the system and how it came to be.

T: So later, these four voices also disappeared, did I get that right?
C: Yes.
T: And a new one appeared?
C: Yes.
T: What is this voice like now?
C: A young guy too, in his twenties or thirties, more or less.
T: How is this voice different from the others?
C: It's just one and it no longer orders me to do horrible things, but he treats me like shit.
T: Could you give me an example?
C: He's asking me to cut myself again. The other four male voices didn't. With the previous ones, I went seven months without cutting myself.

Usually, relevant changes are ways the system finds to deal with something that is not working. By further exploring the logic of the sequence of voice changes, the client can also begin to understand how her internal system evolves to try to help her (TW #6).

T: So, had the cutting escalated?
C: Yes, with the German girl it had already escalated. I had to get stitches and staples several times.
T: So, you started with small cuts, and you ended up with cuts that required staples.
C: Yes.
T: So then, the voice of this German girl disappears, these guys show up, and you don't cut yourself, but they encourage you to do horrible things, which was another type of self-destructive behavior for you.
C: Yes, exactly.
T: Do you know what was happening when they disappeared, and this other voice appeared?
C: No, I don't remember.

Helping the client understand the protective function of the voices is a crucial step (TW #6), but in order for the client to be able to see this, the phobia of the voices also needs to be explored (TW #4), as well as the possible strategies that the client has developed to deal with them (TW #7).

C: I really don't understand why this happens or why I have to have a voice.
T: Usually, the voices try to help in the way they know how, even though it may feel very negative. Did you know that? Have they explained this to you?

C: Not really. One of the psychiatrists said that perhaps it was a support mechanism, instead of true self-destruction. But they don't seem to be very supportive.

T: If they were trying to help, how would they try to do so?

C: (Crying and looking scared.) I don't think they're trying to help me.

T: Of course, this is not easy to understand, especially with voices that tell you to hurt yourself. And that's part of the usual conflict. One of the aspects that maintains conflict is not understanding very well what is going on. But this is what I am here for, to try to understand and help you understand. How does this sound?

C: I would like to understand.

One of the basic steps is to encourage clients to be more curious (TW #2). Once we activate curiosity, we may proceed by exploring other aspects, such as whether the client sees the voices as parts of her or not, how the client tries to deal with the voices, and whether there are phobias (TW #4).

T: Great. Do you see these voices as parts of you?

C: The voices believe they're not parts of me, but I think they are.

T: They don't believe they are, but you do. How is that?

C: I know they are parts of me because they are obviously in my brain.

T: What do you feel towards those voices?

C: I'm tired of them.

T: You're tired, you feel rejection. What do you usually try to do with the voices?

C: I try to make them shut up.

As we pointed out in Chapter 6, this is one of the most common responses we will find. Clients try to get the voices to shut up, to ignore them, or to eradicate them, which will only increase the conflict. This leads to an opportunity to point out how that this strategy is not really helping, that voices have a function we need to understand (TW #6) and allows us to explore possible alternative responses (TW #7).

T: Have you seen that it doesn't usually work too well? Have you noticed that doing this tends to escalate the problem?

C: Yes, but I can't help it.

T: Yes, I know, that is why we are exploring this. Let me explain something okay? (Client nods.) Even though you experience the content of your voices as negative because it makes you feel bad and you end up hurting yourself, they are generally trying to help, but sometimes they don't know how to do it differently. The only way they can find to try to make you feel better or less bad is by repeating the only thing they know how to do. Are you following me?

C: Yes.

T: Many times, they're just trying to communicate something important, but since you don't listen to them because you're scared, the voice has to scream louder, and that's how they finally get you to listen. So, somehow, you may be reinforcing the voice to scream more without realizing it. (Client becomes sad.) But I don't know that; I'm just telling you as a possibility because this is what happens many times when there are voices that end up causing self-harm. They really don't know how to do it any other way. Does this make any sense to you?

C: I don't know, if it's the only thing they learned, I guess it does. It's true that the only way they have achieved something has been by yelling. I've only paid attention to them when they yelled at me.

This is an interesting observation by the client, resulting from modeling or guiding reflective thinking. Realizing that she has not been listening to the voices (TW #2) and the voices have had to reach the point of screaming in order for her to pay attention to them. As always, it is important to check how the system receives this intervention (CS #2.5)

T: So, then it makes sense, right?
C: Of course, because I'm not listening (very low tone of voice.)
T: When I tell you this, what do you notice inside?
C: A bit of sadness, because I may be the one causing the cutting.
T: Well, cutting is the result of something and an attempt to manage something. You tell me that there is a lot of discomfort, great anxiety, and an attempt to feel better. Possibly this is the way you have found to try to calm down, for whatever reason.
C: Yes.

Had we not checked how the system responds to the intervention, we would have not discovered that the client felt guilty when we introduced this information. Identifying this feeling helps us address and repair any issues that may come up during the session (CS #2.4). We can then continue the interview and begin exploring the possible function (TW #6) by asking when do the voices show up (TW #3).

T: Have you noticed when does the voice tend to show up?
C: Usually when I'm feeling bad.
T: The voice doesn't show up when you feel calm?
C: No.
T: Just notice that if the voice doesn't show up when you're feeling well, it makes sense that it's somehow trying to help you because it only shows up when you're feeling bad.
C: Yes.
T: Of course, what would really help you is not saying things that made you feel worse when you're already feeling bad.
C: Of course, there is probably an attempt to help, but the voice is not doing it in the best way.

This is an important point that usually helps the client start to realize that the voices could have a protective function in the system. By asking what triggers the voices to appear, the client increases her awareness of their attempt to protect her (TW #6). Once the client understands this, we can begin closing the session. We have gathered a lot of information for a first interview and we do not want to do too much in a first contact. We close the session by summarizing what has been learned and setting goals for future sessions (CS #3.3). This type of intervention helps with realization and integration of the therapeutic process.

T: So, let me see if I have understood correctly. Initially, the voice of the girl with the nice German accent appears. She seemed to be trying to help you, though the self-harm ends up escalating. When self-harm escalates and you're hurting yourself more, it seems like this voice steps back and other voices show up. The other voices lead to a different behavior that harms you in a different way, though possibly they were trying to avoid you hurting yourself. (Client nods.) *You've told me you've suffered bullying. Generally, voices imitate people that are stronger, those who are in control or more powerful. For example, we saw how those four voices somehow fit with your experience.* (Client nods.) *And then, when the new destructive behavior was causing more problems* (suicidal ideation) *the four voices changed into the new voice you hear now. Is this correct?*

C: Yes.

T: *And we spoke about how difficult it can be to understand that these voices might actually be trying to help* (Client nods.) *When there's something inside of you that tries to protect or help, it usually doesn't come from a calm place. Voices don't usually appear because there is a state of well-being.*

C: No.

T: *We saw how these voices show up when you don't feel well* (Client nods.) *and this is how it usually goes: there's always a state of discomfort that results in an attempt to help. It's a matter of understanding these voices, so they and you, as a whole, can see what you can do differently.*

C: Okay.

T: *If you and I could work on that, do you think it would be helpful for you?*

C: *I don't know. I know that anxiety is what's creating most of my problems.*

T: *I think that trying to understand why anxiety appears could be an interesting goal. If we can understand what triggers the anxiety, we can learn to manage it better. If we understand what makes you feel worse, we can work both with that and with the voice, so it can help you in a more practical way. If it's trying to help, it may be able to learn other ways of trying to help you that don't frighten you.*

C: Yes.

Not only do we close with a reminder of what has been covered in the session, but we also introduce the idea of exploring new options for the system and setting some goals for therapy (CS #3.4). And last but not least, we ask the client if she would like to meet again and encourage her to let us know anything that might not fit, so she knows that she can express her needs and we will adapt.

T: *Would you like to meet another day to try and explore a little bit more about this issue?*

C: Yes.

T: *How are you doing now after everything we've talked about?*

C: Fine.

T: *If there's something that you don't like or that doesn't feel right at any time, it would be great if you'd let me know. If you tell me in the moment, great; if not, you can tell me another day. I would like for you to be as clear as possible with me, so we can avoid misunderstandings. And especially, we can avoid me doing things that others have done and have not felt right to you. Does this make sense?*

C: Yes (smiles.)

The interventions –done in such a way that conveys great respect for the client and models a new way of relating to others–have been mostly oriented towards exploring what has been triggering the voices (TW #3), understanding the protective function of the voices (TW #6), and becoming aware both of the inner phobias (TW #4) and of the fact that not listening to the voices results in more discomfort. We have also helped the client realize that these voices have been trying to help in different ways despite her experiencing it as very negative.

EXAMPLE 2. ALTERNATIVES TO SELF-HARM AND BETTER COMMUNICATION

We begin the next session following all of the steps from the first section (CS #1) of the general structure of a clinical session.

> *T: How did you leave the session the other day?*
> *C: I felt relieved.*
> *T: How about the voices?*
> *C: They were quiet, which is very odd.*
> *T: Odd how? Was it good or bad?*
> *C: Good. Normally, they would give me hell after the session.*
> *T: Great. So, remind these voices that they can also let us know when things do not fit for them.*
> *C: Okay.*

After exploring the effects of the work done in the previous session, we continue exploring and working with issues that came up during the week (CS #2.1). The client gives different examples of moments when the voices talked to her and how she responded to them (CS #2.2), which was mainly trying to ignore them and asking them to shut up and go away. She also states how she managed to avoid cutting for two weeks, except for one day, which is what we need to address as a starting point (CS #2.4). In this part of the session, we explore what happened (CS #2.2) and help the client focus on the positive aspects of those days and on the fact that the voices are trying to help but are still learning (CS #2.4).

> *T: Let's try to understand what happened that day.*
> *C: Nothing out of the ordinary, really. The voices had been telling me to cut myself for a few days. Perhaps I wasn't in fight mode that day, and I just let myself go.*
> *T: So, the voices had been telling you this for a few days.*
> *C: Yes.*
> *T: Why?*
> *C: I think partially because of the exams. I was feeling weaker. It's as if they have more power over me when I feel weak.*
> *T: The other day we talked about trying to understand the voices and why they told you these things. Have you thought about this?*
> *C: I thought about trying to understand the anxiety, and I realized that waiting for people —even if it's in a familiar place— makes me feel very anxious. The other day I was waiting for my sister at the physical therapist, and I had to wait for forty-five minutes. I can't deal with that, and the voices increase in those instances.*

This observation offers us a good opportunity to point out one of the main ideas of the work: helping the client to realize that the voices show up when they feel bad (TW #3) and how this means that they are actually trying to help, which she had a hard time believing in the first session (TW #4).

> *T: Do you realize that, once again, they increase when you feel bad? You feel bad, and the voices show up.*
> *C: Yes, when I feel bad.*
> *T: Yes, when you feel bad. Do you think this may confirm the hypothesis that they're somehow trying to help?*

C: Yes.

T: Let's try to understand. What were they saying?

C: They were just telling me that I could be doing other things instead of being there. I know they were not saying it in a bad way, but I feel bad because it's my sister.

T: The voices were thinking that you could be spending your time differently. That's their way of worrying about you. And the effect on you is that it makes you feel guilty because it's your sister. So, do the voices know that this is not helpful for you?

C: I don't think so, because I almost ended up crying.

By exploring more information about the voices (TW #1), we help the client understand the motivation behind the behavior which, in turn, helps her to be more open to communicating with the parts.

T: Do you have a way of telling the voices that you feel worse when they try to help you like this?

C: Yes, I talk to them.

T: If you try to tell them this, what happens with the voices? Do they understand it?

C: When I talk to them, they usually don't pay much attention to me.

T: Could you try to do it now?

C: Yes, I could try.

T: Go ahead, try to let them know.

C: (Takes a few minutes.) *I did, but they're not answering.*

T: Are the voices listening?

C: Yes.

T: And what do they think about it?

C: Right now, they're quiet.

T: They're quiet. That could mean that they don't object to what we just said.

Later in the session, while exploring what happened the day she cut herself, she mentions that right before doing it, she heard the voices of a younger guy and an older man talking to each other as if she were not there. When we ask the patient how she feels when she hears the voices, we are taking the opportunity to work with the whole system, to understand the dynamics of internal communication and to emphasize the importance of the voices coming to understand that these messages are no longer useful and that we need to find new ways to help (TT-7).

C: They were talking to each other.

T: What did they say to each other?

C: The young one was politely talking with the old man, saying, "You're right, she should cut herself and do as we say, but she's resistant and stubborn." Stuff like that. They were talking about me as if I wasn't there.

T: How was that for you?

C: Bad. I went to bed and covered myself with the blankets and tried not to listen, but it didn't work.

T: No, it didn't work, of course. Remember what I said the other day? That the more we ignore the voices, the louder they tend to get?

C: Yes.

T: *I understand how difficult it must be for you to hear these things. I think it's important to let them know that if they continue to repeat the messages that scare and disturb you, it's going to be harder for you to understand them. If they are trying to help when you're not feeling well, it's important that we to try to help them understand that their messages actually scare you, so you end up feeling worse.*

C: *It is important.*

T: *It is. What happens with the voices when I say that?*

C: (Silence, internal communication.) *Right now, they're quiet.*

T: *Does that mean that they are paying attention or that they don't have a problem with it? Or not necessarily? What do you think?*

C: *Not necessarily.*

T: *Not necessarily. Could you explain this a bit? Since we're starting to know each other, I still don't know how the voices work. Sometimes when the voices quiet down, it's because they're okay with what we're talking about, or because they don't know what to say.*

C: *I think they don't know what to say, yes.*

This can be a good moment to introduce the idea of learned messages and how voices tend to repeat over and over what they learned to say. Notice the voices mostly repeats negative comments or tells the client to self-harm. Remember that repetition was one of the special issues related to challenging voices explained in Chapter 5.

T: *If I understood correctly, these voices seem to be repeating the same comment over and over.*

C: *Yes.*

T: *So, that possibly means they don't have much of a repertoire when trying to convey their concerns.*

C: (Thoughtful.) *Yes, they don't have much of a repertoire.*

T: *I'm not saying this is bad. I'm just saying that it's something that can help us understand. It's like when someone has learned to do only one thing and repeats it over and over, hoping that it will help.* (Client nods.) *And it would make sense that these voices would tell you these things if they learned them from people that told you similar things before. Are you following me?*

C: *Yes.*

T: *Does it make sense to you?*

C: *Yes, because what they're really doing is mistreating me; in a different way, with words instead of actions, but they're really doing the same thing.*

Checking in regularly with the client to make sure that we are not going too fast for her and that we are respecting the pace of the parts is an important point to keep in mind. The message that the voices are trying to help should be reinforced on a regular basis as well.

T: *What do you feel when you tell me that?*

C: *Sadness.*

T: *Sadness. Do you notice something different in the voices?*

C: *No, I feel the same.*

T: *It is also very important to understand that, if they're repeating what they've learned, they are also capable of learning other things. Their attempt to help feels very negative, harmful, and abusive to you; but the reality is that when you hurt yourself, they stop.*

C: Yes, that's true.

T: Isn't that interesting? Just think of that: if a voice wanted you to hurt yourself, it wouldn't immediately stop when you did so. It seems that the voices don't like that too much either.

C: Well, after they're able to make me hurt myself, they don't applaud me, but they do congratulate me. Then they calm down for a while.

We can see that the client is just partially understanding what we are saying. One the one hand she understands this is true, but on the other hand, she interprets that the voices are congratulating her. We continue exploring what she says as a way of modeling healthy curiosity towards the functioning of the entire system.

T: That is really interesting. Why do they congratulate you? What changes after the cutting?

C: That I feel calmer.

T: Do they actually say "congratulations?"

C: No, they don't say that, but they calm down.

T: So maybe what they are really celebrating is that you're feeling better. This is very important because it can help us find other alternatives. (Client nods.) If you find another way of feeling better that does not involve harming yourself, the voices could also help you with that.

C: You think so?

T: Well, instead of giving you such negative messages about hurting yourself, even though it involves relief, they can help you do something that helps you feel calmer and that doesn't involve self-harm.

Once the client can start contemplating the idea that the parts are trying to help (TW #6), we continue to express healthy curiosity while exploring alternatives to cutting (TW #8).

T: Have you tried any alternatives to cutting?

C: Yes, exercising.

T: But that involves doing something physical, and it's not so easy when one is not feeling well.

C: No, it's not.

T: What other things have you tried that may work?

C: Almost all of them imply pain: pulling and releasing a rubber band on my wrist, sticking my hand in the freezer, etc. But my pain threshold is very high, and I don't feel it.

T: Has the rubber band strategy worked?

C: No.

T: I don't like these strategies because, in a way, it's doing more of the same. They don't work for everyone and should be considered a temporary resource, a substitute, to not harm the skin. (Client nods.) You've tried it, and what was the difference?

C: Nothing, I didn't feel anything, but I think this is due to my pain threshold. My cuts are very big.

T: So, the rubber band hasn't worked. What about the hand in the freezer?

C: No, even though my hand turned purple.

T: I haven't heard about the hand in the freezer before. I did hear about ice cubes, though. The idea would be to hold some ice cubes, covering them up with a cloth, so they don't stick to the skin. Sometimes the sensation from the ice cubes feels very similar to what you feel when cutting. Do you think that could work?

C: *Yes, I think so.*

T: *Okay, you can try it out. Obviously, the idea is to use this as an occasional strategy, knowing that our final goal is not for you to hurt yourself to make you feel better.*

If we find a strategy that may work (TW #7), and the client agrees, it will be important to check how the voice reacts to the proposal (CS #2.5).

T: *We should also try to involve the voice. Can you notice that voice inside now?*

C: *Yes.*

T: *What does the voice think about this?*

C: *The voice is not saying anything.*

T: *What does the voice think you need in those instances? Well, if she knows what to do, because maybe she doesn't.*

C: *She doesn't know what to do. She can only think about what we already know.*

T: *Do you realize how important this is? That's where the limitation lies: not being able to help in any other way because she only repeats what she knows. Can you think of something that may have helped you feel a bit less bad in any other situation?*

C: *When I was able to control myself a bit, I used to listen to very loud music on my headphones, because I couldn't hear the voices.*

T: *And how did that work?*

C: *Well, I did hear them, but they overlapped with the song, so it's hard to pay attention to two things at once.*

T: *What sometimes happens in those situations is that the voices scream louder. I don't know if this ever happened to you.*

C: *Yes, they screamed more, but they finally got tired.*

T: *They finally got tired. Let's try to understand this together. If I get too annoying just tell me straight away, okay?* (Client nods.) *So, by the time they got tired, did you already feel calm?*

C: *Well, the message remained, but at least they shut up.*

T: *That's why I am saying this. If you tried focusing more on your music, did the inner disturbance decrease?*

C: *A little bit.*

T: *You may feel that the voice is getting tired, but perhaps it coincides with you feeling a little calmer internally. This is very important to understand.*

It is important to help the client differentiate which resources are adaptive and which are not (TW #7). Many times, her behavior toward the voices may be counterproductive, and it's crucial to understand this. Listening to the voices, with respect and curiosity, is always encouraged (TW #2). This will promote communication and increase understanding for both client and parts.

T: *So, music can be a resource. But doing things to make the voice shut up is not ideal. Did you at least try to listen to the voice before it becomes quiet?*

C: *I don't think so.*

T: It would be interesting to find out if she says other things before it tells you to hurt yourself. Do you think you could try to do this?

C: I guess, but the other stuff she usually says is not good either: that I am useless, that I'm better off just lying in bed. When I'm in bed, they're quiet.

T: And how do you feel when you're lying in bed?

C: Fine, I feel better.

T: You feel better. So, we know being in bed might help sometimes.

C: Yes.

T: Let's try to understand the other things the voice says. Why do you think the voice says that you're useless?

C: I don't know.

T: Can you ask the voice?

C: (Client checks inside.) No answer.

T: Does it sound like a familiar message that you may have been told in the past?

C: Probably. I was told so many things at school...

T: How do you react when you're told that you're useless?

C: I disconnect.

T: It hurts, right? And how do you respond to what they're saying?

C: I usually feel like crying.

T: And when you feel like crying, do you end up doing so?

C: Usually, I do.

T: When you cry, what do you feel aside from sadness? Do you feel any relief when you cry or not?

C: No, just emptiness.

T: That is important, the voice also needs to know that when she says these things about you being useless, you end up feeling a lot worse.

C: I feel empty inside.

T: And how is that emptiness? Just so I can understand.

C: I usually believe that I am useless and it's as if my life made no sense.

T: Then you would be in a riskier situation, right? Because hopelessness is closely related to feeling that there's no way out. It's important for the voice to understand this too. As we talk about it, can she hear it?

C: She keeps on saying that I'm useless.

T: Can you ask her why she is saying that to you?

C: She is saying it's because of what happened today. I met a guy last week.

She explains that she was with a guy who told her that he did not want to go out with her anymore, and the voice started saying negative things. As she talks about it, the voice starts to laugh. Sometimes, it is not easy to see how the behaviors shown by the voices could be helpful, so we have to insist on this point. Understanding this will greatly decrease inner conflict.

C: The voice is laughing at me. I can hear it laughing.

T: What do you think that means?

C: That the voice has fun when I feel bad.

T: Could there be any other possibility?

C: I can't think of it.

T: It's very important to understand this. Can you ask the voice?

C: There is no answer. She's mocking me or something.

T: Well, for now, we don't know why the voice is responding like this. Perhaps she doesn't know how to do it differently. The crucial part of this is how you respond to what you hear. If you hear a mocking voice and you feel terrible because you think it's laughing at you and that's what you deserve, everything becomes more complicated and scarier.

C: Yes.

T: You need to learn to do it differently as well, and you cannot learn that from one day to the next. But as you and I start to understand better, you can also learn to respond in a way that's not as scary for you. Does that make sense?

C: Yes.

T: Is the voice still laughing now?

C: No, it's calm.

It is interesting how the voice calms down as we try to understand the rationale of the laughter. Instead of becoming defensive or critical, we help the client to remain curious (TW #2) and also encourage different ways of responding (TW #8). Once the conflict is reduced, we can explore what could the voice say that would help the client in the present (TW #8). Interesting thing to keep in mind is that the client laughs when she is nervous and there is the possibility that the voice is also doing the same, since it is a part of her.

T: What could this voice say that would be helpful for you? Since the voice doesn't know very well, let's think about what would help you.

C: I wish she didn't abuse me so much. I would feel better if she didn't tell me I'm useless. Sometimes, I would like to hear good things as well.

T: What kind of messages would be useful for you?

C: That I did something right, for example. She could help me increase my self-esteem.

T: That would be ideal and I think the voice can learn, though she may not know how to do it yet.

C: Of course.

T: Of course, and notice that what you're asking for is not easy because, how do you increase someone's self-esteem? It's complicated when somebody feels bad, right? (Client nods.)

It is important to try to be very specific about the type of messages that may be helpful for the client. The more specific, the easier it will be for the voice to start practicing a new way of communicating (TW #8).

T: What helps you increase your self-esteem? What types of messages help you to feel a bit better?

C: I don't know. Right now, probably nothing.

T: Think about someone you appreciate. Do you have a friend that is important for you?

C: Yes.

T: If she feels bad, like you feel now, what would you say to her?

C: That everything's going to be all right and that I'm here if she needs me.

T: And if the voice told you something like that, how would that make you feel?

C: Better.

T: "I'm here, everything's going to be fine."

C: Yes.

T: We're just exploring how to do things differently, or at least trying to avoid criticism. And since she doesn't know how to do it differently yet, I can commit to check in with her every time I see you. I will check with her to see what concerns her, so you and I can take a look at it together. What does the voice think about that?

C: She thinks it's okay, but she says it's going to be hard.

T: Of course, it's going to be very hard. It's about changing a way of responding that is more familiar. She is very used to being critical and it won't be easy, but she can learn the new ways.

The system of parts was initially designed to work as a team with one common goal: surviving in an adverse environment. Introducing the idea of teamwork becomes a crucial aspect of our work. We help the client realize that by going back to functioning as a team, it will be easier to search for adaptive alternatives to self-harm (TW #6). By having shared goals and starting to feel they can learn to work as a team, communication, cooperation, and negotiation are encouraged (TW #10).

T: This is a team. Let's see what can work a little bit better. Does it make sense? : Yes.

T: Could you try with the ice cubes instead of sticking the hand in the freezer?

C: Yes.

T: Let's see if that works for you. What else could we try? Music?

C: Yes.

T: Have you ever tried exercising, even if it's just jumping up and down in your room or maybe going to the pool and swimming?

C: Yes, one day. I was tidying up my room, and I started jumping and things like that.

T: So how was that?

C: It was fun.

T: That's what it's about: learning to change a bad state that can only get worse into something that makes you feel a little better.

One of the main problems after this type of intervention is that clients still do not know how to relate differently to the attitude of the voices. So, when closing the session, we anticipate potential obstacles, which is a way to prepare clients for future difficulties (CS #3.5).

T: Remember that the voice doesn't know how to do it yet, and all of this is about learning. It's like when you start riding a bike, everything we learn takes a series of steps. In the beginning, you must pay attention and later everything becomes automatic.

C: Yes.

T: This is similar. If the voice says something negative, how you respond is going to be crucial. Instead of becoming overwhelmed by it, just keep in mind that she still doesn't know how to do things differently. The most important thing is to understand her and any other voice, to see what is changing, and to notice how they're trying to help you.

EXAMPLE 3. VOICES ARE QUIETER AND ALTERNATIVES ARE WORKING

In the next session, the client comes in looking better and calmer. When we explore how she left the session (CS #1.1) and whether any parts were triggered (CS #2.1), she says she was calm and there was no noise in her head after the session. When checking how the week has been for the entire system (CS #1.2) she says she had a sad week. Adira explains that the voices have been quieter, although she still had difficulties understanding that this is related to the change in attitude that is taking place between her and her voices. We begin this section trying to help her see that this change might be related to the work she has been doing. Then we continue the interview exploring if she followed the indications offered in the previous session (CS #1.3) regarding self-harm.

> *T: So, what do you think about these changes in the voices?*
> *C: They must see I'm in such bad shape that they don't want to kick me when I'm down.*
> *T: But this is great, that means that somehow, they are getting what we are saying and trying to help out in a different way.*
> *C: I guess.*
> *T: Did you try any of the alternatives we discussed?*
> *C: Yes, I tried the ice cubes.*
> *T: And how was it?*
> *C: It works for now.*
> *T: Better than the other techniques?*
> *C: Yes.*
> *T: Okay, so you can use it for now if needed until we find other options. As you feel better and fewer things trigger you, you won't have to resort to that, but it's great if it helps you avoid hurting your skin in the meanwhile.*

After checking if the new alternative worked, we go back to exploring the voices, in this case why they were less active during the week (CS #2.1) with the idea of helping her become aware of the relationship between the changes in the voices and the work we are doing.

> *T: So, regarding the voices, this week you tell me they weren't there.*
> *C: They've been around very little because I've been in bed half of the time. In bed they are calm; they don't feel danger.*
> *T: Do you realize that you have a more understanding view of the voice? Do you realize what you just told me?*
> *C: Yes.*
> *T: They don't feel danger, so they're calmer. And before you were saying that, because the voices see that you are in bad shape, they don't want to do more damage. That's something they didn't do before.*
> *C: Uh-huh.*
> *T: They seem to understand that they were not helping you before.*
> *C: Yes. I'm still in my own bubble and aware of everything that might happen, just in case something bad happens*
> *T: What do you think could happen?*

C: I'm always thinking about every bad thing that could happen.

T: You or one of the voices?

C: Me.

T: And what kind of bad things do you think could happen?

C: They are general, just about anything.

T: And how does that help you?

C: It lets me know they may happen.

Although this might be a way of preventing possible problems, to be continuously on the alert will not allow the client to have a good quality of life. We point this out to the client and try to understand what needs to be addressed (CS #2.4).

T: If I understood correctly, this helps you to be aware of potential threats, but it doesn't allow you to feel calmer or at peace.

C: No, it doesn't help with that.

T: It prevents you from trying new things. It's like a huge alarm that is helping to protect you but, at the same time, you are exhausted.

C: Exactly.

T: And is this related to any part of you, to any of the voices?

C: I wouldn't know. Maybe it is and I don't know.

T: It would be interesting to understand that.

We reformulate the state of alertness as a protection mechanism, as a means to lower the potential defense in any of the parts involved. This intervention is related to exploring the function of the parts (TW #6).

T: When did this protection start?

C: A while back, but sometimes it gets triggered a lot more.

T: Can you identify when?

C: No, it's like a mechanism that triggers something in me.

T: Something automatic?

C: Yes.

T: I have the feeling that it's all so confusing inside, that it's hard for you to think. You're so afraid of what can happen that you try not to think. But if we understand what is related to the peaks of anxiety, we can start to do something about it.

C: Yes. Okay.

T: This week you spent more time in bed, but you didn't have those peaks of anxiety that you mentioned the other day.

C: The day I needed the ice cube, yes.

T: I see.

C: And the next day I also needed one, but I said, "No, no, no, otherwise I'll become addicted to ice cubes."

T: And how did you handle it?

C: I cried and had a hard time, but I got over it.

T: *Of course, it's a nuisance because you suffer and have a hard time, but at the same time you're not running away from the emotions all the time.*

C: *Yeah.*

T: *So that seems like a tremendous breakthrough. And the voices didn't say anything negative.*

C: *No, because they already understood that I was having a hard enough time.*

T: *That's an interesting change, isn't it?*

C: *Humm...*

T: *So, it seems that the voices can understand that when they take a step back, they don't make it worse. Ideally, they would offer a message of support too, but maybe it's too soon for that. What do you think?*

C: *Yes, that would be great.*

It is interesting to observe that simply validating the function of the voices (TW #6) and their stepping back as a resource that does not make things worse is actually helping (TW #7). Then we suggest the idea of how it would be even better if they could give some positive message, just as the client suggested in the previous session, while we acknowledge it might be too soon to do so. This is a way to offer suggestions (TW #8) that can serve both as a reminder of what the client would like and as planting a seed for future collaboration (TW #10). In the next section of the interview, we explore how the voices are doing in the present moment (CS #2.1), which is also a way to explore how the voices are responding to the interventions (CS #2.5).

T: *How do you notice the voices now? Are they still silent?*

C: *They are calm; they haven't been this calm for a while.*

T. *So, overall, this week has been better.*

C: *Yes.*

T: *But you're sadder.*

C: *Yes, and the anxiety is.... phew...*

T: *Do you think it could be related to the fact that you are connecting a little more with what you feel? That you are allowing yourself to do so?*

C: *It could be.*

T: *Because if we think about it, what week has been worse for you: this one or the previous one?*

C: *The previous one.*

T: *The previous one, right?*

P. *Yes.*

T: *Little by little you are resorting to alternatives, you're not hurting yourself, the voices are beginning to understand that criticism doesn't help. I think these are quite a few steps.*

C: *Yes.*

T: *Do you see it too?*

C: *Yes.*

T: *And when I say this, do you notice anything becoming agitated in you as if it were saying "no?"*

C: *No, I don't.*

T: *No? Sometimes it can be scary to think about improving. You want to improve, but at the same time it's scary. Does that ever happen to you?*

C: *Yes, sometimes. To stop being "the sick one."*

T: Can you tell me about that?

C: I don't know, everyone treats you as if you were different. Sometimes you end up getting used to it... I don't know.

T: I understand. You get used to it and it's not easy to change the dynamic.

C: Yes.

T: I think it would be great if you didn't see yourself as a sick person and tried to see yourself as "you".

C: Yes, but it's not easy.

T: I know, it's not. But learning is possible.

Introducing information about the phobia of change and how difficult this can be is a way to validate many of the fears clients may have. Interestingly, right after exploring the possible phobia of improvement in the client (TW #4), the voices appear in the session.

T: How do you feel about the voices now?

C: Now?

T: Yes, now. How do you feel towards them?

C: I don't know, but they are talking to me.

T: And what are they saying?

C: Not to tell you.

T: Why?

C: I don't know.

There are many different interventions we could choose, but in general, a good way to proceed is to respect that the voices do not want to share what they are saying. This does not mean we cannot be curious about this or try to help the client to understand what is happening, which is also a way of addressing issues as they appear in session (CS #2.4).

T: Well, if they're talking to you, that means they have something important to say.

C: Yes.

T: But they don't want to share it with me.

C: With me neither.

T: With you neither. They have not told you then.

C: Let's see if they say anything... (The client takes some time to listen.)

T: What's happening?

C: They're talking to me.

T: They're talking to you. Can you understand what they say?

C: Yes.

T: Oh, okay. Are they just saying, "Don't tell?"

C: Yes. "Don't tell her; it's our secret."

T: Well, they don't have to tell me any secrets they don't want to tell me for now. Things move along at their own pace. Remember the idea is not to force anything. (Client nods.) *Are they concerned about something I said?*

C: No.

T: Are they concerned that we're moving too fast?

C: A little.

T: A little. It's great that you can tell me and that the voices can communicate with us. This way, we can better adjust the pace.

C: Wait. (Internal communication.)

T: What's happening inside?

C: The usual. (Client gets very emotional and begins to cry.) *When I start talking about these things, they show up, and I get anxious.*

This is an opportunity to use a difficulty that arises in therapy (CS #2.4) as a way to gather more information about the internal dynamics of the system. Another relevant aspect here is to remain calm and curious; the best way for clients to learn not to be overwhelmed by what happens inside is through modeling new ways of responding (TW #8).

T: Let's try to use what is happening to try to understand.

C: Okay (wiping her tears).

T: I don't know, maybe I screwed up asking something I shouldn't have asked.

C: No, no.

T: For whatever reason, the voices appear and say, "Don't tell anything; it's our secret." Okay, perfect, I respect it. Do you understand that?

C: Yes.

T: We don't have to talk about anything they don't want to talk about.

C: Okay. (Client is calming down).

T: What happens inside when the voices say that?

C: I get scared.

T: You get scared. So, do you see that the main conflict is your fear of the voices?

C: Yes.

T: And, usually, this is one of the main problems in the beginning. When the parts of oneself, the voices, try to communicate, it becomes very scary because sometimes they're still don't know how to do it. But that's why I am here. (Clients nods and feels much calmer.)

T: I don't want you to feel that we have to talk about things that disturb you, not at all. It's not necessary.

In the previous section, we explored how the system, in this case the client, responds to the voices (CS #2.3) as well as the related dissociative phobia (TW #4). At this point, it would be interesting to check how the voices are responding to the intervention (CS #2.5), so we can understand whether we are on the right track or perhaps other issues need to be addressed.

T: How are the voices now?

C: There's expectation.

T: What are they waiting for?

C: To see what you're going to say.

T: To see what I'm going to say (both laugh). *About what?*

C: About whatever.

T: About whatever. Well, then the voices are listening.

C: Yes.

T: Do they understood that they scare you?

C: Yes, but they don't care; they have been doing it for too long.

T: Is that what the voices are saying or what you're interpreting?

C: Both.

T: Can you tell me what they're saying? Are they literally saying, "We don't care?"

C: They are saying... (Internal communication), "We don't do it to scare her."

T: Good. They don't do it to scare you. And that's what I think too. Do you realize? (Client nods.) They don't do it to scare you, but they do scare you.

C: Yes.

The voices are communicating an important message: they don't want to scare her. We validate the client's feelings (TW #7) and begin exploring alternatives (TW #8).

T: So, we have to help them communicate in a way that doesn't scare you so much (Client nods.) And it seems that they want to learn, that's the feeling I'm getting.

C: Yes. (Client has a sudden expression of guilt.)

T: What do you notice when I say that?

C: I feel bad.

T: Yes, that's what I was thinking, because suddenly you seemed upset, but I wanted to check with you. And you know, when I try to explore the issue of the voices, sometimes I get the feeling that you feel guilty.

C: Maybe.

T: Why is that? Can we explore it a bit? (Client nods.)

C: In a way, I think I could've done something sooner.

T: Oh, I see, it has to do with that then.

C: Yes. (Client begins to sob.) When I started with the voices and the cuts, I could've told someone and now I wouldn't be like this.

This is a common response in clients after many years of functioning in conflict. Once they begin to realize that voices have been trying to help since the beginning, they start to wonder what would have happened if they had understood this and responded differently before. To validate these feelings is very important (TW #7), but we should also help them realize that, for different reasons, they could not do it before. We want them to be able to value how they are managing in the present and to focus on what they can do from now on.

T: But for whatever reason, you couldn't. Do you understand that?

C: I do, but I can't help thinking about how it would have been.

T: It makes a lot of sense and it happens often. When people realize that things can work much better just by changing a few things, they can't help but wonder "what if," but right now, this will not help much.

C: Uh-huh.

T: Beating yourself up with how you should've done things will only make you feel worse. (Client nods.) What is important is that you are here now trying to find ways of improving. And it seems that you feel comfortable here with me.

C: Yes.

T: I feel comfortable with you too. (Client smiles.) *The voices are trying to listen. I'm trying to understand the voices, and you're doing it along with me, despite the fear.*

C: Yes, I am. (Client wipes off her tears and smiles a bit.)

It is interesting to notice how the client calms down when we introduce the teamwork approach (TW #10).

T: So, let's focus on using your mental energy in the best possible way. Now you have very little energy because of the existing inner conflict. The energy is there, but it is used up. All the mental energy you have for doing things right now is being spent on dealing with the conflict.

C: Yes, I notice that too.

T: As we deal with the conflict together, you'll be able to make better use of your mental energy.

C: Okay.

T: It's important that you understand what I mean by mental energy; it's related to what you said in the beginning of the session about feeling weaker. The energy you have available right now is limited because it's spent managing other things. So, if you use it to blame yourself for things from the past, it won't be very helpful right now. (Client nods.) *The idea is that you can use your available energy with me to understand things better. That's more in line with "What can I do from now on?" Do you understand?*

C: Yes. (Client seems much calmer.)

T: I think I understand what you're saying. At times, you might think, "Why didn't I know about this before?" Well, the fact is that you didn't know. So, wondering about it will not help us. What's going to help is thinking about what we can do together—taking the voices into consideration—so that you and everything in you feel better.

C: Yes.

T: So, spend the energy you have on trying to understand yourself and your voices better. And above all, give yourself more messages along the lines of "Well, now I'm doing what I can." You couldn't before, for whatever reason. Do you understand that?

C: Yes. (Client has a firm tone of voice.)

We close the session thanking the client and the voices for the work (CS #3.1) and reinforcing the key message about not knowing how to communicate better before (CS #3.4). In this particular instance, we do not need to check whether the intervention was useful (CS #3.2) or the client is grounded (CS #3.3) because the body language is very clear. She is leaving feeling much more secure and motivated.

EXAMPLE 4. THE VOICES MAKE NOISE TO BOTHER ME

This week has been better in general, but the client comes in saying that she hears a constant noise. As we explore, the first interpretation she offers is similar to what she used to think before. This is a good example of how not only the voices, but also the client, need time to assimilate changes. The tendency is to go back to judging or thinking in negative terms.

In the next segment, we will explore the noise (TW #1) to try to understand the logic of this change, encourage curiosity in the client (TW #2) and explore possible triggers (TW #3).

T: Can you tell me about the noise in your head?

C: It's the voice that, instead of talking, is just making noise, because it knows that it bothers me.

T: Why would it be making noise to bother you?

C: I don't know.

T: When did the noise start?

C: I don't remember exactly.

T: It's interesting to try to notice these things because they can help us understand.

C: Okay, but I didn't pay attention to what was happening.

T: What kind of noise is it? Can you describe the noise a bit?

C: It's not noise. I call it noise, but it's more like a whisper.

T: Uh-huh.

C: I don't understand what they say, but they're whispering.

T: I see. So, it's not really a noise, it's a whisper.

C: Yes.

T: And could this be related to trying not to give you negative messages?

C: Well... (Client seems thoughtful.)

T: Just asking... I don't know...

C: I don't know.

T: Do you hear the whispers now?

C: Not now.

T: Not now. So, when do the whispers appear?

C: Mostly at night.

T: Every night?

C: No, just when I feel angry. I don't sleep very well.

In the following section of the interview, we explore the system using action figures (TW #1). We could continue exploring as we have up until now, but sometimes introducing externalizing techniques can help clients to disclose information that they normally avoid acknowledging due to the phobias.

T: Have you ever tried to make an outline of your inner world using action figures?

C: No.

T: Since you haven't done it, how about trying it so we can see how things might be related?

C: Okay, how do we do it?

T: You see all the little figures on the shelf, right?

C: Yes.

T: Well, tell me which ones you would choose to represent what you notice inside, including the voices and any other parts or aspects of you.

The client selects four figures. This is a useful intervention and one that can easily lead to asking questions about possible missing pieces (TW #9).

T: Is there anything missing? Is there any part that is not yet represented in these figures?

C: (Silence.) Yes, one thing, the one that's next to the kitten.

T: This one?
C: Yes.

After selecting the figures, we ask the client to describe each one. This is important because we want to avoid interpreting what they select. The less information we suggest, the more useful this type of exercise can be to understand the internal dynamics.

T: Can you describe what each one represents?
C: I chose this one because the cuts are part of me. They used to make me sad, but now I have internalized them, and they are part of me. So, I chose it because of that.
C: (Pointing at the next figure.). This is me fighting. And this other one is my inside world. I mean, this is me physically fighting, and this is my inside fighting with the voices with all the anger and everything I hold inside. My inside has to be much stronger, so that's why I chose the one with a machine gun.
T: Uh-huh.
C: (Pointing at the third figure.) This is all the ugliness inside of me. That's why the figure I chose is ugly.
C: (Pointing at the fourth figure.) And this is my voice.
T: And that's your voice?
C: Yes. (Client remains silent while looking at the figures.) Come to think about it, I realize that I have chosen everything bad.
T: That's why I asked before if anything was missing from what was represented there. (Client nods.) Sometimes there is a tendency to choose what concerns us the most, or what we fear the most, or what we reject the most. Sometimes there is also a tendency to avoid choosing what most frightens us. We are interested in everything inside, these aspects too. (The therapist points at all the action figures she has chosen). If something is missing, we want to know.
C: (Silence, thoughtful.) The little one with the lollipop (pointing at another figure).
T: This one?
C: Yes. This is me when I am with my best friend.
T: This is you when you are with your best friend.
C: Yes. It gives me peace of mind and it's as if the voices were reassured as if everything was better. T: Uh-huh.

Once the parts are identified, we explore the organization of the internal structure (TW #1) to get an idea of how the system is organized and whether there are any phobias (TW #4).

T: Is this how things are organized inside? Just as it is?
C: No.
T: Can you place them as you see them or notice them inside?
C: Okay. (She rearranges the figures.)
T: Can you explain it to me?
C: This one is behind everything else.
T: Why is that?
C: Yes, because I don't see him much.

T: Because you don't see him much. All right. And that represents...
C: My best friend.
T: It represents your best friend.
C: Yes.

When clients choose figures that represent people from real life, it is important to explore whether they are talking about a part they notice when they are with this person, a part that is similar to someone from the client's life, or simply the actual external person. This observation offers crucial information when assessing differentiation (TW #5).

T: Does it represent something in you or does it represent your best friend?
C: Something in me, because when I'm with him, it's like I'm someone else, a different person.
T: Uh-huh, and that other person that you are when you're with him, what is she like?
C: She's calmer, as if she were happy.
T: I see, and that part is in you too. (Acknowledging the part that is less visible.)
C: Yes. Sometimes the bad part comes out. It's like I have two parts and when the bad part comes out, she also knows how to control it.
T: And the part that you are referring to as bad, which one would it be? Is it related to any of the other figures you selected or is it a different one?
C: It's a different one.
T: Is it closer to that one there (pointing at the figure)?
C: It's closer to this one.
T: What would you select to represent it, just so we can get an idea?
C: The one that's behind (pointing at another figure).
T: This one. So, where would you place this one?
C: Somewhere around here. (Client places the figure closer to one of the parts that she dislikes.)
T: And this one represents what you call your bad part.
C: Yes, sometimes it's like it's not me. (Client begins to cry. When speaking about this part, her voices trembles.)
T: Can you explain it a bit?
C: It happens to me many times... sometimes I'm like a different person. Often, I don't understand many of the things I do. (Client cries more, with a frightened facial expression.)
T: Uh-huh, and is this part represented here or not?
C: Yes (taking one of the figures).
T: It's that one.
C: Yes, and it's bad.
T: Is that how you see it right now?
C: Yes.
T: Okay. Then this one (going back to the figure which she fears less) *represents what you're like when you're calm. You can be calm in the presence of someone who gives you peace of mind.* (Client nods.) *This other figure represents this part that you define as bad and that you do not recognize as yourself, as it were not you.*
C: Yes.

Every now and then, summarizing what the client has described helps in making sure we are understanding correctly. After checking with the client, we continue exploring to try to understand the needs of each part (TW #7).

> T: *Let's try to see what each one of them may need. What would this part need?* (Therapist points at one of the figures, the one that scares the client less.)
> C: *I don't understand.*
> T: *If she needed something to feel better, what do you think she would need?*
> C: (Silence.) *Do you mean something material or...?*
> T: *Or emotional.*
> C: *For example, to see her best friend more often?*
> T: *That could be. Seeing her best friend would be covering a need. What would that need be?*
> C: *Support.*
> T: *Support. She could need more support. Yes? Does it make sense?*
> C: *Yes.*
> T: *Well, what could this part need?* (Points at another figure.)
> C: (Silence) *I don't know...* (In a very low voice.)
> T: *What would these two need* (the figures she placed together)?
> C: (Silence.) *I don't know.*

We continue exploring the parts one by one. This exercise and the answers of the client help us understand how the needs of each part are completely unknown to her. She is only able to identify the possible needs of the part she fears less, represented by a little girl with the lollypop. This gives us an idea of the internal conflict and why it is maintained. Not only does she have difficulties identifying or acknowledging some of the parts, but she also does not have any clues about their possible needs or functions. Once this is clear, we continue exploring the dissociative phobia (TW #4).

> T: *When you see the part of the little girl, for example, what do you feel?*
> C: *Tenderness.*
> T: *Tenderness?*
> C: *Yes.*
> T: *You can connect with that part and her needs.* (Client nods.) *How about this one?*
> C: *Fear.*
> T: *Fear. And with the one that represents the voice?*
> C: *Also fear.*
> T: *And with this other one?*
> C: *Horror and also fear.*
> T: *Also fear.*
> C: *Yes.*
> T: *Do you notice that the ones that scare you the most are also the ones you have a hard time understanding what they may need?*
> C: *Yes.*
> T: *Yes, fear is really interfering. This is why it's important to try to understand it together.*

Once we have confirmed the dissociative phobias, clearly present towards all the parts except the little girl, we continue exploring the function of each part (TW #6).

> T: *I know this is difficult, but let's try to think of the adaptive function of each of these parts.* (Client nods.) *For example, how does this one help you?* (Pointing at the little girl figure.)
>
> C: *She makes me calm, gives me warmth, tenderness.*
>
> T: *Good. And how can this one* (pointing at another figure) *help you?*
>
> C: *That one doesn't help.*
>
> T: *I know it's hard, it's scary… but if she were trying to help you with something, how would she be trying to do it?*
>
> C: (Silence.) *It makes me aware that I also have that part, even if I don't want to see her.*
>
> T: *It's important to recognize the parts, even the ones that are most frightening.* (Client nods.) *And if this other one was trying to help, how would she be trying to do it?*
>
> C: (Prolonged silence.) *I don't know.*
>
> T: *You don't know.*
>
> C: *No.*
>
> T: *Well, can you ask her? Because it's the one that represents the voice you actually hear, right?*
>
> C: *Yes.* (Silence.)
>
> T: *So maybe she can answer. What is she trying to achieve or how is she trying to help?*
>
> C: (Silence.) *She's not answering.*
>
> T: *She's not answering.*
>
> C: *No.*
>
> T: *Well, she may not know. Maybe she still needs to figure it out.* (Client nods.) *We will come back to that one later or in another session. And would you know how this one* (pointing at the "bad" figure) *is trying to help or how she can help you?*
>
> C: (Silence.) *I don't think she helps me at all* (in a low voice).
>
> T: *Fear interferes a lot with you being able to see it. But if she were attempting to help, even if it seems odd, what would she be helping with?*

The phobia in the client makes it really hard for her to think of options. Since it is so difficult for her to think about this, we can increase her understanding of the protective function by exploring when the part shows up (TW #3).

> T: *When she shows up, what is usually happening?*
>
> C: *I can't control when she shows up.*
>
> T: *Does she show up when you are doing well or when you are feeling bad?*
>
> C: *When I'm feeling bad.*
>
> T: *So, if she shows up when you're feeling bad, she's probably trying to help. That's what we were talking about the other day, remember?* (Client nods.) *It's just that, for now, we don't quite know how she does it, right?*
>
> C: *Uh-huh.*
>
> T: *Would you say that this part shows up when you are not doing well and you can't go on?*
>
> C: *Yes, and many times I don't even remember what I do.*
>
> T: *Does that part remember it?*

C: It's like I don't have contact with her. It's another part of me that takes charge.

T: You know she's a part of you, but you still see her as very separate, as very different, right?

C: Yes. I don't remember what I do when she is present.

T: And does that part ever tell you anything? Does she communicate?

C: No.

T: Would she like to communicate anything now?

C: (Checking inside.) No.

T: Okay, that's fine. We just want her to know that she can share her thoughts and concerns whenever she wants. (Client nods.) And how would these other ones here (pointing at the figures that she can look at) *help you?*

C: They make me strong.

T: Okay, both give you strength.

C: Yes.

T: Great, that's good to know. We will keep exploring the other parts in future sessions to try to understand how they can help out.

After exploring the system with the action figures and having a clearer idea of the internal structure, we can begin exploring the memories the client spoke about, to get an idea of which part holds them and whether it will be necessary to work with them. This is part of the preparation, and though it does not mean we are going to dive immediately into this work, it conveys the message to the parts that we are not forgetting about it and will get to it eventually.

T: So, regarding the memories that you told me about when we met. The ones you know have had an impact on you, remember? If those memories belonged to one or more of the parts, who would they belong to?

C: This one...

T: So, if that part owns the difficult memories, it makes sense for you to notice the anxiety and discomfort. Are you in contact with those memories?

C: I'm trying not to be in contact with them.

T: Does it have anything to do with the part that is so agitated, the one over there? (Therapist is pointing at an action figure.)

C: Yes, that part is nervous and is getting on my nerves.

T: Okay, now that we understand a little better, try to think about what it may need.

C: (Silence.) I think it needs calmness.

T: What tends to work to calm her down?

When exploring alternatives (TW #7), reading comes up as a potential resource, but the client says she cannot read because, with her Obsessive-Compulsive Disorder (OCD), she reads the sentences over and over again. This next section is an example of exploring the symptom to understand how it might be helping the system (TW #3). Often symptoms can be seen as explicit manifestations of how the client or the part are responding to a trigger.

C: I could try to read, but having OCD, I can't do it.

T: Why is that?

C: *Because I re-read the sentences over and over, all the time.*

T: *Who re-reads those sentences?*

C: *Me.*

T: *You. Why?*

C: *If I don't read them a few times, I feel anxious.*

T: *All the sentences or just some of them?*

C: *Some of them.*

T: *Could you give me an example?*

C: *It also happens with the TV. I had to stop watching shows. If I listen to a sentence that I think is funny, I have to repeat it many times.*

T: *If you think it's funny.*

C: *Or if it's nice, I have to repeat it many times.*

T: *Well, it seems that there is something in you that wants you to feel better* (since she is repeating nice things.)

C: *How could that be?*

T: *Notice that it's something that makes you laugh or something nice. There is something in you that wants you to repeat it, right?* (Client nods.) *That seems to indicate that something inside wants you to feel better.*

C: *I guess so* (surprised) *but reading a book like that takes forever* (laughs).

This was an interesting discovery and it's a good example of why we want to be curious about symptoms and what gets triggered inside. If we identify this simply as OCD behavior, we would miss this crucial piece of information. Before closing the session, the therapist tries to use this new information to begin encouraging empathy and compassion for the other parts.

T: *Are you ever able to feel empathy towards the different parts? Even if it's just a little bit of compassion?*

C: *Not too much.*

T: *Not yet. Would you like to be able to feel it?*

C: *I guess so.*

T: *If you're able to have more compassion for yourself and for those different parts that we are trying to understand, including that voice, I think you can feel better. What do you think?*

C: *It could be.*

T: *Yes, just think there are a lot of resources inside of you. If your system was to work as a team, imagine how you could protect yourself.*

C: *I would be stronger.*

T: *That's right.*

EXAMPLE 5. THE VOICES SPEAKS TO ME ONLY IN STRESSFUL MOMENTS

In the two weeks in between the previous session and this one, the client keeps improving. She has been thinking about the possibility of going back to school and has spoken to one of her professors. She has been able to study a bit and has even started organizing her school material. We begin the session, as always, checking how she left the previous session (CS #1.1), and it seems as if the pieces are starting to fall into place. In this section of the interview, we explore whether the voices were active (CS #2.1), what were the triggers (CS #2.2), and how the client is responding (CS #2.3).

T: Have you noticed the voice lately?

C: She was calm these days.

T: Have you heard her?

C: No, she spoke to me at specific times when I was very stressed with my practicum.

T: What did she say?

C: She told me that I wouldn't be able to do it.

T: How did you respond?

C: I lost motivation and stopped studying.

T: And how did she respond to that?

C: She didn't say a word for the rest of the week.

T: Did you try studying after that?

C: Yes.

T: And what happened?

C: Nothing, she said anything.

T: Maybe she understood that her comment did not help.

C: I don't know.

T: Can you ask her?

C: She is not very talkative today.

T: Okay, that's fine. I know it's very difficult, but it would be great if you could try to respond differently. For instance, when she says, "You will not be able to do so and so," you could try to respond how we said the other day, something like, "I'm doing my best, and this does not help me."

C: I forgot about that. I guess I need to practice.

T: It would be great if you could do it. Notice that she shows up again when you are stressed, not when you are calm.

C: I did try to tell her that I can. I try to talk to her so that she learns that I won't give up, but she's blinded.

T: Great, that is the idea. You could even practice some of the options we talked about. For instance, you can say, "I know you're trying to help me, but that doesn't help me right now." The idea is for this voice to learn to communicate using positive messages. But remember she is still learning and needs our guidance.

C: I can try.

It is interesting to see that, after exploring alternatives and offering some suggestions (TW #8), the client feels more capable of trying them out. This exploration helps her to disclose something very disturbing for her. Again, we will explore to understand and address any issues as they come up (CS #2.4).

C: The other day she said something horrible. (Client becomes emotional and it takes her some time to be able to speak about what she wants to share.) *Sometimes I think it's not the same voice, it's another one that comes and says horrible things. Because lately, the noises make me very crazy, very sensitive, very afraid. And the other day there was a baby crying, screaming a lot, and there was a voice inside of me–not that same one, it was more harsh, darker–that said, "You should kill that baby." It sometimes appears when I'm afraid, especially of the noises made by other people. It tells me to hurt people. But it's a totally different voice.*

T: How do you know it's different?

C: It's harsher, with a more powerful tone, darker, harder.

T: Does that voice remind you of anyone?

C: No.

T: No one?

C: No.

We can understand how terrifying these messages can be. Once again, we would need to explore how this voice came to be (TW #1) and what triggers her (TW #3), as well as try to understand the possible function (TW #6).

T: Does it show up in situations such as when the baby was crying?

C: Yes.

T: And in what other situations?

C: When a car honks, for example, it also shows up and says those kinds of things too.

T: Things like what, for example?

C: Well, things like, "You should go down there and hit that woman or that man."

T: Does that sound familiar? Even if it's not the same type of messages.

C: No.

T: Is there anyone you known or anyone in school who got so angry?

C: No.

T: No?

C: No. Well, my grandfather gets angry easily, but he doesn't have that kind of voice, and he would never say anything like that.

T: But is the type of anger similar?

C: No, he would never say those things.

T: Well, it doesn't have to be the same exact message. It could be a learned version, it just goes a little further, right?

C: Yes.

T: When you say that he gets angry easily, I know it's not the same, but just so I can try to understand...

C: Yes, he gets angry, for example, if people honk. He says, "You can go to hell", things like that.

T: So, his version is...

C: Lighter.

T: Lighter, but it's similar. There is a learning process there. When there is a struggle or restrained anger, that kind of messages come up.

C: He would not go that far.

T: I know, not based on what you're saying, he wouldn't. But you get this kind of messages from this voice too.

C: Yes.

T: Do you ever think that sort of things?

C: No.
T: No. And when this voice says this...
C: I get scared.
T: You get scared.

The dissociative phobia is clear (TW #4), so it is not easy for her to think of how this part can be trying to help out. In the next section, we explore the dynamics in the system when this type of messages come up.

T: If she were trying to help, what would she be trying to help you with?
C: I don't know.
T: When she tells you these things, how do you react?
C: The day of the baby, I cried.
T: And, when you cry, what does the voice do?
C: It goes away.
T: It goes away. It seems a bit like the same dynamic, doesn't it? It's something that disturbs you because the baby crying was disturbing you, right?
C: Yes.
T: So that comment appears with a lot of rage. Do you usually get angry?
C: A little more lately.
T: A little more lately, but it's not a usual thing for you?
C: No, I don't usually get angry.

This is an example of how to explore missing pieces (TW #9). In this case, we identify the possibility that there is a hidden feeling of rage in how the part is responding, which is a good point of entry to identify what is missing.

T: Do you tend to keep everything in?
C: Yes.
T: What sometimes happens is just that. Accumulating a lot of anger creates a snowball effect that, in the end, can turn into this type of comments. And, it would be a matter of understanding as well. Notice that when you start crying, the voice doesn't say that again.
C: No
T: Probably, what she's looking for is not for you to cry but trying to stop that baby from bothering you. But of course, what happens to her stems from rage, and with anger and frustration you can't feel calm or say positive messages.
C: I understand.
T: If we start to understand it, she may tell you things in a different way. (Client nods.) Does this voice come up often?
C: No.
T: Does it usually come up when there are noises?
C: Yes, or when something upsets me.
T: When something upsets you. Do those things make you angry or scare you?

C: *Mostly, stuff that upsets me, or actually that scares me, yes, that too.*

T: *Things that scare you or irritate you?*

C: *Both.*

T: *So, when there is something that irritates you in some way or that frightens you, this hoarse voice shows up.*

C: *Yes, hoarse, yes.*

T: *Good. And the other voice, what does it do when this other hoarse voice shows up?*

C: *She doesn't show up.*

T: *She doesn't show up.*

C: *No.*

T: *And you tell me that the other one, the one we were working with trying to understand her better, has been calmer.*

C: *Yes.*

We reinforce that she is starting to differentiate voices (TW #5) and continue trying to help her understand how this voice is helping in the present (TW #6), while exploring possible needs (TW #7) and alternatives ways of responding (TW #8).

T: *It's good that you are now starting to differentiate them. Notice that you started saying, "Well, she said something really horrible" and you automatically said, "No, but I think it was another voice." (Client nods.) You are being able to differentiate them a little better, and that is interesting because sometimes the feeling is that everything is mixed up, so then it becomes more complicated to understand. So, let's try to think together about how this new voice might be trying to help.*

C: *Okay.*

T: *In those situations that irritate you, what would you need to be able to do?*

C: *(Silence.) I would run away, but...*

T: *What would you need in order to deal with it better?*

C: *(Silence.) I can't think of anything.*

T: *You can't think of anything. For example, with the baby, what was the situation?*

C: *I think I was at home. I heard the baby from my room because that boy has some lungs.*

T: *Have you heard him often?*

C: *Yes, but that day he cried and cried. He screamed like there was no tomorrow.*

T: *When you see or hear a baby, how do you usually feel?*

C: *They're cute, as long as they don't scream.*

T: *As long as they don't scream. And what's the feeling?*

C: *I like them.*

T: *You like babies.*

C: *Yes.*

We only explore how she feels towards babies in general; this will help us to rule out whether babies are a trigger. Once she explains that she likes babies, we continue exploring trying to understand what was triggering the voice that day (TW #3).

T: So, it's not so much about the baby. It's about the screaming.

C: Yes, exactly.

T: What happens when you hear the baby scream?

C: I get very nervous.

T: You get very nervous. Can you explain this a bit?

C: The screaming gets into my head.

T: And does that remind you of any situation you experienced?

C: (Silence, thoughtful.) At school, they screamed at me.

T: It may be something similar.

C: Yes, very similar.

T: So, when this hoarse voice appears and tells you something harsh, you focus on what she just told you.

C: Yes.

T: Although you obviously start crying, she may probably be trying to avoid a trigger so you don't make a connection with other memories that hurt and feel worse. I don't know, it's a hypothesis. Does it make sense?

C: Yes.

T: It could be.

The client explains that the kids at school used to gather around her and scream. She covered her ears, trying to make them stop, but the screams "would get in her head." So, if we take this into consideration, we see that the voice is trying to help her by diverting her attention towards the horrible message. It is not an ideal way of helping, of course, but for some reason, it is what this voice learned to do. The next step is helping this voice to find a more adaptive function in the system (TW #7).

EXAMPLE 6. THE VOICES INSULT ME

In the following session, the client brings up some health issues; she lost 20 pounds in two weeks and cannot not eat. The symptom is related to her history, to a specific event from school which took place when she started presenting eating problems. Therapist and client decided to reprocess the traumatic memory that was triggering the symptom, after checking with the system of parts and reaching an agreement. It was an intense but productive session, which led to interesting changes around self-care. The following segment of the interview belongs to the session after the reprocessing was done. We begin by exploring the effects of the work done in the previous session (CS #1) and exploring how she has been in the week between sessions (CS #2).

T: How did you leave the session?

C: Very relaxed, it was as if a really heavy burden had lifted.

T: How was everything inside in these past weeks?

C: Mostly calm.

T: Mostly, okay. How have the voices been?

C: I would say okay, but today my head is spinning.

T: Your head is spinning. Why is that?

C: Things are not well at home. It's as if I noticed everything in me and the voice came through.

T: What is happening at home?

The client comments both parents are not doing well, health wise. The family pressure has activated one of the most hostile voices after an argument with her sister. In the next sections of the interview, we explore the voice that has been active (CS #2.1), the triggers (CS #2.2), how the system responded (CS #2.3), and whether there are any issues that need to be addressed now (CS #2.4).

> T: So, you say your head is spinning because of the voice. What is happening with the voice?
> C: She became agitated tonight. She spent the whole night remembering the moment when my sister got upset. Since this morning, she's been calling me a bitch and telling me I shouldn't exist. This morning I disconnected, and then I realized I had not had one of these spells for a long time. When I came to, I found myself looking at my arms searching for a place to cut. I had the blade in my hand and everything. So, I ran away from the house.
> T: That's good, notice what a difficult situation that was.
> C: The last time (one of the most severe cutting episodes that she does not remember), *I had no recollection of how I put the blade in the backpack. At least I didn't put it in the backpack and didn't take it with me.*

We explore which voice got triggered (TW #3), what it is trying to achieve (TW #6), and how the client has responded (CS #2.3).

> T: What was the voice trying to achieve with that?
> C: I don't know.
> T: Which voice is it?
> C: It's not the usual voice I hear.
> T: Which one is it then?
> C: I think it's the bad voice, the one that said things to me when the baby screamed. That's the one, she doesn't have the same tone as the other.
> T: And she showed up last night.
> C: She showed up after arguing with my sister.
> T: What did she say?
> C: She was just repeating, "Bitch, bitch" ...
> T: How did you respond to that?
> C: I told her to shut up and die.
> T: I see. And how did the voice respond?
> C: She got more aggressive.
> T: I see. It makes sense, aggression leads to aggression, remember? The idea is for you to try to respond differently while the voices learn the new ways.
> C: I know, and I've been doing it most of the time, but that day I couldn't take it anymore. She was driving me nuts.
> T: I know it's difficult. When things get complicated, the tendency is to go back to familiar ways. I am glad you were able to do that most of the time. Do you remember how the voices responded when you responded differently?
> C: Yes, better. I am aware of that. But this voice is very mean.

T: This voice has learned to repeat this type of messages. Remember we talked about how she might not have too much of a repertoire?

C: Yes. The day before that I handled it better.

T: Can you tell me about that?

C: I started to play a game, and then... I can't remember what I did yesterday very well. I know I was doing some stretching exercises and then I was doing some schoolwork.

T: And what was the voice saying?

C: She was saying I was mean.

T: Do you know what she meant?

C: Yes, she was referring to the argument I had with my sister. She thinks I should not fight with her.

T: What do you think about that?

C: I didn't want to fight with her but sometimes I have issues with anger, as you know. It was one of those days. I can't even remember what happened. But I know I was able to deal with the voice better.

T: How is that?

C: I started planning things. I flunked three subjects left at college, so I started to organize my exams and that was a bit motivating. I went to the computer to do some work and she stopped.

T: I see why you say you handled it much better. Good job! And notice how the voice also responding better.

C: Yes, when I started doing useful things, she stopped.

T: That's why it's important that you somehow answer back by, saying to this voice, "This does not help me," "This makes me feel worse." Could you do that?

C: Yes. I already tried it. But since it didn't work, I started doing my school assignments, because she doesn't reason.

T: She doesn't reason.

C: She doesn't listen to me. Sometimes I can talk to her, but other times, I can't. That's why I think they're two different voices, because the one who insults me now doesn't reason. She shows up and just says what she has to say. It's like when someone is pissed off, and rants and raves, and then just leaves, slamming the door in your face. That's how she behaves.

T: Well it's important for you to identify it and understand that, in that moment, she doesn't reason.

C: No, she doesn't.

T: It's important to remind yourself, "I know that this voice responds like this and that in her own way she is trying to help me," and then to start doing things that divert your attention, like what you did then. Notice how it worked.

C: The other voice came back again with the issue of boys, saying that I was the only one who doesn't have a boyfriend and stuff like that. But at least she tries to reason because I can tell her, "Right now I don't want to have a partner, because I am a burden. I am a burden for my friends and I wouldn't want anyone to have to deal with someone like me. I'm sure of that."

T: We would have to modify that message slightly.

C: Why?

T: It's good that you're able to tell her that, right now, you don't want to have a partner. I think that part is very good. But adding that you would be a burden for anyone is treating yourself very negatively, and it's unnecessary. (Client nods.) Think about it. How does saying something like that help you?

C: It doesn't.

T: *It's one thing for you to say, "Right now I'm focused on getting well and I don't want to make my life complicated. I want to be calm and well enough before I even start thinking about a relationship." (Client nods.) But telling yourself that you are a burden for anyone seems totally unnecessary.*

C: *I understand, yes.*

The client is much more able to deal with the voices now, and the voices are also learning to respond differently (CS #2.6). Of course, this is session #7, so the system is still learning new ways of relating and responding. One of the most important aspects in these situations is for the therapist to remain calm, curious, and confident. It's easy to lose motivation and think that things are not really changing, but we need to remember learning takes time. We cannot unlearn years of functioning in conflict in two or three sessions; it is just not going to happen.

We close the session reinforcing the work done (CS #3.1), checking the usefulness of the intervention (CS #3.2), and summarize the major key points of the work done (CS #3.4). We do not check if the client is grounded because, once again, it is obvious by her answers during the previous steps. But we do prepare her for potential obstacles (CS #3.5) since it is very likely that the voices will go back to speaking in the ways they have learned.

T: *I am proud of you.*

C: *Really?*

T: *Yes, I think you are really trying to practice new ways of responding. I think it's fantastic.*

C: *Thank you.*

T: *And the voices are trying too. Do you realize that?*

C: *Well, yes. Things are different now, I know.*

T: *What do you think about the work we are doing now? Is it helping?*

C: *Is it helping? Yes, very much. I felt really lost before. I thought I would never get better. Now I see that change is possible.*

T: *Great. How is it helping? Can you tell me a little about that?*

C: *Well, I can understand myself better, and I can understand what happens inside better too.*

T: *How does that help?*

C: *It gives me more peace of mind. I can think better now, especially since I am not so afraid of my head or my voices. That helps a lot.*

T: *Great. So, remember what we went over today. Voices are still learning. You can see how the voice you normally hear is already responding in a very different way.*

C: *Yes.*

T: *But the hoarse voice seems to need more time to learn.*

C: *Okay.*

T: *Remember, right now, the most important part is how you respond. So, if you hear this voice again, try to remember that it is still learning. (Client nods.) She needs our guidance with that.*

C: *I will try.*

EXAMPLE 7. IMPROVEMENT AND REALIZATION

In the next session, the client walks in smiling, looking proud of herself. We begin the interview exploring how she is doing. Then we explore how she left the session (CS #1.1)

T: How are you doing?
C: Good, I'm good.
T: Yes? Tell me a little bit.
C: Last week I did pretty good.
T: Uh-huh.
C: I even went out with my classmates and everything.
T: That's fantastic! How was it?
C: Very good. I'm happy.
T: I can tell. It's obvious. And you look very good too.
C: Thank you.
T: How were you doing when you left the previous session? Do you remember?
C: Good, yes. The truth is that I felt good.
T: Did you do well after that?
C: Yes, I'm doing much better.
T: I'm very glad, especially because you can realize it and say it. (Client nods smiling).

This is a very positive moment in therapy. However, it can also be difficult for clients, so it is important to explore the phobia of change and improvement (TW #5). It can be a good way to prevent relapses because clients do not know how to be stable; it normally feels weird and unfamiliar.

T: Does it scare you?
C: Well, yes.
T: It scares you. Why?
C: Because I'm not sure I know how to live without being sick.
T: It's something very new, isn't it?
C: I don't remember the things I did before, I don't remember leaving the house or anything, and now that I have a lot of free time, I ask myself, "What did I do before with my free time?" (Client starts crying, moved.) *So far, I'm not able to study as before, at best, I am able to concentrate for a couple of hours or so. But in the meanwhile, I get by.*
T: Yes?
C: When I see I have nothing to do, then I say, "What am I doing with my life?"
T: What would you like to do?
C: I wish I could study and finish those school subjects. They torment me, but I'm not able to file anything in my brain.
T: But is that real?
C: Yes.

T: Isn't it related to your high demands?

C: No, I used to study without a problem. I always did very well.

T: So, you're able to concentrate for two hours and, then, what happens?

When exploring current concentration difficulties, the voice's attempts at helping (TW #6) become obvious and how the system is learning to dialog instead of fighting or arguing (TW #7).

C: Well, the thing is that I was feeling like this, and I thought "If I passed them all now, it would be good" and the voice started to say, "If you pass two now and three in July, that's it, you are done." Later she said, "Then you can start with the project." I was dialoguing like this for a while when I came to, I was surprised to be talking to myself like this.

T: What do you think about that?

C: It's crazy!

T: I think it's pretty good.

C: So, I don't remember about ten minutes or so. I kept moving around the room, but it wasn't really me.

T: Well what you describe implies greater acceptance of yourself. There is no fighting, no attacks.

C: Moreover, when I came to, I was saying, "Well, no big deal, if I don't do the project, I'll do it next year. I can also do it while I work." I think I was talking with the voice.

T: That seems to be an interesting change, and I imagine you see it too.

C: Yes, I was surprised, because for a long time I wasn't able to dialogue like that.

T: Of course, you just stepped into conflict and fought, you got scared. She's is trying to help; she's finding a different way to help you.

C: Yes. I was good, I kept turning things around in my head for a while, and in the end, we were all happy that I was doing the project next year. I don't know, it was weird.

T: Weird, but good, right? Can you see the positive side of it?

C: Yes, before, she would've been shouting at me constantly.

T: Of course, and then you would become frightened and feel discomfort. Now it's a dialogue.

C: Yes.

T: Very good.

C: Aside from the fact that speaking to yourself out loud is very strange because that's what I did and it's weird.

T: Well, but if that helps you, it's okay because it's a way to work as a team.

C: Then yesterday, it came back again. Yesterday my subconscious started thinking about cutting again, but that's the last thing I needed at that time of the night. Of course, I'd been coughing for about an hour, I had already counted all the sheep in the world, so then my brain started to play its tricks on me.

T: Your brain goes to what's automatic, this is pure and simple learning.

C: Yes. For the last four years.

T: Exactly.

C: It's always spinning around the same old stuff. It started saying that it was time, and I found myself looking for places to cut again. It started to tell me that it was a good idea and so and so, and suddenly she even said to me, "If you don't cut yourself, it's as if you were healed."

270

The system still has to continue to practice reaching a more adaptive way of functioning, and clients need our help to internalize the new responses. Remember that it is very easy for parts to go back to functioning in their habitual ways. Old habits are not easily changed. That is why it is so important to check if the learned messages or behaviors are still taking place CS #2.6).

> C: *Another weird thing is that I don't know how to live without depending on people.*
> T: *But you can learn. This is not easy stuff at all, huh?*
> C: *No, but I'm not trusting this either, because when I've spent seven months without cutting myself, it seemed that things were going well and suddenly one day, "boom," I was cutting again.*
> T: *Do you think you felt the way you feel now?*
> C: *No.*
> T: *What is different? Let's try to understand it together, okay?*
> C: *It's like I don't have a huge weight over my shoulders, I have more energy.*
> T: *Yes. That's very good. So then, the issue of yesterday's cuts...*
> C: *Yesterday and this morning.*
> T: *How did you handle it?*
> C: *Well, whatever is inside that speaks to me, asked me if I remembered when I used to cut myself. Of course, I remember it, and I know what it feels like. (Client starts crying, moved.) See? When I talk about it is when I feel bad.*
> T: *Of course, you become emotional. It's normal because you're realizing the difference between then and now, and realization hurts. Becoming aware is a giant step, you can be very proud of yourself. But it's it also like mourning; assimilating and becoming aware is like, "Wow, I've come this far!" So, it's normal to feel emotional and it's great that you can see it here with me.*
> C: *On the one hand, it's great, but on the other hand, I remember everything I went through.*
> T: *Yes, and that's hard, I know. But it's also good that you can realize all of that.*
> C: *I know.*

We close the session talking about preventing relapses (CS #3.5).

> C: *I know that sooner or later I will fall. The good thing is that I know I'm going to fall and it doesn't affect me so much.*
> T: *Sure, and it's mostly about buffering the fall.*
> C: *Of course, and not falling as low as have before.*
> T: *Exactly. The point is not to make things worse. There will be times when you are not feeling well, this is a reality, but what you do with those moments is what can keep you moving forward.*
> C: *I can change things.*
> T: *Exactly, because it doesn't make it worse. The fall is when you resort to behaviors that make things worse.*
> C: *Yes.*

At the end of the session, when therapist and client and setting a new appointment, the client is even able to make jokes about the changes, proudly announcing that she brought her appointment card for the first time since the beginning of the meetings.

C: I brought the appointment card today (laughing).
T: Wow!
C: Yes, yes, yes. I don't recognize myself!
T: Very good!
C: I remembered to bring it. I told you I was improving!
T: Yes, I can see that, great!

This is an example of the type of changes we can achieve in a short period of time. There is still a lot of work to do, and both therapist and client know it. The client feels more stable, there is more control, and there is also hope and motivation. The client went back to school and, within a year, she was able to pass all her pending classes and finish her Bachelor thesis. A year after that, she was working and feeling much better. We continue to meet regularly once a month.

The patient writes this for the book:

I still have a hard time remembering many of the things that have happened to me since that day when everything started to frighten me, the day when a little voice of someone small started to sound in my head. Then several more came along and every time they changed, I felt that something bad was happening inside me.

It was hard to understand what was happening, in fact to this day I still don't understand it, but I have learned to live with those other parts of me that resonate in my brain. With work I have learned not to be so afraid when they appear, to isolate them in a corner and not have them do so much harm. I have learned to deal with them, not to get angry and not to generate more anxiety.

When this started happening to me, I didn't realize how much work it would take to get out of the hole I had fallen into. Now that I'm on the surface I've learned to fight for everything, even if I end up with scars.

CHAPTER 16

HUGO: THE DARK BOX IN MY HEAD

Hugo is a 30-year-old male who is referred by his therapist for an assessment because he hears voices. During an EMDR processing session, the client became overwhelmed by a voice in his head and by an all-encompassing dark box. Initially, the client was curious about this box and tried to get closer and look inside, but he got very frightened when the box repelled him. Right before repelling him, the client was able to see a very sinister image of himself inside.

He is highly intelligent and very creative, yet lately has been unable to function in daily life. He has been locked up in his house for the past three years and has not been able to draw or create anything new. He is very frustrated and feels very limited in his capacity to do anything that can bring about any changes.

BRIEF CASE CONCEPTUALIZATION

History of symptoms and presenting problems

1. **General presenting problems and/or symptoms.** Extreme avoidant behaviors and a tendency to isolate himself. He is not capable utilizing some of his usual abilities, such as drawing or writing.

2. **Previous diagnosis.** Depression, anxiety disorder, and panic attacks.

3. **Attachment patterns.** Avoidant attachment with both parents. Neither caregiver has been abusive, both were focused on his academic achievements and covered his basic needs.

4. **Relational problems**
   a. Family members. The client does not indicate any problems with the family. He understands the relationship is distant, as it has been all his life. No issues around this.
   b. Friends and peers. The client does not indicate any problems.
   c. Intimate relationships. His partner is emotionally unstable; she is attending individual therapy. When his partner is not feeling well, this becomes emotionally contagious for the client.
   d. Work and/or school. Nothing relevant.

5. **Daily life functioning**
   a. Self-care habits. Adequate regarding food and organization but not in regard to emotional self-care.
   b. Financial stability. He gets some support from his family. His partner is working. He also has some savings from previous jobs.
   c. Social, occupational or school functioning. Low, he is isolated.
   d. Overall level of functioning. Low, he can barely leave the house.

6. **Initial onset of problems/symptoms.**
   a. What was happening then? The client says that he was never good at fitting in but does not refer any relevant problematic moments in his life. It seems that minimization and rationalization might be a defense.
   b. What got triggered? He is unable to identify it.

7. **When did symptoms worsen?**
   a. What was happening then? Three years ago, he gradually developed an inability to draw, write, and create in general.
   b. What got triggered? He does not know. He indicates that three years ago, he started staying home most of the time with extreme avoidant behaviors.

8. **When do symptoms increase or worsen now?**
   a. Current triggers. When he has to create or do anything that requires mental energy and creativity.
   b. Degree of awareness of triggers. Average without help, high with help.

Resources

1. **Sources of adaptive information**
   a. Good enough attachment figures in childhood and/or adult life. His parents have offered him enough adaptive information around practical issues and basic care.
   b. Moments of feeling safe and being protected. He can give examples of his older sister.
   c. Moments of feeling cared for. He can give examples of being cared for by his sister.
   d. Other relevant positive figures/models. His partner at the beginning of therapy and his previous therapist.

2. **Emotional regulation capacity**
   a. Self-regulation capacity. The client tends to self-regulate by avoiding any potential conflicts, which is not the best regulating strategy in the present moment. However, he does not get triggered easily, he analyzes and rationalizes difficulties, can understand them and tries to search for solutions.
   b. Co-regulation capacity. Yes.
   c. Tolerance for negative and positive emotions. The client does not connect very well with the body and describes his relationships at a cognitive level. He does not seem to have problems with dysfunctional positive affect.

3. **Social support**
   a. Family members. His sister tries to help him.
   b. Intimate partners. Partner is a source of support when she is doing well.
   c. Friends. A small group of friends.
   d. Work colleagues and peers. Prior work colleagues.
   e. Other professionals. His previous therapist.
   f. Religious/spiritual resources. Not relevant.

4. **Other resources**
   a. Mentalization capacity. The client has good mentalizing capacity and high integrative capacity. He is very bright and can understand complicated concepts and simplify them.
   b. Degree of realization. The degree of realization is not very clear. He seems to realize the events that could have influenced his actual problems, but at the same time rationalizes and minimizes most of them.
   c. Degree of integrative capacity. Very high.

5. **Timeline of best memories.** To avoid disclosing too much personal information, we shall omit this part. The client is able to give examples of good enough interactions, not fantastic or very positively charged but with positive, pleasant elements. Although his parents were never very affectionate or played much with him, they spent time helping him with homework and reading books and novels. Mother would read to him and father would explain some of the readings.

Structural elements of the internal system

1. **Client's degree of awareness of parts**. The client is partially aware of having parts and hearing voices. He cannot admit that he hears voices openly and tries to offer alternative explanations. However, he does experience the voices as parts of him: "It's like talking to myself."

2. **Internal structure**
   a. Approximate number of parts. In the initial intake, the client talks about the voices he imagines and rejects the possibility of talking about parts.
   b. Client's description/representation of the internal system of parts. By using his language, we can explore the system and get an idea of possible parts: a critical part, a creative part, a reasonable part, a fog, a blurry and confusing thing, and a dark square box.
   c. Organization and distribution of those parts that the client can discuss. In the beginning, he does not know.
   d. Any missing pieces in the description. The client presents with flat speech, as if he were emotionally disconnected, but is able to describe in detail what happens inside of him.

3. **Degree of differentiation about the self and others**
   a. Can the client distinguish her/his own thoughts, emotions and needs from what has been imposed by others? With help, he can. No relevant issues with differentiation. He can even question the messages the voices give him with perfectly reasonable arguments.
   b. Is the Is the client confusing any parts or voices with the real perpetrators? No.

4. **Time orientation and current perception of safety**
   a. Is the client confusing what happened in the past with what is happening in the present? The client does not lose time orientation easily.
   b. Does the client know that the danger is over? Yes, he knows he is safe.
   c. Which parts are still stuck in trauma time? The only part that seems to be stuck in trauma-time is the dark square box. Other parts do seem stuck in repetitive ways of functioning that are not useful for the system anymore.

5. **Mentalizing capacities**
   a. Can all parts mentalize? No.
   b. Which parts have higher mentalizing abilities? The Adult Self can mentalize.
   c. Which parts need help with mentalizing? It seems like all of them do. The critical part needs help to mentalize. We cannot be sure about the dark square box or other parts because they did not participate much in the first sessions.

6. **Adaptive information**
   a. Which parts have adaptive information? The client has adaptive information. He is very interested in the human brain and how human beings interact in general. This makes him curious and open to learning new things. Initially, it is unknown which parts have adaptive information, it seems that the creative part and the rational part.
   b. Which parts need help with adaptive information? The rest of the parts do not participate much in the beginning, they could use some help with problem-solving and resolution. These parts do not seem to have too much of a repertoire.

Relational aspects of the internal system

1. **Acceptance of parts.**
   a. Despite the fear/conflict, does the client describe some parts with compassion, acceptance or appreciation? With some help, he can partially accept some voices, or at least show some curiosity towards them, their functions and needs. He understands that the voices are pointing to relevant issues that need to be addressed.

2. **Relationships among parts**
   a. What feelings do the parts have towards each other? Not very clear in the beginning. What we do know is that when we try to explore, all of the voices talk at once. He is not aware that his way of interacting is not helping the system to relate better.
   b. Which are adaptive for the system in the present moment? Unknown. The creative part seems to be the most functional but, at the same time, it is the park most blocked by the critical part.
   c. Which need to improve? All of them.

3. **Degree of cooperation between parts of the system**
   a. Is the client aware of any parts attempting to help the system? Yes. Initially there is no cooperation between parts but, with some help, the client could understand the parts better and negotiate some cooperation.
   b. Can the client accept that there might be an attempt of help even though it may not be clear yet? Yes.

4. **Parts that may have difficulties with therapy.**
   Is there ambivalence or rejection towards therapy? The critical part does not see how therapy can be useful, at least in the first two sessions.
   What are their concerns regarding therapy? To follow indications and have no results.

5. **Co-consciousness between parts.**
   1. If it exists, which parts are co-conscious? He can be co-conscious with most of the adult parts.
   2. When does co-consciousness occur? Does it vary? Quite often the client notices a few parts at a time and the parts interact among them.
   3. How do other parts respond to this? The system is in conflict, they respond critically but with help they are able to soften their messages.

Trauma related phobias and other potential blocks

1. **Phobia of inner experience.** Tolerable.
   a. Can the client check inside? Yes, with help and he can show curiosity quite often.
   b. Can the client notice and tolerate sensations? Even though there is quite a bit of disconnection from emotions, he can notice his body and tolerate some body sensations, except for a blockage that might be related to a part.
   c. Is the client afraid of his or her feelings, thoughts or sensations? Despite having felt frightened when he saw one of the parts, the phobia is not very high. He is not afraid of his thoughts or his mind. He is more afraid of being committed due to the information he is revealing.
   d. Is the client ashamed of his or her feelings, thoughts or sensations? Yes, because of his avoidant attachment, he has learned to avoid sensations and emotions.

2. **Phobia of parts.** Tolerable.
   a. Does the client show ambivalence about the parts or does he avoid talking about them? He is afraid of the critical part because of his way of expressing himself. The parts occasionally feel phobias among them and feel frustrated and disappointed.
   b. Despite the fear, can the client try to explore parts and be curious? He is afraid but is also open enough to explore and understand.
   c. Do any of the parts feel shame or is the patient ashamed of any of them? He does not feel ashamed of the parts. These seem to be more focused on trying to avoid harm, but there is no shame from the patient or from the other parts.

3. **Phobia of attachment and attachment loss.** Tolerable.
   a. Is there ambivalence around trust in the therapeutic relationship? He can trust enough but does not establish a deep bond with the therapist despite being comfortable. This is related to his attachment pattern.
   b. Do the client or any of the parts have difficulties trusting others, ambivalence between wanting to attach and pushing others away? The client does not waste too much energy worrying about relationships; he is not too invested. This is related to his pattern of avoidant attachment.

4. **Phobia of traumatic memories.** Average.
   a. Does the client insist on avoiding any exploration about childhood? The client is very distant from his experiences. He can remember traumatic events, talk about them and understand their potential impact. He does not seem too concerned when speaking about his history. However, he did get triggered during an EMDR session and became very frightened, so maybe some parts are more concerned and phobic.
   b. Does the client show ambivalence about trauma work or even talking about traumatic experiences? The client is not aware of potentially traumatic adverse experiences. He minimizes this possibility.

5. **Phobia of change and adaptive risk-taking.** High.
   a. Is the client afraid of change? He is very avoidant and tends to postpone decisions or opportunities.
   b. Does the client present difficulties trying suggestions that would improve his quality of life? Yes.

6. **Defenses.** Minimization, rationalization and avoidance.

7. **Any other identified potential blocks.** Tendency to remain at a cognitive level. The fact that he has been locked in his house for almost three years signals potential complications in therapy.

EXAMPLE 1. EXPLORING THE SYSTEM

This is an example of both gathering information –by exploring how the voices started and when (TW #1), how the client deals with them, and when do they appear (TW #3)– and helping the client understand the function of these voices (TW #6).

T: My colleague said that during the last session you did not feel good and you heard a voice. Could you tell me about it?

C: Well, this voice isn't a voice that I actually hear. I just imagine it.

T: You imagine it.

C: Yes, I am aware that I'm imagining it, and it's not to be confused with auditory hallucinations or anything like that. It's like when you see an image in your mind, you know that you're not actually seeing it, but it's there. The problem is that I have no control over what it says or when it shows up.

The client, for some reason, seems concerned about hearing voices and denies it. When asked about this, he says that he imagines them. When we find this type of situations, we should not insist on using a specific language. We can explore using the client's language as suggested in Chapter 3. However, it may be helpful to explore with the client how would he feel if he were to actually hear voices, in order to understand the concerns behind the denial. In this next section, we will try to gather more information about the voice, its onset, etc. (TW #1).

> *T: Would you be concerned if you were to hear this voice?*
> *C: Yes.*
> *T: What would you associate this with?*
> *C: This voice that I hear —well, I don't hear it, I imagine it— is associated with a part of my personality that is out of control.*
> *T: When did you start to imagine this voice?*
> *C: I don't know when it started, but I became aware of it during the sessions when I was here with the other therapist.*
> *T: Uh-huh.*
> *C: I think it was there before, but I wasn't aware of it. It was more unconscious. I guess I just thought I was talking to myself. I didn't associate this with a part of my personality that is not functioning correctly.*
> *T: What changed? What makes you think that it is related to a part of your personality that doesn't function correctly?*
> *C: Well the things that it tells me I think are not useful for me. And they are not 100% realistic.*
> *T: What type of things does it say?*
> *C: Negative things. It talks about my flaws, the things I do wrong. It's very strong self-criticism.*
> *T: So, if you could visualize the voice, what do you imagine it would look like?*
> *C: Well, it did show up during a session. We were doing EMDR. First, I noticed that I was in a space that was like a very, very dark vacuum. Then I sensed or saw something like a perfect black box that deep down I knew that shouldn't be there. When I tried to get inside, it repelled me. That's when I saw a very distorted, sinister, and threatening image of myself.*

This illustrates a dissociative phobia in both Adult Self and part (TW #4). Initially, the client was curious about the black box and tried to get closer and take a look. When he did that, the black box (voice) repelled him. And after the voice repelled him, the client became more phobic. This incident also illustrates the risk of using EMDR processing —or trying to do any trauma work, for that matter— without sufficient knowledge about the system of parts or proper preparation. As mentioned in Chapter 2, we cannot stress enough the importance of these two elements.

> *T: So, this happened during an EMDR session.*
> *C: Yes.*
> *T: How did you feel during that session?*
> *C: A bit afraid because I didn't know what it meant or what it was. I even thought that it might be another personality that I would not be able to control and could easily take over. I didn't understand anything, and it scared me.*

Once we gathered more information about the voice, we can proceed by exploring the possible function of this voice (TW #6), so that the client can begin to understand his inner world better and develop a new way of looking at himself and the voice.

> T: *What function might this voice have?*
> C: *I don't know. It does not help me really. I think it could be self-criticism, but it's excessive.*
> T: *If it were to have an adaptive function, what do you think it could be?*
> C: *I think it would be a protective function, because it tries to prevent me from exposing myself to others, so, I don't get external judgments that can hurt me.*
> T: *That's a very adaptive function; it makes a lot of sense.*
> C: *Yes.*
> T: *What do you think about this protective function?*
> C: *It makes sense, but it's excessive.*

As we can see, this client has high integrative capacities and can think about the possible function of this voice, but this is not enough for him to function. Let us remember he has been locked in his house for about three years and that lately he has presented severe limitations. We continue gathering more information and explore the times when the voice gets triggered (TW #3).

> T: *When does this voice that you imagine appear?*
> C: *When I'm working on something, doing things like writing or drawing that require some judgment. I'm constantly wondering if I'm doing it right or wrong. And that's when it tends to appear.*
> T: *Does it help improve your performance?*
> C: *No, I generally lose motivation and stop working.*
> T: *Why would it do that?*
> C: *I don't know.*
> T: *Are you satisfied with the things you draw or write?*
> C: *No, I am never satisfied. I usually think that what I do is no good. It's never good enough.*
> T: *How long has this been going on?*
> C: *For a long time... quite a few years.*

Notice that after identifying the general trigger, we start asking questions about the usefulness of this attitude from the voice; this is a way to start introducing the idea of new alternatives (TW #8). We know that critical voices often repeat messages they have learned in the past and, as therapists, we need to understand where the client learned to be so hard on himself. By doing this, he can begin to understand it too and see that this voice is truly a part of him that is trying to help. It seems that the client and the voice agree on things "never being good enough."

> T: *Where did you learn to be so hard on yourself?*
> C: *Maybe in College, because it was very competitive.*
> T: *How about before that?*
> C: *No, nothing relevant*

Being consistent with his avoidant attachment pattern, the client's response is quite vague. And following the rule of respecting the timing of the client, we do not insist on exploring any issues that he is not yet ready to see or share. We decide to continue exploring the system and the potential dissociative phobia towards what the black box represents (TW #4), trying to understand the underlying meaning.

> *T: What do you notice when you think about this black box?*
> *C: Restlessness.*
> *T: And what does this box mean to you?*
> *C: It symbolizes a part of me –or my head– that is hard for me to access. I can't control it.*
> *T: That is a very good explanation and, psychologically, it makes a lot of sense.*
> *C: In my brain, the box has been the aspect most resistant to external attacks.*

Since this client is not used to communicating with this voice –in fact, he is unable to acknowledge that it is a voice–, we introduce the meeting place procedure as a way to explore the system. The issues that come up while doing this exercise can help guide our next steps in session.

> *T: Let's try something.*
> *C: Okay.*
> *T: It is a visualization exercise to try to understand what is happening inside. You can close your eyes or keep them open, whatever is more comfortable for you. (Client nods.) The idea would be for you to imagine a meeting place; a place where you can invite all the different aspects of yourself. It can be an open space or you can put a table and some comfortable chairs, couches or whatever you like. If you decide to use chairs, check how many chairs you would need for the different aspects of yourself.*
> *C: (After taking his time.) A table and chairs around it sound good. I don't know, I feel that I would need a lot of chairs.*
> *T: That's fine. Imagine there is a door in this room, try to imagine it, and invite the different aspects of yourself, including the dark box and the voices you imagine hearing. Remember that it's a place to dialogue. The purpose is to get to know all the different aspects and have a place for them to communicate.*
> *C: Okay.*
> *T: Take your time.*

The client describes eight parts or aspects. We ask him to describe them (TW #1) and then explore the possible phobia towards these aspects (TW #4).

> *C: (After describing the different parts.) I have the feeling that there are many more, but I'm not too clear about it right now.*
> *T: What do you feel towards the different aspects represented in those chairs?*
> *C: In general? If it's in general, curiosity.*
> *T: Do any of them scare you or make you uneasy?*
> *C: The first one, the dark side, the one that has access to all the rest.*

281

Although it is a bit early to explore missing pieces (TW #9); we do it because the client offered this opportunity when he said, "I feel that I would need a lot of chairs." What the client can see is important, but what he cannot see or look at could be very important as well. Asking about what is missing can be another opportunity for us to help in making explicit the implicit.

After exploring the different aspects, we validate how the critical part is trying to help. We also introduce the idea that, perhaps, this part can learn to do so in a more adaptive way (TW #6).

> T: *It's great that you can think about these different aspects. And it would be even greater if this were less chaotic for you. If everything were in place, there would be no need for this dark part to criticize you in such a way. So it would be able to protect you in a way that's not so hard on you. I think it would be interesting to work on that.*
> C: *Yes, a self-critical part is okay, but not like this.*
> T: *Yes, a critical part is important and can help a lot. The problem arises when there is too much criticism. So, it's important to find out why this part is doing this. Maybe it doesn't know that there are other options.*
> C: *Maybe.*
> T: *We will try to find out. I'm pretty sure this part can learn to help you in a more adaptive way.* (Client listens attentively.) *Do you think it can be interesting to keep exploring these aspects in another session?*
> C: *Yes.*

We close the session reinforcing the work done (CS #3.1). This session led to an interesting change in the client. He was able to start looking at this critical part from a new perspective: as a part that was trying to help but did not know how to do it differently. In the following sessions, we will dive further into the work with the critical part.

EXAMPLE 2. VALIDATION AS A WAY TO MODEL FOR THE CRITICAL PART

In the next session, we begin exploring how the client and the voices left the previous session (CS #1.1) and checking how the week has been for the entire system (CS #1.2). This allows the client to give us more information about the functioning of the parts. He explains how he is unable to do any creative work because the critical part keeps putting him down. The client says it is the part's fault and that he would like it to shut up and leave him alone, which is a clear manifestation of a dissociative phobia (TW #4). We know this dynamic is not going to result in any improvement in the system, so the first step is to try to enhance collaboration (TW #10). To do this, we need for the client to increase his understanding of the critical part, a part that has learned to respond in this way (TW #6), and change his defensive response.

> T: *How did you feel after our meeting?*
> C: *Good, curious, but also frustrated.*
> T: *Can you tell me about it?*
> C: *Well, I was thinking of what you said, that this part was trying to help me somehow. But then nothing changed, it kept being critical, and I couldn't do anything about it.*

T: *Yes, well it's probably doing what it learned to do. Remember we said we would keep exploring today to try to understand it better.*

C: *Okay.*

T: *How was everything inside after our session?*

C: *The critical part seemed to be quiet for a while, but when I tried to draw, it went back to the same old stuff.*

T: *How about the other parts?*

C: *They just want to get rid of the critical part.*

T: *And what do you think about that?*

C: *I agree, it would be a solution.*

T: *You think so?*

C: *Yes.*

T: *If you try to get rid of any of these parts, things will stir up, and you will probably feel attacked again. Do you understand this?*

C: *Yes.*

T: *And why do you think this happens?*

C: *Because they want to self-preserve.*

T: *That's right. Does it make sense to you?*

C: *Yes, it makes sense, but I don't remember making any initial attack towards that part.*

This is a good opportunity to introduce how having such a negative view of any parts will most likely generate more problems and how this is actually creating and maintaining the internal conflict.

T: *Well, if you see this part as something so negative, something that you don't want, something that you fear or something you despise, even if you are not attacking directly, that part of you can feel attacked.*

C: *Yes, I understand that, but it is a part of me that I despise, and I don't like because of his behavior during these last few months, not the other way around. I don't think that it's behaving like that because of my thoughts about him. It's the opposite.*

T: *It would be interesting to find out why he needs to behave like this. That information is inside of you, this part of you knows why. Have you asked this part about this?*

C: *Yes, but nothing. I don't know if I am asking correctly.*

The client sees the critical part as an enemy, so the critical part becomes more extreme with the negative comments, which in turn, generates increasingly more fear in the client. This is a common occurrence, and clients may need time to fully understand this dynamic. One way to guide the next interventions is to promote curiosity towards those parts that the client still does not understand (TW #2), exploring the dissociative phobia (TW #4) and their function (TW #6). In this case, the client rejects the part but, at the same time, he is curious enough about trying to understand what happens inside, which is a good prognosis for therapy and this type of work.

T: *Do you fear getting in touch with other parts of yourself?*

C: *No, I don't think so. I'd like to know myself better.*

T: *You like to know yourself. And would you be willing to see how this part can contribute?*

C: *Yes.*

Working with the meeting place procedure, the visualization exercise that was introduced in the previous session, can help us explore the system in a more organized way. It is important to check which parts are in the meeting place in the present moment and always make sure to extend a general invitation to all the parts, even the ones we do not know. Clients sometimes think that they should go back to the same parts that showed up the last time the exercise was done, and this may increase frustration if some of those parts happen not to be present.

> *T: Could you close your eyes like last time and imagine your meeting place?*
> *C: Yes.*
> *T: And just notice which aspects or parts are there today.*
> *C: I don't know, it's more or less like we left it the other day.*
> *T: Just try to observe. What do you see? How many chairs should there be now?*
> *C: I couldn't tell, practically the same as the other day but with two more extra spaces.*
> *T: Remember all parts are welcome, even the ones we might not know.*
> *C: Okay.*

The parts are practically the same ones that were present in the previous session. Once we made the general invitation, it is important to resume the work with the critical part, the one that was more hesitant towards working and cooperating with the rest of the parts.

> *T: How is the critical part doing?*
> *C: He feels like a victim, basically he feels attacked.*
> *T: Why is that?*
> *C: Because the other parts don't like him.*
> *T: We are working on this. The other parts don't understand them yet. Once they do, I think things could change.*
> *C: I hope so.*
> *T: What do you notice when I say that? What happens inside?*
> *C: He seems more open to listening.*

Showing interest in the critical part is crucial in this case; since it will help the client do the same and will promote empathy toward this complicated voice that he says he imagines. Acknowledging the importance of these voices usually has a pretty fast and somewhat calming effect. This is not to say that the part will immediately trust both therapist and client, but there will usually be some relief, and it can be the beginning of cooperation (TW #10), as we have seen in the previous section.

> *T: Tell him that we know he is a very important part of this process.*
> *C: Okay.*
> *T: And that our intention is not to attack him. We are also going to help him.*
> *C: (Internal communication.) On one side he doesn't seem to believe it.*
> *T: I understand, it's normal, we just met.*
> *C: But on the other hand, he has a sensation of "Finally!" I don't know how to explain it better. He feels that we owe him a lot and we have not been appreciative.*

This is a crucial moment in the session: the part is beginning to communicate feelings. We must acknowledge that, validate it (TW #7) and help the client understand that this is important. Then we check how the parts respond to our intervention (CS #2.5), just as we did in the previous example.

> T: *It is important to thank this part for giving us the opportunity to work with him. He can observe what happens and let us know the things he doesn't agree with. We are going to listen to him. (Client closes his eyes and starts communicating internally.) Is he receiving this information?*
> C: *Yes.*
> T: *What happens when he hears what we just said?*
> C: *He calms down a bit. He doesn't trust very much, but it seems that he might be willing to give in a bit.*
> T: *That's important, it can be dangerous to trust right away.*

Welcoming distrust is a good way to proceed in this type of situations. A critical part might feel better when he or she is seen or acknowledged but trust still needs to develop. After working with the critical part, the client starts noticing some restlessness. Restlessness after receiving empathic attunement from both therapist and client represents a phobia for intimacy/attachment (TW #4). It is possible that the voice is more familiar taking an oppositional, critical and, disconnected stance. The work in this session challenges the part to experience an attunement first from the therapist and then from the client, something that is quite new and unfamiliar for the client.

> T: *Check inside and notice where the restlessness is coming from. Go back to the meeting place and check where this restlessness is located.*
> C: *Well I think it is related to the fear towards this part because it is so resistant.*
> T: *What part would this be?*
> C: *Mainly, the self-critical part.*
> T: *The one that was calmer before? Is it the same part or are they different parts?*
> C: *I think it's the same one, but I'm not sure.*
> T: *Just look at the meeting place and observe if it's the same part or not.*
> C: *Well it's a little bit strange because, on the one hand, I notice this part is calm and, at the same time, there is a lot of restlessness. I somehow perceive two opposite aspects of the same part.*

When continuing to explore the source of the restlessness, we often encounter a common fear that many parts have: they are used to the client wanting them to disappear and tend to assume that this desire is also shared by the therapist. Remember this is one of the special issues in working with challenging parts from Chapter 5.

> T: *Ask him what are we doing now that is making him restless.*
> C: *Well he doesn't want us to expel him or get rid of him.*
> T: *It's great that he can tell us this because it's important to clarify that this is not the idea at all. We are not going to expel him or get rid of him. We are going to listen to him and take him into account. We'll let him play a major role, so he can integrate with you when the time is right.*
> C: *Okay*

In this case, mentioning integration is not an issue. The patient understands the goal is to function in an integrated way and has even spoken about this in the first session. In other cases, when the phobia of dissociative parts is very high, when parts are still seen as "not me," or when there are issues with differentiation, we should be careful about mentioning integration or the possibility of integrating parts. Using metaphors such as teamwork, or words like cooperation and collaboration will be better accepted and are less likely to cause problems.

> *T: Let him think about that and just notice the sensations that go along.*
> *C: Well, he calms down in a certain way, but then he gets back on guard.*
> *T: This is normal, it's okay. Ask him if he wants to focus on that sensation that he notices when he gets on guard or if it's enough for today?*
> *C: I think he can go on, but I don't know.*
> *T: You think he can.*
> *C: Yes.*
> *T: How about this part, does he agree?*
> *C: He feels attacked and wants us to leave him alone.*
> *T: Tell him he can decide, and whatever he decides is okay. We are going to take him into account no matter what, he is a very important part. It's okay if he wants to continue and it's okay if he wants to stop.*

Through the previous intervention, we are letting the critical part know that he has choices and his pace will be fully respected. This models a new way of responding towards this part (TW #8), one that may lower the defensive attitude from this part and, in turn, may also help with collaboration (TW #10), which in this case, facilitates him saying "yes" to continuing forward a bit longer.

> *C: He says that we can continue for a bit.*
> *T: Ask him to focus on the sensations that he is noticing, then.*
> *C: Okay. (BLS)*
> *T: What do you notice now?*
> *C: He seems to calm down.*
> *T: Okay, great.*

After processing the phobia in the critical part (TW #4), we explore the rest of parts, so we can get an idea of the effect of the intervention on the rest of the system (CS #2.5).

> *T: What do you see in the meeting place now? Did anything change?*
> *C: Well, they are not like the other day when they were all arguing and fighting. They are simply paying attention.*
> *T: What do you think about this?*
> *C: It's better for sure.*
> *T: Can you check how these parts are doing?*
> *C: Well, in a way they also felt attacked, so it's normal that they wanted the critical part to go away. The creative part feels more hurt than the other parts.*

When we have the opportunity to explore a part that feels hurt, it is important to take it. The general idea is to be curious about all parts of the system and encourage this curiosity in the client (TW #2), but we also need to take turns to work with the parts that are in more conflict so we can explore possible needs and alternative ways of responding (TW #7 and TW #8).

> T: *Is it okay of we pay some attention to this creative part?*
> C: *Yes.*
> T: *What is he noticing now?*
> C: *That he has always been punished due to the bad behavior of the critical part. He wants to do something and be active.*
> T: *In order for him to do things, he must be a little less frustrated, don't you think?*
> C: *I don't know.*
> T: *Ask him what he would need in order to be able to start doing things.*
> C: *He needs the critical part to shut up.*
> T: *What does the critical part think about this? Remember this is a space intended for dialogue and understanding, where every part can express how they feel and it's okay to do so.*
> C: *He doesn't want to shut up.*

As the communication between parts increases, we try to suggest alternative ways of responding (TW #8) and reach an agreement with the critical part that may work for all of them (TW #10).

> T: *Ask the critical part if he can give some space to the creative part, maybe a couple of days or until the next session?* (Client checks with the part.) *Would this be possible?*
> C: (Client takes time to listen to the part.) *He doesn't want to.*
> T: *Can you ask him why?*
> C: *Because he feels that he would be giving up command.*

The part continues to have trouble understanding or believing that we do not want to get rid of him and, in addition, he repeats what he knows how to do. We cannot force agreements or be critical with a part that only knows to criticize. So, we should model new behaviors (TW #8) by searching for common elements. The Adult Self usually has a more integrated vision than a part that is only focused on what needs to improve.

> T: *He wouldn't give up power or command because he would always be taken into consideration. He has important things to say, and I would make sure I ask him in the next session. This would allow the creative part to be a bit less frustrated and maybe it would also help us to understand the critical part better. Let's see if they can reach an agreement, something that they can agree on, however small.*
> C: (After a few minutes of checking in.) *They're not reaching an agreement.*
> T: *Is there anything in common between these two parts? What could they have in common? An interest, an ability....*
> C: *In a way, they both want to help.*
> T: *Can you ask them both to focus only on that, on the desire to help? And see if they can come up with anything they can agree on.*
> C: (After a couple of minutes.) *They are arguing.*
> T: *What are they saying?*

287

C: Well, the creative part says that in order for me to fulfill myself, I need to do something that I like. And the critical part says that I am no good for that or that I can't do it, and that I am going to get hurt.

T: The critical part is concerned that you might get hurt.

C: Yes.

T: It makes sense, so the idea would be to find out if this critical part can try to collaborate and help while the creative part is doing an activity, without thinking he is going to fail. Perhaps he can try to help with a more constructive attitude, so the creative part doesn't feel paralyzed. Ask him to think about this.

C: Okay.

T: What does he think?

C: Nothing, there is more tension.

T: Who feels more tension?

C: The critical part.

T: Let's trust that this part will find a way to do something. Give him time to think, okay?

C: Okay. (After a couple of minutes.) Well this part is also frustrated because he would also like to be able to do things, but he thinks that all the other parts are useless.

T: Okay, so all parts share a feeling of frustration, right?

C: Yes.

T: Does this part understand that if he says that the other parts are useless, they may become even more blocked?

C: I don't know.

T: Can he understand that he can have more power if he doesn't make negative comments that may hurt other parts? Can he think about this?

C: Okay. (Client takes some time to check with the part.)

T: What happens when he thinks about that?

C: He's calmer now, but he has a very strict and firm personality.

T: Well, this is what he learned. This part has learned a way of doing things to try to help. Let's try to find a way to soften it without forgetting to do what he thinks is important. What do you think?

C: Good.

We check to see how the rest of the system receives our interventions (TCS #2.5) to make sure that we are not going too fast. From time to time, if there is a chance, it is interesting to explore the needs and sensations of each part and we can introduce the processing phobias procedure (TW #4) or the Tip of the Finger Strategy, described in Chapter 2, with each part.

T: We are not going to ask the parts to talk to each other, because they are not ready, but we will keep in mind the needs of each part and try fulfilling them. Let's go one by one. First ask the creative part to focus on his feeling of powerlessness. Does he feel any relief?

C: Not completely.

T: What does he notice?

C: Well, he feels that he has more strength and motivation to do the things that he wants to do. And more frustration for not being able to do them.

T: Does he know we are working on this?

C: Yes.

T: Ask him to focus on his frustration and let him know that we are working on it. What do you notice?

C: He's in a hurry.

T: We understand this, but sometimes being in a hurry might interfere. Let's go step by step so we can achieve the goals. Can you ask this part to give us some time? We won't forget.

C: He says that he has been waiting for a long time.

T: And we are listening to him now. Tell this part that we understand he has a lot of reasons to act like that, and that in all sessions, we will listen to what he has to say.

The therapist's attitude must always include treating all parts equally. This attitude will eventually sink in and it will become a new way of relating for the internal system (TW #8).

T: What happens inside when I say this?

C: They are both calmer. He is calm, but he says he will still remain alert.

T: Great, it's good to be alert, it's a good protection.

C: Yes.

T: What do you notice now?

C: He is calm

This is another piece of work toward collaboration. The system is still in conflict but, with help, the client and the different parts are beginning to learn new ways. Validating the alertness (TW #7) as a protection (TW #6) is a good intervention for this type of parts. We close the session thanking the parts for the work they have all done.

EXAMPLE 3. REACHING AGREEMENTS: TEAMWORK

In the next session, the client comes in with a proposal for working with the different parts. He says the previous work we did got him thinking about how to best work with the internal system and he wants to run his ideas by the therapist to see if he is on the right track.

T: So, you said you had been thinking about our conversations and ways to work with these parts. C: Yes, all parts must participate and contribute with something to the whole.

T: I think it's a very good Idea.

C: Yes, I wrote it after our session. Should I read it?

T: Sure.

C: I'm calling it the Constitution of the Citizens of Hugo's Head and these are the statutes:

1) Each citizen will do whatever they do best.

2) All citizens have the duty and the right to express themselves and inform if needed.

3) No citizen can omit relevant information or prevent others from sharing information.

4) Punishment will not be allowed, only corrections; no threats or scorn will be allowed, only advice.

5) All citizens will search for the overall wellbeing because they search for and want the same things.

6) The tasks of each citizen will be studied if necessary. The goal of the study will be to understand and learn, in a positive way and without punishments.

7) None of the citizens will have absolute power or more power than others.

8) All citizens will be taken into consideration.

9) If there is the need to correct a citizen, his motives will be heard, and he will be supported.

And that's what I wrote so far.

T: Great! It's fantastic.

C: Really?

T: Yes, I would only change one thing.

C: What?

T: The one regarding omitting relevant information.

C: Why?

T: Because each one might have or need a different pace. The idea is for relevant information to come up when the moment is right.

C: Uh-huh.

T: Overall, it's wonderful. It's just that the idea of not being allowed to omit relevant information can make some of the parts feel too much pressure.

C: Okay, I will write it down.

T: What do you think about it?

C: I agree (as he writes it down).

This is a good example of how modeling sinks in: clients understand what is not working out and begin to think of different ways of relating to themselves and the system of parts. Of course, this client is very bright and has high integrative capacities, which helps. After going over the Constitution, we proceed by checking how the parts are doing.

T: How is everything inside now?

C: I think that they're all very tired. There's some confusion, but they're all very tired.

T: Confusion about what?

C: Nothing in particular. What I notice mostly is a general sense of tiredness.

T: There is a general sense of tiredness. Does anyone stand out?

C: The strongest one now is the critical part, but he's not very useful.

Although it is easy to overlook these rejecting messages, it is important to avoid them whenever possible. Whenever clients express negative comments about a part, we should remind them of the therapeutic goals and try to implicate these parts in the work we are doing (TW #10). If we want to model new ways of responding (TW #8), we need to be consistent about the relevance of respect towards all the parts. While we promote curiosity (TW #2), we will be earning the trust from the more distrustful parts.

T: Let's try to remain curious. Remember these comments about not being useful or wanting to get rid of any of the parts are not helpful.

C: Yeah, okay, but this part is what is making the rest tired. The others hoped things could change and he is not cooperating.

T: And we are working on that. You just read out loud a wonderful example of how we are going to keep all of the parts in mind, including this part that has more trouble working as a team.

C: Uh-huh.

T: Ask the critical part if he has any constructive ideas to do something positive.

C: There is nothing I can do. At least that's what he tells me.

T: Ask this part if he can do something to help you.

C: He doesn't know.

T: Okay, he doesn't know. Is this part tired too?

C: He's more tired than usual, but he's the strongest of them all.

Since ordinary exploration is not generating much movement, we can try using the Tip of the Finger Strategy described in Chapter 2 to decrease the negative sensations with very short sets of bilateral stimulation (BLS). Let us not forget that these sensations can be conceptualized as a peripheral consequence of the client's unresolved issues. Remember to always ask for permission and constantly check whether the work can move forward or it is best to stop at any given point.

T: Let's try something. (Client nods). Ask this part is he is willing to focus on the tiredness that he is noticing.

C: Okay. (Client checks inside.) Yes.

T: Ask him to just notice what happens. (Client nods. BLS.)

T: What do you get?

C: He is like desperate, angry... He doesn't want to do anything

T: Can you ask this part to focus on his sensation of anger?

C: Okay. (BLS)

T: What do you get?

C: Everything is useless; there is nothing I can do.

T: Are you saying this or is this part saying it?

C: I am. I feel frustrated about not being able to do things.

T: Okay, we will work with your frustration in a while. What happened with this part?

C: He is less angry, but he is still angry at us.

T: Can you ask him if we can work a little bit more with this sensation?

C: Yes.

T: Does he agree?

C: Yes. (BLS)

T: What does he notice?

C: The same.

T: And you?

C: The same, but I feel the tension more in my head now.

T: Okay, focus on that sensation a little bit more. (BLS)

T: What do you get?

C: He feels a lot of pressure. He feels like blowing up and ending everything.

T: Can we continue? Does it think it's positive to work on such an intense sensation?

C: Yes. (BLS)

T: What do you get?

C: He feels very frustrated.

T: Is he feeling it now?

C: Yes.
T: Can we continue?
C: Yes. (BLS)
T: What do you get now?
C: He's disappointed with the other parts.
T: Can you ask him why?
C: Yes, because they are not good enough.

The previous section is an interesting example of the typical dynamic we can observe in these parts: "Nothing works, everything is useless." But notice how the part keeps saying that it is okay to continue, even though he is venting a bit, which is much better than exploding outside of therapy. Despite the apparently negative feedback from the part, the client's body language shows that he is much more at ease than at the beginning of the session. Therefore, we validate how the part feels (TW #7), suggest the possibility of exploring alternative ways of responding and begin to model a different attitude towards the parts (TW #8), which will help the critical part to learn other ways of communicating.

T: Ask him if it would be possible for him to give us information about how he feels in a less negative way. That usually works better.
C: Okay. (Client checks inside.) He doesn't know that what he says are negative things, he doesn't find a positive way.
T: Isn't that interesting? He is not aware that he is actually saying negative things.
C: I know. No, he is not.
T: Well, this is what this part learned to do. What do you think about this?
C: I didn't know he wasn't aware of that. Now I understand what you mean about teaching him new ways.

This is a wonderful step towards greater realization. The fact that the part was not even aware of the negativity behind his attitude is quite a discovery for the client, who can be more empathic with this part once he understands his difficulties. Once curiosity is online, we can validate the intention and begin exploring the possible function of the part (TW #6).

T: Great. So, let's try to understand why he is so critical. What is he trying to achieve by doing that?
C: He wants the rest to work harder.
T: Ask him if it's okay to ask the other parts what they can do or how they can help.
C: He says that he already asked them, but it doesn't work.
T: We can try to ask them now. (Client makes a gesture.) That is okay, he is not too sure yet. He is still learning the new ways. Which parts are more active now?
C: The reasoning part and the creative part.
T: Can you ask the critical part what he would need to see from the other parts?
C: More effort.
T: How would he recognize the additional effort?
C: He doesn't know.
T: Let's check in with the other parts. Could you ask them both if they have any idea of what they could do? Perhaps one little thing, something feasible.

C: They don't know. They feel discouraged.

T: Why is that?

C: They have lost the desire to do things because they think that, no matter what they do, it will be no good.

T: I see. And can the critical part hear this?

C: Yes.

T: What does he think about it?

C: He doesn't know what he is supposed to do.

T: Well, this is related to what I was suggesting in the previous session. To maybe give the other parts some space to do things, without criticizing them. I understand this is how this part learned to respond, but it's not really helping now.

C: No, it's not working.

T: What do you notice inside when I say this?

C: They are all listening.

T: Great. I am glad they are curious about finding new ways of responding. Let's see if we can think of something together. What do you think the other parts could do?

C: I don't know; something is blocking me. Every time we try to do something with any of the other parts, I feel pressure in my head, and I can't go any further.

T: Is this block that you notice related to any of the parts?

C: I don't know.

T: Can you ask? (Client nods.)

C: Nobody answers.

T: Where do you feel the block?

C: In the back of my head.

This is another opportunity to work on an element that seems to be getting in the way. First, we explore it to see if it is related to any specific part. If it is, we will try to find out what is happening with this part. If it is a general sensation, it can be helpful to process it with very short sets of bilateral stimulation (BLS).

T: Can you focus on that block? (Client nods.) (BLS)

T: What do you notice?

C: I feel bad in general because I think I did everything wrong.

T: Now you feel bad, but the idea is to work with something that can help you, and make you and all the parts feel better. I think the block is important; we should take it into account. Can you focus on the block again? (Client nods.) (BLS)

T: What do you notice now?

C: That it's all my fault; they are all negative messages.

T: Where are those messages coming from?

C: I think they are coming from the self-critical part.

T: Can you ask, just to be sure?

C: I'm not really sure that they come from the self-critical part.

T: Okay, go back to the meeting room and check if there is any part that knows where this is coming from.

C: I feel that all the parts are pretty calm now.

T: Uh-huh. So, let's keep working with the block you were noticing. How is the block now?

C: It's about a 5, maybe lower in certain moments.

T: Can we focus on the block again? (Client nods.) (BLS) What do you get?

C: Guilt.

T: Can you focus on that?

C: Yes. (BLS)

T: What do you notice now?

C: It's a strong sensation, but I don't really know what it is.

T: Where do you notice it?

C: In my head and my chest. I've got the feeling that something is hiding, but I don't know what it is.

T: Check if any part knows what it is. (Client checks inside) What do you get?

C: They feel it's there too, but they don't know what it is either. I don't know if it's myself or another part that was not there before.

T: Can you focus on that? (Client nods.) (BLS)

T: What do you get?

C: It's mental, pretty strong; it's unpleasant negative energy.

T: Do you think it's a good idea to focus on this energy?

C: Yes. (BLS)

T: What do you notice?

C: The block. A very negative description of myself. I feel very bad, guilty, that I don't deserve anything.

T: How would you describe this block that you notice?

C: I don't know. It's like a dark stain, and I can't see beyond it.

T: It must be something important, try to be curious and check what is happening with this block.

C: It objects.

T: Well, maybe it has a good reason to object. Ask if something is bothering it.

C: It doesn't answer, it's just there.

T: Is the sensation in the same place? Is it more intense?

C: Yes, it has increased.

T: What do you think this means?

C: Either it's protecting itself or it doesn't want to allow us to go forward.

T: How do you feel about this block?

C: Mostly worried.

T: Focus on the worry that you feel towards the block. What do you get?

C: I'm worried that it might be a part with negative intentions, self-destructive, with no practical use.

Throughout this session, in addition to promoting curiosity (TW #2) and asking for permission before moving forward, we are constantly moving from processing bits of sensation with the Tip of the Finger Strategy to checking how the different parts are responding to the interventions (CS #2.5). We now explore the phobia (TT-4) and once we detect that it is present, we process it, hoping it might help decrease the fear toward this new part or whatever this stain represents that the client is concerned about. If the work seems to be flowing, we should always try to move forward unless we encounter the sensation of needing to stop. In other clients, the appearance of dark parts can create major blockages that would alert us to the need to slow down the pace of work.

T: What are you noticing now? Fear? Rejection?

C: It's more like fear or concern.

T: Okay fear. Should we focus on that fear that you feel?

C: Yes.

T: Focus on the block and the fear you notice towards this something that has shown up. (BLS) What do you notice?

C: I am not sure.

T: Does it have the same intensity?

T: It's lower now.

C: Shall we do a bit more?

C: I don't know, I'm afraid of thinking that it's something that wants to hurt me. The sensation increases if I think about focusing on it again.

T: So, it seems like the block is telling us to leave it alone for today and we will respect this.

C: Yes.

T: Let's go back to your sensation. What do you notice?

C: I don't know. I'm worried, and I want to know what's happening.

T: Blocks usually have a protective function, and it's important to respect them, but we can work on your sensation of fear as you keep in mind this information.

C: Okay. (BLS)

T: What do you notice?

C: The block is increasing.

T: Interesting, so when we leave it alone, the block increases.

C: Yes.

T: Okay, go back to the meeting room and see if any part has information about the block or if anything has changed. Just observe for a while. (Closes his eyes to check inside.) What do you see now?

C: It seems that they are all waiting for something to happen as if they were waiting for instructions or something like that.

T: How is the block now?

C: It's calmer.

T: It seems that, in a way, it wants to be taken into consideration. It doesn't want to be ignored.

C: I suppose so.

After reducing the blockage, we can explore the internal conflict better. The client needs to do things he enjoys, but some parts get nervous with this idea and block him. We close the session asking for permission from the internal system to allow him to do things that he likes doing without criticism until the next session and to notice how he feels (TW #10).

C: When we talked about doing something this week, it started to increase again.

T: Right now, it seems as if there is a need for a change.

C: Yes.

T: But this possibility of change causes disturbance.

C: Yes.

T: Check if the parts that are feeling disturbed can agree to give us some time. We won't forget about them; we would just be trying something different.

C: (Client checks inside.) *They agree to try.*

T: How are the parts now?

C: Calm.

T: How are you feeling now?

C: Calm too.

T: Okay, so all of you are calm, and they all agree to try this out until the next session.

C: Yes.

T: You have done a great job today. All of you.

C: Thank you. It feels that way, yes.

After working with the different issues that came up as we explored (CS #2.4) things improved for the client. We cannot say this is a conflict-free inner system, but there is more cooperation and respect as we move forward. It was good enough that, by the end of the session, the system of parts was able to accept trying new ways of responding (TW #8) and agreed to give the client some time (TW #10).

EXAMPLE 4. HOW ABOUT ASKING FOR A TRUCE?

After having reached agreements (TW #10), we should always explore whether the client and the parts were able to follow the indications offered (CS #1.3) and inquire about the results. In the following session, the client explains that things are calmer in general. He was still not able to feel very creative, but he had started getting some ideas and there were no critical responses from the parts. He also says how he would like to move forward but is afraid of the critical part's response. When exploring what he would like to do, he explains that what he likes the most is also what blocks him (e.g., drawing, doing creative work).

We use this difficulty as a point of entry towards exploring and understanding what the client might need from the critical part to be able to put his ideas in practice.

C: I feel trapped. I don't like it, I feel small, useless.

T: I understand, and you say that it's in reaction to this part. (Client nods.) *What do you feel towards this part now?*

C: Lack of understanding and concern.

T: Would you be able to give this part any positive message?

C: No, I can't find anything positive.

As is to be expected with this type of dynamic, the client also has difficulties in communicating something positive or expressing himself in a non-critical way, which could help him to better understand the difficulties that the part presents when it comes to saying positive messages. Offering possible options (TW #8) can be useful in this type of situation.

T: How about something like, "I'm going to keep on trying to understand what's happening?"

C: Yes, I can do that. (Client looks more motivated.)

T: Try telling him that and see what you notice.

C: He's not too sure.

T: He's not too sure, that's fine. What can we do to help him feel a little bit more confident?

C: He's afraid I might get hurt.

T: Can you ask him if you can do something about it?

C: Yes. (Client checks inside). He says I've done things wrong many times, so he's not going to change his mind easily.

T: That's understandable. If we look at it in that way, it makes sense.

The first thing we want to do is validate how the part feels, without necessarily having to agree with it (TW #7). After we do this, it is interesting to ask for exceptions. Critical parts are good at doing their job, which is to focus on what is not working right or what can be improved. By exploring exceptions, we are helping the client and the parts think of alternatives that might have worked before (TW # 8).

T: Ask the critical part if there were moments when you did do things right.

C: He says I always do things halfway.

T: He has trouble appreciating the times when you did things right. It seems like he is not able to see them or recognize those moments.

C: No, the only thing he says is that I always do things halfway.

T: Okay, ask him what he thinks is influencing you doing things halfway?

C: He says that I have a weak spirit and I lack consistency, among other things.

T: Ask him how this could be improved. Let's see if he can give us any clues.

C: He says that if I have not accomplished this until now, it will be difficult.

T: Of course, it will be difficult. All of you have to think differently and try to focus on what can be done differently now. I am wondering if this part would be willing to let you try out drawing or doing other tasks without interfering with comments.

C: He says, "Try if you want."

T: He doesn't seem too sure. Can you ask him if he is willing to try?

C: Nothing, no answer.

T: Could this part give you some time, so you can find a way to start something and finish it?

C: I don't know.

T: Can we ask him?

C: It says that it's still going to tell me if I do anything wrong.

T: Okay, but could you ask if he can be a little bit less harsh?

C: He says that he only mentions what he observes.

T: So, again, he is not able to see the good things that you do?

C: He says that I do everything wrong.

T: You know something? It's very hard for a person to do everything wrong. Perhaps, he just doesn't have access to the information or is too used to focusing on what needs to be improved. (Client is listening with interest.) How about you? Do you remember the last time you did something right?

C: Not really.

T: You don't. Okay, so you too have trouble seeing it. This is why we need to think of different ways of doing and seeing things.

C: I see.

T: Check if any other parts can remember anything you may have done right.

C: It seems like this part is not allowing them to give their opinion.

As usual, we try to help the client and the system of parts to listen to the voices and parts (TW #2) but the critical part does not seem to be up for this, so we need to address this issue (CS #2.4) and see if we can achieve some cooperation (TW #10).

T: Okay, can you ask this part if it would be possible to listen to what the other parts have to say? I understand he is trying to help, but we agreed to listen to all of the different opinions. The critical part can be there observing too.

C: He's not going to go away so easily.

T: I don't want him to go away.

C: I mean, to leave some space.

T: I know it's not easy, because he's not used to that, but can he try? I know it's hard, let's give him some time.

C: He's very resistant.

This is another opportunity to use what is happening as a point of entry. Sometimes it is useful to process the resistance that comes up while exploring. When there is resistance from any of the parts, there is usually some type of phobia involved (phobia of other parts, phobia of the therapeutic work, phobia of the therapist). If we identify the resistance as a phobia, the processing phobias procedure can be very helpful. Once we identify the resistance, we can also measure it and add short sets of bilateral stimulation (BLS) to desensitize it. Although measuring is not absolutely necessary, it can help us assess the result of the intervention, especially in those cases where we want to check whether the resistance is increasing or decreasing.

T: Do you think we can focus on the resistance a bit?

C: Yes, he agrees to that.

T: Where do you notice the resistance?

C: Mostly in my head.

T: Where does the part feel this resistance?

C: I don't know; it's just a general feeling.

T: From 0 to 10, what level of resistance do you feel?

C: A 7 or 8.

T: Okay focus on the resistance for a while. (BLS.) What do you get?

C: I feel more pressure in my head.

T: You feel pressure when you pay attention to the resistance. Okay, can you ask him what's good about having this resistance?

C: It likes to be there.

T: Being there is good.

C: It's positive but negative because he likes to hold the power.

T: Okay, so that gives him power.

C: Yes, so even though it's positive, it's not convenient.

T: It's something that makes him feel better, with more power and control.

C: Yes.

T: Does he know that there are other ways to feel power and control?

Remember that one of the major issues with challenging parts is related to power and control. If these parts understand that they can keep control, they may be more willing to listen to new ideas and possibilities. Their willingness to listen will be even more pronounced once they understand that they can have more control by learning new more effective ways of dealing with current situations.

C: No.

T: Well, there are actually.

C: He denies it.

T: I understand the resistance gives him power and control. But if this part is willing to help you , he would have even more power because he could help you achieve something that all of you would like to achieve.

C: I don't think he knows how to do that.

T: Probably not, because he didn't learn other ways. But I think he can learn. What do you think about this?

C: It's not easy for him to help me; he says that he only knows how to send me negative messages.

T: Do you understand that it's the only way in which he knows how to act for now?

C: Yes, I understand, but I don't think he wants to help when all he does is punish me or hurt me. That's not a way to help me.

T: I understand you feel that way, maybe this part really needs to hear what you just said. Does this part know that this actually hurts you?

C: He says that his purpose is to educate me and shape me.

T: Yes, I understand that his intention is good. Ask him if he thinks those ways are working now?

C: He says that it has not worked very well.

T: Yes, that is what we are trying to figure out: ways of helping that will really work now. Probably those ways worked years ago when this part learned to respond like this. But now they are really not working and it's good that you both realize that. What do you think?

C: This part is very disappointed with me because I didn't meet his expectations.

T: What would you answer to that? He told you that it had a good intention to educate you and shape you.

C: The only thing I can think of is to apologize, but I tend to apologize a lot, so I don't know if that's positive either.

T: Try to apologize only to this part, and only about this. Also, thank the part for his good intention, and let him know that you are sorry for not being able to do it, but now you are doing your best and you need his help. Just see if this works.

C: He says that being sorry doesn't fix anything.

T: No, but it's important.

C: Yes.

T: Ask him what you could do to start to fix things.

C: My attention is completely gone.

T: Where did it go?

C: I don't know.

T: He might not know what to suggest. How do you notice the part now?

C: He is not saying anything.

T: Now you have more information about this critical part. Does it help you understand him better?

C: Yes.

T: And maybe it will help you to remember that at the beginning of the session, you also had trouble thinking about anything positive.

C: Right, yes.

Once the critical part is calmer, we can try to introduce a visualization exercise and have the client imagine how he would draw if he were ever able to do it again. This exercise is based on the idea of the future template from EMDR Therapy.

T: I'm going to ask you to do something, but we need your inner system to collaborate. Is it possible?

C: (Clients checks inside.) Yes.

T: It's a visualization exercise. The idea is for you to imagine all the steps you would need to take to make a drawing. Imagine what the space looks like and how you do the drawing. It's important that all the parts allow this without interfering, we know their intention is to help and educate but at the moment we would need them to just observe. All parts can be there but only observing, without interfering. Do you think it's possible?

C: Yes, I think I can try.

T: Do all parts agree?

C: Yes.

The client closes his eyes to visualize himself drawing. After a few minutes go by, he begins to make gestures. We explore what is happening (CS #2.2).

T: How is it going?

C: I'm not able to visualize what I want to draw.

T: What were you able to visualize?

C: The moment I start to draw, but I'm not happy with it, so I erase it or throw it out and start all over again.

T: Is that what usually happens when you try to draw?

C: Yes.

T: Could you visualize yourself doing it without throwing away what you don't like?

C: I can try.

T: Try it.

C: I can't keep what I don't like.

T: Were you ever able to imagine keeping the things you don't like instead of throwing them away?

C: I never like to see things that I've done wrong. I erase them or throw them away.

T: This is one way of doing things, but you can also learn from the things you don't like. And maybe here is where the critical part can be helpful.

C: How?

T: Have you ever tried to draw taking into consideration the critical part instead of blocking it?

C: I don't know how to do that. If the critical part keeps sending negative messages, I'm not able to do it. That makes me stop drawing.

T: Yes, this is what would need to change a bit. The idea would be that the part could be there to help with constructive criticism, instead of sending such critical messages.

T: I don't know, I haven't thought about it.

T: Can we ask him?

C: He has no intention of doing it.

T: Why is that?

C: He thinks it's a waste of time.

T: I see, but is he willing to try?

C: I guess so.

T: That would be great. What do you think?

C: I would like that, but he says he doesn't know how to do it.

T: It's great that he can say this. Check if any of the other parts know how to do this.

C: There is a lot of confusion; nobody really knows how to do it.

T: I see. This is why it is so important to learn new ways of doing things. What does your inside think about this?.

C: I get that it's important to do it, that's all.

T: Where is that coming from?

C: I think it's coming from the creative part.

T: Okay, so we have the critical part that criticizes to help and, when we ask him to guide you, he says he doesn't know how. It takes a lot of courage to say that. And this is allowing other parts to think about it too. Could the creative part help with this?

C: I am not sure this part knows either.

The above excerpt illustrates how to validate the responses of the different parts, especially of the critical part. With this type of new communication, he can start to recognize that he does not know how to do it even if he wants to. The fact that he can express that he has no idea how to do it is great progress, since one of the goals for these parts is to be able to communicate that they need help and that they can be more vulnerable than usual. Once the conflict has been reduced, cooperation improves (TT-10). We seize the moment to ask for something new: a truce with the critical part so the creative part can help him to draw again.

T: Well, each part has a different function. I am wondering if the creative part would be willing to try to help while the critical part stands by and observes until the next session?

C: The creative part is willing to do it.

T: How about the critical part?

C: He doesn't like this idea very much.

T: Ask the critical part if he can just take note of what can be improved without telling you all the time. I'll remember to ask him about it in the next session. Then we can see if this new response can bring about any changes.

C: Okay (internal communication). Yes, he says that he can do it.

T: That would be great. What do you think about this?

C: That we can try.

T: Please thank him and thank all the other parts. This is great!

This is a good way to close a session with a system that is not used to collaboration. We thank the critical part, but we also thank the rest of the parts (CS #3.1) since they usually feel ignored and bullied by the critical part. We cannot know how this exercise will turn out, but it is a step towards working as a team. At the very least, there is the intention of trying to do things differently by both parts involved in the capacity to draw. The fact that both parts involved in the ability to draw intend to try to do things differently is something new and positive. The step of preventing future obstacles could have been added (CS #3.5), alerting the patient that if he is not able to do the exercise, he should keep in mind that parts are still learning to try other ways of responding and to take note to see what can be improved. In this case, we chose not to do so because there were many doubts in the system around this possibility. The critical part could take it as a lack of confidence in their ability. Taking into account that it is the first time ever that the critical part seems have lowered defenses and that he is not a patient at risk of harm if expectations are not are completely fulfilled, we can wait to see the result.

EXAMPLE 5. THE TRUCE IS WORKING

After the work done in the previous session, the critical part complied with the agreement and allowed the client to begin to draw again without pressure or negative comments. We find out about this because we explore the effects of the work done in the previous session (CS #1.1 and CS #1.2) and we check if the client and the parts have followed the indications that were given (CS #1.3).

T: How did you leave the session the other day?

C: Good, as if something different could begin.

T: How was the week?

C: Good.

T: Were you able to draw?

C: Yes.

T: How did you feel?

C: Very good, to be honest. I just hope it lasts.

T: Did the creative part help with this?

C: Yes, without that part, I can't get things done.

T: How does the creative part feel helping with that?

C: Good.

T: How is the critical part doing now?

C: I don't know. I suppose he is waiting to give his opinion.

T: Great, that was the idea. We agreed we would ask him for his opinion. Can you ask him?

C: Okay (internal communication). He is not completely happy. It says that I didn't do much, that it's not good, and it's not enough.

This type of response is very typical in these cases. Critical parts can step aside but are still learning "positive" ways of communicating what could be improved. The therapist needs to model how to focus on what is working instead of what is not. In the following section, we work with the critical part; we do not need to focus on the creative part that is already cooperating and feeling good about it.

T: *I see, can you ask him if what you are doing now is better than what you were doing before?*

C: (Client checks inside.) *He says it doesn't matter.*

T: *Why does he say that?*

C: *Because he thinks what I have done is the same as doing nothing.*

T: *Ask him if he understands that, in order to do things, there must be a process.* (Client nods, while listening.) *The first step is to be able to work calmly so you can continue to improve, but if you don't manage to calm down it's going to be very hard to do.* (Client nods.) *This part would like for the process to be finished, and so would you, wouldn't you?*

C: *Yes.*

T: *But both of you can understand that there must be a process.*

C: *Yes.*

T: *Does he understand that what he did this week made things easier for you and has been useful?*

C: *I get the feeling that he's testing me to see if I can do something useful.*

T: *Okay, we can thank this part for allowing you to draw this week.* (Client nods.) *And can you explain that this is a process and that his help is crucial for it to work?*

By helping the client and the part to focus on the positive aspects, both can continue this exploration without much difficulty. After reinforcing the work done by the part (CS #3.1), we can keep exploring if something else needs to be addressed (CS #2.4).

C: *Yes* (internal communication). *He doesn't know what we want from him.*

T: *Anything he can do to contribute is good, any kind of cooperation he can offer.*

C: *He doesn't like the idea of being pushed aside.*

T: *He will not be pushed aside at all; we will always ask for his opinion and his point of view. This is very important, that is why we are asking for his help; he plays a very important role in improving things.*

The fact that this part can openly express what he feels and thinks means that things are evolving well. By validating the "critical part" and giving it a more adaptive function (TW #6), it starts to negotiate, be flexible and collaborate with the rest of the system (TW #10). This allows us to explore alternatives (TW #8) to continue improving.

C: *He's negotiating and says that will let me do things as he did these past few days, but with some conditions.*

T: *Fantastic. What are those conditions?*

C: *If I want to do something like drawing, whenever I do it, he wants me to truly do it.*

T: *Do you know what that means?*

C: *Yes, it means that I can't get distracted or look at something else.*

T: *What do you think? Does this sound reasonable?*

C: Yes, it's something I have to do, but it's very hard for me to focus only on one thing.

T: Well, it makes sense. Is there any way you can get organized to be more focused?

C: I can clean up my desk and buy a new light bulb.

T: You can do that, great. Let's see what he thinks about that.

C: He seems to agree. (Client checking inside.) *Yes, he says I can do things like that, and maybe follow some type of schedule, an order.*

T: What type of schedule would that be?

C: I don't know.

T: Can you ask him? That's interesting.

C: He says that the time of the day doesn't matter, but it must be at least 2 hours, sitting down, being focused, and not changing activities.

T: Great! He's proposing something flexible. This is great.

C: Yes.

T: He has done a great job thinking about how he can help. The week before, he was very critical and that made you feel nervous.

C: Yes.

T: And now this is very reasonable, it makes a lot of sense. Anything else?

C: That's good enough for now.

T: Yes, very good. Please, thank him.

The previous section is a good example of reaching agreements with parts that are in conflict. We involved the part that was interfering with the client being able to draw, appreciated his function (TW #6), validated the opinions he was sharing (TW #7), and asked for suggestions (TW #8). We end the session thanking the part for the work done (CS #3.1) which is a good way to help the Adult Self become more aware of this new collaboration from the part (TW #10).

EXAMPLE 6. WHEN FEELING GOOD FEELS ODD

After five sessions with Hugo, the system is functioning much better. The truce from the critical part was a turning point in therapy. He was able to draw and is now able to function much better. As in many other cases, when this point in therapy is reached, he finds that adapting to this new way of being feels somewhat odd.

C: I'm a little bit upset with myself because I had a very good week, and that's not normal for me.

T: Why does that upset you?

C: Because I can't recognize myself in the things that I do. I went out with people, and I don't have the attitude that I used to have. I'm more open now, I'm different from how I used to be.

T: What do you think about this change of attitude?

C: It's odd.

T: Do you like it?

C: Yes, but I don't like that it's so sudden. I don't think it's natural to make such a change from one day to the next.

T: I don't think it's so sudden. I've noticed changes in you since the day we met. Maybe you were not aware of them. The way you relate and express yourself has changed a lot throughout the sessions.

C: I don't know.

T: Maybe you became more aware of this when you went out and related to others. It's possible that you are integrating the abilities that belong to the different parts and this is helping you.

C: It's pretty odd. I've started to exercise; something I've never liked. I was always lazy; I never liked sports or exercise and, all of a sudden, I feel like doing it.

T: It sounds like a good thing to me.

C: I even bought sneakers and some sports clothes, and I never like to buy anything for myself. They are good things but things that I would never do.

As usual, it is important to check with the system about how every part feels in regard to all these changes because even though they are positive, it usually feels very new and strange for clients and their system of parts. When we check how the system has been and whether the voices have been active during the week (CS #2.1), it is also important to remember to identify what has triggered them (CS #2.2).

T: What does your inside think about this change?

C: It's okay with it, but it's wary.

T: Which part is wary?

C: I don't know.

T: How has it been inside?

C: It's been calm.

T: Have you heard anything?

C: Just a few times, in certain moments.

T: Do you remember when?

C: No, it was just a couple of times during the week.

T: What did you hear?

C: It was like a warning call.

T: A warning call. Did it help?

C: I didn't pay much attention to it, but yes.

T: How do you know it helped then?

C: It was related to staying focused.

T: I see, good.

In the next section, we can see how with a little bit of help, the critical part is beginning to appreciate the efforts made by the Adult Self and other parts, and the client, as a developing Adult Self, is starting to value the critical part and its role in the system. Once the conflict is reduced a bit, it is interesting to check how the parts are responding to the intervention (CS #2.5).

T: How is this part doing?

C: He is doing better, but he wants more.

T: He is doing better. Does he appreciate the efforts that you are doing?

C: Yes, he's positive, but he's always going to want more.

T: What do you think about that?

C: I don't see this as negative, it's just a certain level of demand so I don't become careless, but he's not extreme like before. I think I should try to take more time to talk to him.

T: Have you been taking some time to talk to him?

C: Yes.

T: What did you talk about?

C: It depends, before I start working, I dedicate ten minutes to talk to him. "I am going to work now, take it easy, don't say anything while I work. When I finish, you can say whatever you want." Just like we did here in session.

T: Great.

C: Or I say, "Well, I spent almost four years doing nothing, so I have to pick up the pace little by little to make up for the time I've lost."

T. And is this working?

C: He stays calm, but sometimes he strikes back.

T: You are both getting used to a new way of functioning, it can take some time. But it sounds great. Do you know what I think is working?

C: What?

T: You try to listen and understand, then you give him information, and you don't reject how he responds.

The changes in the internal system are obvious. Parts are trying to reach common goals, so collaboration has improved greatly within the system. It is important to also check with the rest of the parts (CS #2.5).

T: How are the other parts?

C: Calm, there's no arguments like there used to be. In fact, they're quiet.

T: And what do they think about all of this? Do they see the benefits and how this is helping?

C: Yes. I think they are all trying to reach common benefits. They understand that the problem we had was that no one allowed the rest to do what they had to do.

T: Okay, great.

From time to time, it might be interesting to check if there is phobia towards any of the parts (TW #4) and if there are any missing pieces (TW #9). As the client is more able to look inside, they might need help identifying other aspects that were not described before. The client draws a picture of how he is doing inside.

T: Do you have the feeling that something is missing?

C: Well, I didn't draw fear because it's always there. And I think something is missing, but I wouldn't know how to tell you what it is.

T: Do you notice any uncomfortable sensation towards any of the parts that are there?

C: No.

T: And between them?

C: Not really, there are differences, but not too much conflict. They all have their function, they know what they have to do.

T: Okay and you are listening to all of them, which facilitates the process.

C: Yes.

EXAMPLE 7. THE INNER CONSTITUTION HAS BEEN MODIFIED

The client comes to the next session announcing that the inner Constitution has been modified. This is a good example of the results that take place through modeling. Some clients might take longer to achieve this type of change, but clients with high integrative capacities can move forward once they understand what works. In Hugo's case, he just needed help to reduce the conflict and some guidance so he could function better with his parts.

C: I made a few changes in the Constitution.

T: Really, what changes?

C: I added a couple of clauses. Should I tell you about it?

T: Yes, of course

C: There's three. 1) Citizens should neither work excessively nor under strict and hard conditions because this would hurt the whole. 2) No one should do anybody else's tasks, especially if the other part is more capable of doing them. 3) All rules may have exceptions if reasonably questioned or justified. That's it.

T: Great. It makes a lot of sense.

C: Yes.

T: How are you doing now?

C: Some days I feel that the things we work on here are real and, other days I feel like nothing of this exists. I don't exactly know the hierarchy of the things that I have inside. I drew a line there to try to explain it.

T: Uh-huh. What does this line represent?

C: I'll draw it if you want.

T: Okay.

C: I've thought about different options about how things are organized in my head. The simplest one would be everything in a circle, this is me and the parts are the small parts, each one of them with their own feelings. Another option would be two parallel "MEs," each one with his own parts. And the last option has some type of layer over it.

T: Uh-huh. Can you tell me a little bit more about this external layer option?

C: It would be like a very big me and inside there are one or more little "MEs," each one of them with their parts. It's as if it were one personality that is composed of two smaller ones, each one with its own parts.

T: How interesting. All of these are representations of how you function at different times, right?

C: Yes.

T: It makes a lot of sense and it certainly helps me understand how things are organized. But it's important to understand that there is only one you.

C: If there is only one ME, I don't understand how I can change from thinking one thing to thinking another one so fast and without realizing it. My personal goals change from one day to the next.

T: *Imagine that our purpose is for you to be this "ME" that has and extra layer. We can work with what's inside through this "ME" which is yourself as an adult in the future accomplishing what you want. He would integrate everything that is inside you. What do you think about this possibility?*

C: *It sounds good, yes.*

T: *What's important is to understand what is happening inside and how it can affect you as a whole. I know it can be very confusing, but you are one, regardless of how all of this is organized. Usually, the parts, even the voices you imagine hearing, contain different aspects or emotions. Sometimes one part contains the rage that has been suppressed for whatever reason; another part may contain the painful memories, etc. We will keep working on finding out how everything is organized, but there are many things about your life that you don't remember, and we need to do this work at a pace that fits well with all the parts.*

Later in the same session, the client talks about how he often feels disconnected, as if he was not experiencing things himself. In order to understand this disconnection, we explore the internal system using the meeting place procedure.

T: *Can you imagine your meeting place?*

C: *Yes. In the meeting room there is a long table. The table has no end in sight. It has a privileged spot where the self-critical part is sitting. The rest of the parts are sitting on the sides. The fear part is in a corner.*

T: *Sometimes there are more attendees, sometimes less. Notice that the fear part is always in a corner.*

C: *Yes, it's always there.*

T: *We should explore that part at some point.*

C: *Yes, I see more parts though, I can see the faces; sometimes I can change the angle and see their faces or what they are conveying. I don't have a clear image of each one of them.*

T: *Tell me more about the faces you can see. What do they look like?*

C: *Most of the time it's like looking at myself. I know they are different parts, but I can't really distinguish them.*

T: *Do you notice anything different, maybe a smaller or younger you?*

C: *I feel that fear is younger, and I do see the self-critical part different.*

T: *How is it different?*

C: *It's a damaged version of myself, his appearance is neglected and disheveled.*

After exploring and getting more information about the different parts (TW #1), we continue the work with the critical part just as we had agreed to do. In the next section, we can see there is a better understanding of the parts. The client is able to communicate with the critical part and even apologize.

C: *I carried out two hours of drawing for a couple of days. Everything seemed okay, but other days I was really tired and couldn't do anything. I don't think he's happy about it, or at least I don't feel he's happy.*

T: *And despite this, the part didn't complain?*

C: *I tried to communicate with him, and I noticed he was unhappy. He told me that I'm not consistent and that he gave me a chance and I wasted it, those types of things.*

T: *So, the criticism is lighter.*

C: Yes, at certain times.

T: Ask the part how he's doing now.

C: I know he's mad. He tells me that I'm good for noting and that I'll never do anything because I'm not consistent.

T: How does he feel about the first days, when you did manage to accomplish things?

C: I don't think he really trusted me.

T: What was he concerned about?

C: About me giving up. So, I said, "Thank you for giving me the chance, I'll try again."

T: What did he respond to that?

C: At first, I didn't notice much but afterward he was calmer.

T: Are you going to try again?

C: Yes, I want to try again.

The critical part agrees to give him another chance, so he can try again. At this point, it is important to validate the efforts from the part and to help the client appreciate them (CS #3.1), as well as to keep modeling cooperation and teamwork (TW #10).

T: So, is he willing to give you more chances as long as he sees that you are trying?

C: Yes, but I don't know how many.

T: Can you ask him if he can keep observing to see what happens this week?

C: Yes, he can, but he doesn't really feel like doing it.

T: Okay let's thank him for his efforts. Does he have any suggestions so you can be a little bit more consistent?

C: No, he doesn't. He says he doesn't trust me.

T: Okay, but is he willing to let you try so you can restore that trust? We're going to keep on trying.

In spite of the apparent setback, the critical part has greatly softened his ways, allowing the client as a whole to continue trying to draw. Notice how. Even though the part does not trust him fully, he is willing to keep trying and is not as difficult to reach agreements as it was before. To facilitate the process, we show confidence in the Adult Self and the critical part and keep modeling new ways of responding.

EXAMPLE 8. MORE CONNECTION AND INTEGRATION

During the week, Hugo is called in for a job interview and is hired immediately. He comes to the session and says that he is increasingly able to notice positive changes in the internal system. There is more connection and integration.

C: In a way, I feel positive changes because I feel more optimistic. I look at it as a great opportunity. In this new job, I have a very good shift, from 8 am to 4 pm every day. I'm free in the afternoon to do whatever I want, to draw or to work on my own projects. Since it's in Barcelona, I have more choices.

T. Congratulations, I think it's great! So are you looking forward to it?

C: Yes.

309

T: How is everything inside with this change?
C: Better, calmer, as if it were more united,
T: Do you notice more connection inside?
C: I do.
T: What do you notice?
C: I don't know how to explain it, but I feel more confident in general.
T: How do you notice the parts internally?
C: Very calm.

Looking back and helping the client realize all the changes he has achieved during the three months of therapy is always positive. Summarizing what the client has learned or achieved can also be introduced in the middle of a session; it is not meant to be used exclusively during closure.

T: This is a major change. (Client nods.) You had been inactive for a long time.
C: Yes, for more than three years, almost four.
T: I get the feeling that you are not very aware of this.
C: Yes, as I told you before, I still can't really believe. But I'm drawing again, and I seem to be doing it better than before. I showed my work to a coworker, and he said it was a lot better. I'm much more optimistic about everything. Now I feel like doing things, but even with all the changes, I have the sensation that no changes are taking place.
T: Notice that even with all the changes, you are handling things great. There is a reasonable amount of worry inside, but in general, things are calm. How is the critical part handling this?
C: He's handling it well.
T: Is he helping you?
C: He's there; he's at ease and not looking for mistakes. I think he's doing his job right. He's not crushing me and, if I'm lazy at certain times, he lets me know. He tells me: "Go to work, you have things to do."
T: What do you think about this?
C: I can even thank him now. He helps me focus.

Hugo is a good example of what can be achieved by following this line of work with a client with high integrative capacities. Despite his limitations, by helping him to become curious about what was happening inside, he was able to improve in very few sessions. The client was already curious enough to try to observe what was taking place inside the dark box, but his way of being curious was also critical; which lead to more conflict between the parts. Another aspect that was getting in the way of improvement was his reluctance to acknowledge that he heard voices, but by respecting his choice of words – "the voices you imagine"– he was able to openly talk about these voices and even dialogue with them.

CHAPTER 17

GABRIELLE: I'M NOT BAD, SHE IS BAD

Gabrielle, a 47-year-old client, asks for an urgent appointment during a crisis. Her therapist is on vacation, and she attends a session with another member of the same team. Client and therapist had already met on several occasions, all of them while the primary therapist way away and she was in a crisis. This is a good example of the type of work that can be done following this method even with a client that we are not visiting frequently.

In the initial session, the client explains that she is completely overwhelmed because a voice keeps telling her she is "bad" and encourages her to self-harm. She also refers becoming very dysregulated due to the hostility of the messages she hears, "Kill yourself, you would be better off dead," "Problems would end if you took all those pills," "If you die, your family won't suffer anymore. You are a burden." She states hearing second- and third-person auditory hallucinations.

Gabrielle is afraid of her own reactions and feels she has no control over the situation. Before this episode, she suffered different episodes of severe self-harm: she once banged her head until she cracked it open and, on another occasion, beat herself up with an iron bat and ended with severe wounds.

BRIEF CASE CONCEPTUALIZATION

History of symptoms and presenting problems

1. **General presenting problems and/or symptoms.** Severe self-harming behaviors, frequent suicidal ideation, critical voices, difficulties to function in daily life, frequent disorientation and difficulties remembering what she does. The client was in admitted in the ICU several times due to self-harm and suicide attempts.

2. **Previous diagnosis.** Borderline Personality Disorder.

3. **Attachment pattern.** Avoidant attachment with mother and ambivalent attachment with father. Disorganized attachment with a close relative that often took care of her.

311

4. **Relational problems**
   a. Family members. The client has some family support. She has a close relationship with two sisters that are always checking up on her but in a way that she perceives as critical and invasive. Her daughters try to support her but are too young to understand what is going on with her mother.
   b. Friends and peers. None at the time of the intake.
   c. Intimate relationships. *[Avoids romantic relationships due to her trauma history.]*
   d. Work and/or school. She had to quit her job because her voices would get very aggressive in stressful situations.

5. **Daily life functioning**
   a. Self-care habits. Very limited. When she is not overwhelmed by the voices, she manages to cook, eat healthy meals, and keep her house neat, which gives her peace of mind. When voices are active, she cannot function, forgets to eat, and cannot even keep basic hygiene habits.
   b. Financial stability. She gets some support from her siblings and has a small pension from ex-husband. She is receiving unemployment benefits.
   c. Social, occupational or school functioning. None.
   d. Overall level of functioning. Very low.

6. **Initial onset of problems/symptoms**
   a. What was happening then? The voices started when she was very young. She is not aware of what was happening at the time. She has amnesia for many episodes in her life. She describes having emotional issues for as long as she can remember.
   b. What got triggered? She is not aware of what got triggered.

7. **When did the symptoms get worse?**
   a. What was happening then? Her symptoms got worse when she remembered that one of her main caregivers sexually abusing her.
   b. What got triggered? The fact that no one realized what was happening.

8. **When do symptoms increase or worsen now?**
   a. Current triggers. She associates her symptoms with the voices but is not aware of what might trigger them. The most aggressive voices are the most dangerous for her because she ends up hurting herself in severe ways.
   b. Degree of awareness of triggers. Low.

Resources

1. **Sources of adaptive information**
   a. Good enough attachment figures in childhood and/or adult life. As a child, none. As an adult, what she learned as a mother taking care of her daughters and in her previous therapy, where she had been working with psychoeducation and social abilities.

b. Moments of feeling safe and being protected. She does not remember any.

c. Moments of feeling cared for. The client does not have many memories from childhood, but she remembers having her basic needs met.

d. Other relevant positive figures/models. No.

2. **Emotional regulation capacity**

a. Self-regulation capacity. Severely impaired, does not have self-regulation capacities.

b. Co-regulation capacity. She can co-regulate slightly, but it very difficult for her. *(She learns to do it in therapy.)*

c. Tolerance for negative and positive emotions. She can tolerate positive emotions but has many difficulties with negative emotions.

3. **Social support**

a. Family members. Her daughters and brothers. She cannot rely consistently on their support because she feels they get angry at her whenever she is not feeling well.

b. Intimate partners. No healthy intimate partners.

c. Friends. No friends, she is very isolated.

d. Work colleagues and peers. None

e. Other professionals. Her therapist, psychiatrist, and family doctor.

f. Religious/spiritual resources: Not relevant for her.

4. **Other resources**

a. Mentalization capacity. Very low and limited.

b. Degree of realization. Very limited; she can hardly speak about the few experiences she can remember.

c. Degree of integrative capacity. Very low when triggered. It improves when not triggered [improving with therapy].

5. **Timeline of best** memories. She barely has positive memories. A good memory, for example, was when her grandmother would make her clothes. She could describe other moments when her father was affectionate, but they only lasted as long as she did not get upset, angry, scared, or demanding.

Structural elements of the internal system

1. **Client's degree of awareness of parts.** The client is aware of having parts and can understand that they are parts of her, but she has more difficulties with some of the aggressive voices. **She experiences them** as "not me."

2. **Internal structure**

a. Approximate number of parts. In the initial intake, the client described two bad voices, a little girl part and an old man.

b. Client's description/representation of the internal system of parts. The client is very phobic and cannot describe too many details. She says the little girl is always hiding.

c. Organization and distribution of those parts that the client can discuss. The old man is near the little girl, controlling her.

d. Any missing pieces in the description. It is obvious that there are missing pieces; she never gets angry and is unable to feel sadness.

3. **Degree of differentiation about the self and others**

   a. Can the client distinguish her/his own thoughts, emotions and needs from what has been imposed by others? Yes, with help, she can.

   b. Is the client confusing any parts or voices with the real perpetrators? No.

4. **Time orientation and current perception of safety**

   a. Is the client confusing what happened in the past with what is happening in the present? Client loses time orientation easily.

   b. Does the client know that the danger is over? She often feels in danger.

   c. Which parts are still stuck in trauma-time? All of them.

5. **Mentalizing capacities**

   a. Can all parts mentalize? The Adult Self is learning to mentalize, the rest of the parts cannot.

   b. Which parts have higher mentalizing abilities? None

   c. Which parts need help with mentalizing? All parts need help with this.

6. **Adaptive information**

   a. Which parts have adaptive information? The Adult Self has some adaptive information from the previous work done in therapy and from her experience as a mother

   b. Which parts need help with adaptive information? The rest of the parts do not have adaptive information and need help developing it.

Relational aspects of the internal system

1. **Acceptance of parts**

   a. Despite the fear/conflict, does the client describe some parts with compassion, acceptance or appreciation? There is some acceptance of her child part. She is able to feel compassion, acceptance, and appreciation for this part but gets overwhelmed when it gets triggered and she does not know how to help. She gets angry at herself when she notices that the little girl is present and she, as the Adult, finds herself acting like a little girl. She describes that she feels as she were in the background observing what is taking place and feeling a lot of shame. Neither acceptance of nor interest in the other parts and voices.

2. **Relationships among parts.**

   a. What feelings do the parts have towards each other? Except for the little girl, the rest of the parts are experienced as a problem and something to eliminate. It also seems as if there are at least two parts that think the client should disappear or die. The little girl part is phobic both of the other parts and the Adult Self. The Adult self is phobic of all the other parts. The voices say the client is weak and useless; all the voices and the old man tell her that she is a burden and would be better off dead.

b. Which are adaptive for the system in the present moment? None.

c. Which need to improve? All of them

3. **Degree of cooperation between parts of the system.**

a. Is the client aware of any parts attempting to help the system? No.

b. Can the client accept that there might be an attempt of help even though it may not be clear yet? Even if there is no cooperation between parts, the client can accept that it may be possible that they are trying to help, once the therapist suggests it.

4. **Parts that may have difficulties with therapy.**

a. Is there ambivalence or rejection towards therapy? In the beginning, this was not clear.

b. What are their concerns regarding therapy? It is unknown if they agree with therapy, but she has trouble difficulties attending regularly.

5. **Co-consciousness between parts.**

a. If it exists, which parts are co-conscious? There is no co-consciousness.

b. When does co-consciousness occur? Does it vary? In the beginning there is no co-consciousness

c. How do other parts respond to this? Unknown in the beginning.

Trauma-related phobias and other potential blocks

1. **Phobia of inner experience.** High.

a. Can the client check inside? Yes, even though She becomes scared and confused by the answers from the aggressive parts, she is able to do it with help.

b. Can the client notice and tolerate sensations? The client can notice the body and tolerate some body sensations.

c. Is the client afraid of her feelings, thoughts or sensations? The client is terrified of her thoughts and her mind. She is very much scared of the feelings of the parts.

d. Is the client ashamed of her feelings, thoughts or sensations? She is not ashamed of her feelings.

2. **Phobia of parts.** Extremely high.

a. Does the client show ambivalence about the parts or does she avoid talking about them? Yes, in the beginning of therapy she is terrified of the parts.

b. Despite the fear, can the client try to explore parts and be curious? Yes, but can only do it in therapy with help.

c. Do any of the parts feel shame or is the patient ashamed of any of them? The part is ashamed her reactions when the child part is triggered.

3. **Phobia of attachment and attachment loss.** Tolerable.
   a. Is there ambivalence around trust in the therapeutic relationship? The client is able to trust the relationship, the therapy, and the work. She is even able to trust a co-therapist when her usual therapist is not available.
   b. Do the client or any of the parts have difficulties trusting others, ambivalence between wanting to attach and pushing others away? No significant issues around trusting others. *[Maybe the opposite. One of her problems is trusting too soon.]* The little girl has issues around distrust and touch. She does not want others getting close to her in any way. A part of the client does not want her to go to therapy.

4. **Phobia of traumatic memories.** Very high.
   a. Does the client insist on avoiding any exploration about childhood? The client tries to find out what happened in the past, but often becomes overwhelmed. She is not aware of the relevance of respecting the pace of the system. *[She is improving this in therapy]*.
   b. Does the client show ambivalence about trauma work or even talking about traumatic experiences? Yes, the client avoids talking about these issues when she feels better, but when she is triggered, she usually tries to find out what happened *(which makes other parts angry)*.

5. **Phobia of change and adaptive risk-taking.** Initially low.
   a. Is the client afraid of change? The client is open to change and adaptive risk-taking, but some parts seem to get triggered with this.
   b. Does the client present difficulties trying suggestions that would improve her quality of life? Yes, essentially because other parts are interfering.

6. **Defenses.** Self-blame and avoidance.

7. **Any other identified potential blocks.** Amnesia for big blocks of time, a lot of missing information about her trauma history.

EXAMPLE 1. A VOICE ENCOURAGES HER TO SELF-HARM DURING A CRISIS

The client comments that this week she began to remember something she did not know and that one of the voices she hears is very aggressive. We begin the interview exploring the voices (TW #1) and encouraging the client to become more curious about the voices (TW #2), the triggers (TW #3), and their possible function (TW #6).

T: Can you tell me about this voice?
C: It's very mean. I can't stand it.
T: Mean how?
C: It says horrible things. I am afraid of listening to it.
T: Well, we can listen to it without acting on what it says, that's a good option for now.
C: What do you mean?

T: The idea is to try to understand what the voice is trying to say, but this does not mean that you have to do what it says.

Reminding clients that listening and being more curious about what the voice says does not mean that they have to do what they say, is very important; often clients confuse listening to them to having to follow commands. Doing such an intervention is one of the best ways to reduce fear enough for the client to try to be curious.

C: I cannot understand what she is trying to tell me.
T: Okay, I will try to help you understand this voice but can you tell me a little more about it?
C: Like what?
T: How does the voice sound?
C: Mean.
T: How does mean sound?
C: She is dry and aggressive.
T: Dry and aggressive, I see. Is there more than one voice?
C: I think so, but right now she's the only one talking.
T: Okay, so let's try to understand this voice today.
C: Okay.
T: Does this voice appear when you feel good or when you feel bad?
C: When I feel bad.
T: Is it when you feel overwhelmed, anxious or something different?
C: When I feel sad.

Notice that the voice shows up when the client is sad. Voices and parts usually repeat very similar responses to those of the adults that were around when clients were growing up, so it is very likely that sadness was not handled well when she was a child. This is a great opportunity to help the client understand how the voice might have internalized the responses of the adults and learned to respond towards sadness with negative comments as a way to self-regulate. Remember that we never offer the client our interpretation. Instead, we try to engage curiosity and reflective thinking, asking clients about where they learned this type of responses.

T: When you are sad.
C: Yes.
T: What happens when you are sad?
C: It's not good. The voice gets crazy.
T: Maybe there is a part of you that is afraid of feeling sad, and she doesn't know what to do when you are sad.
C: Maybe.
: How did people react when you felt sad as a child? I know you don't remember many things, just answer from your sensation. How did others react when you felt sad?
C: My mother didn't pay much attention to me.

T: *Maybe she couldn't be there for you; maybe she didn't know how. Did she have any problems?*
C: *Her relationship with my father was not good, and she had many difficulties.*

We offer psychoeducation to help the client understand where the part learned to do that without blaming caregivers. The therapist knows that the mother of this client had emotional issues and could not do things differently with their lack of resources. By inquiring if mother had any problems, we are also introducing the idea of parents doing the best they can, which is not meant to justify them but rather allows us to understand the limitations of the caregivers or other relevant people in the client's life.

T: *Was there somebody in your past who didn't tolerate you feeling bad or who didn't know what to do when you felt like this?*
C: *Yes, my mother. She didn't respond well.*
T: *Then it's possible that a part of you has learned to react in a similar way when you are sad.*
C: (Nodding.) *She probably copied my mother's behaviors, but I don't remember that. I do remember times when my mother left me alone at home. I remember sitting next to the window, so I would have an escape route just in case somebody broke in. I always did the same thing when my mother left me at home. I was very afraid. The fear of somebody breaking into the house is somehow an obsession for me, as well as the fear of being alone, and missing my mother for a long time.*

Before we continue, it is important to check how the voices are experiences our message (CS #2.3) since this can guide our work. Sometimes voices understand quickly, but other times they need more psychoeducation to really understand. In addition, in these situations, it is important to be careful with parts that idealize caregivers. The goal of the intervention is to generate empathy and understanding, not to trigger any conflict within the system.

T: *Does this make sense to this voice too?*
C: (Internal communication for a couple of minutes.) *Yes.*
T: *This is not about judging or blaming your mother. You are aware that she has problems. This is just about understanding.*
C: *Yes, so I can understand things that have happened to me or that are happening now.*
T: *Exactly, what do you think about that?*
C: *I would like to understand, yes.*

Once the client is able to be more curious, we can try to search for the adaptive function of the voice (TW #6). Then we can begin helping the client and the voice with what is not working (TW #7) and exploring how the part can help in a more adaptive way (TW #8). As usual, our way of relating to the client and asking questions attempts to encourage reflective thinking and promote empathy.

T: *This voice may need to understand that she can help you in a more effective way by learning different ways to respond* (Client nods.) *Do you think that she knows how bad you feel when she says these things to you?*
C: (Thoughtful.) *No, she probably doesn't.*

318

T: How could this voice help you in a way that actually would make you feel better?

C: Well, she doesn't know.

T: So maybe you can help her with some suggestions.

C: It would help if she didn't tell me that I am "bad," and didn't blame me. When I was a child, I was called "bad" without having done anything bad. For example, if I cried, they would tell me "you are bad" just because I was crying, or when I was afraid of going somewhere, things like that.

T: Do you see how important this is? It's important that you, as the adult you are now, can realize that a little girl is not bad because she is crying. A little girl may cry because she is sad, afraid, hungry, frustrated; she can cry for many reasons. A little girl does not cry for no reason or because she is bad. The fact that you can understand this will probably help this voice to understand it as well and to try to change the things she says. (Client nods, paying attention.) How could this voice help you? What type of messages would be helpful?

C: Telling me that she understands me, that she understands what is happening to me. But in order to do that, it would be necessary to investigate the past, to know what happened to me before.

Notice how we reinforced the adult perspective that the client just shared. The previous section is a good example of helping the system reflect on the current functioning and how to improve the relationship between parts as a way to begin to work as a team (TW #10).

In the next section, we will introduce the idea of how respecting the pace of the whole system is one of the basic premises that should always be kept in mind. Notice how the client, on the one hand, answers and, on the other hand, brings in a typical issue in cases that show amnesia: clients who tend to oscillate between not wanting to know about the trauma and trying to find out what happened.

T: We will deal with things from the past when the time is right. I imagine your therapist and you have already talked about this. (Client nods.) In order to know what happened, all of your parts need to agree. It's important that you all work as a team, and they may have different emotions, insecurity, fear, etc. Maybe this voice is not ready for this work now because this part getting triggered is related to the new memories that you have been getting, right?

C: Yes and no.

Asking about aspects related to memories can be a complicated for some clients. If they are very phobic of traumatic memories, we should be very careful before introducing this type of questions. In this case, we explore it peripherally, as a way to help her understand the possible triggers of the voice (TW #3).

C: Well, actually, yes, because she appeared saying, "You are bad" when I remembered those childhood situations.

T: So, it's possible that this voice has some of the memories that you don't have, and maybe she thinks that it's not a good time to work on those memories. Perhaps because your therapist is not here, or because many things have happened recently, and you are more nervous. (Client nods.) There could be many reasons, maybe she is afraid, or she is trying to help you avoid getting in contact with those memories, and in order to do this, she says what she has learned to say.

Once again, before we continue, it is important to explore the system's reaction towards the intervention (CS #2.5).

> T: *How is your internal system now, after our conversation?*
> C: *Better.*
> T: *How do you know?*
> C: *Because she is calm, and I am calm*

The main goal of this session was to understand what was happening with the system (TW #1 and TW #2) and what was triggering the voice (TW #3), in order to stabilize the client. Once the system is calmer and we have enough information, it may be a good idea to close the session (CS #3). The fact that the system is doing well does not mean the client is ready to delve too deeply into the internal structure. We must remember that in these cases, slower is sometimes faster.

> T: *Is this enough for you or would you like to explore a bit more?*
> C: *Yes. I am much calmer because I know that we will discover relevant things.*
> T: *When the time is right, okay?*
> C: *Yes.*
> T: *Remember that when there is an internal conflict, if one part is afraid of how you may feel if you retrieve more memories, we need to work with this part, so she can feel safe enough and know that there will be control and containment.* (Client nods.) *It's important for her to know that we won't go into anything without complete agreement from all of you and not until all of your parts want and can do so. We will work with all those things, but when the moment is right for all of you.*
> P: *Okay.*
> T: *Do you have any questions? Or is there anything else that you need now?*
> C: *No, no. I liked this final part.*
> T: *Okay, great.*

We close the session insisting on the importance of respecting the timing of the different parts, reaching agreements, and encouraging cooperation (TW #10). This intervention was very effective; the client left with a better internal sensation and no need to use more medication or return to the Emergency Room. Not all the work is done, but this is a good beginning to reduce internal conflict. The capacity shown by the Adult Self is a good modeling example for the voice (TW #8) that did not learn to communicate things more adaptively. This is an example of an intervention that can be done during exploration, when we interview a dissociative client who self-harms and/or during the stabilization phase.

EXAMPLE 2. SELF-CARE WORK AFTER A SEVERE SUICIDE ATTEMPT

After seven months of stability, Gabrielle committed a severe suicide attempt. She was in a coma for almost a month. This session takes place after she is discharged from the hospital. At the beginning of the interview, the client describes what happened when she tried to kill herself and how everything is different now.

C: *Now it's as if all the voices have united into one. Before it was more like my conscience, but now it's somewhat disconnected. It doesn't feel like me. When I left the hospital, I felt it more like myself, now I see it as something else.*

T: *What do you think is happening?*

C: *I don't know but it's totally against me. It says, "You are useless, you are better off dead." At a certain point, the voice said, "You have 200.000 pills, if you take them all, it should work. And I said, "No, not again please!"*

T: *Do you know why this voice is saying those things now?*

C: *It keeps on saying that I am a burden. That if I were not here, others (referring to her family members) wouldn't have to suffer. It thinks that everyone (again in reference to her family) is suffering and it's my fault. It thinks that if I die, the problem is solved.*

T: *And what do you think?*

C: *I don't feel good, I feel guilty. So, although I don't agree 100% with the voice, I do feel guilty for many reason's*

We start by encouraging the client to pay more attention and listen to the voice (TW #2), so we can explore possible triggers (TT #3 as well as the function of the voice (TW #6).

T: *It would be interesting to know why this voice is trying to help in such ways. We know it's trying to help, but why in this way?*

C: *I don't know, I don't think she is trying to help.*

T: *I understand why you see it that way, but do you remember what we talked about the voices that are trying to help?*

C: *Yes, I remember, but I don't know.*

T: *Do you remember when the voice shows up?*

C: *I'm not sure, I know it's been in the last few days. And something else is happening too, and I'm ashamed of it. You know how when we get cuddly, we talk like little kids? Well, that happens to me, and I am very ashamed of it. I am 47 years old and, when I'm very sad, I talk like a little girl. It's as if somehow, I become a little girl and I need cuddling. This happened last night, and I said to myself, "This is ridiculous, you should be ashamed of yourself!" My inside was saying, "What are you doing? Your daughters are here, and you are acting like a little girl!"*

T: *Is it possible that there is a little girl part that gets triggered?*

C: *Yes, I think that something inside of me that did not grow up gets triggered.*

T: *Well, that is different from acting like a little girl. And it's important to understand it.*

C: *I'm 47 years old, and I need cuddling! How embarrassing!*

T: *I don't think it's embarrassing; I think we should listen to what is getting triggered and try to understand what is happening.*

Exploring the dissociative phobia (TW #4) when working with parts that are challenging for the client is a must. By exploring how the adult feels towards the little girl part, we can identify the presence or absence of dissociative phobias and, from there, guide the focus of our intervention. Remember that compassion helps the work flow naturally; rejection, anger, shame or disgust will require more interventions.

T: How do you feel towards this "something" inside that did not grow up?

C: I don't know. I think that I lacked affection when I was little. Obviously, my mother didn't know how to give me affection. Maybe that's why I give so much affection to others: people, animals, bugs, anything, I don't care what it is.

Notice that the client did not answer the question. So, for now, we change the focus to how the Adult Self feels and explore briefly whether the little girl is oriented in time (TW #5).

T: How do you feel now?

C: When I am not with the kids, I feel very lonely. That's why I don't like to be home, because I'm all by myself, and I feel like an abandoned little girl.

T: So, it's possible that the little girl got triggered. And when she does, it's important not to get mad at yourself or be ashamed. There is nothing to be ashamed of. It is important to understand this so the little girl can calm down. (Client nods.) Can you see the little girl?

C: No, but I can imagine her. Last night she was like my little self, like me when I was little. If you heard me talking, I was a little girl. Until I realized it, and I said to myself, "Don't do that, how embarrassing!" It was as if I were divided in two, the little girl and the adult that I am.

T: Do you think that "something" knows that it has grown up?

C: No, because this happens to me often.

Before we decide how to proceed, we need more information on the little girl, her needs (TW #7), and her function (TW #6). Remember our main goal is to find out what is happening and how it is helping. Exploring the internal system (TW #1) helps us guide our interventions and develop cooperation and teamwork (TW #10).

T: How do you imagine this little girl?

C: She is a little girl that needs to be hugged; she needs to be held and supported.

At this point, it could be tempting to suggest the adult to offer a hug. However, hugs may be triggering for the child part (TW #3). For that reason, before we suggest this type of intervention, we explore how the client would respond to it (TW #7) and check the reaction of the system. We need to make sure that it is an intervention that the little girl can accept.

T: So, when you imagine the little girl, you sense that she needs affection. As the adult, what would you say to this little girl if she is sad and feels lonely?

C: I also feel helpless and unprotected. I lack all of those things that the little girl needs. I need them too. So, I don't feel capable of protecting her.

T: That's why you're working with your therapist to learn how to take care of yourself and the different parts in you.

C: Yes, I would like to learn to do that.

Realizing that the little girl's needs are her needs too generates an important change in the emotions that the adult feels towards the child. It is a good time to explore the dissociative phobia (TW #4) to guide our work.

T: When you imagine this little girl, how do you feel about her?

C: I love her. She is helpless, and I would love to help her.

T: As the adult you are now, what would you say to the little girl?

C: That I would protect her and take care of her. She can be calm with me. I can help her.

T: Sounds good. Can you try to say that to the little girl?

C: Yes.

T: If you try to say this to the little girl, does she receive the message?

C: Yes.

T: So, when you say this to her, what happens inside?

C: She doesn't want to listen to me.

Even though the client shows a positive attitude towards the little girl and is willing to do the procedure, this is not always enough. By exploring how the child part responds to the intervention (CS #2.5) we can detect the need to help the system with this emerging difficulty (CS #2.4). And then, to guide our work, we model a different way of responding (TW #8) while exploring the adult's response to the child part's reaction (CS #2.3).

T: She doesn't want to or is she unable to do so?

C: She doesn't want to. She is behaving like a bad girl.

T: Oh, and how is that like? What's her reaction?

C: As if she was the bad part that tells me to hurt myself.

T: The one that you hear lately?

C: Yes, she says that she doesn't believe me.

When the adult tries to help the little girl, the part does not believe her and apparently sends her messages to hurt herself. Before continuing we explore if the voice she has been hearing lately is related to the girl (TW #1). If this is the case, it will be necessary to help the Adult Self understand the child and, as much as possible, respond in a healthier way (TTW #8) so that the conflict can be reduced, and the negative messages changed.

T: Is the voice that you have been hearing lately related to the little girl?

C: It seems so. That voice is her.

T: How is that girl feeling?

C: She is pushing me away and doesn't believe me. She doesn't let me help her.

T: What would you do with a little child that is nervous and is pushing you away if you know that she really needs help? What would your Adult Self do?

C: I would try to talk to her, but she took me by surprise.

T: If you just see this as a bad reaction, we won't be able to understand why the little girl is responding like this. You know that when children get upset, they can react like that.

C: Yes.

T: So, what would the little girl need from your Adult Self?

C: A lot of understanding and for me to really try to find out what is going on with her.

T: Are you curious? Would you like to know what is happening?

C: Yes, but I don't know how to do it.

Gabrielle: I'm not bad, she is bad

This type of response is indicative of the presence of a dissociative phobia in the young girl, which manifests itself as rejection (TW #4). The best intervention would be to get the adult to understand and accept how the child feels. By validating needs and feelings (TW #7) and modeling a new way of responding from the Adult (TW #8), the little girl might become more receptive.

T: *What do you see now?*
C: *The little girl is angry.*
T: *Tell her that it's okay to be angry, that there is nothing wrong with that, and that you would like to help her.* (Client nods and starts internal communication.) *What happens when you do this?*
C: *She just stays there; she's quiet.*
T: *What does that mean?*
C: *I don't know.*
T: *Does she seem confused?*
C: *No, she's just there; she's quiet. She's just waiting to see what happens.*

This is a very interesting dynamic. The girl has stopped saying negative messages and seems to be waiting for something. This means the curiosity system is back on online. We continue exploring the needs of the child (TW #7) and suggest some alternative ways of responding, which will be modeled first by the therapist (TW #8).

T: *So, she is quiet and waiting to see what happens.*
C: *Yes.*
T: *What do you think she needs?*
C: *To feel heard and for someone to get close to her. Maybe to receive a hug.*
T: *You can offer a hug, but only if she wants you to. We cannot force it.*
C: *Okay* (internal communication).
T: *How does she react?* (Client remains silent while internal communication seems to be taking place.) *Whatever she does is okay. Her way of responding can help us understand.* (Client nods.) *What do you notice?*
C: *She doesn't like me getting close to her.*
T: *It's good that she can say this. Can you understand why?*
C: *Yes.*
T: *She might need you to respect this distance for now.* (Client nods.) *How do you feel when you realize that she doesn't like it when you get close?*
C: *Well, sometimes I don't like it either. I don't like being touched.*
T: *You can understand her then.*
C: *Yes.*
T: *So now that you understand her reaction better, what would you say to her?*
C: *That I understand her. That sometimes when others try to give me affection, I don't like it either.*
T: *And how does she react?*
C: *Fine. She's calm.*

T: It's great that you can understand and that she can tell you what she needs. This is the only way to understand what is happening. (Client nods.) She must be having a very hard time if she doesn't see another way out besides suicide. Don't you think?
C: Yes.

By exploring what the little girl needs now, we are helping to develop present-moment differentiation (TW #5) and promoting empathy and cooperation (TW #10).

T: Can you ask the little girl what would help her now?
C: She wants me to be there for her. She doesn't want me to go away, but she doesn't want me to touch her.
T: Are you okay with that?
C: Yes.
T: What happens when, as the Adult, you understand that maybe it's too soon to get close to her?
C: She feels comfortable too.
T: Wonderful.

Since the adult self tries to understand and there is greater acceptance of the feelings and responses of the child part (TW #7), the little girl seems to be able to open up a bit and can express how she feels.

C: She says, "I don't want you to hug me. I want you to be there because I know you protect me by being there. But I don't want you to touch me or say anything."
T: Okay. Where do you notice the little girl in your body?
C: In my chest. She likes to be there, protected.

Helping the client feel that she is somehow taking care of the little girl is a good step towards increasing compassion. A simple experiment like placing her own hands over the part of the body where she notices this part, as a self-care gesture will usually have good results. Once we implement the intervention and before continuing any further, it is important to check how the little girl responds (CS #2.5).

T: Could you place your hands there and try to notice the little girl?
C: Yes (client closes her eyes).
T: What happens with the little girl when you do that?
C: She feels good.

Now that the little girl feels better, we can try to promote empathy and integration through a positive message from the Adult, making sure the little girl knows that nothing will be forced.

T: What would you say to her now?
C: That she can calm down, that. I will help her grow up.
T: Can you let her know that you won't force anything, and that you are not going to hug her unless she wants a hug?

C: Yes.

T: Let her know that you are going to be there for her.

C: Yes (warmly).

T: How do you notice her now?

C: She is fine; she likes being like this. (Client still has her eyes closed and her hands over her chest.)

T: What is the little girl doing now?

C: It's as if she is hiding so nobody can touch her.

T: Let her know that it's okay, and give her all the time she needs.

C: Now she feels as if all the bad things that happened this week are colliding with my hands and can't reach her, as if my hands were a shield.

T: What do you think about that?

C: I think it's good because it means I can protect her.

T: Great. Notice how important this is.

Before closing the session, we try to reach an agreement regarding the negative messages (TW #10). This way, we may anticipate common problems outside of therapy (CS #3.5).

T: So now that she knows you can protect her; do you think we can ask her not to say those messages that scare you so much?

C: Yes.

T: Can you ask her how she feels about this?

C: She is much calmer now. She is smiling and says she is going to be nicer (La client uses a warm tone of voice and smiles).

T: What do you notice now?

C: Peace.

T: Can you describe what you see when you look at the girl now?

C: She is like me when I was little. She has long hair and wears the dresses that my grandma used to make for me.

When the client looks at the little girl now, she feels acceptance and warmth. A small step towards their integration has taken place. We close the session helping to promote further realization (CS #3.4).

T: It's nice that she can notice how you smile when you look at her, don't you think? How is the little girl now?

C: Good, she is calm. She likes that I smile when I look at her.

T: Okay, take the time you need to notice that.

T: Did you notice that by calming yourself, the little girl also calms down, and that makes you feel even calmer?

C: Yes.

T: What have you realized with this work?

C: That it's really a part of me. Well, that she's me when I was little, so I can deal much better with it.

T: *Great. Now, if you get blaming messages, try to remember that children tend to repeat what they hear. Sometimes they repeat things without really knowing what they are saying. So, if she gets nervous and sends those messages again, try to respond from the Adult. (Client nods.) Let her know that you are there, that it's okay. You can offer her a hug, but she can say no. This can probably help her calm down. What do you think about this?*

C: *It makes sense because she is much calmer right now.*

T: *How about you?*

C: *I am calmer too.*

In this session, the client has been able to take small steps that by the end of the session become huge progress. We begin exploring the conflict she brings in, after a severe suicide attempt, with an aggressive voice that tells her to hurt herself. By being curious and helping the client and the voice understand what is not working, we turn the conflict into a new learning opportunity for the system of parts. It is interesting how we could even access the little girl that was getting triggered and do some self-care work with both the adult and the little girl. Now both parts can be in more contact and even look at each other with more acceptance and warmth.

This is an example that illustrates, on the one hand, how external triggers can be complicated for a system that is still learning to function differently and, on the other hand, the fact that staying focused and not giving up are the keys to working with these kinds of parts and voices.

EXAMPLE 3. NEW AGGRESSIVE VOICE

Gabrielle has been relatively stable for a while. But as integration takes place, she keeps connecting with more memories. This is an example of a delicate moment in therapy. On the one hand, the client is more integrated and is more capable of working with the internal system; on the other hand, she is tired of the conflict and wants to lead a normal life. Although the principles are the same, we need to be aware of potential complications in this new stage.

C: *Lots of memories are coming up, and I relive them exactly as they happened. I also remembered other things that I did not remember before. Two weeks ago, I went to London. It was my niece's first birthday, and we were all sitting at the table... Of course, he (referring to the perpetrator) went too because he's her grandpa. And I was wandering around, hoping not to have to sit down near him, and I ended up having to sit right by him. He was on one side of the table, and I was in that corner.*

T: *I see.*

C: *I have been remembering very hurtful things about other people and thinking about things that happened; I've been putting them in place. Since the last time I was hospitalized —I can't remember what month it was—the voice hadn't shown up, so I was calm. But when the voice showed up in my head, in addition to dealing with everything that I have to keep under control to remain calm, it was just horrible.*

Once we know that the voice was active during the week (CS #2.1), we need to explore what was happening when the voice showed up (CS #2.2). Remember that voices usually show up when something is not right or when the client or other parts are triggered and need help.

T: *Do you remember what you were doing when the voice showed up?*

C: *There were new episodes aired of my favorite TV show and it was great, I was super happy, and when I went to bed, suddenly my head said, "You should have gone through that, having all your bones broken." And I said, "No." And then my head said, "Yes, they should've hurt you like that because you are very bad. You should have had all your bones broken, and you should've been left at the hospital, useless."*

T: *Uh-huh.*

C: *At that moment, I didn't even realize it was the voice talking, because she hadn't been around for so long. I do know that I said, "No, no, no!" I had already taken my pills and said, "I have to sleep, I have to sleep!" And so, I went to bed and thought, "Tomorrow I can't go to the family reunion, because I have my period. It hurts a lot, and I can't have this in my head, I can't fight against this, with the pain and everything. I have to sleep and rest, so this gets out of my head."*

T: *A way of taking care of yourself, right?*

C: *Yes.*

T: *What was the episode about?*

C: *It was an episode of Criminal Minds.*

T: *Was there anything in the episode that could've been triggering?*

C: *No, I like that TV show.*

T: *I am just asking because, if I understood correctly, the voice showed up right after the episode.*

C: *(Thoughtful.) I don't know... In the episode, there was a girl who got raped and was brutally beaten, that's why her bones were broken.*

T: *I see. So even though you know this is fiction, it's possible that something in you got triggered.*

C: *Maybe.*

As we keep exploring to understand this change in the voices she hears, the client explains what happened two days later, a relevant trigger that would not be easily understood if we do not actively explore whether voices have shown up (CS #2.1) and what lead to the voices showing up (CS #2.2).

C: *I had been doing many things at once. So, after I finished everything, I went into the room, sat down and said, "Okay, that's it." And, suddenly, I heard music from a horror movie, and I said, "What's going on?!" I heard a laugh and I said, "No!" And I heard the laugh again, and she said, "Yes!" and I said, "Why do you have to come?" and she said, "Because you can't live without me," and I said, "I hate you," and she said, "You can't hate me. Dolores always tells you that you can't hate me." "Well, I hate you, I've done many important things and you weren't there, I hate you. I'm going to talk to my therapist because I'm not able to love you," and she said, "Well, you have to love me, because I'm a part of you, and you have to love me." And then I got really nervous.*

T: *That's when you called me.*

C: *I got really nervous because she reminds me of all the bad things.*

We can see how a situation that was more or less under control for some time can quickly get complicated when voices show up in ways that are frightening. In these instances, it is important to explore how the system –in this case, the client– responded to the voice (CS #2.3) and address the difficulty that is arising (CS #2.4). We need to pick up the work where we left it the last time there was conflict and continue modeling what has been working so the client can remember the benefits of working as a team (TW #10).

> T: *Notice how contradictory the voice is. On the one hand, she communicates in a way that scares you, but on the other hand, she is also telling you that you cannot hate her. Do you think her true intention is to scare you?*
> C: (Thoughtful.) *I guess not.*
> T: *But you get scared.*
> C: *I got scared because when I heard she was back, I remembered the last things I went through with the voice: mostly the feeling of "I can't go on," when she was telling me to cut myself and I ended up hospitalized. She comes when she's desperate.*

Since these types of situations can be destabilizing and generate a major relapse for the entire system, we explore how the other parts are doing (CS #2.1) and how they are responding (CS #2.3).

> T: *And how are the rest of the parts doing with this?*
> C: *When these things happen, everything becomes agitated.*
> T: *What is agitated now?*
> C: *Everything, it's not one specific part.*
> T: *Do you remember that we had been exploring the voice once and it seemed to be related to a child part?* (Client nods.) *How is that child part doing?*
> C: *The girl is there; she's grown up a bit, she's not so vulnerable, but she's there. And the poor thing is a bit abandoned because I have so many things on my plate.*
> T: *How is she doing?*
> C: *She knows I take care of her, I told her I would take care of her and she is there waiting.*
> T: *Could it be that the other voice is showing up because the girl has not been taken care of? If you had been taking care of the little girl and now, since so many things are happening, you are not doing it... Could this be the reason why the voice has come back?*
> C: *But this voice does not belong to the girl. It's an adult voice.*
> T: *Is it similar to any of the voices that you've heard previously?*
> C: *Yes, it's a voice that's like my other self. She scares me because she hadn't been around for a long time. And even though she doesn't want to scare me, I notice that she laughs at me often.*
> T: *And why does she do this?*
> C: *I don't know.*
> T: *Have you tried asking her?*
> C: (Checking in.) *Because I think she copied many things my mother said and did when I was young. She would laugh at me often.*
> T: *So, then we understand a bit more now. This is what she learned to do.*

We continue trying to promote understanding and empathy since it will lead to decreasing internal conflict and increasing collaboration between the different parts (TW #10). Many times, in their efforts to protect by doing what they have learned to do –without being aware that the past is over–, parts do not realize they are generating discomfort and often scaring the client. Once communication among parts has begun, letting them know about this is usually helpful.

> *T: So then, when she laughed, is that what she learned?* (Client nods.) *And can you tell her that this hurts you and scares you?*
> *C: Yes.*
> *T: Great, try telling her.*
> *C: Okay.*
> *T:* (After internal communication.) *And how does she respond if you tell her that?*
> *C: At the moment, we are a bit conflicted.*
> *T: Why is that?*
> *C: Because she scares me when she does that.*
> *T: She is not trying to scare you, but it scares you a lot, and you can't help it. What else is happening? It seems like there is something else on your mind.*
> *C: Because I was not expecting her so suddenly, and I thought that perhaps she would not come back.* (Client seems thoughtful.) *Why didn't she show up when I did all those important things?*
> *T: Well, let's see if this makes sense to you. Possibly because since you're managing everything well, and you did very important things, she didn't see that you needed any help.*
> *C: And now?*
> *T: And now possibly she noticed that you were more nervous, for whatever reason, and she came back to try and help again. Part of the work is to help the voice realize that this is not helping you and remind her of things that do help.*
> *C: So, am I doing it wrong?* (Client starts crying.)

The attempt to help her understand the part has generated guilt in the client. Thinking that she may be doing things wrong is a trigger for the client, so she begins to cry and get nervous. The therapist explores and repairs using another example that can help the patient understand what she was trying to convey.

> *T: No, I don't think you're doing anything wrong. In fact, I think that what you're doing deserves great credit. Why do you get that impression?*
> *C: Because everything was going well, so if she shows up...*
> *T: Do you think you were doing it wrong because of what I said?*
> *C: If she shows up it's because she thinks I need her help.*
> *T: Of course, but look at me for a moment.* (Client looks up.) *At times, you want to help your daughter, right?*
> *C: Yes.*
> *T: Do you only help her when she does things wrong?*
> *C: No.*

T: Do you help her whenever she can use some support, even if she's doing things right? (Client nods.) *So then, it doesn't have to mean that you're doing something wrong. Do you understand that?*

C: Yes.

T: The voice shows up as support, not because you're doing things wrong. I did not express myself correctly. I am very sorry, because I didn't want you to feel bad. Do you understand when I say that when your daughter can use your help you are also there and that doesn't mean that she's doing anything wrong? (Client nods.) *Do you understand it better now?* (Client nods.)

After such an intense reaction from the client, we should explore how the system receives the message (CS #2.5).

T: What do you notice inside when we talk about this?

C: It makes me nervous. I'm scared that she will come back and things won't turn out right.

T: Since there is fear about different things, I was thinking that we could try to process the fear just a little bit, to see if it calms down. What do you think?

C: Okay, yes.

T: Now, if you think about the voice, take a look and see what you notice. (Client nods.) *What do you notice?*

C: Fear that things may go back to how they were, I don't like that.

Remember that checking with the system is how we know the effect of the interventions we are doing and how we can identify any phobias that are showing up (TW #4). Once the dissociative phobia towards this part is identified, we suggest processing it by using the processing phobias procedure, which the client is already familiar with.

T: Let's process that fear a little bit. Where do you notice the fear?

C: In my chest.

T: Can you focus on the fear that you notice? Nothing else. (Client nods.) *Ready?*

C: Yes. (BLS)

T: What do you notice?

C: She's standing there.

T: Should we do a bit more? (Client nods.) (BLS) *Very good, breathe... What do you get now or what do you notice?*

C: She's standing still.

T: When you say, "She's standing still," are you talking about the voice? (Client nods.) *And how do you see this voice?*

C: I see something like a train station, and it's as if I had to walk, and she was right there. I want her to let me walk and, for now, she is standing still.

T: Okay, but she's not preventing you from walking, is she?

C: No.

T: You would like for her to let you walk, and for now she's just standing there. And when you think about this, do you still notice the fear?

C: No.

T: And what do you notice now?

C: That, for the moment, she is there, and she is going to let me walk.

T: Let's go with this for a bit. (BLS) Breathe.

C: She tells me that she is going to let me walk.

T: What do you notice when she says that?

C: Relief.

T: Let's go with that. (BLS) And now?

C: Better.

T: What is better? What do you notice is better?

C: The feeling of relief. I feel it's brighter. She is going to let me walk.

T: Should we go with this for a bit? Do you think it's a good idea? (Client nods.) (BLS) And now?

C: Good. (Client smiles.)

T: What else is happening inside? You seem to be very thoughtful.

C: I'm imagining the train station and it's more open now, there's more light.

T: And how do you notice the voice? Or how do you see it?

C: She's there waiting for me to walk.

T: And what do you think about her waiting for you to walk?

C: I like it.

T: Let's go with that. (BLS)

C: Now she's happier.

T: And you?

C: Me too, because she's more relaxed, so I can trust her more.

T: Let's go with that. (BLS) And now?

C: She's there, and she's calm and so am I. I trust that she will let me walk.

T: How do you see the voice now?

C: Calmer.

T: And what do you notice?

C: I'm calmer, too.

T: And how is the level of fear now?

C: I'm not scared now.

We can see how the system resolved this conflict through a metaphor: the part is letting her walk. We neither interpret nor interfere, we just trust the process and check in with the client (CS #2.5).

T: What do you think about what just happened? What do you think it means?

C: That perhaps she didn't feel well because I didn't feel well either.

T: That makes a lot of sense. And does that change the way you view her?

C: Yes, of course.

T: What changes in your view?

C: I can't hate her anymore.

T: And what is there instead of hatred?

C: Understanding, what seemed to be one thing was really something else.

T: It is, isn't it? (Client nods, smiling.)

The previous section is an example of how to start to close the session reinforcing the positive change in attitude that just took place, enhancing realization (CS #3.4). Then we continue trying to use this change to improve adaptive communication. Increased understanding is a gateway to compassion and empathy, which as previously mentioned, will help reduce internal conflict and promote collaboration (TW #10).

T: What would you tell the voice now that you understand her a bit better?

C: I would ask for her forgiveness, for getting angry at her the other day. And that, from now on, I will try to understand her better when she talks to me.

T: That's wonderful. If you can let her know, that would be great.

C: Okay. (Client closes her eyes and establishes internal communication.)

T: When you tell this to the voice, what happens? Check and see how she receives this.

C: She is happier now.

T: And you, what do you notice?

C: I feel calmer.

T: Do you think this is a good way to close the session?

C: Yes, definitely.

We close the session making sure she is grounded (CS #3.3), although it was quite obvious things were better. Nevertheless, after any high conflict situation, it is always a good idea to check.

T: How are you leaving today?

C: I am leaving happy with the voice, I'm leaving calm.

T: And do you notice the voice now?

C: It's in the train station, calm and waiting for me to start walking.

T: What feeling do you notice now?

C: Calmness, with her.

T: And with yourself?

C: Also with myself because I see myself closer to her. I think we can walk together.

T: What does the voice think about that?

C: She is the one that suggested it. (Client smiles.)

As we have seen in previous chapters, timing, empathy, and collaboration (TW #10) are crucial in the work with voices, but they become even more important when we are dealing with voices that encourage self-harm or do not see any other way out of the current situation. Our goal was to illustrate the type of work that can be done even with clients that we see occasionally, as support to another colleague or team member. These interventions led to a much better functioning in the client.

After the work done in this session, the client sends the following message:

Hello Dolores.

I want to share something very important with you; something that happened after our session yesterday, which was very intense. When I went to bed, I started thinking about how the voice would act. Then she spoke to me in a very sweet and calm tone of voice and told me, "Do not be afraid, I will always be there to support you, because I am you. I am no longer that helpless little girl, but an adult woman who can speak up and ask for help, and this you have given to me. That's why now we're one and the same. I am you and you are me."

I still had my doubts, so she repeated, "Trust me, because I am you and you are me, and together we will achieve whatever we set our minds to do."

I remember something I have heard many times, "The power lies within."

I am very happy. Thank you very much for your help.

CHAPTER 18

KENDRA: THE LITTLE GIRL IN THE DARK ROOM

Kendra is a 34-year-old female who was referred to our clinic from a town in a different province, 800 kilometers away. She had been in treatment for over 20 years, had received numerous diagnoses, and had remained in a catatonic state for almost 2 years.

Gathering history was not possible in the beginning since she had a very hard time sharing any information whatsoever. Over time, she managed to disclose that she had been sexually abused, humiliated, and beaten almost daily from ages 10 to 24. It all happened within a religious organization that was expected to be a safe space for her and other young people who attended. Her main perpetrator would say things such as, "If you just behaved, we wouldn't have to do this," thus framing the abuse as a punishment for her actions. As a consequence, she felt responsible and learned to mistreat herself by self-harming in ways that resembled those of her abusers.

One of her main problems was the terrifying voices she heard, mostly because she was unable to differentiate them from her main perpetrators. Mapping the system of parts with the client was not an easy task. It took her two years to be able to talk about the voices, which were mostly second person auditory hallucinations. The transcripts of the sessions included in this chapter belong to the period when she started to be able to talk about the voices and some of the parts.

BRIEF CASE CONCEPTUALIZATION

History of symptoms and presenting problems

1. **General presenting problems and/or symptoms.** During the initial intake, she could hardly speak, would not look at the therapist, and seemed to be in a mixed state of hyper-alertness and collapse. She appeared not to be present, but was startled at the slightest noise, such as a nearby closing door or the therapist shifting in the chair. The client hardly speaks in the first interviews; she is able to share some information through email and by filling questionnaires.

She describes severe difficulties tolerating emotions, both negative and positive. She presents with frequent self-harming behaviors that she experiences as punishment and out of control. She can neither look at mirrors, set boundaries, nor express opinions. She cannot enjoy pleasant activities or feelings. The client describes moments where she seems to lose contact with reality, and everything becomes confusing and scary. She presents thought disorder and passivity phenomena, believing one of the perpetrators can still control her from the distance.

2. **Previous diagnosis.** Unspecified Personality Disorder, Reactive Disorder, Paranoid Schizophrenia, Psychosis, Catatonia, and Borderline Personality Disorder.

3. **Attachment patterns.** Avoidant pattern with mother and disorganized attachment with father. Disorganized attachment with an external caregiver.

4. **Relational problems**
   a. Family members. Mother is distant. She expects the client to take care of her and does not give her space to have her own life. She criticizes her and gets angry when the client goes to therapy or does any pleasurable activities and does not seem to understand that Kendra has her own needs.
   b. Friends and peers. She has a hard time opening up to new people.
   c. Intimate relationships. She does not have a partner.
   d. Work and/or school. She has a hard time with some peers due to her fear of saying anything inadequate or hurting others.

5. **Daily life functioning**
   a. Self-care habits. Her safe-care habits are quite limited when she first comes in. She maintains a basic self-care, but has difficulty doing anything that can benefit her. She would like to exercise, but since she does not tolerate the positive affect it generates, she becomes blocked. She often hears critical voices that do not allow her to do anything pleasurable.
   b. Financial stability. When she comes in for treatment, she is working and financially independent. *(Later on, in therapy, she is forced to leave her job, but has a good income from her retirement funds, since she did work for many years.)*
   c. Social, occupational or school functioning. She occasionally engages in some social activities and goes to the gym. She spends most of the time at home, looking after her mother.
   d. Overall level of functioning. At a personal level, very low; towards others, medium.

6. **Initial onset of problems/symptoms.**
   a. What was happening then? Problems started at age 7, after she started being abused by a close relative and nobody noticed. The fact that nobody noticed was the worst part of the experience.
   b. What got triggered? She does not know.

7. **When did symptoms worsen?**
    a. What was happening then? At age 11, when a trusted teacher brutally raped her "because of how she was dressed, to teach her a lesson." As years went by, abuse and maltreatment continued happening on a regular basis; escalating the amount of verbal and physical aggression and sadism.
    b. What got triggered? Previous abuse by a close trusted relative. She thought it was her fault, that there was something in her that "causes the people I trust to behave like this."

8. **When do symptoms increase or worsen now?**
    a. Current triggers. Any trigger that reminds her of the sadistic abuse and negative internalized messages. She gets triggered when looking in the mirror, when something bad happens in the news, when there is an accident (always thinking she has caused it, even if it is something as remote to her as a plane crash), when she feels good, when she eats something she likes, etc.
    b. Degree of awareness of triggers. Low. She is aware of her general sense of feeling bad and in danger but is not aware of the triggers. Phobia of internal experience does not allow her to pay attention to what could be happening. She becomes blocked and occasionally paralyzed.

Resources

1. **Sources of adaptive information**
    a. Good enough attachment figures in childhood and/or adult life. A very close friend in her adult life.
    b. Moments of feeling safe and being protected. She can give some examples of moments in which someone helped her leave the religious organization where the abuse took place.
    c. Moments of feeling cared for. She talks about basic caretaking.
    d. Other relevant positive figure/models. Her spiritual support group.

2. **Emotional regulation capacity**
    a. Self-regulation capacity. In the beginning of therapy, she self-harms frequently to stop the guilt. She indicates punishing herself, repeating what one of her perpetrators told her to do.
    b. Co-regulation capacity. She was unable to co-regulate, she wants to trust the therapist, but she cannot, and this is even more distressing for her.
    c. Tolerance for negative and positive emotions. Severe limitations related to positive affect: activated with any positive feeling or thought. She cannot tolerate most of her emotions or physical sensations.

3. **Social support**
    a. Family members. Her sister, but in a limited way due to the lack of information. She is willing to help and could be a good support figure if she knew what happened.
    b. Intimate partners. None.

   c. Friends. Her best friend.

   d. Work colleagues and peers. None.

   e. Other professionals. A therapist from the day center she attended when she was admitted.

4. **Other resources**

   a. Mentalization capacity. The client has very limited mentalizing capacities. Integration capacity is severely affected by her trauma history and her internal conflict. She is a bright, smart woman. Despite all her limitations, she managed to finish three college degrees and work for many years.

   b. Degree of realization. Very low at the beginning of therapy. *(Improves with therapy.)*

   c. Degree of integrative capacity. Low. *(Has improved with therapy.)*

5. **Timeline of best memories.** To avoid disclosing too much personal information, we will omit this part. The client is hardly able to think of any positive memories or experiences in her life.

Structural elements of the internal system

1. **Client's degree of awareness of parts**. In the beginning of therapy, the client is not aware of having parts. She feels overwhelmed just by the mere thought of having them. She believes two perpetrators are still controlling her, despite having left the religious organization where the abuse happened about 10 years prior.

2. **Internal structure**

   a. Approximate number of parts. At intake, it was impossible to determine how many parts there were. The client could only speak about the two perpetrators, which made it likely that there were two parts of her that she was confusing with the real perpetrators. *[Later in therapy we could explore parts and there are two little girls, a teenager, three parts that mimic the main perpetrators of her life, a dark beast, a shadow, and a helper part that only appeared in three very difficult moments of her life.]*

   b. Client's description/representation of the internal system of parts. She is not able to describe or represent her internal system. She becomes blocked when we try to explore it.

   c. Organization and distribution of those parts that the client can discuss. Not possible to gather this information.

   d. Any missing pieces in the description. It is obvious that there are missing pieces, since she is unable to connect with many emotions.

3. **Degree of differentiation about the self and others**

   a. Can the client distinguish her own thoughts, emotions and needs from what has been imposed by others? No.

   b. Is the client confusing any parts or voices with the real perpetrators? Yes.

4. **Time orientation and current perception of safety**
   a. Is the client confusing what happened in the past with what is happening in the present? Yes. The client has trouble remaining present and grounded. She loses dual attention easily and has many difficulties coming back to the present moment. From time to time, she even confuses the therapist with the perpetrator.
   b. Does the client know that the danger is over? She cannot distinguish between what happened in the past and what is happening in the present, so she continues to feel in danger.
   c. Which parts are still stuck in trauma time? All parts are stuck in trauma-time.

5. **Mentalizing capacities.**
   a. Can all parts mentalize? The client can mentalize whenever she is not feeling activated. We cannot assess the capacity in other parts since it is not possible to explore them.
   b. Which parts have higher mentalizing abilities? Not possible to determine this in the beginning.
   c. Which parts need help with mentalizing? Not possible to explore this initially.

6. **Adaptive information.**
   a. Which parts have adaptive information? The Adult lacks very basic adaptive information. Her knowledge about self-care, love, support, fun, and emotions is very limited.
   b. Which parts need help with adaptive information? We cannot assess this initially.

Relational aspects of the internal system

1. **Acceptance of parts.**
   a. Despite the fear/conflict, does the client describe some parts with compassion, acceptance or appreciation? The client cannot accept that they are parts. The voices she confuses with the perpetrator are experienced as "not me."

2. **Relationships among parts.**
   a. What feelings do the parts have towards each other? From her description, we can hypothesize that the parts that mimic the perpetrators are controlling everything she does, feels, and thinks.
   b. Which are adaptive for the system in the present moment? Not possible to explore this initially.
   c. Which need to improve? It seems that all parts need help. Not possible to explore.

3. **Degree of cooperation between parts of the system.**
   a. Is the client aware of any parts attempting to help the system? No.
   b. Can the client accept that there might be an attempt of help even though it may not be clear yet? No, she has a hard time trying to let the idea in and becomes blocked.

4. **Parts that may have difficulties with therapy.**
   a. Is there ambivalence or rejection towards therapy? More than likely. All parts have trouble believing she has the right to ask for help.
   b. What are their concerns regarding therapy? She does not know.

5. **Co-consciousness between parts.**
   a. If it exists, which parts are co-conscious? Not likely.
   b. When does co-consciousness occur? Initially, there is no coconsciousness.
   c. How do other parts respond to this? Unknown.

Trauma-related phobias and other potential blocks

1. **Phobia of inner experience.** Extremely high.
   a. Can the client check inside? The client cannot even take a look inside. She is not open to exploring parts, she is unable to do so.
   b. Can the client notice and tolerate sensations? Whenever she notices her body or any emotion or thought that frightens her, she becomes blocked and starts crying like a very small child. This frightens her even more.
   c. Is the client afraid of her feelings, thoughts or sensations? She is terrified.
   d. Is the client ashamed of her feelings, thoughts or sensations? Yes.

2. **Phobia of parts.** Extremely high.
   a. Does the client show ambivalence about the parts or does she avoid talking about them? Yes, it is obvious that the client would like to talk about what happened, but she is unable and constantly avoids the issue.
   b. Despite the fear, can the client try to explore parts and be curious? In the beginning it is not possible due to the intense fear, rejection and shame.
   c. Do any of the parts feel shame or is the patient ashamed of any of them? Client is ashamed of what she considers incomprehensible reactions related to the parts and the internal conflict.

3. **Phobia of attachment and attachment loss.** Very high.
   a. Is there ambivalence around trust in the therapeutic relationship? The client is barely able to trust the relationship. She engages in therapy with much difficulty, remaining completely silent for very long periods of time in every session.
   b. Do the client or any of the parts have difficulties trusting others, ambivalence between wanting to attach and pushing others away? Yes, very much so.

4. **Phobia of traumatic memories.** Very high.
   a. Does the client insist on avoiding any exploration about childhood? When the client tries to talk about her experience, she collapses. It is very difficult to bring her back to the present moment.

b. Does the client show ambivalence about trauma work or even talking about traumatic experiences? Yes.

5. **Phobia of change and adaptive risk-taking.** Very high.
   a. Is the client afraid of change? Yes, very much so.
   b. Does the client present difficulties trying suggestions that would improve their quality of life? Yes.

6. **Defenses.** Dissociation and absorption.

7. **Any other identified potential blocks.** Loss of big blocks of time due to amnesia, strong self-hatred, and minimal capacity to experience positive affect.

EXAMPLE 1. I DARE NOT LOOK INSIDE

As we have already mentioned, this series of examples belong to approximately the third year of the patient's therapy, once she has been able to start talking about the parts. We start this transcript exploring whether the voices were active during the week (CS #2.1), how the client responded (CS #2.3), and if any issues need to be addressed (CS #2.4). While doing this, we take the chance to explore the system (TW #1).

T: Have you heard voices in your head lately?
C: It happened to me once at night.
T: What did you hear?
C: They called me by my name.
T: What did you do?
C: I played the music louder and tried to ignore it.
T: And how did the voices respond?
C: He told me I would never be happy.
T: Is it okay if we explore the voices to try to understand? (Client nods nervously).
T: How many voices did you hear?
C: I heard him.
T: One voice?
C: Yes.
T: How did the voice sound?
C: It was a male voice.
T: A male voice. Was it a familiar voice?
C: I think so.
T: Yes? Can you tell me a little bit more about this voice? (Client looks down, nervously.)

Since the client has difficulties responding, it is obvious that the phobia towards this part is high (TW #4). To help the client do this calmly, the therapist resorts to one of the other exploration methods described in Chapter 4, the use of drawings, which is a way to externalize the internal dynamics and get some distance. The therapist pulls out a blank piece paper and draws a circle representing the client's internal system.

> T: *Imagine that this is your mind, your inside. Where would you place the voice? Just draw whatever comes up. I don't expect a specific answer.*
> C: *Yes, but... the only thing I see is as if he* (referring to the perpetrator) *was inside* (pointing at the central part of the paper.) *Everything else is confusing.*
> T: *Inside, where? Where inside this circle do you notice him?* (Client points at the spot.) *Let's put a dot here, to represent this part. And what about the rest of the voices that you hear? Where would they be?*
> C: *This is very confusing...*

It starts to become apparent that Kendra has some trouble with differentiation, so the work in the next section will be aimed at assessing and improving her differentiation capacities (TW#5).

> T: *We are exploring this precisely because it is very confusing for you. It is related to an important issue, differentiation and understanding it can generate important changes. There is no correct answer, it is about understanding how things are represented internally and how you experience them. There is no wrong answer, don't worry about it, just write whatever comes to mind, this is what really matters.*
> C: *What was the question?*
> T: *The question is: if this* (pointing at the drawing) *is you, where would you place the voices that you hear? Where would they be? Would you place them inside of you or outside?*
> C: *Inside.*
> T: *How many dots would you draw in there to represent the different voices you hear?*
> C: *I don't know, I don't know how to do this.*
> T: *How many different voices do you hear?*
> C: *There are several.*

With much difficulty, she states hearing three voices: the main perpetrator, a female perpetrator who worked with him and was aware of what was happening, and God. To continue helping her with the issue of differentiation, when she says "him" and "her" in reference to her real-life perpetrators, we reformulate as "the voice that reminds you of..."

> T: *So, you hear a voice in your head that reminds you of this man, and a voice that reminds you of this woman who was also there, and the voice of something that represents God.*
> C: *Yes.*
> T: *Are there any other parts?*
> C: *The little girl.*
> T: *What is the little girl doing?*
> C: *Nothing, she cannot move. She has to wait for him* (main perpetrator) *and do what he says.*

Once the voices are identified and based on the history we have previously gathered from the client, we can point out the inner conflict, the function of the parts (TW #6), and validate the feelings and need of the parts (TW #7).

T: I see, there is a conflict here. There is one part that wants to protect herself; she wants to fight and escape. And there is another part that cannot do so, because if she tries to escape, the result could be even worse, and your life could be at risk. Does this make sense?

C: Yes.

T: You told me that, at a certain point, you complained, and this person threatened to throw you off a cliff. Am I remembering correctly?

C: Yes.

T: So, what was the result of you complaining or trying to stop him?

C: Things got worse.

T: Worse, that's right. Remember that we have spoken about how there are parts that had to attach to this man in order to survive? (Client nods.) *And how there is another part that is furious but cannot show it, because she has learned that things could get even worse? And since this furious part cannot fight this man, she turns against you and blames you for not having done something different.* (Client is listening.) *Does this make sense to you?*

C: Yes.

It is important to always keep the whole system in mind. Once the client understands the dynamics between the parts that lead to the internal conflict, the therapist can start, on the one hand, helping the part understand that repeating the strategies that were learned in the traumatic past is not adaptive in the present and that this way of responding is not really helping now (TW #6) and, on the other hand, offering the Adult Self new possibilities of responding (TW #8).

T: What I am trying to explain is that this part that seems to have turned against you carries a lot of anger and pain, and she has learned to protect herself and to protect you by constantly criticizing you. But I believe that we can work with her so she can feel better and learn to help you in a less critical way. Does this make sense?

C: Yes.

Even though the client is responding well, it is always a good idea to check how the system responds to any intervention (CS #2.5).

T: Check inside now for a moment. If this part were able to hear me, how would she receive what I just said?

C: I think that she blames me.

T: She blames you. Can she understand what I'm explaining?

C: I think so.

T: So, does she understand that the anger she wasn't able to express to the person who harmed you, she has been expressing towards you? (Client nods.) *Do you think that this part would like to feel better and not have so much accumulated anger?*

C: Yes.

The importance of validation cannot be underestimated. It is one of the most crucial interventions and should be used often. All parts are important, and this message needs to be clearly conveyed. They have all been created for a reason and have helped the client to survive a dysfunctional and dangerous environment in the past. This implies that they bring some resources along, which can be recycled to be useful in the present (TW #7).

> *T: And does this part of you know that she is an important part of the system?*
> *C: No.*
> *T: Can we let her know that she is an important part and that we are going to try to understand her and listen to her? We are going to need her help and the resources she brings.*
> *C: Yes.*
> *T: How does this critical part respond to what I say?*
> *C: I don't know.*
> *T: How do you receive it?*
> *C: I think it can help me.*
> *T: Yes? Does it bother you that I try to understand this critical part?*
> *C: No.*
> *T: Does it scare you?*
> *C: Yes.*

In the following session with Kendra, we kept working on differentiation and focused on some psychoeducation that could help her understand how these parts came to be.

EXAMPLE 2. PROCESSING PHOBIAS AND EXPLORING SELF-REJECTION

Three sessions later, Kendra comes to session saying she cannot stand herself. She is beginning to understand that rejecting parts of herself is not really working, but she cannot help what she feels towards the parts and voices. In the next section, by asking whether any parts were active during the week (CS #1.2), we can start exploring the rejection (TW #4) and what has triggered it or is triggering it in the present (TW #3).

> *T: Can you tell me about the rejection you notice?*
> *C: I notice rejection towards myself. I can't stand myself; I lose patience.*
> *T: Why is that?*
> *C: Because I feel like... I don't know. I was thinking about what you wrote to me a long time ago when you said that if I have something that I do not accept or a part of me that I don't accept, that it turns against me or something like that.*
> *T: Yes, I remember that conversation. Is that what happened?* (Client nods). *Did you notice any parts this week?*
> *C: Yes.*
> *T: What happened?*
> *C: I got frustrated, I just wished they would disappear.*
> *T: So, you do understand that if there is a part of you that you reject, this part is going to become agitated, right?*
> *C: Yes.*
> *T: What part would this be? Have you identified it?*
> *C: Not really, not much.* (Client grabs a pillow and squeezes it.)

344

Grabbing and squeezing a pillow is something the client has learned to do in therapy when she is nervous. Since the dissociative phobia is very clear at this point, we remind her of the usefulness of working with the phobias and suggest processing the rejection she is noticing in the moment (TW #4).

> T: *There was something that worked well for you in a session where we were working with the fear towards those parts. Do you think it would be good to work a little with that to see if something is clarified? Because it seemed that things became a bit clearer.*
>
> C: *A little yes.*
>
> T: *That rejection that you notice, where do you notice it?*
>
> C: *In my head and chest.*
>
> T: *Take the tappers, focus on that rejection a bit, let's do short sets.* (Client nods. BLS.) *What do you notice?*
>
> C: *A little bit of pressure on my chest.*
>
> T: *Notice that.* (BLS)
>
> T: *What do you notice now?*
>
> C: *I don't know.*
>
> T: *What are you getting?*
>
> C: *I don't know.* (Client seems confused or concerned about something.)
>
> T: *Are you okay?* (Client shrugs her shoulders.) *Something seems to be upsetting you.*

Notice how the therapist is not only attentive to the words of the client, but also her body language. By pointing out what we are observing in the moment and exploring it, we can help her identify what is upsetting her. This is particularly important in a client who has such difficulty identifying, understanding, and accepting her emotions. Through this intervention, we are encouraging the client to pay more attention to her system (TW #2), as well as exploring the reaction of the system towards the voices and parts (CS #2.3).

> C: *Yes, but I don't know what it is.*
>
> T: *What worries you? Is it related to this that you reject?*
>
> C: *It may be that, yes.*
>
> T: *Focus on that sensation and try to be curious about it. Try not to reject it, just observe and see what you notice.* (BLS) *What do you notice?*
>
> C: *I notice a lot of violence.*
>
> T: *Are you noticing violence or is that part of you noticing it?*
>
> C: *I don't know.*
>
> T: *Do you notice violence towards this part?*
>
> C: (Client takes a few minutes to check.) *No, I think the part is the one noticing violence.*

Regardless of whether it is her own phobia or the part's phobia, our goal for the session should include addressing the issue of violence (CS #2.4). For this, we continue to use bilateral stimulation and process the phobia (TW #4).

> T: *Let's try something. If the violence comes from this part, we're going to ask this part of you to focus on that feeling to see if she notices a bit of relief.*
>
> C: *I don't understand.*

T: If that part of you is restless inside because it feels rejected, we're going to ask her to focus on that feeling, to see if she notices any relief.

C: Okay.

T: Does the part agree? (Client nods. BLS.) *What do you get now?*

C: I notice as if it were a black dot that I'm not sure how to handle.

T: Where do you notice that black dot?

C: In my head.

T: Do you think it's a good idea to focus a bit on that dot?

C: Yes.

In the next section, we continue to encourage the client to pay more attention to the parts (TW #2), so we can understand both their function (TW #6) and their needs (TW #7).

T: We are going to try to do this while showing interest. There are parts of you that can scare you because you do not understand them or because you do not understand their function. It is important that we can pay attention to everything in you because everything that is inside you interests us. Focus on this black dot and let whatever comes, come. (Client nods. BLS.) *What do you get?*

C: I notice fear.

T: Where do you notice that fear?

C: I don't know.

T: Focus on that fear that you notice. (BLS) What comes up?

C: I'm a little restless, but I don't know why.

T: Do you still notice the black dot?

C: Yes.

T: If that black dot could talk, what would it say?

C: I don't know.

T: Take your time, think about it. If it could talk, what would it say?

C: It's as if it covered me completely, leaving me completely black too.

T: What do you notice when this happens?

C: Shortness of breath.

T: Can you focus on that? (Client nods. BLS.)

C: I don't know who I am.

T: What is happening inside? I'm interested in understanding.

C: It's as if it covered me completely.

T: Do you know why? Try to listen to it, if it could talk, what would it say? That black dot has stopped being a black dot or is it still a black dot?

C: No, it still is.

T: That black dot that you notice, is it afraid?

C: I think so.

T: Would you know what it's afraid of?

C: I don't know.

T: Why do you think it's afraid? What makes you think that?

C: I think it makes me feel afraid.

T: *Then it makes sense for it to be afraid too, that's why you notice that fear. Let's do something, you are both going to focus on the fear and let's see what comes up.* (Client nods. BLS.) *What do you get?*

C: *As if I was afraid of that part.*

T: *It's great that you can identify it. Now focus on that feeling that you have towards that part, to see if we can understand a little more. We're going to try to process that fear a bit, can you?*

C: *Yes.* (BLS)

T: *What do you get?*

C: *As if I do not accept that it is a part of me.*

T: *There you have the conflict: if you do not accept it, this part will feel bad. If it's a part of you that is afraid, what could you say? What helps you when you are afraid?* (Client shrugs her shoulders.)

T: *When you are afraid, does it help you to be rejected?*

C: *No.*

T: *Or to be ignored? Or to have someone get angry at you?* (Client shakes her head.) *It doesn't, right?*

C: *No.*

T: *So, it is important to treat your whole system with the same respect and interest, even if it scares you. There are many things that we still don't understand. The basic and most important thing is to show a lot of respect and interest in the different aspects of yourself. If feeling rejected when you are afraid does not help, what helps? What kinds of messages help you?*

C: *I don't know how to give myself helpful messages.*

Throughout the session, we continuously encourage the client to look at herself more respectfully, helping her develop curiosity and interest not only towards herself but other parts of the system as well (TW #2). Now we will start helping the client to expand her repertoire by exploring new alternative ways of responding toward the system (TW #8), reminding her of behaviors and attitudes previously modeled by the therapist towards her, and helping her become aware of how rejection is related to her history.

T: *When I offer you a message of encouragement or support, how do you receive it?*

C: *It makes me feel better.*

T: *What kind of things that I do or say, help you feel a little better? Can you think of any examples?* (Client takes a few minutes.) *It can be an attitude, some kind of message, etc. Take your time.*

C: *I don't know how to say it.*

T: *It's okay. Something comes to mind, but you have trouble saying it.*

C: *Yes, I don't know how to explain it.*

T: *You don't know how to explain it, but you identify it. This thing that helps you, could you try to apply it with this part of you? Can you try to think about what was coming up for you and try to convey it to this part of you? Can we try?* (Client nods.) *Take your time, no rush.*

C: *If I imagine doing what you do, it's as if the violence that I noticed before stops a bit.*

T: *Good. Should we try doing it again?*

C: *Yes.*

T: *Should I do some tapping while you do it?*

C: *Yes.* (BLS)

T: What do you notice now?

C: I am less afraid to look at that part.

Once the client is increasingly able to look at the part (TW #2), we can also check how the part responds to this change in attitude coming from the client (CS #2.3).

T: I think that's great. How does this part feel when she notices that you are less afraid of looking at it? (Client is silent, but calmer.) *Does this part seem to calm down?*

C: Yes.

T: Can we try a little bit more or do you think it's enough?

C: A little more.

T: Open your eyes to stop me if you need. (BLS. Client opens her eyes.)

C: I don't know. I notice things are separated.

T: Can you identify the things that were all mixed up before? (Client nods.) *That's good, isn't it?*

C: Yes.

T: Could you describe it a bit or is it still difficult?

C: I see that part there, but I don't know how to describe it.

T: What do you see?

C: The part is separated from the black point.

T: Does that part have a form?

C: Yes, it's round.

T: Is that part calmer?

C: Yes.

T: And are you calmer now too?

C: Yes.

We close the session reminding the client the importance of having a more positive perspective as a summary of the work done (CS #3.4)

T: Notice that with curiosity and acceptance, this part has become calmer. This is important, because the more you reject it, the more upset you inside gets. And I think you have suffered enough. (Client is listening attentively.) *Does this make sense?*

C: Yes. (Client seems to want to say something but holds back.)

T: What were you going to say?

C: What I notice is that when I'm alone, I don't know how to do this.

T: Is it as if you didn't know how to do it?

C: I don't know how to look at myself. I feel easily overwhelmed.

T: When you are alone and you are afraid of yourself, you tend to repress or not look or avoid, and that makes you more agitated.

C: Yes.

T: That is why we practice here, so you can learn. Maybe you could try to do just a little part of what we did here today. To try to look at it like "I don't understand what is happening, but I will not judge or reject it, I will just try to understand and observe, so I can tell Dolores when I see her." That would be a huge step. (Client nods calmly.)

EXAMPLE 3. EXPLORING THE SYSTEM WITH THE HELP OF BILATERAL STIMULATION

A couple of weeks later, we again explore if there are any changes in the internal system by simply asking about it (CS #1.2). Notice that we are inquiring about the whole system, not just specific parts or the Adult Self. We begin this session exploring how the client has been, how she left the previous session, the results of the work and if she followed the indications offered regarding trying to pay more attention to the parts if they showed up or if the voices spoke (CS #1.1, 1.2 and 1.3). Then we explore if the parts or voices have been active during the week (CS #2.1).

T: How are things going?
C: Better than other days.
T: How did you leave the session last time?
C: I felt better, things were calmer for a while.
T: How about the rest of the parts?
C: I did not notice them the following days.
T: Did you try to pay a little more attention as we agreed?
C: I think so.
T: How has your inner world been in these last two weeks?
C: Well, I notice that it's a bit confusing. I don't know why.

The aggressive part continues to generate discomfort. The client fears the possibility of reacting aggressively.

T: I remember that you told me about this, and you were very afraid of, once again, reacting as disproportionately as you have in the past, right? In fact, you felt very aggressive, and it didn't seem like you. Do you remember that?
C: Yes, yes.
T: After what we've been seeing, with what would you identify this aggressive part?
C: I don't know.

Exploring the system can be a challenge with Kendra due to the phobia of parts and inner experience. Verbal exploration is very difficult for her, and although externalizing techniques can help, she often gets stuck and feels bad for not being able to follow indications. When we ask her to draw a picture of her inner world, she has trouble with it and gets frustrated because she wants to understand what is happening inside. We suggest, as an experiment, that she try to do the drawing with the help of continuous BLS because it sometimes increases mental efficiency and helps to "think better." We explain the process and check in with the client throughout the exercise.

T: I'm going to ask you to express the different aspects of yourself with a drawing. Just draw whatever comes up, okay? If nothing comes up, no big deal; we have a lot of things to talk about. But I would like to try it. Shall we try? (Client nods.) I'll stand right here and tap on your shoulders. Is that okay?
C: Yes.
T: Take the time you need and just draw whatever you see inside.

C: How should I do it?

T: Any way you feel like doing it. (Client starts drawing.) Very good. Whatever is inside... and when you want me to stop, let me know. You can also draw anything that you see that may be confusing or blurry. Anything. Extend an invitation to your inner world, to see if any information comes up, such as some aspect that may not be represented and wants to be there. And you can stop me any time.

C: I can't see it clearly.

T: You don't see it clearly. Do you notice if there is something specific that you can't see too clearly in there?

C: Yes.

T: Yes, so draw something that is like... something you don't see, something confusing. What do you think it would be like? It could be many things: a shadow, a blotch, a barrier... anything. You can also just write down the word "confusing."

C: It's like a wall, but I don't see it too clearly.

T: Do you want us to go a little further to see if it becomes clearer?

C: Yes.

T: Very well. (Client draws something.) Very good. Is that okay?

C: Yes.

T: Shall we stop for a moment and look at this? Has it helped you to retrieve the information better?

C: Yes.

By asking all these questions, we are both encouraging the client to pay more attention to her inner world and promoting healthy curiosity towards the workings of the inner system (TW #2). This will, in turn, increase her capacity for self-reflection.

T: Great! Tell me a little bit about how this information was coming up for you. Did it come to you from inside? How were you noticing it? I'm very interested in understanding.

C: As if I were inside the things I was drawing.

T: So, these things that you drew here are things that came to you as if you were inside of them. (Client nods.) And you would say they are different parts of you?

C: Yes, some are.

T: Some are. Which ones are not?

C: Those that are not parts.

T: There are many sensations and feelings too, right?

C: Yes.

T: Of these sensations you drew over here, do you see them as parts of yourself or parts that feel those things?

C: It's me feeling those things. I don't know.

T: Okay, then stuff came up that is very much related to things that have happened, right? You were getting this very important information, which is the way you feel.

C: Yes.

So far, the client has offered a lot of valuable information. We have two options now: processing the dissociative phobia represented by the wall (TW #4), since it has shown up in the drawing, or exploring the function of this wall (TW #6). Both options are valid but, whenever possible, it is best to first explore what the wall represents. Then we offer validation (TW #7), modeling a new way of relating to the parts (TW #8) and respecting the pace of the system.

T: *What can you tell me about that wall? What did you notice?*

C: *I notice it when I think of the past. I guess it doesn't allow me to see it.*

T: *Do you think that behind that wall there are more things than on the other side?*

C: *Sometimes I don't dare to look at what's behind.*

T: *So, the wall has a very important function.* (Client nods.) *A protective function that separates things that may be very scary.* (Client nods.) *So, it's important to start with this.* (Therapist points to the drawing.) *Then, when the time comes, the wall will be a good gauge. For now, it tells us that there are things we have to be careful with. So, now and then, we'll see how this wall is doing. When the wall is not necessary, you'll be seeing changes in the wall. As long as it's necessary, we will respect it and take it into consideration because it gives us very important information. Does this make sense?*

C: *Yes.*

T: *It seems that bilateral stimulation helps to access information with less difficulty. Is this true for you?*

C: *Yes.* (The client seems pleasantly surprised.)

T: *Okay, we'll try it more often.*

During closure, we check with the client to make sure everything went well for her and she is stable (CS #3.3). Remember some clients seem to be doing fine and, when we check in with them, they are not noticing their body much and are not very present.

T: *Is it my impression or are you leaving a little bit calmer today?*

C: *Yes.*

T: *Doing it like this is less chaotic for you, right?*

C: *Yes.*

T: *Then we're going to do it like this, okay?*

C: *I put up with it well, I don't know if the tapping is different on the shoulders or the hands, but it's better for me on the shoulders.*

T: *It's better for you there. It's great to know that we have other alternatives. And it's great that you can leave feeling calmer.*

EXAMPLE 4. WORKING WITH CIPOS AND PHOBIAS

The client has had a rough week due to a glimpse of a memory that triggered feelings of loneliness and unworthiness. The initial idea was to work on the intrusive memory and process it, insisting on the fact that, often, less is more. She is already familiar with fractionated processing and is able to tell the therapist when she needs to stop. During the work with this memory, the client connected with a more difficult memory that she was not ready to face. This led to her having trouble staying present, which led us to resort to grounding techniques, time orientation, and CIPOS to stabilize.

351

T: *So, let's try to work on this memory that is bothering you, okay? But we won't do too much. Remember what I told you the other day: it's better to do less than more.* (Client nods.) *So, let's start over and if it's too much, we'll stop, so you can be calm and see that this issue doesn't have to overwhelm you, okay? We'll focus only on this memory with her. Remember that you can stop if it starts being too much for you or any part inside of you.*

C: *Okay.*

After doing a few sets of BLS to process the memory, the client seems unsettled and the therapist inquiries about it (CS #2.4).

T: *What's happening?*

C: *I'm not able to separate it.*

T: *It's okay, try to look at me. It's important that you know you're with me and that we're working on an event from the past, okay? It's the best way to start separating these things. Grab a pillow if you're more comfortable. You've done it before. Hold the pillow and notice it.*

This is a resource that we have used previously to help her stay present and prevent her from pinching her arms. Having something to squeeze helps her soothe and stay more grounded. At the same time, it represents a boundary and helps her feel more protected.

T: *That's right, notice the texture of the pillow. What happens when you hold the pillow?*

C: *I feel a little bit of relief.*

T: *Great. Notice that, okay?*

After focusing on the pillow for a few minutes, the therapist attempts to continue with the processing, but it becomes obvious that another memory is coming up and she has a hard time staying present. As we explained in Chapter 1, the CIPOS procedure is a good option in these cases.

T: *Let's work on that memory that is so hard for you. But instead of using it as a target, which may be too much for you, just think about the memory for a few seconds, okay? And then, you're going to come back here, you're going to notice me, you're going to notice the office, and you're going to orient yourself to where you are: here with me, working on something from the past.* (Client nods.) *With this, we will reinforce your ability to remain present, so it won't be so scary to get into stuff from the past. We're going to strengthen your ability to get out of that situation and be here with me.* (Client nods.) *We will gradually be able to work on these issues, but we'll always do it in a way that's not too much for you. Do you understand this is important for me?*

C: *Yes.*

T: *Why is it important for me?*

C: *Because you don't want me to suffer.*

T: *Is that clear for you? Good. So, first, you're going to think about that moment —the moment when you wanted her to walk into the room— just for a couple of seconds. I will count to two and then you will open your eyes and come back to the room with me. Okay? So, close your eyes and go back to the memory.* (Client closes her eyes and thinks about the memory for two seconds.) *Done. Open your eyes and look at me. What do you see? You can describe my shirt, the situation, or anything you want.*

C: I see... the colors on your shirt.
T: What are the colors on the shirt?
C: Red, gray, pink, and black.

To assess how present the client is after focusing on her surroundings, the Back of the Head Scale is used, which is one of the tools mentioned in Chapter 1 that allows us to explore whether the client is grounded in the present.

T: Are you here with me? From here to here, where this point in the back of your head means you are fully back in the memory and this point out here means you are out here with me. Where would you be now?
C: Halfway, more or less.
T: Okay, then look around again at what's in the office.
C: (Looking around.) *I see I'm here.*
T: How much are you here?
C: Well, I'm a bit more towards the outside. (Placing her hand in front of her face.)
T: A bit more towards the outside. Do you think you need to look around a little more?
C: No, I feel more present.
T: Okay, then you're going to stay with the feeling of being more present, and I'm going to do a little bit of tapping. (BLS) *What do you notice? Could you look at me just so I know you're here? Do you feel more focused here with me?* (Client nods.)

We repeat this a few times until the client feels grounded, oriented in time, and safe. We can end the session here or ask the client if she wants to work a bit more with the memory since we still have time to do more work. An important issue with these clients is to let them know that they have options. Clients with complex trauma usually have not had options; they were stuck in an impossible situation with no way out. Letting them know that they can choose helps with differentiating the past from the present, knowing that things are different now (TW #5).

T: Would you like to think about the memory a little bit more or not?
C: Yes, I'll do it, I'll do it.
T: For how many seconds? You decide.
C: Two or three.
T: You choose, you're the guide. Two or three? Tell me what you prefer, and I'll adapt.
C: Three.
T: Three? Okay. Ready? (Client nods.) *Think about that.* (Client closes her eyes.) *Done. Look at me. Come back here again, pay attention to the office.*
C: I see things... like... empty.
T: When looking at the office?
C: No, the memory.
T: The memory, okay. However, we're not working with the memory itself now f. We're working with your ability to get out of the memory and coming back and being present. So later, when we start working on it, you can feel calm knowing that you can get out of there. Let's throw this pillow back and forth for a bit. (Therapist and client use the pillow to help the client be more present.) *How much do you notice yourself here now?*

C: Not much.

T: Not much. Is the other one better than the pillow? What helps you the most?

C: I'm not feeling well. (Client seems agitated.)

T: Okay, look at me and tell me what's going on.

C: The memory is creeping in.

T: Well, it's okay, I'm here with you. It's fine, just let it out. I know it's creeping in, that's why we're working on being in the present.

C: Yes. It just bothers me that I can't stop my thoughts and all that stuff.

T: Look at me for a second. (Client looks up). If it were so easy, you would've solved it yourself already. If you are working on this with me, it's because this is the space for working on it. Right here you can feel whatever comes up for you, and you can express anything you want, okay? (Client nods.) This is precisely the space for that. If you get angry at yourself for becoming emotional, then you're not allowing yourself the space to work on that, right? (Client nods). So, what do you notice now?

C: Anger.

T: Anger towards...?

C: Anger for reacting like this when I'm here, because this is a safe place.

T: Well, this is about allowing yourself to react like this because you're here with me. So, how about doing a different experiment now? We'll come back to this some other day. Little by little, yes? (Client nods and seems calmer.)

We continue this session processing the secondary emotion (feeling anger for feeling upset). The client calms down and is able to feel relief for having expressed what she felt and needed. We close the session reinforcing the work done throughout the session (CS #3.1) and asking her to reflect on what was most useful, so she can repeat it and maybe do it at home (CS #3.2). Before we finish, we make sure she is oriented in time (CS#3.3) and do a summary of the work done today (CS #3.4).

EXAMPLE 5. A PART WANTS TO HURT OTHERS

After working on the abuse, she suffered from a very close person in the last session, she comes in commenting that she has been very upset lately, with feelings of wanting to hurt her mother. We begin the session exploring the voices and parts (TW #1) and encourage the client to be more curious to understand what is happening (TW #2).

T: Let's try to understand what's happening. Do you hear a voice within you? Is it a sensation or a thought? What is it?

C: What I notice is that I'm very agitated inside, and I'm afraid of losing control at some point.

T: How do you think you could lose control?

C: Well, I do not know, maybe by acting on what I hear. I don't know, everything is very confusing.

T: Then it could be a good idea to try to explore what's happening inside and see what comes up, so we can try to understand this confusion. What do you think?

C: Okay.

T: Can you tell me what you heard?

C: No (looking down).

In the next section, the therapist explores what was happening when the voice showed up, which is the usual way to explore triggers (TW #3) and helps us get an idea of how the voice is trying to help or what it is trying to achieve (TW #6).

T: Okay, I know it's difficult. Can you tell me what was happening when you heard what you heard?

C: I was going over my homework with my English teacher, and she kept telling me that I do everything wrong.

T: And was that when you heard the voice? (Client nods.) *How did you feel when your teacher said that?*

C: Bad. She kept repeating it over and over.

T: I see. So, it seems that the voice didn't like what your teacher was saying either.

C: It could be.

T: It seems like the voice was trying to help you.

C: How could that help me? I got really scared just by having those thoughts.

T: Well, remember when we talked about how some parts try to help in the ways they know? (Client nods.) *Maybe this voice does not know that this is actually making you more nervous. Does this part remind you of anyone?*

C: Yes, of him (perpetrator) *and of the time when I was so aggressive at work.*

T: Let me ask you something. These thoughts from the other day or the behaviors from back then at work, would you say they are similar to the things this man would say or do?

C: Yes, but that's what scares me most. The last thing I would want is to treat others how I was treated.

T: Of course, I understand. And this is one of the effects of trauma. Do you remember when we talked about the different parts that could have different memories, feelings, and sensations? (Client nods.) *Well, one of the most difficult things is to understand those parts that remind us of people who have hurt us. That's why you tend to reject them and get so scared.*

C: I am afraid of becoming that.

T: Of becoming the part that frightens you?

C: Yes.

T: Is this the part that you think could hurt your teacher?

C: Yes.

T: I see.

C: I've noticed a lot of aggression inside, towards her. And this reminded me of something. I've never done such a thing, but it did remind me of times when I had been aggressive.

T: Look at me. (Client looks up.) *This happened a long time ago, and you have worked hard to manage those situations. Remember?* (Client nods.)

The client is blocked with the thought of doing something horrible to her teacher. We keep exploring the system (TW #1) and the phobias (TW #4), so she can understand better and calm down. First, we explore verbally and then we use action figures to get an idea of how the conflict is represented inside.

T: You associate these thoughts and possible behaviors to this part. (Client nods.) *Okay, let's explore those thoughts. How would you describe them? As foreign thoughts? As a voice that you heard?*

C: Well I heard a voice, and then I thought I had to hurt her because she shouldn't exist. (Client starts crying nervously.)

T: Look at me, it's okay, we are exploring something that scares you so we can understand but remember that this didn't happen. Did you feel like yourself in that moment, as you usually are?

C: No.

T: What were you noticing? What was different in you?

C: Well, I was thinking of ways to... I don't know, it was as if I had lost control of myself, as if I could turn into something horrible. (Crying.) I can't say it. It's as if it turned against me.

T: Remember you are here with me. My perception of you doesn't change because of this. I really want this to be clear. I'm just trying to understand, so I can help you understand the things that happen inside of you. (Client nods and seems to calm down a bit.)

T: I know you are not going to hurt her. You have worked hard on that. And the part of you that has those thoughts is trying to protect you, this part is trying to get a message across. But the way this part communicates this message is very scary. (Client looks up.) I am guessing this part might not like the situation that you have right now with your teacher. But thinking about doing something does not mean you're going doing it, it's not the same thing. You said it was as if it turned against you. Can you explain this a bit?

C: Yes. Later, I started to think that I was bad, that I was a bad person, and I felt the urge to hurt myself again.

T: It makes sense, that's what you learned to do. When there was no way to escape from all those feelings you could not express, they would turn into punishments. (Client nods.) And we have worked on that too, right?

C: Yes.

Offering validation for the way in which she has learned to respond (TW #7) is always necessary, as well as repeating the adaptive information that she is still trying to understand and accept.

T: So, let's try to understand how this is related to the four figures that you selected. You said this one (pointing at the figure that represents the part that mimics the main perpetrator) is the one that could hurt others and the rage that turns against you.

C: Yes. It's as if there were two of them. One that wants to hurt others and one that hurts me.

T: I see, it makes a lot of sense. This is what these parts learned to do when there was no other way out. We will come back to these two parts in a little bit. How about these other two parts? What do they represent?

C: This one feels different than the others; it has nothing to do with them.

T: I see, and what does this one represent?

C: It represents time and how the more time goes by, the more I become that.

T: What do you mean by "become that?"

C: Darkness.

T: What does darkness mean for you?

C: I don't know.

After trying to understand what the different parts represent within the inner system of the client (TW #1), we continue exploring her needs (TW #7).

T: Okay. So, would you be able to tell me what this dark part might need?

C: I think that she would feel better if others didn't hurt her.

T: So, is it a part that needs protection or strength?

P: Yes.

T: Okay, how about this other part?

C: Maybe getting to know myself better and understand what is happening with me.

T: Is this part curious about the other parts?

C: Yes.

: What might this part need?

C: This one is more like me. I see myself in this one.

T: What would you need?

C: I really don't know.

T: Don't worry, this is why we are working on this, to try to understand.

When clients appear doubtful about what is happening inside or seem to have trouble defining what they are noticing in a certain part, it can always be useful to explore the possibility that there may be a dissociative phobia (TW #4).

T: What do you feel towards this part?

C: I feel more curious about this other one.

T: Okay great, so with curiosity we can understand little by little. How about these other parts that kind of go together (pointing at the figures that represent the two parts: the one that wants to hurt others and the one that harms the client).

C: Fear.

T: What might these parts need?

C: To be able to see another way out and to see the positive aspects.

Once the client is able to understand these parts a little better and has enough curiosity about their possible needs (TW #1), it is important to validate that the parts are doing what they learned to do with the best intention (TW #7), to search for possible resources for meeting these needs (TW #7), and to model different ways of responding towards the parts (TW #8).

T: This is very interesting. Notice how important this is. Both of these parts need to notice positive aspects and see a different way out. (Client nods.) So, you do understand that these parts have not learned to see things differently.

C: Yes.

T: Great, but they can learn with our help.

C: I would like that.

T: Good. How about this other part, the dark one? What do you feel towards that one?

C: I don't know.

T: Is it positive, negative or neutral?

C: It feels like something that takes over and controls me.

T: How is that?

C: When I notice this part, nothing else moves. It's as if it were controlling me and I turn into nothing.

T: So, when you notice this part, what happens with the other parts?

C: They become still too. Nothing moves.

T: *So, this part is also trying to protect you.*

C: *How?*

T: *Well, I don't know if I understood correctly. Let me run this by you, and you let me know if it makes sense. (Client nods.) I am thinking that when this part shows up, the one that wants to hurt others, then you immediately notice the other part, the one that tells you to punish yourself.*

C: *Yes.*

T: *So, punishing yourself eliminates the possibility of hurting others. (Client nods.) And then you say that when this other part shows up, nothing moves. I understand it's frightening because you feel controlled, but it seems to stop both reactions: hurting others and hurting yourself. Did I understand correctly?*

C: *Well, yes. It's true, when this one shows up, it takes up the entire space.*

T: *So, each part is trying to help in their own way. We just need to help them understand that there are better ways now.*

C: *Okay.*

T: *So, we can both think of ways that can be more helpful in the present moment and share them with these parts.*

Notice how we try to promote curiosity (TW #2) and explore available resources in the different parts (TW #7), which is very new for a client that is used to focus and perceive the negative aspects that frighten her (TW #4).

T: *Can we try to think of the resources that each part brings along? (Client nods.) Alright, let's begin with the part that wants to hurt others, the one that's the most terrifying for you.*

C: *That one is very close to the one that tells me to punish myself.*

T: *They are very close. They kind of go together now, right?*

C: *Yes.*

T: *So, what resources might these parts have?*

C: *I don't think they have any resources.*

T: *Well, these parts scare you and it's difficult for you to think of options.*

C: *Yes.*

T: *Could we think of something that might help them?*

C: *No, I don't see that either.*

T: *I think both of these parts can help, so even though this is difficult, let's try to think about this together. (Client nods.) If they were trying to help, how would they try to do it? Let's think of them separately for a moment, beginning with the one that thinks about hurting others. What is adaptive here?*

C: *Nothing.*

T: *The ways might not seem adaptive, but let's think about what's underneath. What's underneath the idea of hurting others? Does this idea come out of the blue?*

C: *No.*

T: *It doesn't, right? When does this part usually show up? Is it when you feel calm?*

C: *No. It shows up when somebody is hurting me or trying to hurt me.*

T: *So, this part shows up when you need protection. Well, that makes sense. No we need to think of ways that could really help you. What type of messages would help you?*

C: *Maybe to hear that I am not doing everything wrong, or ideas on how to improve what I'm doing.*

T: *That would be perfect. I'm not sure we are there yet, but it's a very good idea. What happens inside when you say that? Does the part say anything?*

C: *No, she's quiet now.*

It is important to check how the part responds to the interventions (CS #2.5). The fact that the part is quiet at this point does not mean it is not cooperating. Quite the contrary, it often means that the part is listening and showing interest in what we are exploring or suggesting.

T: *Okay, so maybe the part can listen to this possibility. I am wondering if we can ask this part to give us some time so you and I can think of ways of setting boundaries with your teacher for instance. How does this sound?*

C: *Good.*

T: *Would you like to work on that?*

C: *Yes.*

T: *Can you understand how this part is trying to help now? And how it gets triggered when you don't feel well?*

C: *Yes.*

T: *How about the one that tells you to punish yourself? Let's do the same thing. If she was trying to help, how would she be trying to do it?*

We continue this session exploring how each part is trying to help (TW #6) and searching for alternatives (TW #8). Notice how the client becomes much calmer as she starts to be able to understand how the part has been trying to help and is currently still trying to help.

C: *I had never seen it like this.*

T: *I know. It's very difficult to understand how parts are trying to help when they use ways that are so frightening. But remember that this is what they learned. And we'll help them think of new ways. So being curious about this is a huge step. I hope you keep your curiosity online to understand and help this part. We have to help it to protect you in a different way, because it's a part of you.*

C: *Okay.*

T: *Everything you notice inside that is now fragmented has useful parts that help you in a different way at certain times. We have to understand these parts and check on their resources. It's not too clear for you right now, but we'll move along together. So, what we'll try to do these days is to understand your system, so you feel calmer about everything that's going on inside. How does that sound?*

C: *Fine, I would like to try.*

T: *Well, to do so, we must not forget any aspect of you. Great work, I'm very happy that you were able to be more curious about other parts.*

After reinforcing the work done by the client and the parts (CS #3.1), we close the session summarizing what was learned (CS #3.4). We always want to prevent possible relapses whenever conflict arises again, so we help the client think of alternatives outside of therapy for when those impulses appear (CS #3.5). In this specific case, we also help her by reminding her about the importance of differentiation (TW #5).

T: So, if you get a thought like that or you hear a voice that says those things, what can you do right now?

C: Well, I think that if I were to think that my teacher is simply being critical, that she is not really trying to hurt me, I would not feel the impulse.

T: So, in a way, this is about differentiating the past from the present. Is it something like that?

C: Yes, she's different with me now, she's not like them.

T: So, could you try to remember what we're seeing here? And say to yourself, and maybe to these parts: "Well, this is an impulse that I feel, a thought that comes up and I'm working on it in therapy, but I know that the situation with my teacher is different now." Would something like this be useful?

C: Yes.

T: It would be like thinking about these situations as useful information for therapy. You can also write me an e-mail when these things happen, and then we can explore the information here.

C: I think that could help.

T: Okay, perfect. So instead of getting frustrated with yourself and the other parts, you can share that with me and think something like, "This is information that will be useful for Dolores so I can understand what happens inside of me."

C: Okay. (Client smiles.)

T: How do you feel now?

C: Better.

T: Great. We will keep working on understanding all of these parts.

EXAMPLE 6. THE MEETING PLACE PROCEDURE

A couple of months later, the client comes to a session very activated. She refers feeling blocked due to certain events from the past but can neither speak about them nor understand what they are bothering her. After trying to explore verbally to no avail, we ask her to draw. She cannot draw what is happening inside either, so we decide to use the meeting place as an alternative way of exploring.

T: Let's do something to see if it helps. Have we ever done this exercise of visualizing a meeting place?
C: No.
T: Then we're going to try it. Right now, you're thinking about those past situations and they bother you. (Client nods.) Let's try to understand what could be getting triggered. Can you try something? (Client nods.) If you don't like it, we'll stop. It's about trying to visualize a space of communication, of understanding. It's neither a space of conflicts, nor arguments, nor judgments. It's about trying to invite all the different parts of you, the different aspects, and trying to see how each one of them is doing in that space. (Client nods). What type of space would you select to have a meeting? What would be more comfortable for you?
C: I don't know.
T: It can be a space with a table and chairs around or it can be a space with couches instead. It can also be outdoors... (Client remains silent.) How would you choose that space to be? (Client remains silent.) Does anything come to mind?
C: I'm thinking that they come in one at a time, but they don't feel comfortable.
T: Okay, think of a place that would be comfortable for you. A place where you can be relatively calm that can help you do this visualization exercise.

C: Right here, for example (referring to the therapy office).

T: Right here. Check and see if you would need this office and perhaps another one, or if we should just stick with this one.

C: Right here is fine.

T: Right here is fine. Okay.

The following instructions are aimed at helping the client keep the whole system in mind, introducing the idea of observing and listening to all parts (TW #2), which encourages and models respect and healthy curiosity (TW #8) and is the foundation to begin promoting dialogue and communication (TW #10).

T: If for any reason, during the visualization, you need to use —or you feel calmer using— any of the other offices, just let me know, okay? It needs to be comfortable for you and it's about you being able to visualize things in the calmest way possible, without judging. If there's a part or aspect of you that is difficult, you can see where this part wants to be, you can see if it needs to be in the next-door office, okay? Try to do that, we have this space. Now I'm going to ask you to close your eyes and we're going to try it.

C; Okay.

T: We're going to invite the different parts, the different aspects of yourself, to walk up to the door and come in. You are only going to observe what happens. Remember that this a space to try to understand. All of the aspects and parts are welcome, each one has its place.

C: (The client closes her eyes to do the exercise and open them quickly, looking frightened.) It's not looking good.

T: What's going on? What do you notice?

C: I'm feeling dizzy.

T: You're feeling dizzy. (Client remains silent.) Tell me a little bit about what happened, it's very important. Did you try to follow the indications?

C: Yes.

T: What did you see? Or what happened inside?

C: That... when you said that all the parts should come in and stuff... everything came in all at once.

T: That means that all these parts want to be heard or want to participate in this. Could that be? But it's hard for you. (Client nods.) Anyway, think about it. You're here with me doing an exercise. We are inviting these parts in order to try to understand what's going on inside, but you're not in there, you are here with me and you are observing. (Client nods.) So, when you invited these aspects or parts of yourself, what did you see?

C: I don't know, it was like... I don't know how to explain it. It's as if they were things that were out of control.

The client is describing two trauma-related phobias, the phobia of dissociative parts and the phobia of inner experience (TW #4). This is a good moment to introduce the processing phobias procedure described in Chapter 1.

T: Out of control things that need to be understood. I know this generates a lot of fear in you. So, is it okay if we do a little bit of tapping with your fear and see if we could take a clearer look at these aspects?

C: Yes.

T: Where do you notice the fear?

C: In my head.

T: Let's do a little bit of work with your sensation. (Short set of tapping.) *Open your eyes. What do you notice now?*

C: It's like everything turned, like... everything. I don't know. (Client looks a bit calmer.)

T: Can you try to visualize it once again? Invite all of those different aspects.

C: Okay.

T: Yes? (Client nods.) *I'm not expecting you to do it, I'm only expecting you to do whatever you think you can do. So, then, check inside and see if it would be a good idea.*

C: If it can help me understand, yes.

T: Yes, in order to try and understand what's there. Check and see what you notice inside, if it's a good idea to continue or not. We don't have to do it.

It is crucial to check that the pace is right for the entire system (SC #2.5) at every stage of treatment, but even more so in the very beginning when the conflict and the phobia of dissociative parts are intense.

C: It's a good idea, it's just that everything is very confusing, it's a bit like how it was before.

T: So, should we try to see what happens if we try again? (Client nods.) *You can do it with your eyes open or closed. You could do it looking towards me or looking at the cushion. Check and see what's more comfortable for you.*

C: Closing my eyes.

T: Closing your eyes. Would it help you if I repeat the instructions?

C: Yes. (Client closes her eyes and signals that she is ready to try it again.)

T: Let's try to invite these different aspects of yourself again, with the intention of understanding what is happening inside. We're not going do anything if it's not the time to do it. We only want to understand what's going on. You and I are here doing a visualization exercise. (Client nods.) *So, try to invite the different aspects of yourself, and see how they would place themselves in the room. Just observe and see who comes in, and where each one of them goes. If they sit down on the big sofa, on the little sofa that's on the other side, if they stand in the corner...*

C: In a corner.

T: Who is standing in the corner?

C: It's like a younger me.

Recognizing and validating what the parts have just done (TW #7) is always a good strategy. Often, clients have trouble when it comes to validating the collaboration of other parts, so it is always a good idea to point it out for them, which also serves as modeling new ways of responding (TW #8).

T: Look how brave is that younger you, isn't she?

C: Yes.

T: Remember that we're not going to judge anything, okay? We are just observing and trying to identify. This younger you is in the corner of the room. How is that younger you? Is she standing?

C: She is crouching.

T: She is crouching. Is she looking up? Is she looking away?

C: She's not looking.

T: She's not looking, but she's there, right? (Client nods.) *We'll come back to that younger you in a moment. Take a look and see what other aspects come in and how they would place themselves in the room and where. Just as information, without judging, we're just going to try to understand.*

C: It's as if... a part had shown up who controls all the rest.

T: So, let's welcome this part, because it's a very important part. It's a part that wants everything to be okay. It's a part that tries to control that nothing is done if it's not a good idea. Is this right?

C: Yes.

T: And where is this part placing itself?

C: In the middle.

T: In the middle. And how is she placed in the middle?

C: She's standing.

T: She's standing. Very well. We'll take this part into consideration. She's in the middle and she can control. It's okay for her to do it if that's what she needs to do. Check and see what other parts come in and where they would place themselves. Anywhere is fine. I know it's scary, but remember that it's information that can help us understand. (Client becomes agitated.) *What happened now? What were you seeing?*

C: It was like... it was like before, something walked in suddenly.

T: Something walked in suddenly. Where did that something place itself?

C: It started running to fight with the part who is in the middle.

T: Let's remember that it's not a space for fighting, okay? It's a space to try to understand. The part in the middle is there and is allowed to be there. The other part is also welcome; look and see where this other one wants to go. She can have her own space, she doesn't have to fight with any other part.

C: It seems that she is covering everything that's in the center.

T: And what does the one in the center do when this other one that covers everything shows up?

C: She can't move.

The following intervention is aimed at helping the client acknowledge the needs of the different parts, to promote understanding so, eventually, she will learn to recognize and meet their needs (TW #7). At the same time, it helps explore the function of the part, which is another fundamental step of the therapeutic work (TW #6).

T: She can't move. We're going to welcome this part that covers everything up. We know that it's another important part of you. I know that sometimes it's scary. Check in with this part that is showing up covering everything. And see why it needs to do this. (Client remains silent.) *Think that, at times, parts act in the way they have learned to act, and perhaps this part is also trying to protect or to prevent is from going too fast.* (Client remains silent.) *When I welcome this part, what do you notice?*

C: It's like if it were something strange.

T: It's something strange for you. Maybe this part is telling us that it's enough for today. Do you think that may be it?

Before we continue working, we explore how this part responds to the intervention (CS #2.3). It is important to check in with the Adult Self and the whole system instead of trying to suggest their response. This is a good way to model how to check inside and respect the pace in every session.

> T: *Is it okay with you if we check this?* (Client nods.) *Let's tell this part that if it's too much for today, we already know that she's indicated it in the only way she knows how. If she doesn't mind continuing for a bit longer, we're going to ask her to move to a different location in the room. She doesn't have to leave. We don't want her to leave. I don't want her to leave.*
>
> C: *Okay.* (Client closes her eyes and remain silent, she looks calmer.)
>
> T: *I think it's an important part and we need to understand why she's doing this. If she thinks that it's a good idea to continue a bit longer, check and see if this part moves elsewhere in the room or not. That way we will know if it's enough for today or if we can continue for a bit longer. Try doing that and take your time. Whatever this part decides is fine with me.*
>
> C: (Client takes her time to check inside.) *It's as if the part in the center accepts it too.*
>
> T: *The part in the center accepts it too. So, then this other part in the center that was covering everything up, is it still covering everything or has it moved elsewhere?*
>
> C: *I don't know.*
>
> T: *Or is it in the same place but the part that couldn't move is calmer?*
>
> C: *Both parts are calmer.*
>
> T: *And both of them are more or less in the middle. Let's thank both parts for allowing us to continue for a bit longer.* (Client nods.) *And let's invite any other parts that want to be there. Check and see if any other part comes in and where it places itself.* (Client makes a gesture.) *Did something happen now?*
>
> C: *It's not another part, it's just that the part in the corner is scared.*
>
> T: *It's scared and that's why she's in the corner, right? Does this part need anything now?*
>
> C: *I think she needs a hug.*
>
> T: *How do you know she needs a hug? What do you notice or what do you see?*
>
> C: *It's as if she were asking for help. I don't know, it's just what it seems.*
>
> T: *Check and see if you would like to receive that hug.*
>
> C. (Client closes her eyes to check in with the part.) *She doesn't say anything, but it seems that she would.*
>
> T: *Okay, and is there a part of you that can give her that hug? Without forcing it. Check and see if there's a part of you that could give it to her. What do you notice when I say this?*

The fact that the patient is considering giving this part a hug is very important. But before going ahead with that idea and suggesting it, we check if the part would be willing to receive that hug. From the answer, it seems like it. This is one way to explore how the system has reacted to this intervention (CS #2.5). Next we explore whether there is a part that can help meet this need (TW#7), because the therapist knows that the Adult Self is not yet ready to do it.

> C: *That there is no one.*
>
> T: *And is there anyone that has not come in yet who can give her that hug or not? Or is there anything else that we can do?*
>
> C: *Maybe if ...* (Client seems uncomfortable.) *Forget it, I think it's silly.*
>
> T: *It's not silly. What is it?*

C: That… if I let you in, this part feels calmer.

T: Can that part know that I am here? (Client nods.) *Yes? Does this part notice that I'm here and I'm trying to help her?*

C: Yes.

T: Does it help her to know that I'm here?

C: Yes. She's calmer.

T: She's calmer knowing that I'm here, okay. What's happening with the other two?

The therapist has followed the patient's suggestion with a slight modification. Instead of trying to go one step further in the visualization exercise, which would possibly be premature to this system, we help the part notice that we're there. Just by doing that, they calm down. Even so, before we continue, we check how the rest of the system responds to the work we're doing (SC-2.5). This is a good way to keep the whole system in mind and to avoid any complications that may arise as a result of the parties not understanding the work or feeling excluded.

C: They are still standing in the middle.

T: They're there controlling and, for now, they're okay there. What do you notice now?

C: It's not like before, I am less afraid now.

Before closing the session, we reinforce the work done and validate what every part involved has done (CS #3.1), in addition to checking that the client is grounded (CS #3.3) and summarizing what has been done and setting goals for the future (CS #3.4).

T: It seemed like you calmed down a bit when you saw that this part was listening and allowed us to explore. (Client nods.) *Okay, let's thank all of these parts for the work they've allowed us to do today. And these parts are going to help us slow down or move forward. We're going to need to be curious. I'll be here to help with that. I can see all these different aspects and parts without judging them, and I'm going to help you understand them too. Is it okay if we work along these lines?*

C: Yes.

T: Okay, thank you so much.

EXAMPLE 7. THE MEANING OF TRIGGERS AND REACTIONS

Most of the work done in previous sessions was geared at Kendra understanding she was not in danger anymore and that the voices were her voices, not those of the perpetrators. In this session, Kendra describes feeling controlled by a voice that she confuses with one of the main perpetrators. She has had a rough week since some specific days, such as Christmas Day, trigger her history of trauma. Not only does she have issues with daily triggers (e.g., certain news on TV or her family's behaviors during those days), but also with the voices she hears, that remind her of the perpetrators. The voices repeat the same messages and have the same tone and attitudes. After the previous session, the client started doing things that made her feel good, and this is one important trigger in her life since she was punished when she felt good or enjoyed things. We begin the following transcript by exploring how the feeling of being controlled starts.

T: How does the feeling of being controlled begin?

C: (Client is silent for some time and seems restless.) *I don't know. Just when I start thinking throughout the day, the idea of being controlled by this person comes up.*

T: Being controlled by this person. How does this feeling come up? Does it come from within? Does it come to you as a voice? How does it happen?

C: The voice shows up.

T: The voice shows up. What does the voice say to you?

C: (Silence, she seems restless.) *That...* (silence).

T: It's hard for you to tell me. Is it because of what I may think?

C: Yes, I think it's as if I was worthless.

T: But it's great that you can tell me. It's about me being able to understand what is happening. And it makes you upset to tell me this. What does the voice say to you? I would like to understand that voice and why it says what it says, whatever that may be. (Client remains silent and seems restless.) *And if the voice gets angry at me, remember that it's not a problem. You can tell me.* (Client seems even more restless.) *What's going on in your head right now?*

C: The voice says that regardless of what I do, nothing will change.

T: And it's possible that this voice believes this. But you feel very bad when you hear something like that, right?

With this intervention we have simply validated the voice (TW #7) while at the same time helping the client acknowledge that this response from the part is not helping right now because it scares her. This is the first step towards introducing the idea of thinking of alternative ways of responding (TW #8).

C: I feel like it blocks me. It doesn't let me do anything. (Client starts crying, very upset.)

T: Kendra, can you look at me? (Client shakes her head as if saying "no.") *No, okay. But you do know that you're here with me and we're talking about something difficult for you, right?* (Client nods.) *If this voice tells you that, it's possibly feeling very hopeless.*

This is a good moment to introduce psychoeducation and adaptive information that the client cannot access when triggered. This information should be realistic and based on information we received from the client, not an interpretation from the therapist. It truly is a reminder of things we have already covered before.

T: Maybe this voice is afraid of feeling hopeful or expecting that you can feel better, because in the past, when you've expected things to go better, you have been badly hurt. Are you following me? (Client tries to nod.) *Did you hear what I said?*

C: I think so, but could you repeat it?

T: Sure. Remember that we've talked about how the different parts have learned to protect you in a way that it's so difficult for you to understand? About how they protect you in a way that is very critical and scares you? (Client nods.) *Perhaps this voice has developed a defense by thinking it's not worth it, that regardless of what you do, nothing will work. It's possible that this voice has seen that, in the past, when you've expected things to improve, you've been hurt. So, a reasonable defense against such experiences is to assume that it's not worth doing anything. Have you been able to follow me now?*

C: Yes.

Although the client gives an affirmative reply, checking how the client and the voice receive the message is recommended (CS #2.5). By asking her to think about what we just said, we encourage reflective thinking and make sure the intervention was understood.

> T: *What do you think about what I'm saying?* (Client remains silent.) *When I tell you this, what happens to the hopeless voice?* (Client remains silent and restless.) *Do you notice whether the voice is more agitated? Do you notice whether it calms down? Is it disconcerted? What do you notice?* (Client remains silent, tries to speak and pinches her arm.) *Here, hold this cushion, you're going to hurt your arm. Can you hold the cushion?* (Client takes the cushion and starts squeezing it.) *I know these issues make you feel tense.*
> C: *I have a hard time understanding the relationship between one thing and the other.*
> T: *You have a hard time.*
> C: *Yes.*
> T: *And what was this voice saying about this now?* (Client remains silent.) *We're going to come back to you now, so you can understand it. But for now, we're taking small steps. What happens to this voice when I tell you that?* (Client remains silent.) *Think about the possible frustration and discomfort that this voice may be feeling to the point of believing that it is better to do nothing,*
> C: *It's as if the voice was saying that it's not worth it..*
> T: *Because that's what this voice has learned to say. Does this make sense?* (Client remains silent and agitated.)
> C: *The voice says that he's stronger than other things.*
> T: *Well this voice has a lot of strength. That's why I'm interested in understanding it, because it can be very useful. It can help you a lot more if it can really understand that there are other ways of helping you that don't imply conveying that it's all worthless.*

By strengthening the positive aspects of the voice, which is a good way of validating, the defensive attitude from parts or voices is often reduced. It is also a way to identify resources (TW #7) and build the relationship with the more defensive parts. The client can listen but is not able to let the information in. By helping the client think why it is so hard for her to understand the voice, we are modeling new ways of communicating (TW #8) and helping her understand part of the existing conflict.

> T: *You tell me that you have a hard time understanding the relationship. Why is it so hard for you?*
> C: *Because... because...* (Silence.) *On the one hand it's like... I feel empty...*

Since the client has trouble moving forward, we help her by exploring when the voice shows up (CS #2.2), which will help us understand the possible triggers (TW #3).

> T: *Would you be able to tell me when the voice shows up?* (Client remains silent.) *It would be important in order to understand this voice, so you and I can understand it.*
> C: *It wasn't just because of one thing... It happened after seeing that my mother doesn't notice the changes in me. Or some days also after going to the pool... and feeling better.*
> T: *When was the voice most triggered? When your mother told you that she didn't notice any changes? Or after going to the pool and feeling better?*

C: I think it got more triggered with my mother.

T: Perhaps this part is frustrated because you're making a big effort. Do you realize this? (Client nods.) *Remember when your brother recognized the changes a while back?* (Client nods.) *You felt good and the voice was not triggered, right?*

C: No, it wasn't.

T: Maybe this voice gets triggered because it feels very frustrated when nothing seems to be enough. Especially when there is criticism, regardless of what you do. Does it make sense? (Client remains silent and seems restless.) *What are you thinking?* (Client remains silent and starts making a squeaky sound with her feet against the floor.) *What's happening inside your head?*

C: I'm getting that I do feel frustrated.

T: Both you and this voice are feeling the same. Is it so? (Client nods.) *It's really frustrating for you that your mother criticizes you and doesn't value the things you do.* (Client nods.) *Can you understand that this voice may also be frustrated?*

C: No.

T: You do understand that you get frustrated, do you?

C: Yes.

Since the client has trouble understanding how the voice might feel in those instances when her mother is being critical, the therapist helps her think of a similar situation in a third person perspective. It is not uncommon that people tend to be more understanding and empathic when thinking about other people in a particular situation than when thinking about themselves in the same situation.

T: Do you know how sometimes it helps to see the situations from another person's point of view? (Client nods.) *Imagine that I make a huge effort, that it's very hard for me to take care of myself. It's hard to get up, and I intend to go to the pool, take care of myself, change my schedule to be calmer... I'm achieving it, and I feel better because I'm achieving it. Do you follow me?* (Client nods.) *Imagine that my family starts to criticize me and is completely unable to see my efforts. How do you think I would feel? Do you think I could feel good about that?*

C: No.

T: Do you think it would make sense for me to feel frustrated?

C: Yes.

T: And even for me to think it's not worth it. Would you understand it?

C: Yes.

By using this type of techniques, we are helping the client develop a more empathic attitude towards herself (TW #8). This is a very difficult goal to reach without external help in cases of complex trauma and severe abuse because clients tend to see themselves through the eyes of the perpetrators in their lives. In the next section, we will link the previous example with what might be happening with the voice, as a way to try to help her understand the triggers (TW #3) and the function of the behavior(TW #6), also a very difficult task because of the phobia towards this voice (TW #4).

T: Well, I think this is what happens to this voice. And this is when what is hard for you to understand comes into play. (Client is moving restless but paying attention.) *Try to look at me so you can understand this explanation, yes? Because sometimes it's hard for you to understand how other aspects of yourself try to help you.* (Client looks up and nods.) *So, you're struggling and doing all sort of things, and then comes a time when you have a sense of feeling better because all of that helps you. Then your brother tells you that he sees those changes and there is a feeling of, "Hey, I'm on the right path."* (Client nods.) *The moment the criticism returns, saying "it's not enough, there is no change," you get frustrated and suffer, right? Do you follow me up to this point?*

C: *Yes.*

T: *Then this voice that is difficult for you to understand becomes triggered right when you suffer. Since you are having a hard time, this voice gets triggered and says, "It's not worth it." And if you notice, this voice gets triggered when you're feeling bad due to this kind of stuff. So, the way this voice has learned to protect you is to convey that it's not worth making any effort because it's more painful to be motivating yourself, to have the feeling that things are going well, and then suddenly, boom! Once again, it's not enough!* (Client is paying attention.) *What's important is that this voice can understand that, even though it makes a lot of sense and it's trying to help you, you end up feeling worse, because it conveys the same messages you received from your family. What do you think?*

C: (After some silence) *Well, I can see it differently now.*

T: *Is it helpful for you?* (Client nods.) *Does it help you to feel calmer about this voice?*

C: *Yes.*

Once the client can understand better, we spend a couple of minutes insisting on how important this is, as a way to help the information really sink in and perhaps have other parts understand it as well.

T: *Do you understand a little better why this voice gets triggered?* (Client nods.) *This is going to take a while, okay?* (Client nods.) *We are going to explore it gradually, and I will do everything in my power to help you understand these parts better, okay?* (Client nods.) *And as we discuss this information, I believe that this voice may also better understand what happens when it starts being critical.*

C: *But I feel that this part is not mine.*

T: *I understand, and that is what usually happens with the parts that scare you the most.*

C: *I see it as an outside part... it's just... like...*

T: *It's okay, you can tell me.*

C: *It's as if it paralyzed me or something.*

The client's attitude shows more curiosity at this point (TW #2) so we can explore the origin of the voice, which will help us understand its function (TW #6).

T: *You have told me that it's a very strong voice. It's powerful, right?* (Client nods.) *If that strength learns to help you in a different way, you may not have that feeling of becoming paralyzed.* (Client nods.) *I know that voice reminds you of someone complicated. That's why, isn't it? This is the voice that reminds you of this man.* (Client nods.) *Try to look at me for a second, okay? Because it's important that you stay with me when I tell you these things.* (Client looks up.) *Do you remember what we talked about how little children learn? As we learn to care for ourselves, to protect ourselves, we do so from the people around us, from the people who are supposed to care for us.* (Client nods while looking at the therapist.) *There's a part of you from when you were in this difficult situation, right?*

369

(Client looks away.) *Try to look at me, try to be with me so you can see me, okay? There is a part in you that has learned to protect by imitating this man.*

C: *To protect me?*

T: *Yes, it has learned to be strong and tries to protect you when something hurts, copying what it has seen in this person, because he was the strongest person in that moment of your life.* (Client lowers her eyes.) *Try to look at me, okay? This person was in control of everything. This person is not in your life right now. Correct?* (Client nods.) *Good. Even though it's hard to tell right now, you know this person is not in your life anymore. He's somewhere else, right?* (Client shakes her head.) *There is a part inside of you that seems like him, but it's not him. Do you follow me? Tell me.* (Client makes a gesture as if saying "more or less.") *Tell me how far you've followed me.*

C: *Up until you said that he's not a part of me.*

We are trying to help the client differentiate between parts that remind her of perpetrators and the real perpetrators from her life (TW #5). Since this is very difficult for the client, we try to keep her engaged in eye contact, which is something that calms her in difficult moments.

T: *Okay, when you become motivated with something, generate expectations, and then feel bad when they criticize you or don't value what you're doing, this part shows up to avoid that suffering. And the way it has learned to do so is by telling you, "It's not worth it." Because this part has learned that, in the past, if you hoped that the situation could change, you felt much worse because there was no way out at the time. Do you follow me now?* (Client nods.) *The reality, although it's hard to see now, is that you're not in that situation anymore. And what may happen is that there may be some part of you...* (Client looks away.) *Stay with me, okay? ¡ It's important.* (Client looks up.) *There may be a part of you that doesn't know that you're no longer there. There may be a part that thinks the danger is still present.* (Client is listening closely.) *So, let's try to find ways for all aspects of yourself to know that you are not there anymore and that this person can no longer hurt you.* (Client looks away.) *Try to look at me for a second, okay?* (Client looks up.) *I would love for this to be a swift process, for me to explain it to you once and have everything be clear, but I know it will take longer. What is clear to me is that all of you is important and that we will eventually understand everything in you.*

The client seems a bit calmer and is now able to let this information in or at least is curious enough to listen. Now is the right time to check how the voice receives this message (CS #2.5). Remember it is important to check how our interventions are fitting for the system but especially with this type of parts.

T: *What does this voice think about what I'm saying?*

C: *It's stronger... as seems stronger.*

T: *Of course, it's stronger. This voice is very strong, and it is a part of you that can help you a lot. And it's a very important part. What is this voice saying to you now? Is it telling you anything now?*

C: *It's telling me not to pay attention to what you're saying.*

T: *Which part of what I'm saying?* (Client remains silent.)

Since it is difficult for the client to respond, we can try to get the voice involved. This will improve the client's ability to communicate internally.

T: *Could you ask this voice what he thinks would be helpful for you?*

C: *Well, what it says many times. That everything would end if I just went back to that place with him* (referring to the perpetrator).

The message "everything would end if I go back to that place with him" is a very dangerous internalized message. The part of her that has bonded with the perpetrator idealizes a situation where she was repeatedly abused and humiliated. The perpetrator did a very good job getting her to believe that "he was the only one who cared for her and loved her." So, it is important to help the client connect with the reality of the situation and dismantle the magical idea of going back to him and feeling well.

T: *When you were with this person, was this voice feeling well?*

C: *Sorry?*

T: *When you were in this place, did the voice think you felt okay?*

C: (Thoughtful.) *I don't know.*

T: *What do you think?*

C: *That I wasn't doing well.*

T: *I see.*

Initially, neither the client nor the voice responds to this; neither can say that she was doing better. The Adult Self is able to say that she was not doing well. Even though complete realization is not there yet, introducing this idea and the voice responding by not getting agitated or upset but it is a start. We continue trying to highlight the positive features of the voice (TW #7) and how it can help more effectively now (TW #6). Once again, it is important for the client and voice to understand that there were no options before, but there are now (TW #5). This is one of the specific issues that should be worked on to help the client to differentiate past from present.

T: *What qualities do you notice in the voice?*

C: *A lot of confidence.*

T: *A lot of confidence. You see this voice as confident and strong.* (Client nods.) *And this is something that could help you very much. This voice is very important and can help you, you know? We are interested in seeing how. What do you think this voice may need?*

C: *Well, for me to surrender.*

T: *For you to surrender to what?*

C: *To her.*

T: *And what does "to her" mean? What would you have to do initially?*

C: *Uh... well... to allow myself to be controlled like this.*

T: *And do you think we could reach a middle ground?* (Client remains silent.) *Let's see, this voice is confident and strong, and in its own way, it's trying to help you. I hold on to my theory that this voice has learned from the strongest person at the time, who was that man, correct?* (Client nods.) *I think this voice can help you even more effectively. I wonder if from now until our next session, this voice can only try to observe how you take care of yourself, without telling you that it's not worth it. If she can give you a break, just to see how you respond. And in our next session, I promise to ask this voice about it.*

371

C: But how do I control it? I don't know how.

T: No, you don't have to control it. I'm asking the voice. (Client is listening.) *What you would have to do... Look at me for a second... The only thing you would have to do is what you've been doing when you've felt better: go to the pool, change your schedule in a way that is helpful for you, do some cooking if you feel like it, but at your own pace. That's what you would do. And I'm telling this voice because I know she's a strong and confident part, and I think she can help you in a different way.* (Client is listening.) *Right now, when I mention this, how do you notice this voice?*

C: As if she felt superior to that.

T: Of course, she can be superior to that, so I think she can help us a lot. Just think of this... Look at me for a second. When you arrived here today you were quite restless, weren't you? (Client nods.) *And we have spoken a little bit about this voice and everything that is going on, right?*

C: Yes.

T: Right now, do you feel as restless as before, less, or more?

C: Hmmm ... not the same. It scares me less.

T: It scares you less, okay. Well, this is important. I know that it's very hard for you and today you've really made a huge effort trying to understand this voice. I congratulate you because you have really tried to see what I was trying to explain, in spite of your fear. (Client nods.) *So, since for now it is hard for you to communicate and understand this voice that you see as not being yours, we are going to allow your internal sensation to guide us a bit. If you are a little calmer now and less scared, this may mean that this voice is willing to try what we have discussed.*

This example illustrates how it may also be difficult for therapists to understand the function of some of the most complicated voices and parts. Sometimes these voices get triggered after feeling something positive or adaptive, such as hope. This can be confusing because parts and voices generally get triggered when something negative occurs, which helps clients to easily see that the response of the part could be an attempt to help, however dysfunctional it may be. Other times, their way of trying to help is so convoluted and apparently dysfunctional, that it is more difficult to understand. These parts, in their attempts to help, resort to internalized messages and behaviors that are threatening for other parts and the client herself.

In addition, parts that imitate perpetrators can be very difficult to understand and accept because of the development of attachment bonds with the real perpetrators that are hardwired in complex ways, for instance, through idealization of real perpetrators and minimization of what really happened. These complications make differentiation a key aspect of our work.

Keeping in mind that voices and parts are trying to help even when it may not be obvious is one of the main ideas of the book; without this basic assumption, both therapist and clients are more likely to remain stuck or the symptoms may even worsen. Curiosity will always be our best ally and perhaps the only way of really finding adequate alternatives for all the different parts of the system.

EXAMPLE 8. DIFFICULTIES WITH PLEASANT ACTIVITIES

The client did better for a couple of weeks; she was able to return to the gym and get back to her self-care routine of healthy eating and exercise. Things were going better until a critical voice started telling her that she should not be doing that. This section focuses on exploring which parts consider self-care as a problem and how to handle this new situation. We begin this section exploring the parts that were active during the week (CS #2.2) to see if anything needs to be addressed (CS #2.4).

T: *So, you say that this is related to a part that doesn't like you to do things that help you. Did I get it right?*
C: *Yes.*
T: *What does this part thing about you doing things that are good for you?*
C: *That I can't let go and I can't allow myself to do things that make me feel better... I don't know.*
T: *That you can't let go and you can't allow yourself to do things that make you feel better? Well, I know sometimes it's hard to understand when there's so much chaos inside. Let's try to find out what is happening inside. Is that okay with you?*
C: *Yes.*
T: *So, you get the thought "I can't do this". Or maybe "I don't deserve to do this"?*
C: *I don't deserve to feel good.*
T: *I don't deserve to feel good. When you think about those words "I don't deserve to feel good," what do you notice in your body?*

Checking the reaction in the body is another way to explore the reaction of the system to the intervention (CS #2.3). In this case, we are trying to see what happens when we challenge the belief indicated by the client.

C: *Everything is squirming inside.*
T: *Everything is squirming inside. How?*
C: *I don't know.*
T: *Try to be curious. I know it is difficult for you, but I would like to understand how everything is squirming inside.*
C: *If I try to notice what happens in the body, everything squirms even more.*

This is a good example of how the body can be particularly difficult for clients with a phobia of inner experience. We proceed by helping the client to stay in contact with the therapist, adding some elements that make the client feel safer so we can continue with the exploration (TW #1).

T: *During therapy sessions, it usually helps you to be in contact with me.* (Client nods.) *It's usually less difficult when you are able to look at me, isn't it?*
C: *Yes.*
T: *Can you try to look at me? Remember the strategies that work for you; you can look at my forehead or my ear. If you can look at me in the eyes, great, since I know this calms you down, but if it's not possible, it's okay. Just try to look at some part of me, okay?*
C: *Yes.*
T: *How about if you hold a pillow? See if that helps.* (Client takes a pillow.) *What do you notice when you hold the pillow?*
C: *I feel safer.*
T: *Would it help if I hold one also?*

C: Yes.

T: Can you look at me now?

C: Yes.

T: Is the distance between us okay?

C: Yes, it's okay.

T: So, you feel safer with the pillow now. Does it feel like some sort of protection?

C: Yes.

T: So now, with the pillow in the middle, may we explore this thought about not deserving to do things that make you feel good?

C: Yes.

T: Ok, so think about that thought for a moment... Is this your thought or does another part think this?

C: It's another part.

T: Can you tell me about this part?

C: I don't know what part this is.

T: Can you ask something to the part that brings this thought? (Client nods.) What is this part concerned about?

C: That there's danger. The part thinks something bad will happen if I do things that make me feel good.

T: I see, this makes a lot of sense. This is what this part learned to do because you were punished when you did things that made you feel good.

C: I never saw it that way.

T: Well, thanks to this part, now we can understand better. And this also means that this part probably doesn't know that the danger is over; that you can do things that feel good now, that there is no punishment for that now. (Client looks up). What happens when I say that?

C: It's as if the part was listening to what you are saying.

After understanding the origin of the part and helping the client realize that the part is responding how it needed to respond when the client was a child and was punished for playing or doing pleasant things, we can move on to working with differentiation (TW #5). However, we will skip this section in the transcript because there are better examples of working with differentiation later on in this same case. In the following section, we will search for exceptions within the system, exploring which parts might believe the opposite of the part that is still stuck in trauma-time. By introducing the adaptive belief, we can identify which parts reject it and work with this rejection. Once again, remember always to check how the system responds to the intervention (CS #2.5).

T: So, we started with the idea of working with the part of you that believes that you don't deserve to do things that make you feel good. Is there is a part of you that knows you deserve to do things that are good for you?

C: I don't see her.

T: What happens if I tell you: "I believe that you deserve to do things that are good for you?" What happens when I say that?

C: Well, it's as if there is a part of me that rejects that.

T: Ok, how about the others? Do all parts reject it?

C: No, not all. Not with you.

T: *Not with me. Did I understand right?* (Client nods.) *So, it's as if other parts accept it.*

P: *At least one part of me does.*

T: *One part of you does. Ok, so when I say, "I think you deserve to do things that make you feel good," there is a part of you that feels better and there is another part that is restless. What makes this part restless?*

C: *I don't know how to explain it...*

T: *Okay, don't worry if you can't explain it; it's okay. Do you notice the restless part now?*

C: *Yes.*

T: *What is happening with the restless part?*

C: *She is mad at me.*

T: *She is mad at you. Why is she mad at you?*

C: *Because I told you.*

T: *So, it bothers her that you tell me that there is a part that rejects what I say. Ah, okay, but you know, it's very important that you can tell me because I am very interested in this part that rejects it. When I talk about listening to your body and listening to your inside, I mean all of you. I am very interested in knowing whether any parts don't receive well or don't understand what I say, because sometimes it's just a misunderstanding. If you —all of you— help me understand what is going on inside, we can work on it.* (Client nods.) *The fact that this part can say what worries her or what bothers her is fantastic. This is very important for me, and it's okay if she doesn't like what I say. I would like to know what this part would need to hear. Let's be curious, you and I and the part that accepts it. What can we do to help the restless part?*

Notice that before moving forward, we check if any needs can be met at this point (TW #7). By taking the entire system into consideration and validating the feelings from this part (TW #7), we can engage the part in cooperating (TW #10) and start to introduce the idea of processing the phobia (TW #4).

C: *We can help her feel less scared.*

T: *To feel less scared. Where is this part noticing the fear?*

C: *Around here* (pointing at her chest).

T: *Around here, okay. Do we know what this part is afraid of?* (Client remains silent.) *Check whether she knows; perhaps she doesn't know. And it's okay if she doesn't know, it's a great step for her to realize that she is afraid and that she needs to lose the fear. And that you can know this too and to be able to tell me; that's going to help. Do you think she knows what she is afraid of or not?*

C: *No.*

T: *Is this part one of the younger parts or is she an older part?*

C: *One of the younger ones.*

T: *Is she related to the little part that was in the corner?*

C: *Yes.*

T: *Is this the same part or is it another one?*

C: *Yes, it's that one.*

At this point, we choose to try an intervention based on a body approach, having the client experience what type of gestures can feel better in order to identify a resource that will not be triggering for her or any other parts of the system.

T: *Okay, it's very important that this part is able to say whatever she needs to say, and I would really like to help her with the fear a bit. So, let's try to be curious again. You notice that this part is afraid, right? But we don't know what she is afraid of yet, and you notice it around your chest. Can you try to find out what motion or gesture she would need to do? Maybe pushing the fear away would help. Maybe trying to soothe the fear. Maybe just knowing that it's okay for her to be afraid right now, that we will keep working on it and we don't have to do anything with it at this point. Do any of the things I said fit?*

C: *I am not sure.*

T: *Should I repeat them one at a time so you and this part can try to notice what fits best?*

C: *Yes.*

T: *Okay, check if pushing the fear away would help.*

C: *It's stronger than me.*

T: *Ok, see if calming down the fear like this would help.* (Client shrugs her shoulders.) *You're not sure? Okay. See if it would help her to be there as an observer. She would just need to allow you to go to the gym and exercise, observe what happens, and the next day, I would ask her about it.*

C: *That's better.*

T: *That's better. Okay, so notice how this part can help us, she can guide us so we can improve.*

The client seems calmer, but she is pinching her hands, which is one of the ways she uses to try to stay grounded. By exploring this automatic resource, we can help her find alternative resources that will not hurt her skin or body (TW #8).

T: *Why are you doing this with your hands? Does it help?*

C: *It relieves the tension.*

T: *This helps you relieve the tension. Can we explore if there is any other motion you can do without pinching yourself? How about trying this movement?* (Therapist makes a gesture of supporting the arms instead of pinching them.) *Just try it out and notice what happens.*

C: *It's like...* (Tension seems to increase.)

T: *It doesn't quite fit.*

C: *It seems like I feel more tension.*

T: *Okay, that doesn't help. Let's try it like this and check if it helps. Is that better? That motion is like pinching yourself. Could you try it like this, without pinching yourself?.*

C: *I think so.*

T: *Okay, now try to hold the pillow.* (Therapist takes another pillow and models the motion.) *Okay, hold the pillow, without pinching. Yes, just like that, perfect. How is the sensation?*

C: *Well, better.*

T: *Better. Do you think you could you try this at home without pinching yourself? It is obvious that your hands need to do something, and we must listen to your hands, but we don't want you to hurt yourself. So how about something like this? Do you have an anti-stress ball?*

C: *I would have to look for it.*

T: *Do you think that could help?*

C: *Yes, it may, at least at night.*

T: *So just hold a ball in each hand, or a pillow, and the idea is to make this motion. This motion is important, it helps you relax. But hold something, don't hurt yourself. What do you think?*

C: *Well, I can try that.*

T: *Okay, great. Let's try it, and we'll see if it helps. It's a simple exercise, but it may be helpful for you. Try it out throughout the week and let me know if it helps. If it doesn't work, we will think of something else. Do you agree? It may be a good resource.*

C: *Okay.*

T: *How are you doing now?*

C: *I feel less scared.*

Although this resource is working, the client tends to pinch her hands. As she is doing this exercise with the pillow, she ends up doing both: squeezing the pillow and pinching her hands. We offer another possible resource: two rubber animal toys so she can squeeze each one with one hand.

T: *Would you like to try these out?*

C: *Yes.*

T: *Take one in each hand* (Client takes the rubber animals and squeezes them.) *How is this sensation? Is it better than the pillow?*

C: *Similar.*

T: *Okay, good. Now you have two ways to relieve tension at home. You can try both and see which works better for you.*

C: *Squeezing the toys.*

T: *They are cool, huh?*

C: *Yes.*

After making sure the client has understood the assignments, we close the session. Later that week, and before her next session, the client sends the following email.

Thank you so much for these toys! They really do work! Every time I feel nervous, I squeeze them, and I can feel how the tension disappears. It's very soothing. I don't have to pinch myself anymore.

EXAMPLE 9. INTRODUCING THAT THE DANGER IS OVER

As we could see from the email the client sent after the session, she started practicing and using the resources at home that same day. In the following session, we check if the client has continued practicing the exercises we suggested in the previous session (CS #1.3) and if they are still working for her. She explains that it is a great resource and that she does the exercises often. As a matter of fact, the client walks in looking much better and brings along her new resource, the rubber animals. Through this session, we continue the work with differentiation (TW #5) since this led to interesting changes.

The client mentioned having had a very rough week and feeling very agitated because she is afraid of a part will not stop crying. In this session, we explore what is happening with this part (CS #2.2) and how the client responds to this reaction (CS #2.3), addressing the issue that came up during the week and is still coming up during the session (CS #2.4). As it becomes obvious that there is a part stuck in trauma-time and the client is afraid of it, we try to get the Adult Self to be more capable of tolerating the possibility of looking at this part and trying to understand what is happening (TW #2).

C: This part scares me.

T: You are afraid of it. (Client nods.) *Are you noticing this part now?*

C: Yes.

T: How do you see this part? (Client remains silent.) *Or how do you notice her?*

C: Hum.... I don't know. It's like a little girl who is crying. I don't know how to explain it better. T: You are explaining it very well. That's what you notice. Are you seeing the little girl too?

C: Yes.

T: Can you tell me anything about this girl? Can you describe what you see?

C: She's by herself, crying.

T: Where is she?

C: In a dark place.

T: So, do you have the feeling that this little girl part seems to be having a hard time?

C: Yes, I think so.

T: And when you hear her crying, you feel scared.

In the previous segment, we explore information about the part (TW #1), validate how the younger part may be feeling (TW #7), and try to help the client understand her, so we can begin exploring the dissociative phobias (TW #4).

C: Yes.

T: What are you afraid of?

C: If I try to help her and I fail, I will take a step backwards.

T: You think that if you try and fail you will take a step backwards. What do you mean when you say, "take a step backwards?"

C: Return to the same situation, to experience that again.

T: Are you talking about your memories?

C: Yes.

T: We don't have to go back to old memories (Client looks down, agitated.) *Can you try to look at me?* (After a few minutes, the client looks up.) *Great. While you look at me, do you still see this little girl?*

C: Yes.

T: What could help her right now? Look at me, let's both try to help her.

We just tried to explore the needs of this part (TW #7), but the phobia in the Adult Self is too high. The client is having a difficult time; she is squeezing the rubber toys she is holding in her hands, the resource from the previous session. We encourage her to squeeze the toys, knowing that it will keep her be more present and oriented while we try to find a way to help both client and part.

T: You can squeeze the toys if it helps. Do you ever feel like the little girl is feeling right now

C: Yes.

T: And when you feel that way, what seems to be helpful?

The client does not know what might help, and the little girl is getting more upset. Perhaps the little girl in the dark room might not know that she is safe now, that the danger is over, and that no one can hurt her. The following intervention attempts to increase the client's level of differentiation between past and present (TW #5).

> T: *I would like to know if this little girl knows that she's not there anymore and that the danger is over.*
> C: (Client looks thoughtful for a few minutes.) *No.*
> T: *Okay, she doesn't know that, so we can help her with this. Let's tell this little girl that she's not there anymore, that you managed to get out.*
> C: *She's still there.*
> T: *She really doesn't know that she's not there anymore, does she? No one has told her that she's not there anymore.* (Client is paying attention.) *So, she doesn't know that they can't hurt her anymore. It's important for her to know that. It's important for her to know that you are not there anymore. That you are here with me and that you, the both of you, left that place a long time ago.*

After introducing the information to help both client and younger part to realize that the danger is over, it is important to check how the client and parts respond to the intervention (CS #2.5).

> T: *What happens when I say that?* (Client remains silent.) *That's right look at me.* (Therapist maintains contact.) *What happens when I say that? What happens to the little girl when she hears what I am saying to both of you?*

There is a long silence, but the client seems to calm down with this intervention. Her body language is much calmer, she is no longer squeezing the toys in her hands, and she is able to look at the therapist. When a client calms down after such an intense moment, it usually means that the part that was upset has also calmed down. And it is crucial that clients realize that by helping their different parts to calm down, they too calm down. This is why we repeat the information several times, while it seems to be sinking in.

> T: *Does she seem to calm down?*
> C: *It's as if there is a little bit of light entering the dark room.*
> T: *If this little girl feels that she is still in a dark place and feeling sad, it's very important for her to know that she's not there anymore, that you were able to get out, and that you can take care of yourself now. Before it wasn't possible. You were able to get out. It's important that you can realize this and that the little can see it too.* (Client remains silent for a few minutes but is very attentive.) *What do you think about this? Does it make any sense?*
> C: *Maybe.*

After checking how the Adult Self is doing, we ask her to check on the little girl (CS #2.5). The Adult is now able to check inside and report back on her impression.

> C: *I think she doesn't trust me to help her.*
> T: *Great, it's important to know this. It's okay that she's doesn't trust us.* (Client seems surprised by this statement and calms down even more.) *Would she like us to help her?*
> C: *Yes.*

One of the most relevant interventions with distrust is validating this feeling as a resource that was once helpful and can still be helpful (TW #7). Parts have very good reasons to distrust, and our response will make a big difference. A little bit later in the session, once things seem to be moving along better, the client feels nervous again because the little girl seems to be waiting for help and the Adult Self does not know what to do.

Since the phobia between parts has decreased with this intervention, we can take another step and introduce an experiment on time orientation (TW #5), promoting co-consciousness between the two parts that are active in the session. If the Adult Self and the little girl can experience or notice something together, this can be a good way to help the system experience what it is to be accompanied and to start working in cooperation (TW #10).

> T: *Could you try to show her the toys by looking at them?* (Client looks at the toys.) *Great, that's it, look at the toys. These are toys that I gave you the last time we saw each other. Can the little girl see the toys?*
> C: *I think so.*
> T: *What happens when she sees the toys?*
> C: *She hopes they can help.*
> T: *It helps you, the adult, to squeeze the toys, doesn't it?* (Client nods.) *Can we try to let her squeeze them with your hands?*
> C: *How do I do it?*
> T: *Just ask her to do it. The little girl is part of you. You have the toys and you can use your hands to squeeze them. You can show her; show her the toys and let her notice how you squeeze them here, in 2019.*
> C: *I think she doesn't trust us.*

When parts do not trust the client, the therapist, or the work we are doing, the client or some of the other parts might get frustrated. It is very important to help clients understand that this is okay. It is actually more than okay: it is a basic feeling that we need to respect (TW #7). The only way to gain the trust of distrustful parts is by respecting their feeling and being curious about why they feel the way they do. When parts realize that we are not trying to force trust, they automatically begin to trust, little by little.

> T: *She doesn't trust. That's okay, and it's important not to force her. Does the little girl see the toys?* (Client nods.) *Is she curious about them? Even though she doesn't trust, does it help her to see them?*
> C: *Yes, it helps a little.*
> T: *What do you think about that?*
> C: *It can be a way to help her.*
> T: *Okay, one way to help her is to let her know that she's not there anymore. And another way is to let her know that she can say, "I don't trust you" or act like she doesn't trust without any negative consequences.*

In the previous section, we saw how validating distrust is a good way to respect distrustful parts and model an alternative way of responding (TW #8). We close the session highlighting and reinforcing the work done by the client and the part (CS #3.1) and reminding the client how difficult it was for her to trust when she started therapy. This is a good way to introduce adaptive information, help her empathize more with the difficulties of this part, and encourage her to become more aware of what helps her feel better.

> *T: Something seems to have changed. Can you notice if anything has changed inside and what is it?*
>
> *C: I didn't know that if I changed my way of responding, she could feel better.*
>
> *T: Okay, it's great that you can know this now, isn't it? Look at me for a second. Do you remember how hard it was for you to trust at all the first time you came to see me?*
>
> *C: Hum... maybe I need to learn not to see her as an enemy.*
>
> *T. Great. Do you see how important this could be?*
>
> *C: Yes, for her and for me.*
>
> *T: Very good. I think it's great that you can realize this.*

As a final closing step, we should always anticipate future problems to prepare the Adult Self for what may occur between sessions (CS #3.5) because, in this case, it is very likely that the little girl could get triggered again.

> *T: If you notice this little girl, restless, remember to try not to look at her as an enemy, because that doesn't help either one of you. Just show her the toys and give her time to calm down, okay? Tell her, "We are here, we are not there anymore." Okay? Nothing else, just remember how we both worked on this. (Client nods.) How do you notice the little girl now?*
>
> *C: She is paying attention.*
>
> *T: Okay. Can you try to show her the toys again? Ask her to look at them, knowing that she's not there anymore. These toys are recent, they are from 2019. Can she see them?*
>
> *C: Yes, I think so.*
>
> *T: How does the girl feel now when she is able to see the toys again?*
>
> *C: You mean, what do I see now?*
>
> *T: Yes.*
>
> *C: She's feels... curiosity, yes.*
>
> *T: Okay, great.*

This session led to a significant change in the client, who was able to look at the younger part of her with new eyes after many years of rejection, shame, and fear. After the session, the client writes an email to express her gratitude for the huge piece of work she was able to do with one of her most wounded parts.

Dolores, I wanted to let you know that today in our session, I noticed that something broke inside of me when I was able to look at this other part of me that I had not even been able to look at until now. Before, it was impossible for me to accept that this part existed and, even less, that she was a part of me and that it was good for me to take her into account. Another thing I wanted to say is that, since I started using the toys, I could not ignore the fact that they were yours. They connect me with you. It's not the same to be alone with myself than to be accompanied by someone who helps me not to be afraid of myself. I think that, today, her wounds were soothed by a new and comforting gaze.

EXAMPLE 10. CURIOSITY AS A FIRST STEP TOWARDS INTEGRATION

After working with the child part, the client is more capable of being curious about her internal system. She comes in looking better and a lot calmer. Curiosity helps reduce the phobia for the dissociative part and it will be important to assess progress in this area. In the following section of the transcript, we explore whether the client has noticed the part lately (CS #2.1) and how the system is responding to these changes (CS #2.3), which will allow us to identify if there are changes in the dissociative phobia.

> T: *Have you noticed the child part lately?*
> C: *Yes, I think that more than other times, but I don't know in which context.*
> T: *We agreed to check and see how she's doing. So, there have been times when she has shown up and you have noticed her, which used to scare you quite a bit.*
> C: *Yes.*
> T: *When she shows up now, would you say you are less scared than before?*
> C: *I think so. I'm less scared than before, but it's also as if I'm not trying to push her away like I used to do.*
> T: *Exactly, this has helped you both feel better and reduce internal conflict. Before, you were so scared that you tried to push her away. Since you started to realize that this didn't make you feel better and stopped doing it, the girl calmed down.*
> C: *Yes. It seems like she is standing in a corner, but she is more present than before.*

When clients are used to a particular way of reacting towards themselves and their inner reality, it is not easy to change things around from one day to the next. The new experience can seem unusual and, for a while, may even be confusing, in addition to the possibility that there may be an underdeveloped capacity to identify emotions. Reinforcing any progress that takes place will be important (CS #3.1).

> T: *More present than before. So, what do you think about that?*
> C: *Well, I don't know, maybe it does make me feel calmer or... I don't know.*
> T: *So initially it doesn't seem to be something negative, right?*
> C: *Right.*
> T: *It's positive that she can be more present. It's good that you can be more in touch with that part of yourself.*
> C: *I guess it is.*
> T: *Are you noticing her right now?*
> C: *No.*

When clients are used to pushing dissociative parts away, stopping and noticing them is usually not an easy task. So, asking the client to just notice what is happening inside (CS #2.3) may help us to continue the work.

> T: *What do you notice now when we talk about this?*
> C: *As if I were on guard.*
> T: *What do you notice that makes you feel that you have to be on guard?*

C: I don't know, it's as if I became more guarded just to protect the little girl.

T: Isn't that interesting? You become guarded to protect the little girl.

C: Yes.

T: That is positive, isn't it? What do you think?

C: Yes.

We are helping the client realize the positive changes (more empathy, curiosity, and acceptance towards this part of herself) and validating this important shift from avoidance, fear, and rejection towards protectiveness. By demonstrating curiosity and interest, and then naming this shift, we offer mindsight and model mentalization for the client.

T: That's so interesting. Now you've become guarded in order to protect something that you couldn't even look at before or see as a part of yourself. That's a very good thing. And what does the girl think about you wanting to protect her more?

C: I think she also feels calmer.

T: Calmer. This is very positive.

Once we reinforce these changes (CS #2.6), we explore the nature of the threat so we can get an idea whether anything else needs to be addressed at this point (CS #2.4).

T: What do you worry might happen if we talk about the girl?

C: If we talk about the girl you say?

T: Yes, or isn't talking about the girl what worries you?

C: No, what worries me is talking about things that can hurt her.

T: So, it would be important not to talk about these things that may hurt her, because at the same time they hurt you, then. I understand.

When the therapist checks to see how the girl is doing (CS #2.1), the client can notice that she is still sitting in a corner, scared and on the alert. We ask permission to process the fear on a general level since both of them are feeling a bit scared at the moment. In order to process this fear, we work with short sets of bilateral stimulation, again using the processing phobia procedure (TW #4). And in this case, since there does not seem to be a conflict between these two parts, we can do it in co-consciousness.

T: It's normal that there is some alertness. Ask the little girl if it's okay to work a little bit on this fear with tapping. Take the time that you need to check with her and see if she agrees.

C: (Client checks in with the part and nods.) Yes.

T: Let me know whenever you're ready, let's work only on the fear.

C: Okay. (BLS)

T: What do you notice?

C: For now, I just see her in the same place.

T: Okay. Was the girl able to notice the tapping?

C: I don't think she did, not yet.

T: *Shall we try a little bit more? Let's see if she can try noticing it through your hands.* (Client nods. BLS.) *What do you notice?*

C: *I don't know, I'm having a little bit of trouble connecting with...* (Client remains silent.)

T: *With the girl? Or with something else?*

C: *With her feelings.*

T: *It's okay. Check on the fear and the alertness. Are they the same? Did they increase? Did they decrease?*

C: *I don't know, there is a little bit of fear that something may come up that could hurt this part.*

T: *We're not going to work on anything that may hurt this part or you. We won't force anything. Check and see how the girl's fear or alert are doing after the tapping we did.*

C: *Perhaps I notice that she is paying more attention now.*

Since the girl is paying more attention, it seems that the fear has slightly decreased. To facilitate dual attention for both of them (TW #5), given that we are trying to process both their fears at the same time, we suggest doing tapping with eyes open so the little girl can see how we are doing the tapping.

T: *Can we try the tapping with your eyes open, so the girl can watch if she can?*

C: (Checking inside.) *Yes.*

T: *You're simply going to try and accept it, knowing that she's a child and that she still feels like she is back in trauma-time, okay? That's why she's anxious.* (Client nods.) *What we are trying to do is help her to get out of the past and realize that we are in the present.*

C: *Okay.*

T: *So, let's work with your fear and the girl's fear. Let me know when you are ready, okay?*

C: *Now.* (BLS)

By modeling curiosity throughout the process, we encourage both the client and the child part to do the same (TW #2). As curiosity starts develops towards one another, as well as towards the outside world, we are helping the client to start becoming more co-conscious and to differentiate past from present (TW #5).

T: *How did it go?*

C: *I think she's trying to look outside, but I'm not sure.*

T: *Well, then, is it possible that you're noticing her feeling more curiosity towards the outside?*

C: *Yes.*

T: *Okay, so try showing her where we are, okay? You can look around the room, you can look at the different things that are here in the office. We can even touch some of these things if that would help her notice it more.* (The client looks around the room, which is the office used for children and adolescents.) *What happens when the girl can see through you?*

C: *She feels calmer.*

T: *And you?*

C: *I think I do too.*

T: *Okay, so take a look and see if there's anything here that is drawing the girl's attention, something that could be positive, something that she's curious about. The girl is looking through you, and you notice whatever the girl notices. Perhaps we can use it. Check and see if it would make sense to hold one of these things so she could notice it through your hands, not only see it.*

C: *That thing that is made out of colorful foam.* (Client points at a square piece of foam in the office.).

Working in a practical and more physical way helps the client to be connected –rather than disconnected or disoriented– to something positive in the present. In addition, it develops co-consciousness and encourages cooperation (TW #10). We should take every possible chance to help the client differentiate the past from the present (TW #5).

T: *Okay, take it.* (Client reaches for the foam.) *Can the girl see it?*

C: *Yes.*

T: *As you hold it, can the girl notice that?*

C: *I think so.*

T: *So, what does she feel when you touch the little square foam and notice its texture?* (The therapist holds and touches another piece of foam, noticing the texture, modeling for the client.)

C: *It's like she feels connected to something.*

T: *I see. And these foam squares were not there, in that dark place, right?*

C: *No.*

T: *No. And does the little girl know that these foam squares were not there in that dark place back then?*

C: *I don't know, maybe not.*

T: *So, can we tell her?*

C: *Yes.*

T: (Pointing at the square foam toy.) *The girl sees this, right?* (Client nods.) *Does she see the one you have?* (Client nods.) *Does she see the one I have?* (Client nods.) *Does she notice what you are doing?*

C: *Yes.*

T: *When you do this, does the girl notice that she is also doing it?*

C: *I think she doesn't notice it.*

T: *And what can we do for her to notice it?* (Client remains silent.) *Tell her that she can do anything she wants with the little square. Let her see it, okay? Let her explore.* (Client explores, takes her time.) *Check and see if she's able to notice it. She doesn't have to do it if she doesn't want to, okay? Only if she wants to.*

C: *It's like she's not changing much.*

T: *How is the girl now? Where do you see her?*

C: *In the same corner.*

T: *How is her curiosity about looking outside doing?*

C: *I don't know. She's more curious, yes.*

T: *Well, that is an interesting change.*

Psychoeducation for the adult about the exploration action system is essential, particularly when clients have not been encouraged to play or be curious and especially when they have been punished in childhood for feeling curiosity. Giving permission to explore not only implies that there is nothing wrong with curiosity but also implies the courage to explore what was once forbidden. This small step means the freedom to do many other things that were not allowed then since it helps the client with differentiating past from present (TW #5).

> T: *When a person lives through situations in which there's no way out, curiosity and the exploration system become completely stuck and can't be used. And when the girl feels curiosity to look outside, to notice, whatever it is, we're activating the same system that she was not allowed to use. For the girl to see that she can explore, that she can touch what is in the here and now is something very new and positive. What do you think about what I'm saying?* (Client is paying attention but remains silent.) *Don't get frustrated, okay? We have more than enough time, and we are re trying to understand.*
>
> C: *It's just that I don't see much change in her.*
>
> T: *Well, she doesn't have to change much. The girl has been stuck there for a long time, right? Lately, the girl is more present with you since we worked a little bit with her and saw that she's not there, right?*
>
> C: *Yes.*
>
> T: *That is already a huge change. So, we have to be very patient and not get frustrated because the girl cannot move any further. As she keeps on learning, as she continues to notice that she can, she will be able to do it, you know?* (Client nods.) *If you get frustrated because the girl doesn't change too much, or if you expect a bigger change that she cannot do for now, the girl will become more anxious.* (Client is paying attention.) *So, for her to feel curiosity is a huge change. It's really good.*

It is important to remember that frustration can serve as a trigger for the negativity that was present in trauma-time. By modeling acceptance of what is and offering a positive frame, we counteract the perspective of failure to which the person has usually resorted to, which helps decrease this frustration, allowing us to resume the work with the girl.

> T: *Okay, is the girl able to touch the little square foam a little bit or notice it?*
>
> C: *She notices it more.*
>
> T: *How do you know?*
>
> C: *It's as if she noticed that it is something from the present moment.*
>
> T: *And what do you think of that?*
>
> C: *I don't know.*
>
> T: *You notice that the girl can notice it more and that she can notice that it is something from right now.*
>
> C: *What difference does it make that she notices that I'm touching this right now?*

The little girl is able to notice that she is touching something from the present, but the adult does not know why this is useful. This reflects a low level of mental efficiency and the degree to which several aspects of the client remain disoriented in time. The need to go over these points again is crucial, in order to increase mentalization.

> T: *Well, the fact that you're touching this now means that you're not there. It means that you are with me touching something from right now, something that was not there.* (Client is paying close attention.) *This was not there in the past, right?*
>
> C: *No.*

T: And that means that the girl is not there either, but she still doesn't really know it. If the girl can touch this, it means that the girl is within you, here, touching this. When the girl can see and touch this, it means that the girl is here, with you and me. It means that she's not there anymore.

Insisting on this point is essential since it helps the girl notice that she is no longer in the past, in trauma-time. Through the use of objects, we can enhance co-consciousness, presentification, and differentiation (TW #5).

T: If the girl is touching this here, that proves that she's here with you. When I explain this to you, what happens with the little girl? (Client remains silent.) *The girl still notices that this is from here in the present, right? It's not anything that was there then. So then —look at me for a second— what do you think about this?*

C: I would like her to be more connected with these things in the present.

T: Why don't you tell the girl that? Why don't you tell her that you would like for her to know that she's here with you? And that you can protect her now, that you have left that place, that you're here with me. Is it asking too much?

C: No, I can tell her.

T: Try telling her that.

C: Okay. (Internal communication.)

T: What happens when you tell her that?

The girl initially likes this message, but then she gets scared because she believes she has to continue complying with the perpetrator, who was in the room from the past. In the next section, we validate what she is feeling (TW #7) and continue introducing differentiation (TW #5) of what is happening now and what happened then.

T: That's what she has learned, notice how important it is to know this. (Client looks nervous.) *It's very important for you to tell the girl that you're not there, okay? For her to know that the man cannot tell her what to do anymore. You are here with me, and that person cannot say or do anything to her anymore. It's important that she knows this. If she doesn't know it, she will feel that she has to comply and stay in that corner. If you tell her and show her that you want her to be here and that you've gotten out of there already, she can come out.*

C: I don't know how to have her be with me.

There are always choice points during the sessions. One intervention could have been to see if she could ask the girl how she would like to be with her. However, in this case, the child is so afraid that it might be too hard for her to engage or to offer any clues about her preference, which increases the frustration in the adult, who does not know what to suggest. So, we simply continue helping the adult to connect with the child.

T: Where are you noticing the girl in your body right now?

C: I think that in my head.

T: In your head. (Client nods.) And do you think it's possible to notice her anywhere else in the body?

C: Here in my chest.

T: Would the little girl like to be here? Would she like to know she's here within you? She would be protected there.

C: Yes.

T: Very good. What do you think if I do a little bit of tapping and you place your hands over the spot on your chest where you notice her? Invite the girl to be here too.

C: Okay.

T: Can you notice the little girl?

C: I can see that I can welcome her.

T: Okay, so then you can close your eyes or leave them open, this is about welcoming the girl. Whenever you're ready, you may invite the little girl, put your hand over your chest, close your eyes to see the girl, and notice her. And I'll do tapping whenever you tell me.

C: Now. (BLS.)

T: How did it go?.

C: I'm feeling a bit dizzy.

T: It's okay, let's check to what is the dizziness related. Look at me again for a second. We're interested in staying here in the present, understanding this, okay? (Client nods.) Does the dizziness have to do with you or with the girl?

C: No, with me I think.

T: What's going on with you?

C: It's like if I reach a point that... (Client remains silent and looks down.)

T: That's a bit scary, right? This is very new for you. How do you notice the girl now?

C: She's more here, present.

T: You notice that she's more present, very good. Do you still see her there or can you notice her here already?

C: No, I see it differently.

T: So, what makes you more agitated: for her to continue being there or noticing her more here?

C: I don't know.

T: You don't know. Is it okay with you to notice her here? Check on that.

C: It's a bit overwhelming.

It is important to be cautious when things become overwhelming for our clients, since there may be new material that threatens to emerge as the client becomes more co-conscious with the little girl. In order to avoid this, given the amount of fear that she is currently experiencing, we choose to postpone paying attention to this other material and try to divert the attention to how the little girl is doing, which may help increase reflection and mentalization.

T: How is the girl doing now?

C: Well, it's as if she's more present.

T: And is that good for the girl? Do you notice if she's calmer?

C: I think she's still very scared.

T: She's still very scared, yes. But does she like being able to be closer to you?

C: I think so.

T: You think so. So, she's still scared. Do you think that perhaps she may be scared because she's noticing that you are scared?

In the following section, we see that the fear that came up is related to the client's fear about what the perpetrator could do to the little girl if she were to leave the dark room from the past. So, we choose to process the phobia (TW #4) in the adult, insisting on presentification (TW #5) and co-consciousness (TW #10), instead of delving into what is generating this fear.

T: We're going to do tapping with your fear. Is that okay with you? Just with the fear, the fear that got activated now, nothing else. Ready? (Client nods. BLS.) What do you notice?

C: I don't know if the fear that I see may be partially due to the fact that they can hurt that part, I don't know.

T: Well, take the square piece of foam again if it helps. Having this part be more present with you and me here can help her keep more distance from what happened then. It is very important for you to tell the girl that the man is no longer in your life. This is crucial, what you just told me is very important. The last time you saw this man you were elsewhere, and you're not there right now. He cannot hurt the girl anymore; she is out of there. The girl is here with you. Do you realize that?

C: Yes, now I do.

T: How does she receive this?

C: She is surprised.

T: She is surprised, right?

C: It's like she doesn't have to continue fearing that he will come back.

T: Of course, that's what I'm saying. Think about it, we have been working together for a long time. During all this time, that man has not come back, he has not shown up, do you realize that? (Client nods.) You and I have been working and now we have more access to the little girl, right? (Client nods.) This is very important, pay attention, because it helps us understand a lot better why you sometimes get triggered.

C: And how does it help us understand better?

T: Well it helps us understand better because a part of you still thought that she was there. A part of you even doubted whether he could still hurt her. But neither the girl nor him are in that room anymore. So, it's impossible. Does it make sense?

C: Yes, because it explains things better.

T: This does explain things better, doesn't it?

C: I see that I can help more so that part doesn't feel she's still there.

T: Exactly, in a way, you have more arguments, more resources. (Client nods.) This is a very important step. And now, how do you notice the little girl? Aside from surprised, which you said before.

C: She's thoughtful.

T: Is she calmer than before?

C: Yes.

T: So, we're also going to thank her for the work she has allowed us to do today, okay? (Client nods.)

After this session, and to her surprise, the client started engaging in positive and pleasant activities and she was even able to feel some joy, which she shared with the therapist through e-mail.

EXAMPLE 11. COOPERATION AND CO-CONSCIOUSNESS

The client reported feeling peaceful after the previous session. She said it had been a completely new experience to be able to look at the little girl she once was with different eyes. In this session, we begin exploring how the client left the previous session (CS #1.1), how the week was for the entire system (CS #1.2), especially for the little girl with whom we worked in session. Then we resume the work and introduce more interventions differentiating past and present (TW #5) through coconsciousness work.

T: *How did you leave the session?*
C: *Very calm and peaceful.*
T: *How was the week?*
C: *Good, I felt much better than other times.*
T: *How do you feel right now towards the little girl?*
C: *Even better than last time. I don't know how to explain it. Perhaps it was important for me. Somehow it was a change. I don't know how to explain it very well, because I don't really know. It's as if I had been able to reconcile myself more with the part we worked on the other day.*
T: *Great, and how is that part doing?*
C: *The same, until yesterday, I was noticing myself more at peace.*
T: *And what happened yesterday that was different?*
C: *Well, I felt like I was crying inside, but I didn't understand why.* (Client seems confused.)

Since the part was obviously active during the week (CS #2.1), we explore what the trigger may have been (CS #2.2) and how the system responded (CS #2.3).

T: *At what time of the day was that?*
C: *In the afternoon.*
T: *Where were you?*
C: *I was not doing anything special; I think I was reading.*
T: *What were you reading? Do you remember?*
C: *"The Karamazov Brothers."*
T: *What's the book about?*
C: *I just started it recently, but it's about a Russian family. I don't know, it was about some stuff that happened with Stalin and the Russians.*
T: *Do you think something in the reading may have caused it?*
C: *Well, now that I think about it, they all gather around this one character asking for advice.*
T: *And they gather around what exactly? What's the character like?*
C: *He is a Russian sage, a monk.*
T: *Okay, and they all get together and ask for his advice.*
C: *Now that I think about it, I think this could be similar to a scene from my past.*

T: Something you have experienced in the past?

C: Well, now that I think about it, yes.

T: If a scene from your own life gets triggered, it makes sense for this part to become more agitated. If we are working on letting her know that she is no longer there, and something gets triggered that brings up a similar feeling, it all makes sense. You were reading that, and you started to notice how the girl got upset.

C: Yes, as if that little girl part became triggered as if she was crying.

The client connects a current trigger with a scene from the past involving the main perpetrator. As a result, both the flight system and the attachment system seem to be triggered at the same time. This is a common phenomenon observed in clients with complex traumatization, who had to both idealize the perpetrator and assume the responsibility for the abuse in order to survive. This ambivalence is a typical example of the conflict clients experience inside. Once the trigger is identified (TW #3), we go ahead and explore how the client responded (CS #2.3).

T: And how did you respond to that?

C: Since I didn't realize that it could be coming from what I was reading, I kept on reading.

T: Well, now you know for the next time. It's important to notice these things and try to see what triggers you. So, you continued reading.

C: Yes, I went outside.

T: And when you went outside, how did you notice her?

T: I don't know, it felt like she was in her usual corner, but more upset than previous days.

T: And where do you see the girl now?

C: Well, she's still in the same place. But it's not like before; she doesn't seem to be so alert.

T: She's not so alert.

C: I think that had already changed a little last time.

T: Okay, so how do you notice her now?

C: The same as last time.

T: And what do you notice when you see her like this now?

C: Well, that perhaps what we did the other day... I would have to tell her that more often.

T: Say it, it's okay.

C: That no one can hurt her.

T: Very good, and are you able to tell her that?

C: It's like I still don't... I don't know... No...

T: Try to finish the sentence, it's like you still don't...

C: Well, when I'm by myself, I can't do it spontaneously.

T: When you're by yourself you can't do it spontaneously, but you're already starting to think about the possibility. That's great.

It is important to continue encouraging communication and cooperation with the girl (TW #10). By using the words "with me" and holding a mutual gaze, the relational resource activates the attachment system, and both parts can be more present during the therapeutic process. Activation of this action system in this way could be conceptualized as introducing a different type of resource (TW#7).

T: And being here with me, are you able to tell her that, just to see what happens? Try to look at me for a moment. What do you notice or what do you feel when you look at her now?

C: I don't know, it's like I feel sorry for not being able to help her see what I lived through.

T: You feel sorry for her? You feel empathy? (Client nods.) *That's very good.*

C: What?

T: This is very good. The fact that you can feel sorry for not being able to help her see it is very positive. Do you realize that it's very different from before? There used to be more rejection. And now you want her to see how things are. Does it make sense?

C: Yes.

T: How is the girl doing now?

C: She's still alert as if she didn't know that there's no longer danger.

T: And when you see that she's alert, you feel sorry that she can't see that. And what else do you notice?

C: I don't know; nothing else.

When the Adult Self starts feeling compassion for the little girl, it is important to help the client to become aware of this (TW #8). From this new way of looking at the girl, we can help the Adult Self to identify those needs that were not met and could now be met through the therapeutic work (TW #7). This could lead to increased cooperation with her younger part (TW #10).

T: Do you have a positive feeling towards the girl now?

C: Yes. But it's as if she were still waiting for me to help her.

T: Of course, it makes sense, the girl is expecting you to help her. Check and see what could help the girl now, okay? Since you're willing to help and the girl is expecting you to help, let's try and see what the girl needs now. (Client nods.) *Ask the girl what she needs now, what would help her.* (Client remains silent.) *Are you getting an answer?*

C: I don't see anything.

T: What do you notice?

C: I don't know. Nothing.

T: So, the girl is expecting you to help her and you would like to help her, but the girl doesn't really know what she needs.

C: No.

We try to engage the Adult Self in order to increase mentalization capacities and activate the care-giving system (TW #3).

T: And you, as an adult, what do you think the girl could need? Try to think about it here with me, okay?

C: I think she needs to know that I don't blame her.

T: I see. Do you blame her now?

C: No, I don't, not at all.

T: Can you let her know?

C: Yes. (Client takes some time to communicate this and then looks up.)

T: How did it go?

C: She is calmer.

T: Great. And how do you feel when you realize that you can actually help her feel better?

C: Better. I feel calmer too.

T: Both of you have done really good work!

We close reinforcing the work done throughout the session (CS #3.1) and checking how the little girl and the Adult Self responded to the work (CS #3.2). We do not check if she is stable and grounded because her body language is very clear about how she feels. She seems much more relaxed, looking at the therapist directly and speaking in a calm tone of voice.

EXAMPLE 12. THE BURDEN OF GUILT

In the previous sessions, we kept working with the little girl and other parts of the system. The client is much more aware of how useful it is to understand the different parts, what they are trying to achieve, and what they might need (TW #7). She is also much more aware of what the parts had to endure. This is an interesting yet complicated moment in therapy with an upside to it (more realization and cooperation), but a downside too (realization hurts). The client has been thinking about what she could have done and did not do. This session focuses on the work with guilt and how to help the client overcome this difficult moment.

C: It's as if I were feeling like I did back then. As if I had to repair something.

T: Repair what?

C: Apologize to him. (Client is referring to the perpetrator.)

T: I see. However, if there is something that you should repair, it would be the damage done to you.

C: I know, but I can't help thinking that. It's as if I need to be punished.

T: Therapeutically, the reasonable goal would be for you to treat yourself well and with respect. That's what you deserve. That's what human beings deserve: to be treated properly and correctly, and not to be punished. Does this make sense?

C: Yes, it does. But in certain moments, this just comes up.

T: Okay, so let's try to understand it. (Client nods.) *You just said that you feel like you did back then, but what are you getting? Is a memory coming up? Is it a sensation? Is it a sentence?*

C: No, I'm getting moments.

T: Moments?

C: Like the one when I thought I had to jump out of the window.

T: So, when you get those moments, how do you get them? As a memory? As a thought? Is it a voice that tells you something? How is it? Just so I can understand it.

C: It's all of that... It's like the response to feeling very guilty about anything, as if I had to punish myself.

T: It's important that we understand this because it seems to be related to control.

C: Control of what?

T: I think this might be about control, about what you learned to do back then; it's pure survival. When a person is in a no-win situation, and someone is doing everything that this person did to you, the only chance to feel some control is by feeling guilty. The reality of the situation is that this person was hurting you, that you had no way out, and he was the only one guilty and responsible for what happened. This is the reality, you had no way out, and you could not admit that, because that would be horrible for any human being. The only way to survive was to think, "I am guilty, there are things I can do better," because it gives you hope that, if one day you do everything right, the bad things could stop happening. When there is a persistent feeling of guilt about everything, it's because the person has learned to take on the guilt and responsibility that nobody has assumed. Do you understand?

C: Yes.

T: Does it make sense?

C: It does.

T: It's related to learning to feel in control when there is no control possible. When someone is in a no-win situation, what they end up repeating inside is what they have learned. It's very important that you understand this so you can separate it, and you can say, "Wait, this is what I learned from this impossible situation, as Dolores told me."

The client seems to understand and has an attitude of curiosity towards the information received through psychoeducation, but before we continue, we check how this information reaches the system (CS #2.5)

T: What do you feel when I explain this?

C: That I would like it to be a possibility for me. I would like to believe it.

T: It makes sense, and you would like to believe it. What prevents you from believing it right now?

C: It's as if I'm unable to separate one thing from the other. It seems like I can't separate what I think about myself from what he thought of me.

We can see that the internalization of how she was seen by the perpetrator still has deep roots, which make it more difficult for the information to become incorporated and integrated. This is one of the reasons why it is so important to remember that our way of looking at clients helps them learn to look at themselves differently and validates their feelings (TW #7).

T: I would like for you to try and allow that explanation to sink in. I would like that the things you repeat to yourself could be those said by others from a place of respect and real interest towards you.

C: I would like that too.

T: Great. I imagine that you notice that I am happy when you are well, when you are able to see positive things in you. I am happy when you are able to enjoy things, because this is natural. This is normal in human beings.

C: I know.

T: The only thing this person was doing was passing on to you the responsibility of his actions, which were completely inappropriate. Together, we have to find a way for these repeated messages to yourself to stop coming from a harmful attitude. They could be messages that you hear from people you know who don't hurt you. Would that be possible?

C: Maybe. I've been able to do it with other things that are not exactly like this.

T: With other things that we have been seeing?

C: Yes.

T: Such as when you repeat certain types of messages or try to look at yourself through my point of view or from your friend's perspective. How beautiful what you once told me, "When I see myself through your eyes, it changes the view I have of myself."

C: Hmm.

T: It is very important that you can continue using this. If you need to do so, ask yourself, "How would Dolores look at me in this situation?" knowing that I am someone you can trust, at least for what you have told me so far.

C: Yes.

T: That would be very useful to repair the damage done to you. What I would like to see is the reparation of all the pain that you have been inflicted. I wish for it to stop weighing so much on you, so now that you are in 2019, you can stop thinking that you are responsible for things that only this person is responsible for.

C: Yes, I would like that too.

Before closing the session, we check how the system receives the information (CS #2.5) since it can help us guide the rest of the work. The system is quiet, and the patient feels more empowered. The patient asks for a summary of the intervention and we close by making a visual outline of the information on a sheet of paper. The patient keeps the outline so that she can review it and remember it outside of session.

It is worth noting that, often, when this type of pervasive guilt is present, it is extremely hard for clients to fully grasp our explanations. In most cases, we will find that we need to repeat this information more than once and also make sure the client truly understands it. A good way to do this is to have clients repeat back to us, in their own words, what they have understood. It may also serve as a way to summarize what was learned in the session (CS #3.4). In addition, any positive feeling of increased realization can also be installed with a few brief BLS sets.

EXAMPLE 13. WORKING WITH ANGRY VOICES

This session takes place a few months later, when the patient is functioning better internally, and the system has become calmer and more collaborative. We begin this session exploring the results of the work (CS #1.1) and how the system was doing during the week (CS #1.2). The first part of the interview is not included because we want to focus on the work that needs to be done when clients are terrified of the voices that get triggered and feel overwhelmed.

Despite all the work we have done until this moment, the way the voices showed up this week has been particularly difficult for the client. She states feeling overwhelmed because the voices she has been hearing in the past week are those that remind her of the two main perpetrators of her life. In the beginning of the session, she has trouble speaking about the voices; she can only say that she has been hearing them. She also describes noticing a familiar sensation of helplessness. We begin this section of the interview by exploring triggers (TW #3), not just the familiar feeling, but also what might be triggering the voices.

T: So, when did you start noticing that familiar feeling?

C: Everything started on Christmas. Something like a voice showed up. It was constantly repeating that I was worthless.

T: Okay. So that day, something was going on, and there was a voice in your head telling you that. Did I understand correctly?

C: Yes.

T: Shall we explore this a bit? (Client looks down.) *Are you able to explore with me those voices that show up sometimes?* (Client remains silent and seems agitated.)

Since the client is so agitated, we suggest that she uses a resource that can help her stay grounded (TW #7), which works very well for her in this type of situations in which the phobia towards other parts is very intense.

T: Did you bring the little resource toys that you always carry in your purse?

C: No, I forgot them.

T: You forgot them. Do you want a pillow instead? (Client looks down in silence.) *Do you think it would help you or not?* (Client shakes her head, looking down.)

T: No? Are you sure? It'll take me a second to grab it.

C: Well, okay.

After helping the client to remain grounded using one of the resources that usually help, we can begin exploring the voices (TW #1) and help her pay more attention to them (TW #2). This is a good example of some situations we can encounter later in therapy after we have already done a lot of work, and how important it is for us to remain calm and focused so clients can calm down and activate their curiosity, after exploration has once again shut down completely.

T: Yes? Let's try to understand what is happening with these voices. Can you tell me how many of them there are? (Client becomes very dysregulated, she is shaking and holding back her tears.) *Look at me, okay? It's all right, it's all right.* (Client tries to look up.) *That's right look at me. If you can't do it, we don't have to explore it. We don't have to explore anything that you can't explore.* (Client continues to look agitated and starts to cry.) *And if any of those voices tell you something negative about me, it's okay, you can tell me. Don't be afraid of that, you can tell me anything.*

C: I feel bad for thinking about those things.

T: Well, that's why we're here trying to understand it. If you can tell me what those things are, we can understand it together.

C: They're always telling me to repeat something like, "Who do you think you are?" (Client says this with difficulties, she is very agitated.)

T: Well, it's okay, don't worry, this can help us understand. So, is it because of something I said?

C: No, it's only when I come here.

T: What are their concerns about coming here?

C: I think it's because they don't want me to think that I'm going to feel better by coming here.

Once we know what the voice is saying, we can understand why the client is getting so upset with the message she hears. Notice that the voices are just doing their job (TW #6), which has been partly to protect the client from ever hoping she or her situation could improve. Although we could just point this out, we use this opportunity to help the client reflect on why the voice might be responding in such ways, by exploring what triggered the voice in the session (CS #2.2), so we can address the issues that are coming up (CS #2.4).

T: Okay, so you think the voice doesn't want you to think that you can feel better. And we want to try to understand why it thinks that, whether there is something I do that makes this voice concerned. When such a voice appears –saying this sort of thing– it usually is because something I said was either not understood or not liked. So, it's okay for the voice to say it. (Client is listening closely.) This scares you very much, I know, but look at me. I'm fine. We can look at it together. It's okay for them to say things about me, it's no big deal. So, right now when the voice told you, "And who does she think she is?" was it after I said or did something in particular?

C: It was when you explained how things were in the past.

T: When I explained how things were in the past. What does the voice think?

C: The voice wonders how you know these things.

T: Well, I don't know exactly what happened because I wasn't there, but I do know how human beings respond to certain experiences that you have shared with me.

Once the client is showing increased curiosity (TW #2), we can start to explore whether parts are oriented in time (TW #5) and to offer psychoeducation or adaptive information if needed (TW #7).

T: Does this voice know that you're no longer there?

C: I think it's as if I'm still there.

T: Then look at me for a second. This means that just as the little girl didn't know that she was no longer in that dark place, this voice doesn't know that you're no longer there either. Since this voice doesn't know it, it repeats what it learned to do there. Because that kept you safer when you were there. (Client is listening closely and is calmer.) This voice really doesn't know that it doesn't have to do that anymore.

C: Maybe.

T: What happens with this voice when I say that?

C: What happens with what?

T: With the voice, how is it doing?

C: I don't know.

T: Is it quiet? Is it angry? Has it calmed down? Is it surprised?

C: I think it's not saying a word.

T: It's not saying a word. What do you notice? Has it quieted down now?

C: Yes.

T: Yes? Well, maybe that means it may be able to hear a little more of what we are commenting. (Client remains attentive.) Do you understand what I'm telling you about this voice not knowing that you're no longer there? And this is why it just repeats what it learned to do. (Client appears restless again.) You're getting scared. It's very scary for you. (Client nods.) Because that's the voice that reminds you of that man.

Once again, we introduce the idea that this part reminds her of a man that hurt her but is not really that man (TW #5). Differentiation with perpetrator-imitating parts can be a very complicated issue for these clients to resolve, due to the vast amount of fear they generate within the system (TW #4).

C: Yes.

T: So, it's a voice that learned to respond in a way that is very similar to this man. Do you remember our conversation about how parts learn by imitating the stronger people? The ones in control?

C: Yes, but it's very difficult to accept.

T: What do you find harder to accept?

C: Well, feeling like it controls me.

T: You feel that you are controlled by this man who is no longer in your life. If we really think about it, it's a voice that represents a part of you that tries to protect you in the way it has learned to do so. A voice that reminds you of this man but is not this man. (Client is listening.) So, what is interfering is your fear, which is normal. It's normal for you to be afraid because it reminds you of this man. That's why we're interested in understanding this voice; so, it can protect you in a way that doesn't scare you. This is a voice that has a lot of strength, right? (Client nods.) And the fear you feel towards this voice is an important interference because you are trying to make it go away. Do you realize this? (Client nods.) And usually, when you try to do that, the voice becomes more agitated.

We kept working to increase differentiation (TW #5) and then introduced the idea that this part is doing what it learned to do, trying to help in the way it knows how (TW #6). Then we remind the client how her own fear is getting in the way of understanding (TW #4). This is very important information that we will more than likely have to repeat quite often. Fear is a very strong emotion that usually dominates the lives of people who live with parts or voices. Wanting to avoid the voices is a natural response, in order to reduce the feeling of fear. However, we need to remind them that trying to shut down the voices is not a good idea since this usually backfires. In the next section of the transcript, once the client is somewhat calmer, we try to explore the voices (TW #1) and help the client be more curious. (TW #2).

T: Now, could you tell me if there is only one voice?

C: Now there is the little girl who just cries and does nothing else.

T: Okay, the little girl cries because she's also scared of this voice.

C: But I feel ashamed.

T: About what?

C: The fact that she is crying now, I don't know.

T: The fact that she is crying. (Client nods.) And why are you ashamed of her crying?

C: I don't know.

T: One of the main problems when there is internal conflict is that the system becomes organized according to what has happened.

C: According to what?

T: To what has happened in that difficult situation that went on for quite a few years. To survive that situation, the system becomes divided into teams: one is in charge of things being under control, in order to avoid more punishment; another one tries to hide everything related to your vulnerability, in order to avoid more damage. It's as if different internal teams were built. And what we are trying to do is for these different teams to be able to function as one team that can help you now, because you are no longer there.

Using metaphors to help clients understand what happens inside is often useful. Sometimes we need to speak to the client in very simple terms. When there are younger parts involved in the process, speaking in a way that could be easily understood by a child can facilitate comprehension.

Then we repeat how they are no longer there (TW #5) in order to insist on the message that things are different now, that life is safer now. Another reason to adapt the language and the amount of information we offer is that the integrative capacities of clients can be affected when they are triggered and frightened.

> C: *It always happens in a situation that is good. It's as if they don't let me feel better.*
> T: *Okay, yes, but let's think together again. So, when you were in this situation of the past, what happened whenever you felt good?*

With the previous sentence, we are trying to help the client to identify the link between learned responses from her system of parts and the way in which she currently responds, and also to distinguish, once again, between past and present (TW #5).

> C: *The man would come and scold me. I had to stop. Feeling good wasn't allowed.*
> T: *It wasn't allowed, you got punished, exactly. Can you see how you learned this?* (Client nods.) *I'm very interested in you understanding this here with me. One of the problems is that there are parts of you that cannot believe that they are no longer in that place.* (Client is listening.) *Another problem is your response to these parts. They frighten you; you reject them, you want them to leave. So, then, the parts feel even worse. That's why I always try to understand everything that is inside of you. Because I think that if you understand it better, your response may be different.*
> C: *Hmm.*
> T: *How is the voice now, after listening to what we are talking about?*
> C: *I don't know. Maybe it's that I don't know how to deal with them.*

Notice how by insisting on differentiation (TW #5) and with the help of adaptive information (psychoeducation), the client can begin to identify that maybe she needs help dealing with these voices differently (TW #8). This is the result of modeling curiosity in the previous sessions. Once curiosity is online, we can start introducing messages that can reach the other parts too. In the next section, we try to communicate to the voice that these ways are not helping.

> T: *Yes, yes, you are doing it well. Yes, I think this is part of the problem. But just as the voice can learn to help in some way that doesn't scare you, you can learn to deal with it in a way that doesn't agitate it. In order to do so, we must be curious and try to pay attention to what the voice says, okay?*
> C: *Okay.*
> T: *So, right now, what voices are there?*
> C: *Well, the voice of the lady.* (Remember that this lady is the client's second main perpetrator.)

Despite the work done towards increasing differentiation, the client still shows difficulties distinguish between real perpetrators and parts of the self. When we run into these types of issues, it is important to point them out and help clients understand that although these parts or voices can remind them of people who hurt them, they are not really those people (TW #5). Even though this may seem repetitive, this is how it needs to be done with these types of clients, especially when their integrative capacity is limited. Insisting over and over on some of the more complex issues presented becomes necessary.

T: And do you understand –look at me, please– that they are voices? Look at me for a second, so you can be with me and not get lost in the inner chaos. (Client looks up.) Do you understand that they are voices that remind you of them, but they're neither him nor her?

C: Fuck!

T: It's very hard. I know, that's why I'm repeating it. And I'll repeat it as many times as you need. What were those two voices saying now? (Client mumbles.) Look at me, I'm fine with whatever they have to say. (Client tries to look up.)

C: It's just that... (Client mumbles.)

T: That who do I think I am, right?

C: Yes.

T: It's okay. So, what bothered them now? Can we try asking them?

C: How can I overcome the fear toward the voices?

Since the client cannot check inside due to the fear (TW #4), we suggest processing the phobia toward the parts; a procedure with which both client and parts are familiar. But they all become agitated, so we need to explore what happened (CS #2.3) and address this difficulty that just came up (CS #2.4).

T: Just so I can understand, look at me, when I talk about processing the fear... (Client looks down and starts moving her legs agitated.) Stay with me, okay? Stay here with me. When I ask you to process the fear towards those voices, the voices become agitated, right? (Client nods.) What happened with the voices? Do you know?

C: They didn't like it. It's as if they became defensive.

T: I see. Possibly, what is happening is that they are afraid to disappear, that I'll try to get rid of them, but that's not the idea. We want to understand the voices. But what happens? That when there is so much fear on your part, you have a harder time paying attention to them. (Client is listening.) What I was trying to do was to help you work with your fear a little bit, so that it would decrease, and you could listen to them a little bit more. I was not trying to get rid of them at all. I understand that they would feel that. (Client nods.) What happens now with the voices when I explain this to you?

C: Well, they say that they're relieved.

As we mentioned before, the fear of disappearing is one of the special issues in challenging parts, such as these ones. When voices believe we want them to disappear, they become more defensive and stick to their ways. In the previous section, the therapist understands and accepts the reaction of the voices (TW #7 and TW #8). By responding in such a way, it is more likely for these voices to calm down. As always, after an intervention such as this one, it is necessary to check in with the parts to see how they have received the message (CS #2.5).

T: Relieved? Good, because it's very much related to that. Look at me, okay? Often, fear does not allow us to listen and makes us not want to ignore them. When I suggested processing the fear, they understood that I was trying to get rid of them. But the idea is quite the opposite. The idea is for you to be able to listen to them with more curiosity. (Client looks down.) Look at me, okay? I know this is very scary for you. Listening to them doesn't mean you have to do what they say. One thing is to listen and try to understand, and another thing is to have to do what they tell you. They are two different things. The important thing is for you and me to understand and for the voices to also understand that you are very afraid of how they talk to you. What is also important for you to understand it that voices generally don't have much of a repertoire; they have not learned many ways of communicating.

C: Hmm.

T: Do you see that these voices having many different responses, or do they usually give you repetitive messages?

C: Yes, they are repetitive.

Just in the previous two paragraphs, the therapist has given the client crucial information about the internal system, since one of the special issues we encounter with challenging parts is repetition. These voices usually have a very small and repetitive repertoire. It is important for the client to be reminded that listening to the voices does not mean complying with their wishes. The therapist also went briefly over the treatment goals: to increase the ability to listen to the voices with curiosity and understand the voices, not get rid of them. It is very important to convey this information and we might need to repeat it many times.

T: Yes, right? Okay, so look at me. Just so you understand, they usually repeat what they have learned. You and I can help them communicate in a way that helps you, so they can protect you when they still feel you are in danger. That's why we have to work with your fear when the time comes. (Client is listening.) Or with their fear, that's another possibility. Look at me for a second. There's the possibility of working a little bit on your fear of them, so you can listen to them without being so scared. And there's the possibility to work with their fear of disappearing because that's not the idea.

C: Hmm.

T: And there is no need to do neither one of them; they are just possibilities.

Giving clients options is always good practice. It is important that they learn that nothing will be forced on them and that they can decide whether to do one thing or the other or none at all (TW #8). This simple intervention can have general powerful effects.

C: Yeah, I just don't know if it can hurt them.

T: No, this is not an exercise that can hurt them at all. Do you remember that we have used this when working with your fear towards the little girl?

C: Yes.

T: And it helped, right?

C: Yes.

T: So that's the idea, to help reduce the fear and improve curiosity. (Client nods.) Check to see if the voices would like to work a little on their fear of the work we do or on their fear of disappearing. And let them know that they don't have to, of course.

C: I think they may be scared of what we may do.

T: Okay, and what do you think? Would you be willing to try? To do a little test to see how it goes?

C: Okay

T: We can do it in two ways, okay?

C: Okay.

T: So now, just check and see what fits best for you and the voices. One way, the first option, is for the voices to focus on the fear of what we may do. Another way is for the voices to focus on the fear of what we may do, and, at the same time, you focus on the fear of what we may do, because talking with the voices worries you and it also scares you. Look and see what fits best both for you and for the voices.

C: I don't know how to separate it.

T: You don't know how to separate it. So, let's do one thing. Check and see if, inside of you, the voices agree with doing an experiment with their fear and your fear.

C: (After checking in.) *We can try.*

Asking for permission and offering choices are basic signs of respect for the entire system. Since we have permission from the voices and the client to move ahead, we can now try to implement the processing phobia procedure.

T: We can try, perfect. Okay, so let's put our hands here on the table so we can do some tapping. I'm going to tap a little bit now. It's just a test. You're going to focus on your fear, and the voices are going to focus on their fear. It's a shared fear. Let's see if it helps. Both you and the voices can take your time. When you feel that we can start, just let me know.

C: (After closing her eyes and taking some time.) *Now.*

T: Very well, so both you and the voices, just the fear, okay? Nothing else. (BLS.) *What happens when we focus slightly on the fear?*

C: I don't know.

T: How is the fear of the voices now?

C: I don't notice any changes.

T: You don't notice any changes. Okay, let's do one thing then. You know I suggested two things initially, right? The fear of the voices, and your fear along with the fear of the voices. Now we are going to try only with the fear you feel toward the voices, just to see if something changes, okay? This is what they accepted initially. What do you notice?

C: I don't know.

T: Could your fear be interfering with letting us work a little bit with the fear of voices? This sometimes happens.

C: Maybe.

T: So, let's try this. You are going to ask the voices if we can work with your fear towards them a little, so you're able to listen more to them. Let's see if that suits them. Nothing else for now. (Client and voices agree. We start BLS.) *What happens?*

C: I feel as if I can look at them more.

T: As if you can look at them more, okay. So now, help me decide. Shall we do a little bit more with your fear, so that you can look at them a little more or not? Or shall we do a bit of work with their fear?

C: Not with their fear.

T: Not with their fear, okay. So, what we're going to do is promise them that I won't forget and that we will work with their fear too, okay? (Client nods.) *So, do you think it would be good to work a little bit more with your fear so you can look at them more? Or is it okay like this?*

C: I think it's good for today.

T: That's fine. So, tell me, what's different now that you can look at them a little more? What changes for you?

C: It's just that I'm less afraid when doing it with you.

T: Very well, I think that's important. How do you notice them? Do you notice whether they are quiet, calm, or agitated?

C: It seems that they're looking at me more.

T: That's interesting. You are more able, and so are they.

C: Yes. I would need to learn to relate to them later, when it happens to me while I'm not here. T: Exactly, exactly. That's what you and I are going to do: you will learn that.

As you have seen in this case, most of the worked has geared towards helping the client understand the different parts and voices (TW #2), identify their needs (TW #7), and explore how they have helped in the past and how are they still currently trying to help (TW #6). We have done a considerable amount of work with differentiation (TW #5), which is a key aspect with fearful and distrustful parts. The client continued to progress as we were increasingly able to work with co-consciousness and she was able to learn to understand and accept parts of herself that she had been experiencing as enemies that she would like to see gone.

A few months after this session, the client was able to follow a suggestion from the therapist meant as a co-consciousness exercise: to watch a tennis match with her little girl part, both of them together. This is the email she wrote after that session:

Hello Dolores.

Yesterday I was able to do what you suggested. I am in shock because of how I felt just by having the girl participate and watch the match with me. I felt light, with much less tension. And I'm not sure if I was feeling accompanied by the girl or she was feeling accompanied by me.

It may be one of the first times that I have allowed her to join me in one of my things, I don't know if you would say the same. At first, I had to get over the prejudice of dedicating this time to the girl and doing something –like watching the match– that, because of what we learned, we have always seen as something "bad," as a waste of time.

I hope I can make peace like this with other parts which I still don't know how to treat. I trust that the moment will come when it comes. Thank you very much. It's been a great idea.

The work with Kendra offers the reader a learning opportunity of different aspects of therapy, given that her difficulties with trust, self-acceptance, and inner parts illustrate the toxic effects of early and chronic abuse. One of the main problems from the beginning was her self-hatred, which was reflected in the way she looked at and treated herself and was also manifested in how she looked at and treated other parts within her. Kendra kept looking at herself and her actions, wishes, desires, emotions, and thoughts through the eyes of her perpetrators, and repeated the toxic messages that she received, which she had ended up internalizing. When she was younger, basically anything she did was forbidden and punished: playing was bad, having needs was selfish, enjoying was a sin, etc.

All of the above led to such internal chaos and conflict that she was too mentally exhausted to function. Her integrative capacity was affected, and she could hardly think straight. So, despite being a bright, intelligent, and sensitive woman, most of the time she could not use any of her capacities. Integrative deficits had increased after so many years of suffering and trying not to think, not to want something different, and not to hope for a way out. By the time she was able to get out of her horrible situation, she could not realize she was free and safe. Most of her parts remained stuck in trauma-time. It took a lot of therapeutic effort for her to begin believing that she was safe, that they could not hurt her anymore, and that she had the right to live in peace and enjoy life. We are still working on it, but she is doing a fantastic job and I thank her for her trust. A few months ago, I asked her to write down her thoughts about the work we had been doing and any improvements she noticed. She has given me permission to share it as a closing statement:

For years and years, I have lived anything positive as negative, as something to avoid. I also believed that the mere fact of interacting with someone is likely to cause irreparable harm to both of us, the other person and myself. All of my feelings were "trained" in blame. I have lived feeling guilty for every positive thing that I felt, saw or did, on my own or, even worse, in relation with others. So, simply enjoying a cappuccino, was something I had to win back with the help of a friend. She came along to the coffee shop to prove to me that it did not hurt her in any way that I also had a cup myself.

I spent a long time trying to avoid the relationship with a person with whom I had already had the experience of being loved unconditionally. The fear of hurting him was overwhelming and, although I started realizing he was on my side without reservations, I always put a barrier so I would not feel anything positive about such a friendship.

I cannot yet allow myself to do things just for me, just for my own interest or enjoyment. Interestingly, if I have to do something for others, I do not have a problem with it. I have lived a long time "looking outwards," getting punished for any behavior that showed I was thinking about myself. So, this made it very hard to allow myself any self-care. My work in therapy all these years has helped me learn not to mistreat myself. Not yet to "love myself," but at least not to feel rejection for what I try to do for me, for my past, for my ideas about life, etc.

In therapy, I have learned not to fear my feelings, both the negative and the positive ones. I was never judged when I arrived at the session crushed under the burden of guilt, fear, shame, fatigue, or doubt. My feelings were always understood and accepted.

The way I was looked at, without judging anything I brought up, has always been an opportunity to move forward, to continue working. The patience I have received in therapy, I have felt it grow inside toward myself in moments of discouragement.

I will not surrender to being unable to experience something good about myself

APPENDIX

BRIEF SUMMARY CHARTS

FROM CHAPTER 1

CLINICAL PROCEDURES AND TECHNIQUES

PROCEDURE / TECHNIQUE	GOALS
Grounding Techniques	To regain a sense of safety and control by learning to anchor themselves in the here and now.
Meeting Place Procedure	To increase understanding of the system, change the defensive attitude for curiosity and observation, and develop reflexive thinking. This helps to improve communication, empathy, collaboration, and cooperation among parts.
Processing Phobias Procedure	To reduce the conflict between parts.
Tip of the Finger Strategy	To progress towards processing the traumatic experiences.
CIPOS	To enhance the capacity of the client to stay present and tolerate entering safely and gradually into the traumatic memories.
The Freckle Technique	To be used when traumatic material comes up during session, this material is intrusive and poses a risk for the client or others, the client is not yet ready to work with trauma processing, and it is not possible to contain the material that has emerged.

Table 1. Quick reference table of the different clinical procedures and techniques described in Chapter 1

FROM CHAPTER 2

GENERAL STRUCTURE OF THE THERAPEUTIC WORK (TW)

1. Exploring the voices (content, tone, message, age, moment of onset, etc.) and parts
2. Encouraging clients to listen to the voices and pay more attention to the parts.
3. Exploring the triggers (what was happening when the part showed up or when the voice spoke)
4. Exploring and processing dissociative phobias
5. Assessing the degree of differentiation and time orientation in client and parts
6. Exploring and validating the function of the voice
7. Identifying and validating resources, feelings and needs
8. Exploring, modeling, and practicing alternative ways of responding. Offering suggestions when needed
9. Identifying and exploring missing pieces
10. Reaching agreements, developing cooperation and team work

GENERAL STRUCTURE OF A CLINICAL SESSION (CS)

1. **Explore the effects of the work done in the previous session**
   CS #1.1 Explore how the client and the parts/voices left the previous session
   CS #1.2 Check how the week has been for the entire system
   CS #1.3 Explore whether during the week the client has followed the indications offered in the previous session

2. **Work on issues that came up during the week or come up during session**
   CS #2.1 Explore if the voices and parts were active or not during the week. Check how the parts are doing.
   CS #2.2 If the voices appeared during the week or during the session, we must explore what triggered them
   CS #2.3 Explore the reaction of the system towards the voices or parts
   CS #2.4 Address any issues or difficulties as they appear
   CS #2.5 After any intervention, check how the rest of the parts feel about what just happened
   CS #2.6 Check whether learned messages or behaviors continue to take place after the voice or part has started practicing new adaptive behaviors.

3. **Closure for the session.**
   CS #3.1 Reinforce the work done throughout the session and validate the efforts made by each part of the system that was active/participated during the work
   CS #3.2 Check on the usefulness of the interventions applied during the session
   CS #3.3 Check that the client is stable and grounded, oriented in time
   CS #3.4 Summarize what has been learned in order to help clients organize the work done during the session and to set goals for future sessions. Enhance realization
   CS #3.5 Anticipate potential obstacles and problems to prepare clients for future difficulties

Table 2. Quick reference table of the different steps to be followed in the treatment work and clinical sessions, which will be found throughout the clinical examples in the book

FROM CHAPTER 3

KEY ASPECTS IN THE DEVELOPMENT OF THE ADULT SELF

- Keep the whole system in mind
- Always be respectful
    - Accept how the client experiences what happens, even if we do not agree with it
    - Respect the feeling and thoughts of every part and do not take sides
    - Use the language of the client
    - Avoid name calling and dismissive comments.
    - Respect the timing of the different parts
    - Encourage clients to make decisions
    - Avoid interpreting as much as possible
- Develop healthy curiosity through modeling
- Validate the entire system
- Be compassionate
- Promote dialogue, communication and understanding of the intention to help
- It's all about teamwork: Promote empathy, cooperation, and negotiation.

Table 3. Key aspects that will help our clients to develop their Adult Self.

BENEFITS OF WORKING THROUGH THE ADULT SELF

- Enhances metacognitive processes.
- Develops new ways of communicating.
- Increases capacity for self-reflection.
- Improves integrative capacities.
- Patients become able to identify and meet their needs
- Fosters healthy self-care patterns.
- Promotes autonomy, generating empowerment and security.
- Parts are less likely to switch during session.

Table 4. Benefits for our clients once they start to develop their Adult Self.

FROM CHAPTER 4

EXPLORING THE SYSTEM AND INTERNAL CONFLICT

- Moment of onset
- Information about the characteristics of the voices
- Identifying the message from the voices
- Exploring communication/interaction style with and/or among the voices
- Identifying where the messages were learned
- Exploring the function of the voices
- Exploring needs in the different parts and in the Adult Self
- Exploring alternatives
- Exploring the logic of the changes in the voices.
- Building resources and reminding the client that this is a learning process

Table 5. Areas of exploration to be taken into consideration when learning about the system pf parts. This can be done through direct questioning or through the use of drawing and Playmobil action figures.

FROM CHAPTER 5

SPECIAL ISSUES IN THE WORK WITH CHALLENGING PARTS

ISSUE / FUNCTION	INTERVENTION
#1: **Repetition:** Endless repetition is used as a defense to manage affects and emotion.	Acknowledge the protective function of the parts. Convey that new ways will make them more useful and powerful.
#2: **Anger:** Showing anger compensates for the fear of disappearing	Repeat the message that voices are important and we do not want to get rid of them.
#3: **Distrust:** Distrust helps them deal with the fear of rejection	Accept mistrust and reframe it as a good protection Convey interest in their needs and what they have to say.
#4: **Control:** Appearing to be in control hides extreme vulnerability	Parts need to know that cooperation will allow them to be in control become stronger.
#5: **Power vs submission:** Appearing powerful keeps both client and parts "in line." Submission helps avoid conflict or retaliation	Explain that all parts aim for the same goal. Cooperation will make them more powerful Explain the importance of being assertive. No need for submission anymore.
#6: **Power struggles:** Client or parts fight back in response to insults and threats from the voices	Ask clients to be respectful with voices Ask clients to rename voices if needed Lay the foundation to initiate respect and cooperation

Table 7. Special issues often encountered when working with dissociative voices and parts

FROM CHAPTER 13

History of symptoms and presenting problems

1. General presenting problems and/or symptoms
2. Previous diagnosis
3. Attachment patterns
4. Relational problems
    a. Family members
    b. Friends and peers
    c. Intimate relationships
    d. Work and/or school
5. Daily life functioning
    a. Self-care habits
    b. Financial stability
    c. Social, occupational or school functioning
    d. Overall level of functioning
6. Initial onset of problems/symptoms
    a. What was happening then?
    b. What got triggered?
7. When did symptoms worsen?
    a. What was happening then?
    b. What got triggered?
8. When do symptoms increase or worsen now?
    a. Current triggers
    b. Degree of awareness of triggers

Resources

1. Sources of adaptive information
    a. Good enough attachment figures in childhood and/or adult life
    b. Moments of feeling safe and being protected
    c. Moments of feeling cared for
    d. Other relevant positive figures/models (caregivers, siblings, nanny, teachers/coaches, family friends, etc.)
2. Emotional regulation capacity
    a. Self-regulation capacity
    b. Co-regulation capacity
    c. Tolerance for negative and positive emotions
3. Social support
    a. Family members
    b. Intimate partners
    c. Friends

      d. Work colleagues and peers

      e. Other professionals (therapists, support groups, teachers, etc.)

      f. Religious/spiritual resources

  4. Other resources

      a. Mentalization capacity

      b. Degree of realization

      c. Degree of integrative capacity

  5. Timeline of best memories (realistic, not idealized; include age, places and people)

Structural elements of the internal system

  1. Client's degree of awareness of parts

  2. Internal structure

      a. Approximate number of parts

      b. Client's description/representation of the internal system of parts

      c. Organization and distribution of those parts that the client can discuss

      d. Any missing pieces in the description

  3. Degree of differentiation about the self and others

      a. Can the client distinguish her/his own thoughts, emotions and needs from what has been imposed by others?

      b. Is the client confusing any parts or voices with the real perpetrators?

  4. Time orientation and current perception of safety

      a. Is the client confusing what happened in the past with what is happening in the present?

      b. Does the client know that the danger is over?

      c. Which parts are still stuck in trauma time?

  5. Mentalizing capacities

      a. Can all parts mentalize?

      b. Which parts have higher mentalizing abilities?

      c. Which parts need help with mentalizing?

  6. Adaptive information

      a. Which parts have adaptive information?

      b. Which parts need help with adaptive information?

Relational aspects of the internal system

  1. Acceptance of parts

      a. Despite the fear/conflict, does the client describe some parts with compassion, acceptance or appreciation?

  2. Relationships among parts

      a. What feelings do the parts have towards each other?

      b. Which are adaptive for the system in the present moment?

      c. Which need to improve?

3. Degree of cooperation between parts of the system
    a. Is the client aware of any parts attempting to help the system?
    b. Can the client accept that there might be an attempt of help even though it may not be clear yet?
4. Parts that may have difficulties with therapy
    a. Is there ambivalence or rejection towards therapy?
    c. What are their concerns regarding therapy?
5. Co-consciousness between parts
    a. If it exists, which parts are co-conscious?
    b. When does co-consciousness occur? Does it vary?
    c. How do other parts respond to this?

Trauma related phobias and other potential blocks

1. Phobia of inner experience
    a. Can the client check inside?
    b. Can the client notice and tolerate sensations?
    c. Is the client afraid of his or her feelings, thoughts or sensations?
    d. Is the client ashamed of his or her feelings, thoughts or sensations?
2. Phobia of parts
    a. Does the client have ambivalence about parts or avoid talking about them?
    b. Despite the fear, can the client try to explore parts and be curious?
    c. Do any of the parts feel shame or is the patient ashamed of any of them?
3. Phobia of attachment and attachment loss
    a. Is there ambivalence around trust in the therapeutic relationship?
    b. Do the client or any of the parts have difficulties trusting others, ambivalence between wanting to attach and pushing others away?
4. Phobia of traumatic memories
    a. Does the client insist on avoiding any exploration about childhood?
    b. Does the client show ambivalence about trauma work or even talking about traumatic experiences?
5. Phobia of change and adaptive risk-taking
    a. Is the client afraid of change?
    b. Does the client present difficulties trying suggestions that would improve their quality of life?
6. Defenses (minimization, rationalization, avoidance, etc.)
7. Any other identified potential block

REFERENCES

Bamberger, W. (2010). *Interpersonal Trust – Attempt of a Definition.* Scientific report, Econiche Universität München. Retrieved 2011-08-16.

Bateman, A. & Fonagy, P. (2004). *Psychotherapy for Borderline Personality Disorder. Mentalization-based treatment.* Oxford University Press.

Blizard, R. A. (1997). Therapeutic alliance with abuser alters in dissociative identity disorder: The paradox of attachment to the abuser. *Dissociation, 10,* 246–254.

Boon, S. (2017). The functions of perpetrator-imitating parts.

Bowen, M. (1974). Toward the Differentiation of Self in One's Family of Origin, In Lanham,

MD: Rowman & Littlefield *Family Therapy in Clinical Practice* (reprint ed.). (published 2004), pp. 529–547, ISBN 0-87668-761-3

Caul, D. (1984). Group and Videotape Techniques for Multiple Personality Disorder. *Psychiatric Annals* 14(1), 43-50

Emde, R. N., Biringen, Z., Clyman, R.B. & Oppenheim, D. (1991). The Moral Self of Infancy: Affective Core and Procedural Knowledge. *Developmental Review,* 11, 251-270

Erikson (2011). *Child Development Institute Parenting Today.* Childdevelopmentinfo.com. Archived from the original on October 2, 2011. Retrieved 2013-01-04.

Flavell, J. H. (1979). Metacognition and cognitive monitoring: A new area of cognitive-developmental inquiry. *American Psychologist,* 34, 906-911. doi:10.1037//0003-066X.34.10.906

Forgash, C. & Copeley, E. (2008). *Healing the heart of trauma and dissociation with EMDR and Ego-States Therapy.* New York: Springer Publishing.

Fraser, G.A. (1991). The dissociative table technique: A strategy for working with ego states in dissociative disorders and ego-state therapy. *Dissociation: Progress in the Dissociative Disorders,* 4: 205-213.

Fraser, G. A. (2003). Fraser's "Dissociative Table Technique" Revisited, revised: A Strategy for Working with Ego States in Dissociative Disorders and Ego-State Therapy. *Journal of Trauma & Dissociation,* 4 (4): 5-28

Gonzalez, A., & Mosquera, D. (2012). *EMDR y disociación.* El abordaje progressivo. Madrid: Ediciones Pléyades, S.A [English Edition, *EMDR and Dissociation. The Progresive Approach.* Amazon Imprint]

International Society for the Study of Trauma and Dissociation (2011). Guidelines for Treating Dissociative Identity Disorder in Adults, Third Revision: Summary Version, *Journal of Trauma & Dissociation,* 12 (2), 188-212

Janet, P. (1928). *L'évolution de la mémoire et de la notion du temps.* Paris: A. Chahine. Jung, C. G., & Baynes, H. G. (1921). *The Psychology of Individuation.* London: Kegan Paul Trench Trubner.

Kernberg, O.F. (1984). *Severe personality disorders: Psychotherapeutic strategies.* New Haven, CT: Yale University Press.

Kernberg, O.F. (1993). *Severe personality disorders: psychotherapeutic strategies.* Yale University Press. Knipe, J. (2017). *EMDR Toolbox* (2nd ed.). New York, NY: Springer Publishing Co.

Korn, D. L. (2009). EMDR and the treatment of complex PTSD: A review. *Journal of EMDR Practice and Research,* 3 (4), 264-278.

Korn, D.L. & Leeds, A.M. (2002). Preliminary Evidence of Efficacy for EMDR Resource Development and Installation in the Stabilization Phase of Complex Posttraumatic Stress Disorder. *Journal of Clinical Psychology.* 58 (12), 1465-1487.

Loevinger, J. (1976). *Ego development.* San Francisco: Jossey-Bass.

Mayer, R.C., Davis, J.H. & Schoorman, F.D. (1995). An integrative model of organizational trust. *Academy of Management Review.* 20 (3), 709–734. doi:10.5465/amr.1995.9508080335.

McKnight, D. H., & Chervany, N. L. (1996). *The Meanings of Trust.* Scientific report, University of Minnesota.

Metzinger, T. (2003). *Being no one: The self-model theory of subjectivity.* Cambridge, MA: MIT Press.

Moskowitz, A., Mosquera, D. & Longden, L. (2017). Auditory verbal hallucinations and the differential diagnosis of schizophrenia and dissociative disorders: Historical, empirical and clinical perspectives. *Journal of Trauma and Dissociation,* 1, 37-46.

Mosquera & Gonzalez (2014). *Borderline Personality Disorder and EMDR Therapy.* Amazon Imprint.

Mosquera, D. (2014). *Working with hostile voices and Parts of the Personality in Dissociative Disorders.* 3rd International Course Organized by the New Frontier in the Healing of Trauma. Venice, Italy.

Mosquera, D. (2016). Why are complex trauma and dissociation relevant in the understanding and treatment of Borderline Personality Disorder? *ESTD Newsletter,* 5 (2), 5-8

Mosquera, D. (2018). The effects of feeling invisible. Understanding the connection with early trauma disruptions and severe neglect. *ESTD Newsletter,* 7 (1), 5-12

Mosquera, D. & Ross, C. (2016). A psychotherapy approach to treating hostile voices. *Psychosis. Psychological, Social and Integrative Approaches,* 9(2):167-175

Mosquera, D. & Ross, C. (2016). Application of EMDR Therapy to Self-injury and Self-harming behaviors. *Journal of EMDR, Practice and Research,* 10 (2), 119-128.

Mosquera, D. & Steele, K. (2017). Complex Trauma, Dissociation and Borderline Personality Disorder: Working with Integration Failures. *Journal of Trauma and Dissociation,* 1(2017), 63-71.

Nathanson, D.L. (1994). *Shame and Pride. Affect, Sex, and the Birth of the Self.* New York: Norton

Nijenhuis, E.R.S, Van der Hart, O. & Steele, K. (2002). The emerging psychobiology of traumarelated dissociation and dissociative disorders. In H. D'haenen, J.A. den Boer & P. Willner (Eds)., *Biological psychiatry* (pp. 1079-1098). Chicester, UK: John Wiley & Sons. Paulsen, S. (1995).

Eye movement desensitization and reprocessing: Its cautious use in the dissociative disorders. *Dissociation,* 8 (1), 32-44.

Paulsen, S. (2009). *Looking Through the Eyes of Trauma & Dissociation: An Illustrated Guide for EMDR Clinicians and Patients.* Bainbridge Institute for Integrative Psychology.

Phillips, M., & Frederick, C. (1995). *Healing the divided self.* New York: Norton.

Romme, M., & Escher, S. (1989). Hearing voices. *Schizophrenia Bulletin, 15*, 209–216.

Romme, M., & Escher, S. (2000). *Making sense of voices a guide for professionals who work with voice hearers*. Oakland, CA: Mind Publications.

Romme, M., & Escher, S. (2006). Trauma and hearing voices. In W. Larkin & A. Morrison (Eds.), *Trauma and psychosis* (pp. 162–191). London: Routledge.

Ross, C. A. (1997). *Dissociative identity disorder: Diagnosis, clinical features, and treatment of multiple personality* (2nd ed.). New York, NY: Wiley.

Ross, C. A., & Halpern, N. (2009). *Trauma model therapy: A treatment approach to trauma, dissociation, and complex comorbidity*. Richardson, TX: Manitou Communications.

Schwartz, R. C. (1995). *Internal Family Systems Therapy*, New York, NY: The Guilford Press.

Shapiro, F. (2001). *Eye Movement Desensitization and Reprocessing. Basic Principles, Protocols and Procedures.* 2nd edition. New York, NY: The Guilford Press.

Shapiro, F. (2018). *Eye Movement Desensitization and Reprocessing (EMDR) Therapy: Basic Principles, Protocols, and Procedures.* 3rd edition. New York, NY: The Guilford Press.

Shapiro, F. & Solomon, R. M. (2010). EMDR and the Adaptive Information Processing Model. Potential Mechanisms of Change, *Journal of EMDR Practice and Research*, 2(4), 315-325

Steele, K, Van der Hart, O. & Nijenhuis, E. R. S. (2001). Dependency in the treatment of complex posttraumatic stress disorder and dissociative disorders. *Journal of Trauma and Dissociation*, 2(4), 79-116.

Steele, K, Van der Hart, O. & Nijenhuis, E. R. S. (2005). Phase-oriented treatment of structural dissociation in complex traumatization: Overcoming trauma-related phobias. *Journal of Trauma and dissociation*, 6(3), 11-53.

Steele, K. (2009). Reflections on Integration, Mentalization, and Institutional Realization. *Journal of Trauma & Dissociation*, 10(1), 1-8.

Steele, K., Boon, S., & Van der Hart, O. (2017). *Treating trauma-related dissociation: A practical integrative approach.* New York: W. W. Norton.

Van der Hart, O, Solomon, R. & Gonzalez, A. (2010). *The theory of structural dissociation as a guide for EMDR treatment of chronically traumatized patients.* Paper presented at the annual meeting of EMDR International Association, Minneapolis, MN

Van der Hart, O, Nijenhuis, E. R. S. & Steele, K. (2006). *The haunted self: Structural Dissociation and the treatment of chronic traumatization.* New York: Norton.

Watkins, J. & and Watkins, H. (1997). *Ego States: Theory and Therapy.* Norton. New York. Young, J.E. (1990). *Cognitive Therapy for Personality Disorders.* Sarasota, FL: Professional Resources Press.

Young, J.E., Klosko, J.S. & Weishaar, M.E. (2003). *Schema Therapy. A Practitioner's Guide.* NY: Guilford Press.

Made in the USA
Middletown, DE
06 April 2021